LONDON LIVE

From the Yardbirds to Pink Floyd to the Sex Pistols:
The inside story of live bands in the capital's
trail-blazing music clubs
By TONY BACON

London Live
From the Yardbirds to Pink Floyd to the Sex Pistols: The inside story
of live bands in the capital's trail-blazing music clubs
By Tony Bacon

A BALAFON BOOK
First edition 1999

Published in the United States by Miller Freeman Books
600 Harrison Street, San Francisco, CA 94107
Publishers of Guitar Player and Bass Player magazines
Miller Freeman Inc. is a United News and Media company
Published in the UK by Balafon Books, an imprint of Outline Press Ltd,

ᴜᴎ Miller Freeman
A United News & Media company

115J Cleveland Street, London W1P 5PN, England.

ISBN 0-87930-572-X

Printed in Singapore

Art Director: Nigel Osborne
Design: Sally Stockwell
Editor: Siobhan Pascoe
Production: Pip Richardson

Print and origination by Tien Wah Press

99 00 01 02 03 5 4 3 2 1

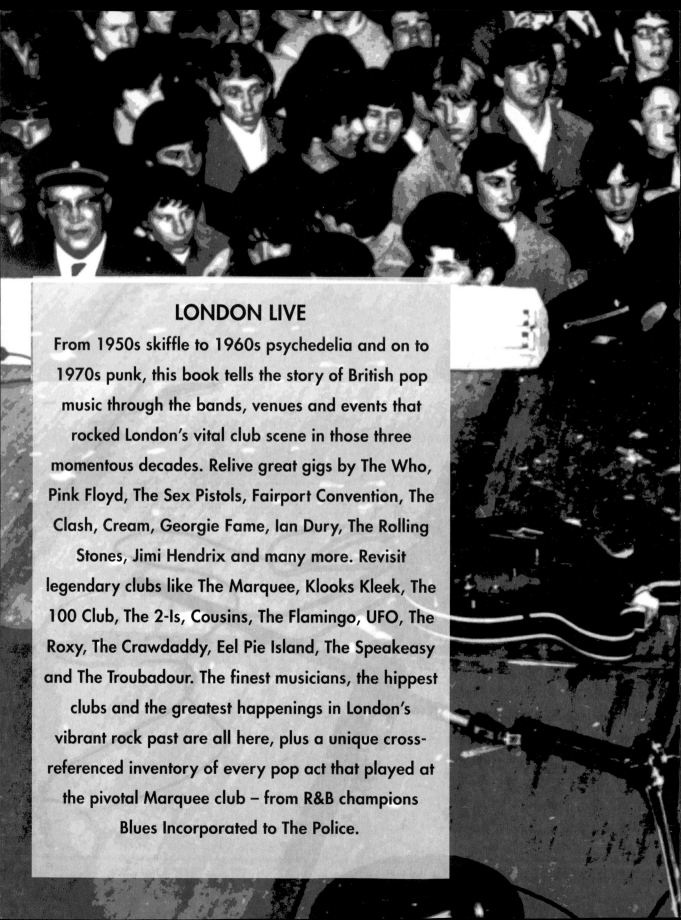

LONDON LIVE

From 1950s skiffle to 1960s psychedelia and on to 1970s punk, this book tells the story of British pop music through the bands, venues and events that rocked London's vital club scene in those three momentous decades. Relive great gigs by The Who, Pink Floyd, The Sex Pistols, Fairport Convention, The Clash, Cream, Georgie Fame, Ian Dury, The Rolling Stones, Jimi Hendrix and many more. Revisit legendary clubs like The Marquee, Klooks Kleek, The 100 Club, The 2-Is, Cousins, The Flamingo, UFO, The Roxy, The Crawdaddy, Eel Pie Island, The Speakeasy and The Troubadour. The finest musicians, the hippest clubs and the greatest happenings in London's vibrant rock past are all here, plus a unique cross-referenced inventory of every pop act that played at the pivotal Marquee club – from R&B champions Blues Incorporated to The Police.

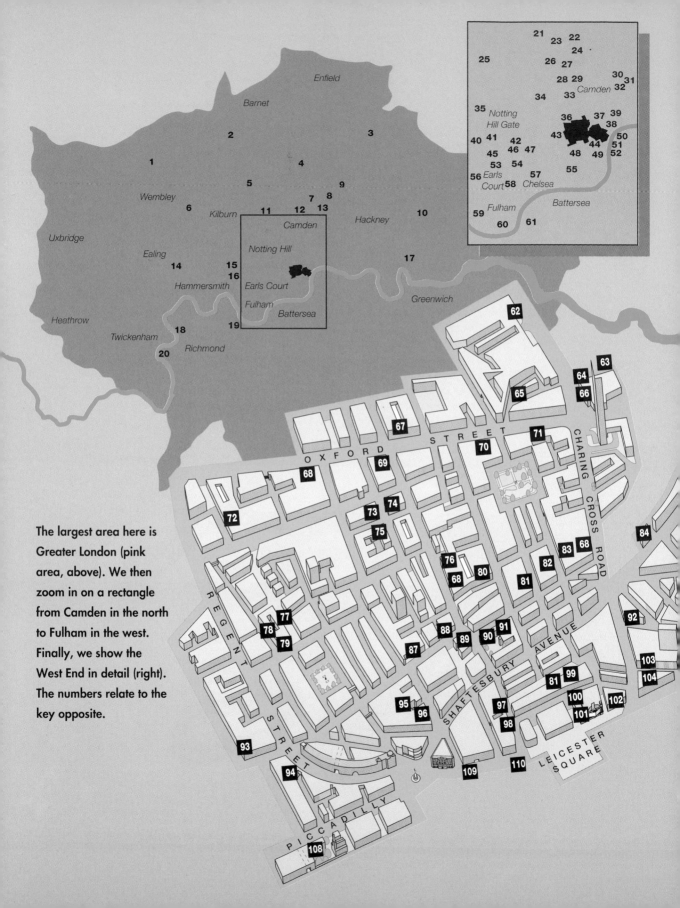

The largest area here is Greater London (pink area, above). We then zoom in on a rectangle from Camden in the north to Fulham in the west. Finally, we show the West End in detail (right). The numbers relate to the key opposite.

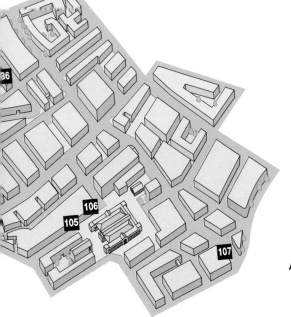

Above and to the right is an A-Z listing of all the venues and their associated key numbers relating to the three maps nearby. More information on the various locations is available on pages 144-145.

PLEASURE GARDENS
AND JAZZ CLUBS

IT IS JULY 14TH 1956, AND THE STORY OF LIVE POP MUSIC in London is about to get properly underway. Wally Whyton has a skiffle group and they have been invited to play as part of the second annual Soho Fair, an event organised to celebrate Bastille Day by French restaurant owners in the lively square mile of central London known as Soho. The musical entertainment will also include New Orleans marches, the oriental charms of the Hong Kong Restaurant Ensemble, and jiving to Cy Laurie's jazz band.

"The parade followed its route around Soho," Whyton explained later, "and eventually came to a standstill outside the 2-Is coffee bar in Old Compton Street, close to the corner of Wardour Street.

Jiving in the street (above) at the Soho Fair in summer 1956, just along from the 2-Is coffee bar.

❝ We went inside for a coffee and asked Paul Lincoln, one of the two Australian wrestlers who had just taken it over, if we could do a bit of busking. I realised he'd only been open about three weeks and was doing no trade whatsoever. So he agreed and we went into the basement. It was very steep going down, and led to a room that could only have been about 16 feet wide and probably 25 feet long. We started playing, and suddenly the place had come to life. It seemed to work well and Paul asked us to make it a regular stopover. Within a short time the place was jumping; in a few months they were queuing around the block. The 2-Is was certainly the first place to have that regular music and I think other places wanted to have some of this. Everybody joined in.[1] ❞

Of course, popular music had been played in London before this. Street balladeers, variety performers, revivalist jazzers, even music-hall singers – all could to a greater or lesser degree be described as purveyors of popular music. But pop music?

Skiffle, a peculiar British interpretation of American folk-blues, was Britain's first modern pop music, even if it was often ramshackle and turned out to be shortlived. At the time of

Whyton's experience at the 2-Is, skiffle was already being played in other coffee bars in London, and Lonnie Donegan had displayed the music's public face six months earlier when his 'Rock Island Line' 45 had gone into the charts. But in July 1956 Whyton and his skifflers opened up the 2-Is coffee bar to live music, beginning a series of steps that would transform British music. The pop-music club had, in embryonic form, arrived.

London's role as an entertainment centre had arisen naturally if slowly from its position as England's capital city. Early troubadours and minstrels flourished in the streets and taverns of London, and from the middle ages street hawkers sang melodic ads for their wares, adding to a rich cacophony accompanying everyday life. City Waits developed in the 15th century from night-watchmen who would mark hours of the night by sounding musical instruments, and the Waits went on to form musical bands that welcomed special visitors and accompanied ceremonies and plays.

Broadside ballads appeared from the 16th century, an effective way to spread news and satire, recycle folk songs and continue the minstrel tradition. Verses were printed on a sheet called a broadside or broadsheet and the tune was sung by the seller (or made up by the buyer). Street balladeers proliferated in London well into the 19th century.

Elizabeth I apparently encouraged music in London — William Byrd and Thomas Tallis were among some 30 musicians she employed – while William Shakespeare enjoyed fame in the London theatre with plays that abounded in original music, dancing and songs. Byrd and lutenist John Dowland found popular success for their songs and pieces, many of which were assumed to be folk songs.

A large central portion of London was rebuilt after the Great Fire of 1666, and six years later the world's first paid-entry public concerts were announced at the house of violinist, composer and entrepreneur John Banister, in the Whitefriars area (between Fleet Street and the Thames). Banister presented music on a daily basis, and an account exists of one such concert. It remains a relatively timeless portrait of a music club:

> [There was] a large room [with] a large raised box for the musitians, whose modesty required curtaines. The room was rounded with seats and small tables, alehous fashion. One shilling was the price, and call for what you pleased; there was very good musick, for Banister found means to procure the best hands in towne, and some voices to come and perform there, and there wanted no variety of humour, for Banister himself [and others] did wonders upon a flageolett to a thro' Base, and the several masters had their solos.[2]

Evidence of public concerts in London proliferates from this time onward, with Covent Garden emerging as the main centre. But it was in the pleasure gardens of London that popular songs gained most early currency. The New Spring Gardens at Vauxhall (later Vauxhall Gardens) was probably the biggest, and boasted ad hoc performances of the day's pop songs among its varied entertainments. A concert hall was added in 1758; Thomas Arne and later James Hook were hired to write songs for it. James Boswell described the music he heard at Vauxhall in the 1790s as "vocal and instrumental, not too refined for the general ear". Vauxhall Gardens closed in 1859 and was built upon; another Spring Gardens on part of the site was reinstated in the 1990s. Other musical gardens included Ranelagh, opened in Chelsea in 1742 (now part of Chelsea Hospital gardens), and Marylebone, opened in about 1650 (its site now including parts of Devonshire Street and Beaumont Street).

By the 1860s popular music in London had moved from the outdoor pleasure gardens to

the indoor music-halls. The "halls" ranged from singing-saloons in pubs to the later and grander variety theatres. Music had been popular in English pubs and taverns since the earliest times, and from the 17th century and into the 19th was sometimes organised into regular events known as a "Free and Easy" or a "Harmonic Club". Hackney-born publican Charles Morton bought The Old Canterbury Arms in Upper Marsh, Lambeth, in December 1849 and started concert performances three nights a week, and these became so popular that in May 1852 he added next to the pub a concert hall, often described as the first music-hall. Evans's Music-and-Supper Rooms in Covent Garden began in the 1840s and is another contender, although as an all-night haunt for "wealthy bohemians"[3] it sounds a little different in character to what emerged as the popular music-hall.

Music-halls mushroomed everywhere in London and other major cities. By 1866 there were 33 in London; by the 1890s, at the peak of music-hall popularity, over 14 million tickets

The Selmer musical instrument store of Charing Cross Road highlighted a number of central London's musicians' landmarks in this 1937 ad (right). To find out what was where, check the key below.

"Where there's a job...there's a Selmer"

Prime working locations of late-1930s dancebands (main picture): 1 Savoy Hotel; 2 Berkeley Hotel; 3 Café de Paris; 4 Dorchester Hotel (opposite number 5); 5 Grosvenor Hotel; 6 Mayfair Hotel; 7 Lansdowne House; 8 Piccadilly Hotel; 9 Embassy Club; 10 Romano's; 11 Ciro's Club; 12 BBC Broadcasting House; 13 The Casino; 14 Murray's Club.

were being sold in the capital city each year. In the West End, big halls included the Palace at Cambridge Circus, the Tivoli in the Strand and the Alhambra on Leicester Square (more or less where the Odeon cinema now stands).

Music-hall audiences were generally young, with a significant proportion under 25, and largely upper working class and lower middle class – although "perhaps only in London, where the cheapest seats could be 2d [1p] compared to the normal 6d [2.5p], were the lower working class able to attend in sizeable numbers".[4] Music was part of a range of entertainment which also included dancing, circus-type acts and comedy. The musical programme centred on "serious" music at first, but gave way to the music-hall song: 'A Little Of What You Fancy (Does You Good)', 'Two Lovely Black Eyes', 'My Old Dutch' and so on. There were hundreds of others; virtually all had verse/chorus structures, a simple melody with

a limited range, an obvious persona adopted by the singer, and escapist subject matter. In short, they were what we would now call pop songs. The music-hall also produced its pop stars of the day, the likes of Marie Lloyd, Albert Chevalier, George 'Champagne Charlie' Leybourne, or Gus Elen.

Meanwhile, jazz had been brewing away in the United States since the late 19th century, a rich mixture originating in the cultural melting pot of New Orleans. London waited until 1919 to get one of its first live and genuinely American tastes of the hot new music, albeit in ersatz form. The Original Dixieland Jazz Band was a group of five white musicians playing drums, cornet, trombone, clarinet and piano. Based in New York, they helped to popularise the jazz of the black originators, not least by being the first outfit to record the music commercially.

They also travelled to Europe to spread the word, and in April 1919 debuted at a revue at the Hippodrome in Charing Cross Road, moving on to the London Palladium in Argyll Street. In October they played at the opening of the new Palais de Danse in Shepherd's Bush Road, Hammersmith, west London, a venue soon better known as the Hammersmith Palais. Some of the audience at the Palais were surprised by what they considered to be no more than a curious gimmick; a few were affronted by the un-musical noise coming from an unusual line-up; and probably still fewer recognised the historical significance of this early display in London of the potential – if not the true embodiment – of real live jazz.

Duke Ellington and his Orchestra visited England for the first time in 1933, amazing crowds who had never before seen such assured American jazz on home territory. This programme (above) was sold at Ellington's date at the Trocadero Cinema in the Elephant & Castle, south-east London.

R E V I E W

ORIGINAL DIXIELAND JAZZ BAND

HIPPODROME, APRIL 7TH 1919

"The Dixieland Jazz Band appeared in *Joy Bells* at the Hippodrome last Monday... On the occasion of their performance they gave us a demonstration of undiluted jazz, and it must be admitted, despite all that has been thought and said to the contrary, there was a certain charm in the mournful refrains, dramatically broken up by cheery jingles and a miscellany of noises such as one generally hears 'off'. At one moment the whole orchestra would down tools while one member tootled merrily or eerily on his own account, and the whole would resume again, always ready to give a fair hearing to any other individual player who had suddenly developed a stunt. The conductor was most urbane about it all, but everybody was perfectly happy, not excluding the audience who appreciated a novelty not unartistic."

TOWN TOPICS, APRIL 12TH 1919

At the Palladium the Dixieland Band's audience "was a music-hall crowd – certainly not composed of jazz enthusiasts, if they existed at all in those days," as a visitor remembered it many years later. He also saw them at the Palais, and noted that "almost without exception the crowd was in evening dress; admission was by ticket only. Hermione Baddeley, the actress, made an opening speech, and Harry Pilcer and partner gave an exhibition of ballroom dancing."[5] Clearly no wild jazz-age scenes here.

During the Dixieland Band's extended trip, which lasted into 1920, the Americans also played at Rector's Club in Tottenham Court Road (in premises to which we will return much later for the 1960s UFO club). Rector's was one of a number of small clubs, select restaurants and up-market hotels in London that presented jazz-flavoured dance-music in the early 1920s. The Savoy Hotel in the Strand was in the upper bracket, and briefly, late in the decade, the resident band there was Fred Elizalde & His Music, one of the pioneering British jazz bands. The Cafe de Paris in Coventry Street was among the most fashionable and expensive of the dining-clubs, while adjoining Shaftesbury Avenue a little further up the street – and a world away in style – was Lyon's Corner House. But both featured jazz-inclined musicians in their

dancebands, as did Haymarket's Kit Kat restaurant/club and Old Bond Street's Embassy Club, one of London's first nightclubs when it opened around 1922.

The musicians at these and other venues, had to wait until the early 1930s before they could experience the real thing. Louis Armstrong played at the London Palladium in 1932. *Melody Maker* described the black American jazzman's performance as "uncanny", despite some second-rate pick-up players for a backing band and some negative audience reaction, and praised Armstrong's vocal energy, trumpet technique, tone and instrumental mastery. "He works with a microphone and loudspeakers, except for his trumpet playing which varies from a veritable whisper to roof-raising strength, mostly the latter. The amazing thing is his personality. He positively sparkles with showmanship and good humour... He is in short a unique phenomenon, an electric personality – easily the greatest America has sent us."[6]

Danceband dives and jazz clubs grew up quickly in 1930s Soho. One of the earliest was The Bag O'Nails in Kingly Street. The picture (right) shows the house-band there in 1937. Drummer Phil Cozzi led the outfit, with Solly Reid on clarinet and baritone sax, Art Thompson (standing) on piano, and Joe Boyd on bass. Thompson had hit the musicians' job centre in nearby Archer Street as soon as he arrived in England from his native Canada, landing the Bag gig. "This business is just what you make it yourself," he told an interviewer. "The only ambition I got is to make a living."

And then a second coming: Duke Ellington and his famous orchestra visited in 1933, debuting at the Palladium. Fast becoming the venue of choice for such visitors, the Palladium was in Argyll Street, on the site of a couple of previous theatres and a "skating palace" dating back to 1870. The existing Palladium Theatre had been finished in 1910; by 1934 it would officially be named The London Palladium. In June 1933, Ellington and his band simply blew the place apart. Here was a ensemble of supreme black musicians playing stylish, orchestrated jazz in a startlingly new and original way, and London marvelled at the Duke's assured display.

After this landmark, one might have expected an influx of yet more American bands to show homegrown musicians how to really play jazz, and to demonstrate to London audiences the wealth of musical delights on offer. But such a development was effectively ruled out in 1935 when the Musicians' Union in Britain decided to defend the jobs of home musicians by barring American infiltrators. No musical judgement was made; it was simply a matter of maintaining jobs for our boys. The Ministry of Labour decreed that in future a reciprocal swap between the MU and the equivalent American Federation of Musicians of one British musician to the US for every American player visiting the UK must be made.

With such a one-sided proposal, American and British musicians by and large stayed where they were for the next 21 years. American jazz master Coleman Hawkins was already

in Europe when the order was made, but managed some British appearances by masking his shows as commercial "demonstrations" of his favoured Selmer saxophones. But this was a rare exception. Live music now meant British-played live music – and the most popular variety in London's clubs, restaurants and hotels was swing-based danceband music.

British bandleaders drew their personnel from the hundreds of jobbing musicians who gathered every Monday to seek work at the traditional "hiring fair" held in the open along the length of Archer Street, just off Shaftesbury Avenue. In the late 1930s and early 1940s there was good work for the chosen players: top dancebands included the outfits of Carroll Gibbons and "Tango King" Geraldo, who entertained the well-heeled at The Savoy, while Jack Jackson took the baton in front of the similarly elevated clientele at The Dorchester in Park Lane. Bert Ambrose orchestrated at nightclubs such as the Embassy or Ciro's (in Orange Street), Edmondo Ross went Cuban at the Coconut Grove in Regent Street, and Sid Phillips smoothed his band's path through the "blasé socialites"[7] at Le Suivi in Stratton Street.

As for jazz, the possibilities were less assured but still relatively numerous. There was a range of seedy jazz dives in and around Soho, including Jigs and The Shim Sham in Wardour Street, The Blue Lagoon in Frith Street and The Unity in Dean Street. Musicians played in dancebands in ritzy places to live, and played jazz in basement dumps for fun.

Soho is roughly a square mile in central London bounded by Oxford Street (north), Charing Cross Road (east), Leicester Square and Piccadilly Circus (south) and Regent Street (west), and by the 1930s was already openly displaying a colourful, exotic surface over a village community. J B Priestley had caught its flavour in 1930 when he described "the glimpses of foreign interiors; the windows filled with outlandish foodstuffs, Chianti flasks and bundles of long cheroots; the happy foolish little decorations; the dark faces; the girls leaning out of the first floor windows".[8] Clubs for live jazz, considered risqué music, began to fit with ease alongside Soho's prostitutes, restaurants, and strip-tease joints.

On the western border of Soho was The Bag O'Nails club, in the basement of 9 Kingly Street, established as a music hang-out around 1930. A profile in 1937 said that "hundreds of well-known musicians have busked on its rostrum. It is to the history of British swing music what Hampton Court Palace is to the history of England. It is the show shop of promising musicians; the rendezvous of successful ones".[9] The Bag was also significant at the time as a base of the first Rhythm Club to be inaugurated in Britain. It acted as an early-evening meeting place where keen jazz enthusiasts could listen to live jam sessions as well as serious record recitals of the latest American recordings, activities still imbued with novelty and excitement in mid-1930s London. Significant too was the fact that consideration was being given for the first time to those who wanted to come to a club not to dance but to listen. London club-owners would worry constantly over the coming years trying to decide whether to provide for both kinds of visitor or one type exclusively.

When the war came in 1939 many of the upmarket nightclub revellers at first behaved as if nothing had changed. "For all the difference there is [in many of the clubs] in any way," noted one observer, "there might not be a war on."[10] But reality struck during a German air-raid in March 1941 when the Cafe de Paris took a direct hit. Bandleader and dancer Ken "Snakehips" Johnson as well as club-owner Martinus Poulsen were among those killed.

One of London's longest-lived music-club premises started in 1942 soon after Robert Feldman, a jazz fan and budding clarinet player, took a break from his rag-trade job in Soho for a snack at Mack's Restaurant in the basement of 100 Oxford Street. "I remember when I first went down the stairs to the restaurant," he recalled years later. "There were posts all over

Wreckage is searched (above) after a German bomb hit the Café de Paris nightclub in March 1941. The explosion killed bandleader Ken "Snakehips" Johnson, sax-player Dave Williams, proprietor Martinus Poulsen and several club-goers.

LEADING WEST-END JAZZ VENUES (map, right)

Club 11's Tony Crombie, Leon Calvert and Ronnie Scott (left to right, below) plus guest. Cy Laurie blows a storm at his club (centre) as two nattily-dressed visitors approach the entrance. House-band at the Bar Of Music club (centre, below).

the place, holding up the ceiling. Suddenly I imagined them turning into palm trees and thought it would make a nice little club."[11] After doubtless tricky negotiations with the fearsome Old Ma Phillips who ran the place – she was later known by club-goers as The Dragon – the Feldman Swing Club opened in October 1942. *Melody Maker* said it supplied "a long-felt want by giving London enthusiasts what they have always lacked – a regular home of swing where they can meet, dance, and listen to the music of the stars".[12]

One of the attractions was a trio consisting of Feldman on clarinet and his brothers Monty on accordion and eight-year-old Victor on drums. The percussive prodigy was dubbed "Kid Krupa" after American legend Gene Krupa; Victor later enjoyed a successful career in the US as a fine vibraphonist and pianist. Feldman's club was a lacklustre dive, but gradually the premises began to attract better musicians and bigger crowds, and benefited from the popular "revivalist" jazz evenings which began in 1950 as the London Jazz Club and in 1951 as the Humphrey Lyttelton Club, with Lyttelton's band often in residence. The Feldman club name itself ceased in 1954, but the premises continued to host revivalist jazz under the Humphrey Lyttelton banner. Ten years later it would change its name to The 100 Club, of which more later.

The war raged on and on, and ground to a bloody halt in 1945. In Britain, despite the ruins and the indelible marks of suffering, many people were determined at last to enjoy themselves, to celebrate survival. One obvious way, as the 1940s drew to a close, was through music. Jazz in Britain had split into two factions around this time. On one hand there was revivalist jazz, a throwback to the traditional Dixieland style of the 1920s, which also became known here as "trad". On the other hand, there was modern jazz. This aped the intricate rhythms and expanded harmonic possibilities of the freshly-minted New York bebop style, and became the province of the "modernists", or "mods".

A new clutch of London clubs catered for one or other of the factions – there was little love lost between the rival fans – and another source was seized to provide club space. Rehearsal rooms, used by dance troupes and theatre groups during the day, were temptingly empty most evenings and nights. Some were ideal for the new jazz clubs. Frank Richardson's rehearsal basement in Gerrard Street was one such dive turned into a number of different clubs on various nights. Richardson no doubt welcomed the extra cash. Many clubs would occupy his premises over the coming years, but if you went to 44 Gerrard Street on a certain night in the early years of the 1950s you might well have discovered the West End Jazz Club and its secretary George Melly – who sang with the resident Mick Mulligan band.

"We were on the road all the time," Melly wrote later, "[but] tried to keep some foothold in London [by running] our own club in a rehearsal room in a Gerrard Street basement and, on the rare occasions we were in town on a Saturday night, organised all-night raves.

Mick and I were the first people to organise all-night raves, and they were an enormous social success, but a financial loss... Anyway, we didn't really run the all-nighters to make money. Although today the idea of spending a whole night in a crowded, airless basement at a small loss appears extraordinary, it was very exciting then. Forced as we were by commercial necessity to occupy most of our lives playing strict-tempo music for dancing, the all-night sessions were an escape back into the jazz atmosphere of our beginnings. We could dress in shit order, fall about, and tell people who criticised our music to get stuffed.[13]

Among the first modern-jazz clubs was Club 11, named for the ten musicians (including Ronnie Scott and Johnny Dankworth) plus one "organiser" who started it in 1948. It was based in another rehearsal room, this time Mac's at 41 Great Windmill Street, opposite the Windmill Theatre and a drumstick's throw from the musicians' alfresco job centre in Archer Street. Although it became a focus for the modernists' jam sessions and was novel in its jazz-only policy, Club 11 was shortlived. In March 1950 it moved to 50 Carnaby Street, and the Great Windmill Street premises were soon turned by clarinettist Cy Laurie into a successful revivalist club that lasted to 1961. Club 11, however, didn't last long in its new location, closing a few months after the move following a police raid for drugs. One of those arrested, an RAF servicewoman, said, "It left me filled with resentment of the police, because I was accused of possessing a low moral standard, fraternising with (to recall a certain lieutenant's phrase) 'buck niggers', and the likelihood of becoming a drug addict."[14] This was in fact the very first demonstration of the popular equation that a music club and its musicians, plus lively young audience, equals bad things and especially drugs. Thus formulated, it would recur on a regular basis.

Studio 51 was another of the early modern clubs, started by bassist Joe Muddel and compere Tony Hall in 1951 in (would you believe) a basement rehearsal studio, at 10-11 Great Newport Street, which had hosted earlier jazz clubs. Trumpeter Ken Colyer also launched a successful revivalist club here three years later on a different night, and his New Orleans Club was the recognised "home of purist traditional jazz"[15] for many years, today recorded by a Westminster City Council commemorative plaque outside the long-ago-converted building. As this book demonstrates, there is surely scope for many more such plaques. We'll discover shortly how Colyer himself was also instrumental in the skiffle boom, and a little later how the Great Newport Street dive – with its various club names – would be a significant venue in the story of early rock'n'roll and R&B.

First we'll visit a trio of jazz clubs launched in the 1950s that would have a big effect on the development of live music in London. The Flamingo was a modern-jazz venue set up by film-salesman, pianist and jazz enthusiast Jeff Kruger. His West End job made it easy for him to visit clubs like Feldman's and Studio 51. Kruger liked the music but found the places dirty and claustrophobic, and wondered why a jazz club couldn't be held in the nice sort of venues that he went to for Sunday-evening dances in north London. "They were advertised in the *Jewish Chronicle* each week," Kruger recalled, "and were held in up-market locations such as a nightclub or hotel ballroom."[16] Then he happened to eat at a restaurant in the Mapleton Hotel at the corner of Coventry Street and Whitcomb Street. Chatting to the manager, he discovered an unused basement room.

The 21-year-old Kruger opened his first club there in August 1952 with the Johnny Dankworth Seven and Kenny Graham's Afro-Cubists. It started as "Jazz At The Mapleton" but a few months later saxophonist Graham's theme tune 'Flamingo' provided Kruger with a better name for the new venture (Graham had already run a shortlived club with that name in 1950 at the Great Newport Street basement). A number of clubs occupied the Mapleton site over the coming years, but Kruger shifted the Flamingo from the Mapleton in 1956 to a series of brief temporary homes – the Cafe Anglais at Leicester Square, the Doric Rooms at 10 Brewer St and the Pigalle Restaurant at 190 Piccadilly. He also opened a club called the Florida, before moving the Flamingo early in 1957 to its best-known premises in the basement of 33-37 Wardour Street, opposite the end of Gerrard Street. The Flamingo lasted here until 1970, and its offshoot the All-Nighter Club that began in 1959 would host some important R&B developments in the early 1960s. At first, though, jazz prevailed.

The Marquee, probably the best-known club name in London, also started life as a jazz venue, in the basement of the Academy cinema at 165 Oxford Street. On the site of a Roman road, Oxford Street began to develop into a shopping street toward the end of the 19th century and, while today the heyday of this now charmless street is clearly well in the past, in the mid 20th century it was a major place to shop. Cinemas and places of entertainment sprang up, the Academy Picture House that appeared around 1930 being one among many.

In the 1950s the Academy's owner, George Hoellering, added a couple of further attractions to his cinema: a restaurant, the Pavilion, and in the basement the Marquee ballroom. The Marquee's interior was devised for Hoellering by Angus McBean as a circus masquerade, complete with striped marquee-style awnings. McBean designed theatre sets, but was better known for his theatrical portrait photography – and later for his famous photo of The Beatles leaning over the balcony of EMI's London offices which was used for the cover of their first album, *Please Please Me*.

Hoellering's Marquee ballroom was not a success, despite McBean's ornate decorations. So at the end of 1957 Hoellering agreed to let it out on Saturday and Sunday nights to pianist Dill Jones and his manager Peter Burman. They presented the first "Jazz At The Marquee" gig on Saturday January 4th 1958 with the bands of Jones, trumpeter Kenny Baker, and busy saxophonist Kenny Graham. However, despite ads that boasted of the Marquee's espresso coffee lounge, Steinway piano, Western Electric sound system and "a wonderful step forward in atmosphere and luxury", still the public failed to crowd the basement under the Academy cinema.

Enter Harold Pendleton, a young Merseyside chartered accountant who'd moved to London in 1948 with a passion for jazz and a new job in the capital's financial district. He soon met bandleader-to-be Chris Barber, and became so enamoured of jazz that he decided to leave his secure job and concentrate on music as a business. In the early 1950s he became secretary of the National Federation of Jazz Organisations of Great Britain, an important-sounding and terribly British set of committees and hierarchies that aimed to slap the fast-growing and dissipated jazz club movement into a disciplined nationwide organisation. "First meeting," Pendleton recalls, "they disagreed on everything. 'Rubbish! That's not jazz!' and so on. To cut a long story short, I threw the lot of them out and took the damned thing over. First thing I did was to shorten the name to the National Jazz Federation, the NJF. My intention? A career. Number one, I thought this has to be run properly, and two, profitably."[17]

Pendleton's NJF company included Chris Barber as a co-director – Pendleton was by now managing Barber's band – and the two began organising concerts and gigs under the NJF banner. These included "workshop" dates at the Royal Festival Hall's recital room, with revivalist- and modern-jazz bands on different nights, as well as a number of concerts in the main hall.

Then one day in 1958 Peter Burman came to see Pendleton at the NJF office in Carlisle Street, Soho, explaining about his Marquee nights and, more pointedly, how he was losing money and couldn't pay the rent. Perhaps Pendleton would be interested in taking over? Burman's timing was good: a few years earlier Pendleton had lost the premises at 14 Greek Street where he'd run the London Jazz Centre, and was now keen to start a new club.

Pendleton went to see Hoellering at the Academy and agreed to take over the rental of the Oxford Street Marquee, which began in its new NJF guise on Saturday 12th and Sunday 13th April 1958. "I was now in the perfect position," Pendleton recalls. "I was midway between 100 Oxford Street, which was on the other side of the road, and the Flamingo, which was down at the bottom of Wardour Street. I was the third party; I could build in the

Cy Laurie opened his club in a
huge basement in Great Windmill
Street, opposite the Windmill
Theatre, soon after the modern-
jazz Club 11 had left in 1950.
When not being used as a club the
basement was Mac's Dancing
Academy, a hoofer's school and
rehearsal space. Laurie was a
clarinettist whose band played in
the revivalist or "trad" jazz style,

which harked back to the Dixieland originators of the 1920s. The style was much ridiculed by the "modernists", who preferred modern-jazz. "An overdose of technique doesn't make up for an absence of spirit," countered Laurie, who called his jazz "blue hot". Laurie's club specialised in trad, regularly presenting his own and other trad bands (like those in the pictures, left). Some typical trad fans (below) are seen settling down at the club in the mid 1950s, just four among some 6,000 devotees on the club's bulging membership books of the time. Laurie's club lasted until the early 1960s when the basement began to host the Piccadilly Jazz Club, and then became mod R&B club The Scene.

middle. Humphrey Lyttelton at the 100 was putting on traditional and not modern, the Flamingo was putting on modern and not traditional – so I was going to have both. It's all jazz!"[18] Pendleton refers to the Oxford Street Marquee as "mark one" to distinguish it from its later Wardour Street location, and describes its physical layout at the time:

> **It was a basement, straight underneath the cinema. The Academy cinema had a standard foyer, and then alongside it to the left was a very narrow door and steps down, just enough for one person up or one person down. You'd reach a flat point at which there was a cash desk, above which was the front half of a carousel horse stuck to the wall, looking at you as you came down the stairs. Turning to the right you'd emerge at the same level at the top of another flight of stairs, and these would take you down into the ballroom. It was quite big – it could hold 600-plus – and had a sprung floor. When you came down there was banquette seating going in a big oval to the stage. The stage was in the middle of the longer wall on your right: you could get more of an audience in a curve around it than with a stage at one end. All around there were green and white stripes or red and white stripes, like the inside of a marquee, with scalloped edgings around the lights. When you see a photo of a band with that tilted, striped roof above them, you know it's the Marquee mark one.[19]**

Pendleton stuck at it and gradually the Saturday and Sunday Marquee audiences grew. Toward the end of 1958 a Friday night was briefly added, but a big coup was bringing modern-jazz stars the Johnny Dankworth Orchestra to the club for a Sunday night residency starting in 1960. More nights were added over the years, and by the time Alexis Korner's Blues Incorporated added Thursday-night R&B there in 1962 the Marquee was working every night except Monday and Tuesday.

Just qualifying for a 1950s birth was Ronnie Scott's jazz club. Scott had been hankering for his own modern-jazz dive since Club 11 had folded, and visits to the great New York clubs hardened his resolve. Ronnie Scott's Club opened at 39 Gerrard Street on Friday October 30th 1959, with the Tubby Hayes Quartet headlining. Scott and Peter King as co-owners of the new club also played, and the advance publicity noted this in a style heralding Scott's comedy routines that became a fixture of the club's entertainment: "A young Alto Saxophonist Peter King and an old Tenor Saxophonist Ronnie Scott, plus first appearance in a Jazz Club since the Relief of Mafeking of Jack Parnell."

Ronnie Scott (above) leans on the bar at his jazz club in Gerrard Street, about to be interviewed for TV by journalist Steve Race. The shot was taken in 1965 a few months before the club moved to Frith Street.

Scott had his Gerrard Street club newly-decorated and reopened in April 1961 with a licensed bar, a rarity among London music clubs then, and couldn't resist boasting about how this made it "the first British jazz club on American lines".[20] Scott moved his club in December 1965 to its present site at 47 Frith Street, continuing the Gerrard Street basement as The Old Place until the late 1960s. Ronnie Scott's has hosted performances of most of the greatest jazz musicians, and in the early 1960s the club was instrumental in presenting more American jazzmen in London. Ronnie's is still functioning today in Frith Street, with Pete King at the helm since Scott's death in December 1996. The old Gerrard Street basement, now in the heart of modern Soho's Chinatown, is, inevitably, part of a Chinese restaurant.

The Marquee club started life in a lavishly decorated ballroom under the Academy cinema in Oxford Street, and for years presented a programme devoted to jazz. For a few months after its opening in January 1958 (ad, right) the club was run by jazz pianist Dill Jones and his manager Peter Burman. In April Harold Pendleton and the National Jazz Federation took over, running the Marquee at Oxford Street until 1964 and subsequently at another location into the 1980s. Trumpeter Kenny Graham is shown playing at the opening night (far right) with bassist Joe Muddel, below the club's distinctive striped decor. Chris Barber (with trombone, below), a co-director of the NJF, was tireless in encouraging and advancing jazz, skiffle and blues in Britain.

PETER BURMAN & DILL JONES
invite you to

JAZZ AT THE MARQUEE

165 OXFORD STREET, W.1
(Next Door Academy Cinema)

The Sensational Star-Studded Opening This Week End

SATURDAY & SUNDAY
JANUARY 4th & 5th
presenting

KENNY BAKER
DILL JONES TRIO
KENNY GRAHAM
QUINTET

Your Compere **DILL JONES**
of B.B.C. JAZZ SERIES

Your Host **PETER BURMAN**

invite you to meet the stars at the most Modern Jazz Rendezvous in the World. 7.30-11.30 p.m.

ESPRESSO COFFEE BAR
FREE MEMBERSHIP THIS WEEK END

MAKE THIS YOUR REGULAR SATURDAY
AND SUNDAY RENDEZVOUS

JAZZ, SKIFFLE & ROCK'N'ROLL

22

At first, skiffle was popularised through feature spots in jazz band concerts. Here the music's main ambassador Lonnie Donegan (right) plays an interval spot during a Chris Barber concert in 1954. Barber is on bass while Pat Halcox claps.

SOHO SKIFFLE AND ROCK'N'ROLL VENUES

1 Chiquito's
2 The Dominion
3 Sam Widge's
4 Freight Train
5 Cat's Whisker
6 Skiffle Cellar
7 Round House pub
8 2-Is
9 Heaven & Hell
10 The Cave
    44 (Skiffle) Club
    Good Earth
11 The Stork Room
12 Café de Paris

More info pages 144-145.

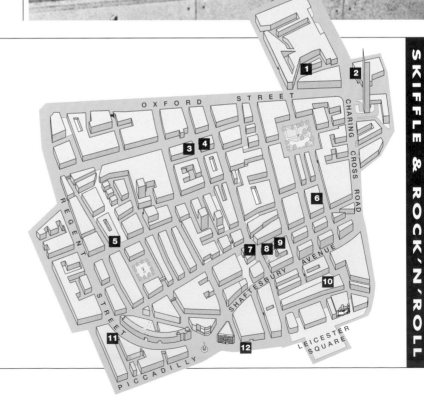

SKIFFLE & ROCK'N'ROLL

VIPERS, SKIFFLE, STEELE AND ROCK

THE STORY OF SKIFFLE IS THE STORY OF LONDON IN THE 1950s and the experiments of jazz musicians like Ken Colyer, Chris Barber and Lonnie Donegan. It's also the story of the coffee bar scene and the ad hoc groups such as The Vipers that blossomed there.

Whatever the origins of the word itself, the music that came to be called skiffle in Britain in the 1950s derived originally from the fascination that a handful of British jazzmen and music fans developed for the American folk-blues and country-blues of Leadbelly, Big Bill Broonzy, Woody Guthrie and others. It developed into a brief but intense national pastime thanks to hit records and the additional influence of early American "spasm" bands, jug outfits and washboard groups who used improvised instruments to fire their brand of homemade music.

Not that many of these antecedents could be heard too easily in Britain at the time. The occasional American blues or folk record might somehow turn up buried deep in a BBC radio programme, although such broadcasts were a distinct rarity. However, a handful of the more committed London-based aficionados did come upon a cache of genuine records at the US Information Service library in the American Embassy at Grosvenor Square. Lonnie Donegan and Wally Whyton both remember plundering this treasure trove; Donegan – an expert story-teller today – even says that he sort of "forgot" to return a record or two, while Whyton recalled the joy of handling and playing real Muddy Waters records and discovering "songs you could learn in ten minutes and they'd last you a lifetime".[21]

Lonnie Donegan was born Anthony James Donegan in Glasgow but grew up in east London, and had edged his way into an amateur band with Chris Barber in the late 1940s by pretending to be able to play banjo. By the early 1950s Donegan had his own revivalist jazz outfit, and in summer 1952 they landed the support to American blues guitarist Lonnie Johnson at an NJF concert at the Royal Festival Hall, a large new venue by the Thames built for the previous year's Festival Of Britain. Inspired by NJF compere Harold Pendleton who confused the names of Donegan and Johnson at the concert, Tony Donegan decided to adopt his hero's forename, and from that time on was Lonnie Donegan.

By early '53 Donegan was in a band with trombonist Chris Barber and trumpeter Ken Colyer. Recently Colyer had illegally jumped a merchant-navy ship to get to New Orleans, which as the birthplace of jazz he considered his spiritual home. Colyer played successfully with a number of local musicians, but was soon caught, arrested, imprisoned and then sent back to England – where many considered him a hero for undertaking such a wild musical adventure. The homecomer's new revivalist band, Ken Colyer's Jazzmen, was the one with Donegan and Barber, plus a drummer and clarinettist from Colyer's previous outfit, the Crane River Jazz Band, and a bassist.

It was from Ken Colyer's Jazzmen that a small offshoot skiffle group was formed to play some folk-blues and provide an occasional light interlude in contrast to the band's otherwise full-pelt jazz. The skiffle group centred on Colyer, Donegan and Alexis Korner on guitars, either Barber or the band's regular bassist Jim Bray on bass, and Colyer's brother Bill on washboard. They could lay claim to being the first skiffle group regularly performing in public in Britain, exemplified by their interval spots during the Colyer Jazzmen's gigs at the London Jazz Club, which by now was based near Marble Arch at 34 Bryanston Street, in a hall next to a church around the back of the Cumberland Hotel. One of the earliest reviews of a skiffle date highlighted a performance by Colyer's men at the LJC in summer 1953. Alan Lomax was mentioned; he was the son of US folk-music scholar John Lomax who was one of those

rare voices on BBC radio in the 1950s praising and playing American folk music. Both helped maintain the Archive Of American Folk Song at the Library Of Congress.

R E V I E W

KEN COLYER SKIFFLE GROUP

LONDON JAZZ CLUB, (PROBABLY JUNE) 1953

"The Skiffle Group which takes over during the intervals at the London Jazz Club is obviously going to be the success of the year. It's getting so that more people flock into the Club for the interval than for the rest of the session. The group varies in personnel, but is always based on the guitars, banjos and vocals of Ken Colyer, Alex Korner and Lonnie Donegan. Other recent participants have been Chris Barber and Jim Bray on bass, Ron Bowden on drums and Bill Colyer on washboard. The idea came from Alex Korner and Ken Colyer, and was first suggested before Ken went to New Orleans, but neither of them could have guessed what a large potential audience there was. The repertoire includes such numbers as Trixie Smith's 'Freight Train Blues', 'Long Gone John' and Woody Guthrie's 'New York Town'. If you don't believe that this kind of music could be a draw in London – and I don't blame you for doubting – drop in and feel the electric atmosphere that builds up during Lonnie Donegan's version of 'John Henry' or Ken Colyer's 'How Long'. Any time now the Library Of Congress will be coming across from Grosvenor Square to take the whole thing down on tape for Alan Lomax."

BRIAN NICHOLLS, *JAZZ JOURNAL*, JULY 1953

Alexis Korner was born in London in 1928, his parents originally from Greece and Austria, and seems to have spent most of his early life travelling around Europe, although the war brought the family back to the relative safety of England in 1940. In the army, Korner ended up at the BBC's British Forces Network based in Hamburg, already with an interest in music and playing guitar. Back in London he started knocking around the Soho jazz clubs in the early 1950s, playing where he could, all the while developing his interest in obscure blues records. He joined Colyer's outfit, and in 1955 landed a job as a trainee studio manager at the BBC.

In September of that year a blues and skiffle club was opened in a room over the Round House pub in Wardour Street at the corner of Brewer Street in Soho, among the first regular clubs in London formed to present such music. The players involved included Bob Watson, Pete Korrison, Cyril Davies and Korner. The club was in "an elongated room upstairs holding about 125 people, although on some nights there were more people waiting to play than pay," wrote Korner's biographer. "For the early birds there were seats in front of the stage, which had a piano to one side and a large mirror on the wall behind. A guest would open the evening about 7.30, then Cyril on 12-string and Alexis often on mandolin would play as a duo, and as the evening wore on other musicians would be invited up."[22]

Cyril Davies was a 23-year-old scrapyard panel-beater who loved the blues. The big man was a mean blues singer, played a wailing blues harp, strummed his distinctive Grimshaw 12-string guitar, and is described by many who knew him as the most convincing British bluesman of his time, compulsive about singing and playing folk-blues in general and the songs of Leadbelly in particular. With Korner, Davies would form the backbone of the club over the Round House, which drew gradually bigger audiences during the rest of 1955 and into 1956.

Ken Colyer had left the Jazzmen in 1954, and the outfit naturally turned into the Chris Barber Band, retaining for the moment Donegan and the skiffle group in its midst. During the summer of 1954 they'd put out an LP that included a couple of skiffle numbers among the jazz, and late in 1955 Decca issued a series of singles culled from the LP's tracks: by

RIVER CITY JAZZMEN. Admission 3/-. New members welcome.

SKIFFLE AND BLUES
SKIFFLE AND BLUES
opening September 1. featuring Ken Colyer, Bob Watson's Skiffle Group and guests.—" Round House," Wardour Street. 8-10.30. Admission 2/-. Free membership opening night.

One of the first clubs to offer the exotic attraction of regular skiffle and blues was started in 1955 by Bob Watson, Cyril Davies and others at the Round House pub in Soho.

February 1956 the Lonnie Donegan Skiffle Group's 'Rock Island Line' had become a tremendous success and shinned up the *NME* sales chart to peak at number eight. Starting then and lasting a good few years, skiffle became a national sensation – *Woman* magazine carried tips to achieve that perfect outdoor skiffle party; Kellogg's Rice Krispies offered a free "skiffle whistle" in each pack; the *Daily Herald* sponsored skiffle contests at Butlin's holiday camps; and even the jaunty music-hall-to-TV singer Max Bygraves put a verse in his recording of 'Fings Ain't Wot They Used T'Be' that went: "We used to have stars, singers who sung a Dixie melody, they're buying guitars, clickety-clop, backing themselves with three chords only." Kids everywhere were forming skiffle groups.

But where to play beyond the bedroom? London teenagers had already found the answer. Around the time that 'Rock Island Line' hit the charts some coffee bars were already echoing with the sounds of skiffle's optimistic ensemble vocal, cheap acoustic guitar, tea-chest bass (an upside-down packing case "body" with a broomstick "neck" and a piece of string attached) and washboard (a metal washday device pressed into percussive service by rapping it with fingers and knuckles).

Coffee houses had been popular in London for hundreds of years. Samuel Pepys often wrote in his famous *Diary* of the 1660s about visits to his local in Lombard Street, one among over 80 such establishments in London then. But almost 300 years later London coffee shop owners had something new to sell: genuine Italian espresso and cappuccino. Italian coffee king Achille Gaggia had revolutionised espresso-making in 1948 by introducing a pump-driven machine that worked by passing a powerful jet of hot water rather than steam through the coffee, producing a smoother-tasting drink. As part of the fashion for all things Italian, Gaggia's impressive new chromed machines began to arrive in England in the early 1950s. A number of the London coffee bars had the added bonus of genuine-sounding Italian immigrant families for owners, especially in the already cosmopolitan mix among the French and Swiss and Jews and Greeks and Irish in Soho. In 1953 the Moka Bar at 29 Frith Street had become the first coffee house in town with a Gaggia.

Teenagers were a new phenomenon, and businessmen had not yet learned to target their already significant spending power. The youth market did not exist, so the entertainment industry largely ignored them. Ballrooms were, by and large, for ballroom dancing. Pubs held little appeal. Apart from being too young to go in them, kids had little incentive to enter dreary, smelly drinking-holes designed for their parents and with an occasional drunken pensioner bashing out music-hall songs on an out-of-tune piano. And youth clubs were little better, run by parents with clearly parent-inspired agendas.

The attractions of the coffee bar, that peculiar amalgam of pine, caffeine, bamboo and bullfight posters, were legion. The coffee bar offered teenagers a warm, welcoming meeting-place. Not a parent in sight. You could sit nursing a single cup of coffee for hours, with no one suggesting a cross-country run in exchange for a badge. And music might come in the form of a stunning jukebox full of hip records, or live skiffle. Coffee bars were simply irresistible. "They were the first places where you could hang about for an evening, spend a shilling on a coffee, go in at nine and come out at eleven, and nobody bothered you, nobody said you had to have a second cup of coffee," Wally Whyton recalled. "It meant that you met strangers and socialised with them. 'What do you do?' 'Oh, I'm in advertising, I play the guitar.' 'Oh really? I play as well. What about bringing it down next Wednesday?'"[23]

Among the earliest of the central-London coffee bars noted for skiffle were the Bread Basket and the Gyre & Gimble. The Bread Basket was at 65 Cleveland Street, a half-mile or

JAZZ, SKIFFLE & ROCK'N'ROLL

25

Skiffle-blues-folk fusion in 1956! The City Ramblers skiffle group (Skiffle Music ad, above) rub shoulders with bluesman Cyril Davies and folk singer Peggy Seeger at the Princess Louise pub in Holborn. Not too far away, at the Bread Basket coffee bar, The Vipers Skiffle Group was forming, centred on a loose amalgam of Wally Whyton, Tommy Steele, Lionel Bart and others.

so north of Soho, beyond Oxford Street. It opened around the end of 1955, and soon had skifflers like Alexis Korner, Johnny Yorke and Nancy Whiskey playing downstairs. Wally Whyton again: "Spotting other budding entertainers in the basement of the Bread Basket, just five minutes from home, I decided to take my guitar along, and within a few weeks the nucleus of a group was formed."[24]

Whyton's band shuffled its members almost weekly, and became known as The Vipers Skiffle Group. Early line-ups included Tommy Hicks, whose employment as a merchant seamen made his appearances necessarily erratic (Hicks later became Steele), and Mike

PAUL LINCOLN & RAY HUNTER present

THE NEW 2 I's CLUB at 44 Gerrard St., W.1

The Old Place with the NEW FACE.

OPENING FRIDAY, OCTOBER 19th with a SENSATIONAL
JAZZ WEEK-END NON-STOP. JAZZ — SKIFFLE — ROCK 'N ROLL
& BLUES.   8-11 p.m., FRIDAY, SATURDAY and SUNDAY.

Join at the door, 2/6 yearly or at the 2 I's Coffee Bar,
59 Old Compton Street, W.1

Pratt, who worked with Whyton at an advertising agency, and was later better known as Jeff Randall in the TV series *Randall & Hopkirk Deceased*. Hicks, Whyton and Pratt, along with Lionel Bart (later renowned for his stage musicals), also called one of their aggregates The Cavemen; Hicks in later Steele mode had his first hit with a song they wrote together, 'Rock With the Caveman'. For the Vipers proper Whyton included partners such as bearded Belgian guitarist Jean van den Bosch and Canadian beatnik/guitarist Johnny Booker (aka Johnny Martyn).

The Gyre & Gimble was a little further from Soho than the Basket and in the other direction, a mile or so south at 31 John Adam Street, off the Strand near Charing Cross railway station. One habitué later described the tricky sequence of events that led to a night at the Gyre: "We'd take the Piccadilly Line [Underground] from Southgate and travel to Leicester Square with 12/6 [63p, about $1] in our pockets. It was very important to look right: black jumper, open-toed sandals, one red sock and one black sock, slim-jim tie and college scarf to finish the look off.

In those days skiffle music was all the rage and it wasn't booze but espresso coffee bars and cellar clubs that were the attraction… We would cruise down Charing Cross Road to the Gyre & Gimble. If you were in the know you would go through a scruffy bookshop… through a back door and down a long flight of stairs to where a dim cellar and candle-light awaited you. As you descended the stairs you were met by the sight and sounds of a chrome coffee-machine on the counter. There were nearly always three or four guitarists sitting around learning blues guitar riffs, and the occasional clarinet player.[25]

The Gyre & Gimble had started business in 1955, and was run by John St Crewe, and it was in this smokey all-night coffee bar that the formative Vipers met their first managers, Roy Tuvey and Bill Varley. They owned Trio Recording Services in Denmark Street, a studio that a few years later became Central Sound, and were enraptured with the skiffle on display at the coffee house.

So smitten were Tuvey and Varley that on a number of occasions they dragged a bulky professional tape recorder plus mixing desk and various microphones all the way from Denmark Street to what Whyton described as the "seedy hive of bohemian culture" in Charing Cross, in order to capture the sound of acts such as Chas McDevitt, Jim Dale, and Whyton's Vipers. Varley recalled: "We thought, let's try and make a programme out of this. We weren't really thinking money, I promise you, we were only thinking about the aesthetic qualities, if you like.

WHEN IN LONDON
visit
THE 2 I's
COFFEE BAR
59 OLD COMPTON ST., W.1
★
Home of the Stars—
TOMMY STEELE
THE VIPERS
TERRY DENE
★
Presenting every Night
SKIFFLE
at its best with
LES HOBOUAX
THE COTTON PICKERS
THE EASTSIDERS,
etc., etc.

The 2-Is coffee bar in Old Compton Street became a mecca for skiffle bands and fans. Ex-art-school skiffler Lionel Bart painted the eyes on the basement wall, seen behind the Vipers (below).

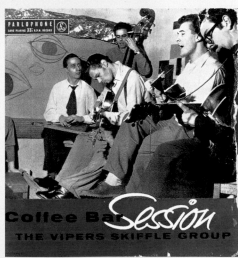

Coffee Bar *Session*
THE VIPERS SKIFFLE GROUP

Vince Taylor (right) ran his own shortlived coffee-bar club, the Top Ten. In later years his 'Brand New Cadillac' would be covered by The Clash, while Taylor himself was apparently David Bowie's model for the Ziggy Stardust character.

Fifties coffee-bar kids could hardly believe it when they were allowed the freedom to be themselves in their new subterranean meeting places. Amid loud jukeboxes blasting out very good music, the teenager was slowly coming to life.

❝ We thought the public generally should know about these people. Because who of the general public would be sitting in a very pungent sort of place at one o'clock in the morning listening to these people? Nobody seemed to be interested in it at all, strangely enough, until about the time the Lonnie Donegan record of 'Rock Island Line' was released as a single, that then sparked off the interest. Our coffee-bar-society tape had sort of gone into oblivion by then, so [we decided to manage these artists]. We thought they had something going for them.[26] ❞

The Vipers had a hit in February 1957 with 'Don't You Rock Me Daddy-O', and might have done even better had not Lonnie Donegan put out a version of the same song at the same time. The Gyre & Gimble became a betting shop in 1963, while the Bread Basket was closed and later demolished – almost the entire block is taken up today by college buildings.

We've already heard briefly (page 8) how the 2-Is coffee bar at 59 Old Compton Street stumbled on good business when, soon after opening in 1956, it began hosting live skiffle sessions. It became the best-known of the music coffee bars, in the heart of Soho, publicly forging links from skiffle to British rock'n'roll through the efforts of and publicity about performers such as Tommy Steele and Wee Willie Harris, and even hosted a live edition of TV's earliest teenage-music show, *Six-Five Special*, in November 1957.

But in its early months the 2-Is struggled to stay afloat. Paul Lincoln had arrived in Britain from his native Australia in 1951 with £20 ($31) in his pocket, and along with fellow Australian Ray Hunter began looking in London for a more reliable source of income than their wrestling bouts allowed. "We were able to rake up enough money to take these premises over in Old Compton Street in the West End," Lincoln recalled years later. "It was owned by three Iranian brothers and they called it the 3-Is. Apparently one of them left and so it ended up [as the] 2-Is. That's the name we took over and remained with."[27]

Lincoln and Hunter opened the 2-Is as their new coffee bar, probably in April of 1956 – and immediately began losing about £40 ($63) a week. Then another coffee bar opened right next door at number 57, called Heaven & Hell and owned by Eric Lindsay and Ray Jackson. "Heaven" was the brightly-lit ground floor, "hell" the dark, moody basement. As a result of this novel competition the early summer of 1956 saw business at the 2-Is go from lousy to non-existent. Then in July Wally Whyton and his Vipers popped in during the Soho Fair, and suddenly the 2-Is had a new attraction. Before long kids were queuing around the block, eager to pay their shilling entrance (5p, about 8¢) to the tiny skiffle basement.

The official capacity down there was 80 people, packed very tightly and sweatily into the tiny basement; more often it seemed like – and may well have been – several hundred. So popular did the Old Compton Street coffee bar become that owners Lincoln and Hunter hired a second 2-Is at 44 Gerrard Street before the end of 1956, presenting skiffle, jazz and rock'n'roll. But for most visitors, it was the original Old Compton Street basement or nothing. Another 2-Is regular, Adam Faith – then still Terry Nelhams and a member of The Worried Men Skiffle Group – well remembered the heaving mass of music-lovers jammed in front of him in the packed club.

If anybody fainted, because it was so hot in there, they would lift them up, and as you were singing you could see bodies being manhandled in the small gap between the heads and the ceiling, and being pushed out on to the pavement through the skylight. Five minutes later they'd have a cappuccino upstairs, they'd be refreshed and come back in again.[28]

It wasn't only budding musicians from London and its environs who were drawn to the 2-Is. National publicity in 1956 meant that youngsters from around the country flocked to it intending to play – and the astute Lincoln started holding audition evenings where hopefuls played for free (while punters, of course, still paid to get in).

Two such out-of-towners were Bruce Welch and Hank Marvin – originally Bruce Cripps and Brian Rankin – fresh down from Newcastle upon Tyne, some 300 miles to the north of London. "The upstairs was a bit like a glorified ice-cream parlour, I suppose," Marvin remembered of the 2-Is, "but the attraction really was the cellar downstairs. There was a tiny stage the width of the room, deep enough to get a drum kit on, that's all. So the drum kit went to one end of the stage and the other musicians, the guitars and singers, stood in line along the stage, because you couldn't stand one in front of the other. There wasn't room."[29] Marvin

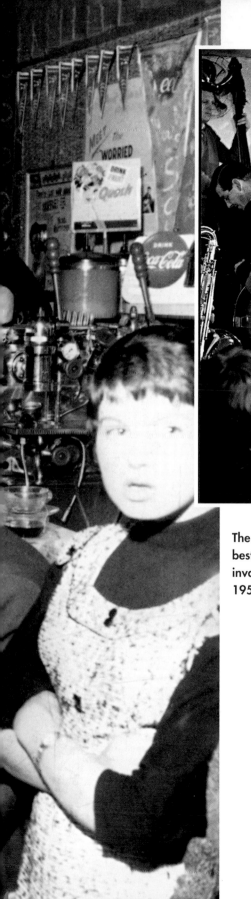

The 2-Is was never spacious at the best of times, so when BBC TV invaded the premises in November 1957 for a live broadcast of their new pop show Six-Five Special, cats were unswingable. Wee Willie Harris (with bow-tie, above) was among the performers.

and Welch soon got a break, toward the end of 1958, when Cliff Richard needed an injection of players into the backing band for his first tour. Manager John Foster went to the 2-Is to find some suitable candidates. Marvin said he'd do it, but only if Welch was in the band too. The Shadows were almost there. "Lincoln's policy of 'giving kids the opportunity to show just what they could do', as he was reported in a national newspaper as saying, had a double effect," Welch wrote later in his autobiography. "The 2-Is became a haven for agents, managers and impresarios on the look-out for new talent to discover. It also brought over 5,000 teenage hopefuls flocking to his door each year for that opportunity. If they were lucky they were auditioned and given a booking; if not, they moved on to the next coffee bar or club, and there were plenty of them. Hank and I were two of the lucky ones."[30]

One of the music-business professionals attracted to this hot-bed of potential pop-stars was George Martin, who would later become a household name as The Beatles' producer. Since 1950 Martin had worked for EMI, and was in effect the talent scout – as well as a good number of other things – for the small Parlophone label. Martin was tipped off by his friend Noel Whitcomb of the *Daily Mirror* and one evening in 1956 they visited the 2-Is together to see Tommy Steele playing with The Vipers. "We sat with our coffee and watched this genial young man bounce on to the stage with his guitar over his pelvis, and my immediate impression was that he was a blond cardboard imitation of Elvis Presley," Martin wrote years later.

> Noel thought the same. Tommy had a lot of energy, but his voice didn't sound that great – what little I could hear of it: for the Vipers were extremely loud and he wasn't. By today's standards the act was positively matronly, but for those days it was quite shocking, rather like musical masturbation; the pelvic gyrations quite turned me off, especially as I was still thinking only in terms of voices. Noel agreed... so I let Tommy Steele pass. On the other hand I liked [The Vipers] and thought they had great guts, so I signed them to a recording contract... But passing over Tommy Steele was obviously a big goof, especially since Decca came down [soon afterwards], signed him up, and made a great star out of him.[31]

These were examples of what soon became customary: a record-company scout visiting London clubs with the hope of finding raw live acts to turn into potentially lucrative recording stars. Martin, on his part, made two top-ten hits in 1957 with The Vipers: 'Don't You Rock Me Daddy-O' and 'Cumberland Gap'. "They used to jangle away on the acoustic guitars and make the most enormous sound," Martin wrote of The Vipers. "The style was really the forerunner of the electric guitars which came later – in a way the precursor of The Beatles."

As for the 2-Is in Old Compton Street, it limped on to 1970, when it became the Bistingo restaurant. Today the converted premises are occupied by a bar. It's often said that Tommy Steele was "discovered" at the 2-Is, and this probably has its roots in the account that Steele's co-manager, John Kennedy, gave in *Melody Maker* in May 1958. This was prompted by Kennedy's wish to distance himself and his charge from the contemporary stage musical *Expresso Bongo* (later a movie with Cliff Richard) which portrayed a witless coffee-bar singer turned into a star by a devious agent. Kennedy, on the fringes of the newspaper and PR worlds, said in *Melody Maker* that he first met Steele at the 2-Is while the budding singer was on shore-leave. This was probably around September 1956. The Vipers were playing, but "every time they finished a number, a kid with a tousled head would chip in with a rock'n'roll song and really get the other youngsters going".[32] Steele was by now an ex-Viper, explained

RICHARD GUNNELL (Entertainments) LTD.
Presents

ROCK 'N' ROLL

Starring

RORY BLACKWELL'S ROCK 'N' ROLLERS

CLUB HALEY

EVERY THURSDAY

Commencing SEPTEMBER 27th, at the

TAVISTOCK RESTAURANT BALLROOM

18 Charing Cross Road   8–11 p.m.

Summer 1956 saw rock'n'roll appearing in London's clubs and dancehalls for the first time, but the bands, like Rory Blackwell's, were mostly composed of jazzmen.

Kennedy, and was thus keen to show the group how he could make a mark on his own.

Steele moved on to another (unnamed) coffee bar; Kennedy followed and saw the same spontaneous reaction, and pointed out to Steele that he should exploit his personable, vital talent. "I'll tell you what," Kennedy reported Steele's answer, "you fix me up something before I go back to sea, and we'll talk business."[33] Kennedy told how he used his newspaper background to get Steele his break, posing the singer with pretend-debutantes for the cameras and convincing socialites that Tommy was their newly-adopted working class hero. Kennedy also noted that Hugh Mendl of Decca Records had already seen Steele at the 2-Is and was "so impressed that Tommy got a three-year [recording] contract", while impresario Larry Parnes was brought in "to help us on the business side".

Parnes offered a different set of recollections when interviewed in the 1980s for a book on pop-music managers.[34] In summer 1956 Kennedy met Parnes apparently by chance at the Sabrina coffee bar at 15 Wardour Street and enthused about Tommy Hicks, who he said just happened to be playing at the Condor Club, next door to the coffee bar at number 17. How about going upstairs to see him? Parnes however was tired, having just flown home that day from a holiday, and left – but not before Kennedy had insisted he come to Hicks's performance at The Stork Room, 99 Regent Street, the following week.

Parnes duly turned up at The Stork Room and, he said, recognised Hicks as an artist he'd already seen at the Gyre & Gimble three months earlier. Hicks was even better here. "It was a very hard club," Parnes recalled. "They weren't teenagers and this was a nightclub with a tough audience, but they loved him. He brought the place to life. He had charisma and a great personality." Parnes was introduced to Steele afterwards, and a management contract was signed a few weeks later, in September '56. Kennedy and Parnes proceeded to steer Steele away from rock'n'roll, turning him into the dreaded all-round entertainer – despite the musical leanings of his number one hit of January 1957, 'Singing The Blues'. A TV journalist wrote later of Steele at the Stork: "The management allowed Tommy to sit with me though not to buy a drink, treating him with barely concealed contempt. This was adult curiosity of the worst kind, good for a giggle but without sympathy."[35]

Part of Kennedy's and Parnes's method of creating a household name with Tommy Steele was to send him out to play for the general public in tours of civic halls and variety theatres, and to line up films and pantomimes for the lad, while continuing to promote the idea that he was the idol of the wealthy set by presenting him at top-notch central-London venues. Perhaps the team's biggest coup was to have Steele play in January 1957 at the Café de Paris, a fashionable, expensive dining-and-floorshow club in Coventry Street on the southern fringes of Soho. "It was that Café de Paris engagement that really made Tommy a star," Kennedy asserted. "It was worth a great deal of publicity. There was no difficulty in getting columnists there. I told them confidently that the first-night audience would be distinguished. I was amazed to find I was right." The socialites – and newspaper columnists – turned up to the Paris, and as Kennedy boasted, "His press notices the following day hailed a new star."

Steele might have started the idea that Brits could be rock'n'rollers too, but had quickly been diverted to the more familiar path of showbiz success. A number of other British rock'n'roll outfits began to appear, starting in summer 1956, following Elvis Presley's first assaults on the UK charts with 'Heartbreak Hotel' in May and 'Blue Suede Shoes' in June. Almost all of these early British "rock'n'roll bands" were composed of danceband musicians and jazzmen who spotted the potential for quick earnings from a passing fad.

Consequently the places to see rock'n'roll in its early British guise were usually dancehalls or jazz-club premises that switched to rock'n'roll for a night or two. Some of the earliest jazz

Despite the gleaming proximity of the hallowed Gaggia espresso machine, many coffee-bar kids opted for the hip prop of the distinctively waisted Coca-Cola bottle or, as Vince Taylor demonstrates at the 2-Is (below), the cool green 7-Up variety. But all drinks were best put aside during hip-twitching practice (left).

clubs advertising rock'n'roll were Studio 51 in Great Newport Street, which promised a "Rock'n'Roll Club" from August 23rd but didn't specify performers, and the Tavistock Restaurant Ballroom at 18 Charing Cross Road, which hosted Rik Gunnell's new Club Haley and presented Rory Blackwell's Rock'N'Rollars starting September 27th. Among the dancehalls, Wimbledon Palais put on a "rock'n'roll jamboree" in November with Blackwell and others.

Among the first British rock'n'roll bands was Tony Crombie's Rockets, with a six-man line-up of vocals, tenor sax, piano, bass, guitar and drums. Crombie was a modern-jazz drummer, one of the founders of Club 11, and had played with Ronnie Scott and Victor Feldman as well as leading his own outfit. Most of his fellow Rockets were also dumbed-down jazzers out for some welcome cash. Their agent was Jeff Kruger, founder of the Flamingo club, who'd added artist promotion to his activities and was specialising in rock'n'roll bands.

It's not so surprising that early British rock'n'roll was largely in the hands of jazzmen. After all, who else would be able to approximate this American invention? True, Larry Parnes's stable of 1950s British rock'n'rollers did include the fine guitarist Joe Brown among its singing frontmen, while Billy Fury's backing band numbered keyboardist Georgie Fame in its ranks and Marty Wilde's outfit boasted guitarist Big Jim Sullivan. However, the notion that untrained players could offer something worthwhile was limited to skiffle and some revivalist jazz; the acceptance of talented amateurs as pop musicians would have to wait a few years until the R&B boom of the early 1960s.

SUNDAY IS ROCK-'N'-ROLL NIGHT
AT
WIMBLEDON PALAIS
★ A STAR GROUP EVERY SUNDAY ★
2nd DECEMBER — RORY BLACKWELL'S ROCK 'N' ROLLARS
MEMBERS 3/- — JOIN OUR CLUB NOW — 7.30—11.0 p.m.

Meanwhile, the British Musicians' Union had at last reached an agreement with its American counterparts for an exchange system of US-for-UK visitors and vice versa. The effective ban on US musicians playing in Britain that had begun in 1935 was lifted during 1956, and the first American rock'n'roller to appear in Britain was 32-year-old Bill Haley, who debuted with his Comets at the Dominion Theatre in Tottenham Court Road in February 1957. Then in March of the following year came Buddy Holly. Budding British pop musicians turned out in droves to observe at first hand the working methods of Holly and his band, making ready for their own breakthrough that was now only just around the corner.

R E V I E W

BUDDY HOLLY & THE CRICKETS
TROCADERO, ELEPHANT & CASTLE, MARCH 1ST 1958
"Despite a Presley film across the road, they drew 1,500 into the first house and 3,000 to the second. And I might as well say now that, though it's an excellent show, I was disappointed that [they] were on stage little more than 20 minutes. With tickets up to 10/6 (53p, about 85¢) shortweight is hardly forgivable. Still, this was the first show. Strangely enough, they unload all their disc hits with feverish speed... by having them at the beginning, the act seems to end on an anti-climax. They are fortunate in being able to sit both sides of the fence: country and western fans need to look no further than the best-selling 'Peggy Sue' – and Buddy Holly is every bit as good as o the disc; and for the rock'n'rollers 'That'll Be The Day', 'Oh Boy', 'Rip It Up' and so on are given plenty of punch. I didn't feel quite at home with Buddy Holly when he added the Presley movements. He seems so obviously out of his depth. But – though I did detect a few scornful laughs – it produced the usual screams from the usual bevy of teenagers. There's no doubt about it, the outdated Variety halls could learn a lot from these teenage coast-to-coast tours... It's strictly pop music, but the customers are not likely to grumble about that. As Buddy Holly says, 'We like this kind of music – jazz is strictly for the stay-at-homes!'" **BILL HALDEN,**
MELODY MAKER, MARCH 8TH 1958

FIRST LONDON THEATRE APPEARANCE!

ROCK with **TOMMY STEELE**

DECCA'S DYNAMIC RECORDING
STAR singing his best sellers — "Rock
with the Caveman", "Doomsday
Rock" and "Singing the Blues".

Presented by HAROLD FIELDING

ALL NEXT WEEK!
**FINSBURY
PARK EMPIRE**

Twice Nightly at
6.25 & 8.40 p.m.

"He's Great, Great, Great"
— Ker Robertson, Daily Sketch

Paul Lincoln, owner of the 2-Is, stumbled upon Willie Harris selling drinks at the coffee bar with Mickie Most. Lincoln helpfully offered to make Wee Willie (above) a star, but the budding singer first had to dye his hair shocking pink. While the tinted Wee Willie was recording 'Rockin At The 2-Is', Tommy Steele was singing the blues at his first London theatre dates (poster, left).

FOLK CLUBS: FROM FINGERS-IN-EARS TO ELECTRIC GUITARS

38

Work songs of Britain and America blues, calypsos and folk-jazz.

Ballads & Blues

Ken Colyer's Banc
Isla Cameron
Ewan MacColl
A. L. Lloyd
Margaret Barrie
Fitzroy Coleman
Alf Edwards
The Two Gormor
Bruce Turner

ROYAL FESTIVAL HALL

Monday, July 5, at 8 p.m.

Ewan MacColl's influential Ballads & Blues folk club was presented at a number of London venues through the years. Occasionally the name was used for a bigger concert such as the Royal Festival Hall event announced in this 1954 ad (above). Bert Jansch (opposite) was among the "contemporary" folk players who created an alternative to MacColl's strict traditionalism.

MOST OF THE ORIGINAL SKIFFLERS had been inspired by American folk music, but there were others playing in London at the time who were in search of a British-based expression. From the 1950s the Scottish-born singer Ewan MacColl and others around him helped fire a new folk-music revival that centred on MacColl's Ballads & Blues club and later Singers Club.

These clubs were based at various times at a number of venues around central London, but MacColl was relentless in his touring around the whole country to present folk-song to everyone he could possibly reach. He wrote later that by the end of 1968 he and his American folk-singing wife Peggy Seeger had performed at no fewer than 482 clubs in Great Britain. MacColl, the son of an iron-moulder, was also strongly involved in radical theatre, having helped to establish The Theatre Workshop in east London.

The Ballads & Blues name was borrowed for the club from some successful radio work that MacColl had undertaken for the BBC, creating a series of themed programmes with illustrative songs performed by the likes of Big Bill Broonzy, Alan Lomax, Bert (A.L.) Lloyd, MacColl and others. "The main objective of the series," MacColl wrote, "was to demonstrate that Britain possessed a body of songs that were just as vigorous, as tough and as down-to-earth as anything that could be found in the United States. Against American songs like 'Frankie And Johnny' and chain-gang chants like 'Another Dead Man Gone' we juxtaposed traditional murder ballads and treadmill songs."[37] This mixed programme devised for MacColl's radio series accurately set the agenda for his clubs and the resulting folk-music revival. Later in the 1950s he instigated with folklorist Alan Lomax and producer Charles Parker the *Radio Ballads*, another influential set of BBC programmes, this time highlighting the documentary power of folk songs. The Ballads & Blues club's best-known London location was

FOLK CLUBS

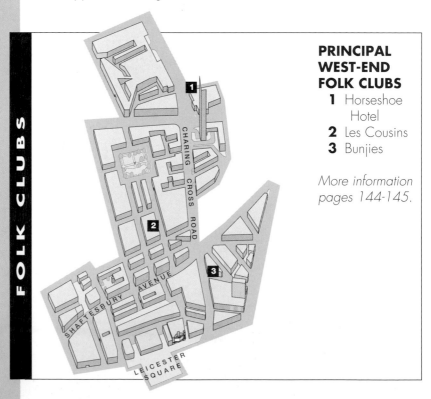

PRINCIPAL WEST-END FOLK CLUBS

1 Horseshoe Hotel

2 Les Cousins

3 Bunjies

More information pages 144-145.

at the Princess Louise in High Holborn, a big Victorian pub that's still there today. It was the first regular club of this MacColl-led traditional folk revival. From 1954, in an upper-floor room, the club would provide an often unpredictable mix not only of the club's stalwarts – MacColl, Seeger, Bert Lloyd, Seamus Ennis, Rory McEwan, Fitzroy Coleman – but a floorful of ordinary visitors who were encouraged at various points during the evening's entertainment to get up and sing a song or two.

MacColl's folk-club music was as pure and unadulterated as that of his radio programmes: work-songs, miners' laments, sea shanties, all underpinned by his passionate Communist

Ewan MacColl and his wife Peggy Seeger not only organised the Ballads & Blues gatherings but also the later Singers Club (pictured).

beliefs and celebrating the voice of the people. When MacColl or Lloyd sang, it was unaccompanied, with one hand cupped over an ear, the better to judge their accuracy of pitch. This gave rise to the sometimes derogatory description of the clichéd "finger-in-the-ear" folk singer: the kind who would set forth in nasal-toned voice on a 24-verse marathon about the appalling results of a mining disaster.

The Ballads & Blues club managed to absorb skiffle players and singers as that American-inspired music boomed in 1956 and 1957, but the skifflers who visited found themselves being turned on to their own native folk music. In a sense, the folk revival came directly out of skiffle. Folk singer and one-time skiffler John Hasted exemplified the link. "All along I had a

rather ambivalent attitude to skiffle," Hasted wrote later. "What I really dreamt of was a folk-song revival, but the skiffle craze was the next best thing. I called my group a 'Skiffle and Folksong Group' in the hope that a folk-song revival would grow out of skiffle. It did."[38] Jimmy McGregor was another regular at MacColl's clubs, and would later popularise folk music on TV in duet with Robin Hall. He said, "That easy, swingy American music got [the skifflers] going first of all, but then they graduated to more interesting music, if you like, more complicated music: their own traditional English, Irish and Scottish folk music."[39]

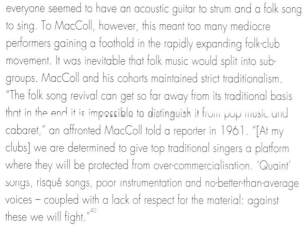

The revival took hold, many skifflers moved over and, as the 1960s got underway, everyone seemed to have an acoustic guitar to strum and a folk song to sing. To MacColl, however, this meant too many mediocre performers gaining a foothold in the rapidly expanding folk-club movement. It was inevitable that folk music would split into sub-groups. MacColl and his cohorts maintained strict traditionalism. "The folk song revival can get so far away from its traditional basis that in the end it is impossible to distinguish it from pop music and cabaret," an affronted MacColl told a reporter in 1961. "[At my clubs] we are determined to give top traditional singers a platform where they will be protected from over-commercialisation. 'Quaint' songs, risqué songs, poor instrumentation and no-better-than-average voices – coupled with a lack of respect for the material: against these we will fight."[40]

In the early 1960s, at odds with MacColl and his traditionalists, came the new wave of "contemporary" folk players, generally younger and more open to new directions. The key man among the contemporary guitarists was Davy Graham. He freely combined jazz, blues and folk, as well as occasionally throwing in a stately baroque melody or a modal Indian drone, spinning a skilful, finger-picked style that inspired Bert Jansch, John Renbourn and others and was sometimes called "folk-baroque". Graham's best-known piece was the instrumental 'Angie' which many 1960s folk converts would aim for, gaining little more than sore fingers.

Akin to the folk-baroque pickers was the new breed of singer-songwriter, strumming rather than picking their guitars, and singing their own songs in the wake of Bob Dylan's quickly-growing influence. Dylan had first come to Britain in 1962, just after the release of his first album, to contribute to a play for BBC TV, and took time out to visit The Troubadour at 265 Old Brompton Road in Earls Court, west London. The Troubadour was a coffee bar opened around 1955 that by the early 1960s was hosting live folk music in its basement. The Troub's Anthea Joseph remembered Dylan's visit.

❝ **I saw these feet coming down the stairs, cowboy boots and jeans which was quite unusual, and I thought: oh God, it's one of the Southend hillbillies, I can't bear it. Then he came down a bit further and I saw the face and thought: I know that face. He pushed some money at me and said, 'Can I come in?' 'Hang on, you are Bob Dylan?' 'Yes, I am.' 'Right, if you play, you can come in for nothing.' Half the audience loved it, the other half hated it.**[41] ❞

● **SATURDAY** ●

A CLUB Calendar announcement last week gave the impression that Don Rendell was appearing with his New Buffet, Alto and Tenor at the "Flamingo" on Wednesday, February 1st. The date was, in fact, Saturday, January 28th, and Don will be at the "Flamingo" again on Saturday, February 4th.

AT THE TROUBADOUR, 265, Old Brompton Road, Earls Court, 10.30: **SHIRLEY COLLINS** and **MARTIN CARTHY.**

The Troubadour was a coffee bar in Earls Court that became an integral part of the folk scene in the 1960s. The ad from 1961 (above) is an early indication of its new role. Martin Carthy (silhouetted in the inset picture, right) was a popular performer at the Troub, which became important as a meeting place as well as for its live music. Charlie Watts met Alexis Korner here, and Korner invited him to join Blues Incorporated.

REVIEW

By the middle of the 1960s *Melody Maker* was describing The Troubadour as "probably the oldest [folk] club still going and one of the few non-alcoholic ones", adding that it was "a place to arrive early, otherwise you either don't get in or you suffocate at the back of the basement where the singing goes on".[42] One of those appearing before the regular throng was Martin Carthy, another skiffle convert. Carthy soon began to carve out his own path somewhere between the well-trodden traditionalism of MacColl and the newer ground of the singer-songwriters. He also formed an inspiring duo with fiddler Dave Swarbrick, who would go on to wider fame in Fairport Convention, and the two dug deep into traditional material for many of their rousing Troub sets.

Bunjies was at 27 Litchfield Street, another coffee house opened in the mid 1950s that began to present folk – but earlier than The Troubadour. Among the first to play at Bunjies was Davy Graham, in 1956. Sometimes called The Folk Cellar, Bunjies was run in the 1960s by Lou Hart and Theo Johnson. Dylan also dropped in here during his '62 visit, on this occasion parting with entrance money even though he sang a couple of songs. Paul Simon had a flat a few doors away during his mid-1960s stay in London, and Al Stewart started playing here in 1965 with a residency that ran almost uninterrupted for two years. Stewart reckoned he accidentally stumbled into folk music when a friend took him to Bunjies.

> Somehow I got conned into playing something. I only knew two songs: one of my own and a Dylan number. The manager heard me play and booked me as a resident. So I went home and learnt two Dylan LPs off by heart. Next week at Bunjies I played them straight through in the same order as the record. Gradually I made up more songs of my own to go alongside the Dylan numbers.[43]

The other big name in folk clubs in central London at the time was Les Cousins (usually anglicised to plain Cousins). It was housed in the old Skiffle Cellar premises in the basement of 49 Greek Street and run by Andy Matthews, whose parents had a restaurant nearby. During the early 1960s Cousins was (not forgetting the Flamingo) one of the few clubs to stay open all night, and together with The Scot's Hoose pub near Cambridge Circus it quickly became a popular folk hang-out. Players who appeared regularly through the 1960s included Bert Jansch, John Renbourn, Ralph McTell, Paul Simon, John Martyn, Al Stewart and Roy Harper.

Greeted by some famously hostile audiences, Dylan's visit to Britain with The Hawks and

Cousins club presentations loom from the 1960s "Folk Forum" listings in Melody Maker, not least London resident Paul Simon strumming 'The Sound Of Silence' in August 1965 (top) or Bert Jansch grappling with 'Angie' the following week.

a selection of amplifiers in May 1966 had alerted some British folk musicians to the possibilities of electric instruments. Two of the earliest British folkies to explore the world of pickups and volume controls were Jansch and Renbourn, who started a club in February 1967 at the Horseshoe Hotel, a pub next door to the Dominion Theatre in Tottenham Court Road. From the very first Horseshoe date they began to amplify their own guitars and add miked vocals, amplified bass, and drums. It was the start of what soon became Pentangle, a group that merged folk, jazz and rock. A surprised reviewer described that opening night at the Horseshoe: "The third session [of the evening] was switched-on and plugged-in! Renbourn played electric guitar and Jansch fitted an electrical pickup to his instrument. They were joined by bass and drums. It all seemed disorganised – 'under-rehearsed' said one fan – but happy."[44] It wasn't long before Pentangle had organised themselves and made sense of the new balance required between Jansch and Renbourn's acoustic and electric guitars, Jacqui McShee's lead vocals, Danny Thompson's amplified upright bass and Terry Cox's drums.

By summer 1967 folk players' interest in electric instruments was spreading. Columnist Karl Dallas, noting Al Stewart's new "experimental" residency at the Marquee, wrote: "Does this mean that folk-rock, the hybrid musical form that arose from the demise of the American folk scene and manifested itself in the shape of The Lovin' Spoonful, The Byrds and the electric Dylan, may happen here?" Stewart agreed that pop and folk were moving closer together, concluding: "Within the next year a whole stack of folk singers are going to switch to electric guitars."[45]

Fairport Convention had come together in north London during 1967 as a group mainly hooked on the west-coast rock of bands like Jefferson Airplane, and they soon began seeking gigs. They sprinkled some hopeful ads through *Melody Maker*'s Club Calendar listings in May. Friday: "Fairport Convention stays home tonight", Saturday: "Fairport Convention stays home again patiently awaiting bookings"; and Sunday: "Fairport Convention gives up hope, goes to Highgate Odeon". By June, however, they were playing an audition night at the Happening 44 club in Gerrard Street, and soon after were spotted and signed-up to their first record deal. But the additions of folk singer Sandy Denny to the group early the following year and then fiddler Dave Swarbrick saw them switching to folk-rock, mixing rearranged traditional material and contemporary songs. They quickly became the genre's leading outfit, surviving multiple changes of personnel through the decades.

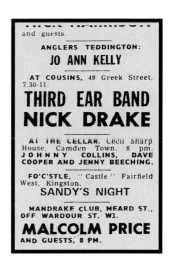

More Cousins ads to transport one back to the golden days of purely acoustic entertainment in Soho. Needless to say, Al Stewart was a regular in 1966 (below). Those who recall this April 1970 show (above) may have seen Nick Drake perform songs from his forthcoming second album, Bryter Later.

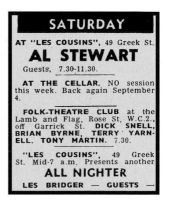

REVIEW

FAIRPORT CONVENTION

ROYAL FESTIVAL HALL, SEPTEMBER 24TH 1969

"Fairport Convention have put an ingredient back into folk music that has been missing for a long time now. The ingredient? Excitement. At their packed first major appearance for six months they proved the possibility of fusing a traditional form with the modern setting of electric instrumentation, still retaining a musical integrity and taste that in other hands may well have gone by the board. Their treatment of ballads… has brought traditional folk music into a far more plausible perspective and given it a more tangible relevance with what is happening musically

today than half a dozen revivals could hope to do. Fairport [have also] moved into the dance music area of traditional folk. They included two sections of jigs and reels, mainly featuring Swarbrick, but outstanding was [one with] a brilliant Richard Thompson guitar solo that shifted the accent from British to American country music… The Fairport, of course, didn't stick to an entirely traditional programme [but included contemporary songs too]. The audience reacted very favourably to the Fairport's new direction, and it will be interesting to see if there is any reflection of their approach to traditional music from the folk scene in the near future."

TONY WILSON, *MELODY MAKER*, OCTOBER 4TH 1969

BRITISH R&B: BORN IN THE LONDON CLUBS

"RHYTHM-AND-BLUES", OR R&B, WAS A TERM invented in the US at the end of the 1940s by *Billboard*. The music-trade magazine coined it to replace "race records", a chart grouping they'd used since the 1920s to separate the work of black artists. Today, music historians tend to use R&B as a catch-all description for the best black American pop made between about 1945 and 1960 – from Louis Jordan to Ray Charles, Bo Diddley to Muddy Waters, Howlin' Wolf to Chuck Berry.

In the early 1960s, Britain developed its own version. But at first it wasn't easy to hear much of the original stuff here. Radio was, with rare and honourable exceptions, closed to it. Occasional records came back with enlightened travellers, the American Embassy in London had some gems in their disc library, and Pye's valuable "R&B Series" of US recordings started to appear around 1960.

But we did get a few precious visitors. Despite the continuation of what amounted to a union ban on almost any US musicians playing in the UK, some enthusiasts managed to bring in a bluesman or three during the 1950s. Josh White was more slick showman than R&B artist, but in July 1950 he became the first black American solo singer-guitarist to play in the UK. And guess who was at the head of the queue to study him up close? "Over at the Chiswick Empire," reported *Melody Maker*'s club columnist, "following his shows, the dressing-room of Josh White was jammed with club members from all over town listening to impromptu sessions by this great folk-singer. Guitarist Alex Korner received a signal honour when Josh invited him to provide the accompaniment backstage."[46]

Others came: Big Bill Broonzy, Lonnie Johnson, Sonny Terry & Brownie McGhee, Sister Rosetta Tharpe. Chris Barber and the NJF often facilitated these visits, and their biggest coup came in presenting Muddy Waters in October 1958. Muddy brought his piano player Otis Spann... and his Fender Telecaster guitar. The sonic bombardment of real, loud, aggressive rhythm-and-blues came as a shock: the audience could hardly believe their (sore) ears.

Alexis Korner and his blues-wailing partner Cyril Davies had early in 1957 renamed their skiffle-and-blues club above the Round House pub in Wardour Street as the Barrelhouse & Blues. Korner explained later, "Cyril said to me, 'I'm fed up with all this skiffle rubbish, I want to open a blues club. Will you run it with me?' I said yes. One week we shut down with a full house, the next we opened the Barrelhouse & Blues club and three people turned up."[47] As he'd done with a number of previous visiting bluesmen, Korner persuaded Muddy Waters to drop by the Round House, and the American cheerfully blasted out some beer-glass-rattling R&B on his Telecaster.

Korner, spurred on by these first-hand experiences, was invited by Chris Barber toward the end of 1961 to rejoin the Barber band for another "interval act"; not this time to play skiffle, but electric blues. Korner had also resolved to put together his own group, Blues Incorporated. Barber's outfit had a regular gig at the Marquee, and in the first few days of January 1962 an early version of the R&B interval act appeared. *Jazz News* caught the whiff of something new: "The Marquee club last Wednesday night was the scene of great excitement when guitarist Alexis Korner combined with Barber-band trumpeter Pat Halcox on piano and harmonica player Cyril Davies to play a set of rhythm-and-blues numbers. Following the success of the session Korner will make regular appearances at the Marquee. Korner's own newly-formed R&B band plays a concert with the Acker Bilk band [in January at Croydon]."[48] Bilk was the bowler-hatted

---

The earliest evidence of a venue calling itself an R&B club is this ad (above) from 1960 for St Mary's Hall in Putney. Around 1963 some up-and-coming groups such as The Rolling Stones and The Detours (later The Who) would play there.

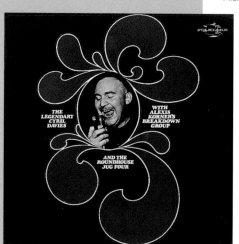

Rare recordings of Cyril Davies and Alexis Korner in 1957 at the Round House pub were reissued on this LP.

Cyril Davies (below left) and Alexis Korner were the prime movers of the British R&B movement. Both loved the blues and spread its infectious power by any means possible, not least their forming in 1962 of Britain's first successful R&B group, Blues Incorporated. Their first-ever gig in March 1962 at The Ealing Club was advertised in Jazz News (near right), while December dates included the Oxford Street Marquee and La Discotheque.

Cyril Davies (harp) and Alexis Korner (electric guitar) seen making musical history with Blues Incorporated at The Ealing Club in west London in 1962. Just visible in the shadows is their drummer, Charlie Watts.

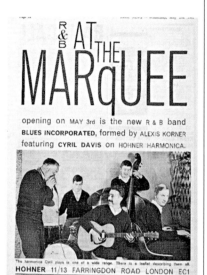

opening on MAY 3rd is the new R & B band
BLUES INCORPORATED, formed by ALEXIS KORNER
featuring CYRIL DAVIS on HOHNER HARMONICA.

The harmonica Cyril plays is one of a wide range. There is a leaflet describing them all.

HOHNER 11/13 FARRINGDON ROAD LONDON EC1

Blues Incoporated moved to the Marquee in May 1962 and began the first regular R&B dates at what had been solely a jazz club. The

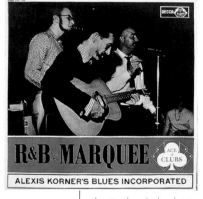

R&B from the MARQUEE

ALEXIS KORNER'S BLUES INCORPORATED

line-ups varied but included (top of page) Charlie Watts on drums and Jack Bruce on bass, and (above) Dick Heckstall-Smith on sax. The band's "R&B From The Marquee" LP was actually a studio recording.

R E V I E W

MUDDY WATERS

ST PANCRAS TOWN HALL, **OCTOBER 20TH 1958**

"There were some who could not hear [Muddy's] voice properly over the powerfully amplified guitar, and others who simply do not care for the electric instrument at all. But whichever way you looked at it, Muddy's concert was remarkable. For an hour and a quarter he sang and played with a fierce intensity... His right-hand man and half-brother, Otis Spann, who has worked with him for ten years or more, complemented the vocal and guitar parts with rolling blues piano such as we have never heard before in this country. [Chris Barber's bassist Dick Smith and drummer Graham Burbidge] supplied the required extra sock. It was tough, unpolite, strongly rhythmic music, often very loud but with some light and shade in each number, such as you could have danced to with confidence. The repertoire was pure blues, and the style was vital, uninhibited and decidedly 'down South'... I liked some of the violent, explosive guitar accompaniment – although there were times when my thoughts turned with affection to the tones of the acoustic guitar heard on his first record... At a guess I'd say this was the nearest we'll get to a Chicago South Side blues performance in London. Muddy seemed able to forget where he was standing as, eyes closed, he built up patterns, sometimes walls, of electrified sound." **MAX JONES,** *MELODY MAKER,* **OCTOBER 25TH 1958**

figurehead of trad, the popular early-1960s version of revivalist jazz, accurately described by *Melody Maker* in 1961 as "the new rage". Clarinettist Bilk had a series of hit records, peaking with 'Stranger On The Shore', and was a big concert draw for many years. While Korner was plugging in his amplified guitar and making the first moves toward the music that would displace it, trad was everywhere in London's clubs (notwithstanding modern-jazz mainstays at Ronnie's and the Flamingo). Trad outfits such as Kenny Ball's Jazzmen, The Temperance Seven, Terry Lightfoot & His New Orleans Jazzmen and The Mick Mulligan Band played to enthusiastic audiences at packed venues like the Jazzshows Jazz Club (as 100 Oxford Street was now known), Eel Pie Island (an ancient, shabby ballroom on the Thames at Twickenham) and the Ken Colyer Club (at the Studio 51 premises in Soho).

Meanwhile, Korner shifted and changed the line-up of his new band almost gig by gig, striving for the right musical balance. For example, ex-Screaming Lord Sutch singer Andy Wren didn't work and was soon replaced by Art Wood. Korner, frustrated by the short Barber interval spot, wanted a regular gig for his Blues Incorporated; new boy Wood, who'd been at Ealing art school, suggested the Ealing Club as a possibility.

The Ealing Club at 42A The Broadway, Ealing, in west London, had opened in January 1959 as a jazz dive, first advertised as "a backstairs session at the Moist Hoist" because of the club's location in a leaky basement reached down some steep external steps. Blues Incorporated opened there in March 1962, and Korner recalled a few years later how he'd persuaded the Ealing Club to "take a gamble and open its doors to R&B". It was an unforgettable opening night: "I had Cyril Davies on harmonica, Mick Jagger and Art Wood singing, Charlie Watts on drums, and even Paul Jones hitchhiked down from Oxford to help out. Week by week more people arrived."[49] This concertina'd recollection puts more people on that first-night stage than is likely, but certainly the Ealing Club, as London's first regular R&B venue, very soon attracted

almost every budding R&B musician from miles around, some of whom would become architects of a new British pop structure. Ealing regulars included Jagger, Watts and Paul Jones, as well as Keith Richard and Brian Jones, Jack Bruce and Ginger Baker, Graham Bond and Long John Baldry. Jagger, already in a bedroom-only R&B band, remembered:

> **[Blues Incorporated didn't play] the kind of rhythm-and-blues that we had expected, or liked to play ourselves; it was more of a jazz band, in our opinion. Alexis [sang] these funny blues interpretations in what seemed to us a very upper-class English accent. We used to hoot with laughter about this. Cyril played very good harmonica – I'd never seen anyone play it like that before – and, of course, Charlie was playing drums. It was a Mecca for anyone interested in the blues. We went every Saturday... and soon got up the courage to get up and have a go ourselves. I saw people my own age getting up – like Paul Jones and Brian Jones – and I thought to myself, 'They're not that brilliant, I can do as well as that.' So I got up and sang 'Got My Mojo Working'... and before I knew what was happening, I was one of the band's featured vocalists. Then Keith would come up and we'd do a couple of Chuck Berry things... That's how it all started.[50]**

In May 1962 Blues Incorporated moved their regular gig from the damp, distant Ealing Club to the prestigious, central Marquee. The Marquee was now open four nights a week presenting a mix of trad and modern jazz, but for Blues Incorporated an additional Thursday-night slot was opened. As the weeks went by, Thursday nights at the Marquee would reveal new recruits to the band, including Jack Bruce on bass and Ginger Baker on drums. Toward the end of 1962 the group were regularly attracting audiences of 700, but with Korner leading them to ever-jazzier territory Davies felt further from the pure country-blues he loved, and left the group.

Korner moved Blues Incorporated to the Flamingo in January of the new year, probably for more money, while Davies continued the Thursday-night slot at the Marquee with his new band, the R&B All-Stars, soon with the bonus of vocalist Long John Baldry. One club-goer described the contrast between the frontmen: "Cyril Davies, who played the harmonica brilliantly, [looked] near 40, balding, and wore lumpy jackets and baggy corduroys. The singer, Long John Baldry, was about 6' 6" tall, incredibly thin and young-looking, and wore an immaculate silver-grey mod suit."[51]

While Korner faced the volatile Flamingo crowd, the All-Stars played successfully in a number of clubs where R&B was attracting increasing audiences. Studio 51 in Great Newport Street, the Railway Hotel in Harrow and Eel Pie Island at Twickenham served them well, while another strong venue was Len Weston's new Roaring 20s club, in the erstwhile Club 11 basement at 50 Carnaby Street. It was one of the first London clubs that had a notably black clientele (although the Flamingo too attracted a good number of Afro-Caribbeans) with the sound-system of Count Suckle a distinct draw. *Jazz News* reported in January 1963 that "velvet excitement" erupted when "Peggy Phango and her girls from the *King Kong* cast joined Cyril Davies and his All-Stars in an evening of rhythm-and-blues unsurpassed so far in London".[52] The four black singers from the West End show frequently joined the All-Stars after that Roaring 20s debut, billed as backing vocalists The Velvettes.

Meanwhile, Ealing Club regular Brian Jones was busy forming The Rollin' Stones (no "g" at this stage), an R&B group of shiftin' personnel that rehearsed in various Soho pubs. In July

Cyril Davies split from Korner and formed his R&B All-Stars in late 1962. Charlie Watts also left and formed Blues By Six. Saxman Dave Gelly: "Charlie lived in a place so small there wasn't room for him and the drums. So he used to keep them in the left-luggage office at Leicester Square underground station. That meant that wherever we were going we had to go via Leicester Square to pick up the drums. He'd produce the left-luggage ticket, and out would come Charlie's drums."

RHYTHM & BLUES EXCITEMENT
AT THE **MARQUEE**
EVERY MONDAY AND THURSDAY
THIS THURSDAY, 3rd JANUARY
CYRIL DAVIES R & B ALL STARS
WITH THE **ROLLING STONES**

A SHOT OF RHYTHM AND BLUES!
THE ROLLIN' STONES
EVERY SATURDAY AT THE EALING CLUB.
7.30 p.m. — 11.00 p.m.
(Opposite Ealing Broadway Station)

The Rollin' Stones (usually no 'g' at this stage) played the Marquee in 1962 (Richard and Jones pictured there, left) as interval act for Blues Incorporated. In September they played the Ealing Club, and performed another interval spot, this time for the All-Stars, early the following year (ads, above).

MERRY CHRISTMAS!
From **Ken Colyer &
the Jazzmen**
MAC DUNCAN IAN WHEELER JOHN BASTABLE COLIN BOWDEN RON WARD & RAY FOXLEY

**Come along and hear us
every Fri., Sat., Sun., Mon.**
at STUDIO '51, 10/11 GT. NEWPORT ST., W.C.2 7.30-11 p.m.
Piccadilly or Northern Line to Leicester Sq. Buses 1 24 29 39 134 176

Another early gig for the Stones was at Studio 51 in Great Newport Street. The premises also hosted a regular trad-jazz club run by Ken Colyer. His band, the Jazzmen, were of course regular attractions there.

1962, with Jagger and Richard on board, the group played its first gig, as Blues Incorporated's interval act at the Oxford Street Marquee. They lasted there until later that summer. The club's boss remembers a TV interview on the subject years later. "They said, 'Harold Pendleton, 20 years ago today the Rolling Stones first appeared at your club, the Marquee. What did you think of them?' I said well, I can't say, because I'd gone to the pub.

> **The Stones were the interval group: we put them on to fill up time while we all went for a drink – the club wasn't licensed then. I explained how I always went with the main band to have a drink, so I never saw the Stones. 'Stop the cameras!' But I said I do remember their last appearance at the club [in January 1963]. I was coming out with Cyril Davies, who was leading the real band, and there was a band loading on the other side of Poland Street. So I said, 'Good night,' and they said, 'Fuck off!' back. I said to Cyril, 'Who are they?' He said, 'Oh, they're difficult, the Rolling Stones; sacked 'em, no good.' Oh, I said. They're a bit upset, aren't they?**[53]

These were still early days for British R&B. Brian Jones tried to help by defining the music in a letter to *Jazz News* late in 1962. He concluded: "It would be ludicrous if the same type of pseudo-intellectual snobbery that one unfortunately finds contaminating the jazz scene were to be applied to anything as basic and vital as rhythm-and-blues."[54] *Jazz News* ignored the slight and sided with Jones, starting a regular R&B column the following month and regularly logging London's six most active R&B bands: Blues Incorporated, Cyril Davies's All-Stars, Blues Plus Six, The Rollin' Stones, The Wes Minster Five, and Dave Hunt's R&B Band.

THE
NEW CRAZE
IN BEAT
MUSIC
RHYTHM
AND
BLUES
DAVE HUNT'S
RHYTHM & BLUES BAND

OPENING THIS FRIDAY
41, GC Wardour St Soho

DAVE HUNT'S R & B BAND
R & B — NEW YORK STYLE
● FEATURING HAMILTON KING ●

PICCADILLY CLUB — EVERY FRIDAY P.M.
Richmond Station Hotel — EVERY SUNDAY P.M.

NEW YEAR'S EVE AT THE PICCADILLY
8 p.m. — 12.30 p.m. : STAR GUESTS

Dave Hunt (above) was a jazzman who defected to R&B when it became popular. His band was the first R&B outfit to play the Station Hotel in Richmond, which soon became the Crawdaddy. Hunt was moved aside when the Stones started playing there early in 1963, but continued for a while to perform at the Piccadilly, a new club in the old Cy Laurie premises in Soho.

In Richmond, south-west London, various jazz clubs had run at the Station Hotel pub in Kew Road since the early 1950s. Giorgio Gomelsky was a Russian émigré, working as a film editor at Shepperton Studios, and a fan of jazz and R&B – he'd made some jazz documentaries since arriving in Britain in 1955 at the age of 20. At the end of 1962 Gomelsky began promoting regular Sunday R&B evenings at the Station Hotel, first by transforming the resident trad band, Dave Hunt's Confederates, into Dave Hunt's R&B Band – with a pre-Kinks Ray Davies alongside trombonist Hunt. Davies later described the band as "a combination of mainstream jazz and big-band-style blues players".[55] Hunt himself summed up the confusion at the time: "R&B," he explained, "is what the rockers call jazz and the jazzmen call rock'n'roll."[56]

Early in 1963 Gomelsky became frustrated by the unreliability of Hunt's band. "The young Brian Jones was always bending my ear," recalls Gomelsky. "He'd say with his lisp, 'You mutht help uth, we have the betht blueth band in the land.' So when Hunt goofed it, I called up the Stones pianist Ian Stewart at his work at ICI – that's how you contacted the Stones then – and asked if they wanted a residency on Sunday night. Of course they did. The first night three people came."[57] However, the Stones audience soon began to grow steadily.

Local journalist Barry May visited the club to write a piece during April 1963 and asked Gomelsky for its name; in the absence of anything else Gomelsky reeled off the name Crawdaddy, recalling Bo Diddley's song 'Doing The Craw-Daddy'. That same month Andrew Oldham and Eric Easton also came to see the Stones at the Crawdaddy, and signed them to a management deal, ending Gomelsky's hopes in that direction.

53

Dancing at the 100 Club (left). Still in action at the time of writing, 100 Oxford Street is one of London's longest-running music-club dives. It opened in 1942 as The Feldman Swing Club. Jazzshows took it over in 1959, but this series of ads from 1964 (below) shows its changing status that year: introducing regular R&B in January (left); soon splitting club names for jazz and R&B (centre); and permanently changing the name to The 100 Club in September (right).

Jazzshows Jazz Club

EVERY NIGHT AT 7.30
100 OXFORD STREET, W.1

Thursday, January 16th
BOB WALLIS' Storeyville Jazzmen
Friday, January 17th
ALEX WELSH & HIS BAND
JOHN CHILTON'S QUARTET
Saturday, January 18th
THE AVON CITIES JAZZ BAND
with CHRIS MARLOWE
RAY BUSH R & B GROUP
Sunday, January 19th
TERRY LIGHTFOOT'S JAZZMEN
Monday, January 20th
ALAN ELSDON'S JAZZ BAND
MICK EMERY'S FOLK GROUP
DOUGGIE RICHFORD'S TRIO
Tuesday, January 21st
MONTY SUNSHINE'S JAZZ BAND
with VAL WISEMAN
DICKIE BISHOP'S FOLK GROUP
Wednesday, January 22nd
BACK O' TOWN SYNCOPATOR
DOUGGIE RICHFORD'S TRIO
★ **Thursday, January 23rd** ★
RHYTHM & BLUES with
★ **THE ANIMALS** ★
JIMMY POWELL & THE
★ **FIVE DIMENSIONS** ★
★ Members 5/-, Guests 6/- ★
Full details of the Club from the Secretary

Jazzshows Jazz Club
100 OXFORD STREET, W.1
AT 7.30

Friday, February 28th
MONTY SUNSHINE'S
with VAL WISEMAN   JAZZ BAND
DICKIE BISHOP'S FOLK GROUP
Saturday, February 29th
THE BACK O' TOWN
SYNCOPATORS
Sunday, March 1st
THE MIKE COTTON BAND
Monday, March 2nd
ALAN ELSDON'S JAZZ BAND
MICK EMERY'S FOLK GROUP
Wednesday, March 4th
THE BACK O' TOWN
SYNCOPATORS
Full details of the Club from the Secretary
J.J.C., 22 Newman St., W.1 (LAN 0184)

100 CLUB
100 OXFORD ST., W.1
7·30 to 11 p.m.
RHYTHM AND BLUES

Thursday, February 27th
JIMMY POWELL
AND THE FIVE DIMENSIONS
JOHN LEE AND THE GROUND HOGS plus
THE PRETTY THINGS
Tuesday, March 3rd
THE ANIMALS
JOHN LEE AND THE GROUND HOGS
Thursday, March 5th
THE ALEX HARVEY SOUL BAND
THE WES MINSTER 5
Full details of the Club from the Secretary
100 Club, 22 Newman St., W.1 (LAN 0184)

100 CLUB
100 OXFORD ST., W.1
7·30 to 11 p.m.

Thursday, September 3rd
THE GRAHAM BOND ORGANISATION
THE KING B FOUR
Friday, September 4th
THE MIKE DANIELS BIG BAND
THE DELTA JAZZMEN
JOHN CHILTON'S QUARTET
Saturday, September 5th
ALEX WELSH and his BAND
JOHN MADDOX TRIO
Sunday, September 6th
TERRY LIGHTFOOT'S JAZZMEN
Monday, September 7th
THE BIRDS
THE BLUES BY KNIGHT
Tuesday, September 8th
THE PRETTY THINGS
BRIAN KNIGHT'S BLUES BY SIX
Wednesday, September 9th
Wednesday Night Beat Session
THE KINKS
DANNY AND THE TORINOS
Thursday, September 10th
THE GRAHAM BOND ORGANISATION
THE KING B FOUR
Full details of the Club from the Secretary

54

Another kind of British R&B began at the Flamingo, known for modern-jazz (above). Georgie Fame & The Blue Flames began at the Flamingo (below) in 1962 and recorded a live LP at the club the following year.

THE ROLLIN' STONES

CRAWDADDY, RICHMOND, (PROBABLY APRIL) 1963

"A musical magnet is drawing the jazz beatniks away from Eel Pie Island, Twickenham, to a new Mecca in Richmond. The attraction is the new Crawdaddy rhythm-and-blues club… the first club of its kind in an area of flourishing modern and traditional jazz haunts. Rhythm-and-blues, gaining more popularity every week, is replacing [trad] all over the country, and even persuading the more sedate modernists to leave their plush clubs. The deep, earthy sound produced at the hotel on Sunday evenings is typical of the best of rhythm-and-blues that gives all who hear it an irresistible urge to 'stand up and move'… The membership book lists more than 700 names of rhythm-and-blues devotees from all parts of London and west Surrey… The Rollin' Stones, a six-piece group, were formed just ten months ago [and] although 'pop' numbers are sometimes played, songs written and recorded by the American rhythm-and-blues guitarist Bo Diddley are the Rollin' Stones' favourites… The Rollin' Stones and the Crawdaddy Club have put the Station Hotel on the map as far as youngsters are concerned." **BARRY MAY,** *RICHMOND & TWICKENHAM TIMES*, **APRIL 13TH 1963**

The Stones recorded their first single a few weeks later; by September they were touring the country as support to their hero Bo Diddley, and in December had the first British R&B chart hit, 'I Wanna Be Your Man', written for them by Lennon and McCartney after Oldham had steered the Liverpudlians to a Stones rehearsal at Studio 51. Meanwhile, at the end of June, Gomelsky had moved the ever-popular Crawdaddy out of the Station Hotel's overloaded back room to a new home at the clubhouse of the Richmond Athletic Association.

Back in the centre of town a four-piece group called The Blue Flames had been sacked from their job as Billy Fury's backing band, piano player Georgie Fame moved to the Soho flat of his friend Mike O'Neill, pianist/vocalist of Nero & The Gladiators, not far from the

FLAMINGO

33-37 Wardour Street, London, W.1
Gerrard 1549, Guests welcome
Dance or listen in comfort
Sam and Jeff Kruger present:—

★ **FRIDAY** (1st) 7.30 - 11.30
TONY SHEVETON
AND SHEVELLES

★ **SATURDAY** (2nd) 7-11.30
DON RENDELL QNT.
FEATURING IAN CARR
DICK MORRISSEY QRT.
COMPERE: TONY HALL

★ **SUNDAY** (3rd) 7 - 11
TONY SHEVETON
AND SHEVELLES

★Membership **NOW** until January
1964 now only 5s. **SAVES YOU**
2s. EACH VISIT. Send P.O. and
s.a.e. to Hon. Sec. at above
address.

ALL-NIGHTER CLUB

33-37 Wardour Street, W.1
Tony Harris and Rik Gunnell
present:

★ **FRIDAY** (1st) 12-5 a.m.
GEORGIE FAME
and BLUE FLAMES
TONY SHEVETON
AND SHEVELLES

★ **SATURDAY** (2nd) 12-6 a.m.
GEORGIE FAME
AND BLUE FLAMES
TOMMY WHITTLE
QUARTET
FIRST TIME FOR 3 YEARS —
RONNIE SCOTT
(SCOTT CLUB PROPRIETOR) —

★ SUNDAY AFTERNOON 3-6 p.m.
GEORGIE FAME

★ **MONDAY** (4th) 8-1 a.m.
GEORGIE FAME
AND BLUE FLAMES

★ **THURSDAY** (7th) 8-1 a.m.
GEORGIE FAME
AND BLUE FLAMES

ALEXIS KORNERS
BLUES CITY
OPENING NIGHT
FRIDAY 1st NOV.

Georgie Fame stands by a wall at
the Flamingo decorated with pictures
of visiting musicians – and no
wonder the young organist looks
slightly dazed. A typical week from
December 1963 (above) reveals
Fame and band clocking up a
shattering total of hours at the All-
Nighter, pumping out a stirring mix
of R&B, soul, modern-jazz and ska.

Georgie Fame with manager Rik Gunnell (above, right). Gunnell also ran the All-Nighter at the Flamingo in Soho where Fame & The Blue Flames played regularly from 1962.

Although line-ups of the Blue Flames changed regularly over the years, this version of the group (right) includes on congas Speedy Acquaye who, apart from one short break, played with Fame from 1962 to 1966. During just one month in 1963 the band played 43 bookings, including 13 at the Flamingo, eight at the All-Nighter, four at the Roaring 20s, three at The Scene, two at Klooks Kleek and one at Eel Pie Island. "The busiest band in town bar none," said a convincing ad taken by manager Gunnell.

Flamingo club. Jeff Kruger had moved his Flamingo to its Wardour Street location during 1957, and in May 1959 an offshoot called the All-Nighter Club was started there by Rik Gunnell and Tony Harris. The All-Nighter was open Friday and Saturday nights, starting at midnight and continuing through to the small hours, as well as on Sunday afternoons. Both clubs are often called "the Flamingo" because they were at the same premises, but they operated at different time-slots and had separate promoters. Both at first presented mostly modern-jazz, although the Flamingo proper did start to include R&B, and the All-Nighter audience – notably black American servicemen and white insomniac mods – also wanted more dance-oriented entertainment. "Pills would be popped to help keep the dance going," confessed one visitor. "The Flamingo wasn't licensed, but if the barman knew you then he'd slip you a short of whisky to liven up the ubiquitous Coke."[58]

Fame got to know Rik Gunnell (who became Fame's manager) and the Blue Flames got their chance at the All-Nighter Club in March 1962. They suited well: by September the band was playing the Friday and Saturday midnight-to-dawn sessions, the Sunday afternoon date, and new Monday and Thursday 8pm-to-midnight spots. No doubt they slept occasionally as well. By now with Speedy Acquaye on congas, Mick Eve on tenor sax and John McLaughlin on guitar, the Blue Flames started to follow their own musical inclinations as well as those of their audience, and gradually came to mix soul, funk, R&B, ska, Motown and modern-jazz into a distinctive strain of British R&B.

At the end of 1962, Fame made a significant instrumental move. "They wouldn't let me play the piano that was in the Flamingo because it was reserved for great British jazz pianists," Fame recalled. "So they had to rent me a little old upright piano which they stuck in the corner.

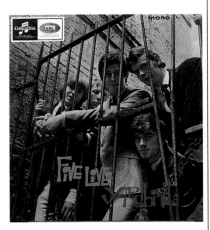

The Yardbirds recorded their first album (above) live at the Marquee in March 1964. "Before long the vagueness had become a 'sound'," wrote manager Giorgio Gomelsky in the sleevenote, "urgent, precise and real." The group are pictured (opposite) sharing a joke at the Marquee. They are (left to right) Jim McCarty (drums), Paul Samwell-Smith (bass) hiding Chris Dreja (guitar), Eric "Slowhand" Clapton (guitar), and at the mike Keith Relf (vocals/harmonica).

There I was, quite happy. Then one night an American GI by the name of Carl Smith from Grand Rapids, Michigan, who became a great friend of mine, walked in and said, 'Man, you ever heard of Mose Allison?' I said no, and he gave me my first Mose Allison record. [Then] I think in the space of 48 hours I heard three organ records by Richard 'Groove' Holmes, the great Jimmy Smith, and Booker T & The MGs – and I didn't play piano for years after that. I went around to Boosey & Hawkes [store] the next day and bought myself a Hammond organ.[59]

Fame and the Blue Flames, weathering frequent line-up changes, built an enviable following and were resident at the club for several years, blowing a powerful organ-and-sax-fuelled storm. Club-goer Annette Carson recalls the excitement of their All-Nighters: "I was really impressed by Georgie Fame's sound there. What with the brass in the band it was a terrific sonic assault, not just a booming rhythm section," she remembers. "They seemed much more professional than the R&B combos I was used to, and swung like crazy. I was completely blown away and stood rooted to the spot throughout their set – although the dancefloor behind me was crowded with dancers doing ultra-cool moves. The crowd were in fact a little intimidating: mature, sophisticated and impressively well-dressed for a night out dancing."[60]

Unfortunately the keen sound was not reproduced well on Fame and the Blue Flames' live LP *Rhythm & Blues From The Flamingo*, recorded in summer 1963. It barely reached bootleg quality – although compère John Gunnell's interval announcement directing the audience to spend money on Coca-Colas and hot-dogs was captured in marvellous fidelity.

In Richmond, less than an hour's tube ride from Wardour Street, Giorgio Gomelsky had taken on a new R&B band, The Yardbirds. Toward the end of 1963 Gomelsky replaced the

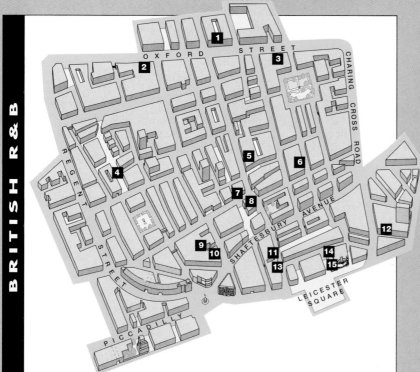

More info pages 144-145.

BRITISH R&B

SOME WEST-END R&B VENUES

1 The 100 Club
2 Marquee (Oxford St)
3 Beat City
4 Roaring 20s
Top Ten Club
5 Marquee (Wardour St)
6 Ronnie Scott's (briefly)
7 Jack of Clubs
8 Round House pub
9 The Scene
10 Piccadilly Jazz Club
11 The Flamingo
12 Studio 51
13 La Discotheque
14 The Ad Lib
15 Notre Dame Hall

resident Stones at his Crawdaddy club with The Yardbirds: bassist Paul Samwell-Smith, drummer Jim McCarty, vocalist/harmonica-player Keith Relf, rhythm guitarist Chris Dreja, and lead guitarist Top Topham. Eric Clapton replaced Topham in October. Gradually the group developed their live show at the Crawdaddy, inserting longer "rave-up" passages into their blues fare. "People had simply never heard music that would let them rip like that," Jim McCarty reckoned. "At the Crawdaddy, people would actually swing from the rafters."[61]

Gomelsky added another couple of venues, presumably with the intention of building a Crawdaddy "circuit", opening at the Star Hotel in Croydon, on the southern fringes of London, and (briefly) Edwina's Club in Seven Sisters Road, north London. He also maintained links with Chris Barber and Harold Pendleton at the NJF – they'd helped him find the new Crawdaddy location at the same sports-ground where they held their annual outdoor National Jazz & Blues Festival, which had first been staged there in 1961. The NJF were still bringing over American bluesmen to work in the UK, and in October 1963 presented Sonny Boy Williamson, Muddy Waters, Memphis Slim and others. Williamson stayed on and the Yardbirds backed him on a lacklustre live recording made in December at the Crawdaddy, released later as the *Sonny Boy Williamson & The Yardbirds* LP.

Gomelsky's NJF connection also helped him land a Friday-night residency at the Marquee for his new charges, beginning in February 1964. They recorded a show there the following month which was released at the end of the year as their debut LP *Five Live Yardbirds*. Recorded in front of what manager Gomelsky's sleevenote called "hundreds of mody-bodies" it captured the group on better form, and offered a reasonably effective band-in-a-room sound. Keith Relf's dad Bill, who acted as the group's roadie, helped by holding a boom-mike out over the stage "as if it were a Watusi spear in a tribal punch-up",[62] while Gomelsky's assistant Hamish Grimes, compère for the evening, apparently needed several attempts at his tongue-twisting introduction: "Now it is time for the birdmerising, yardmerising, in fact most blueswailing Yardbirds!"

Chris Dreja said later that the band sensibly approached the recording as just another gig at the Marquee, despite the chore of a soundcheck in the afternoon. "We played twice as loud and fast as normal," he recalled.

> **It was a great night! Eric broke his usual number of strings: that's why he was known as 'Slowhand'. It started at the Marquee, in fact. He used to buy these incredibly thin strings, and at least every two numbers he'd break one, and in a good-natured way the audience would slow-handclap. That went on the whole time he was with us.[63]**

Yet another kind of R&B had developed in London clubs during 1963 in the hands of one Michael Lubowitz, a trained musician born in South Africa who'd moved to Britain in 1962. Lubowitz soon renamed himself Manfred Mann, and later that year formed the Mann-Hugg Blues Brothers with drummer Mike Hugg, adding guitarist/saxophonist Mike Vickers, bassist Dave Richmond and singer/harmonica-player Paul Jones.

In December the Blues Brothers passed auditions to secure gigs at the Marquee and the Roaring 20s, and were soon delivering distinctly jazz-tinged and musically impressive blues sets all around town. Co-leader Manfred Mann, beatnik-bearded and a precise, serious jazzer at heart, was asked by *Melody Maker* – curious in the first few months of 1963 about this weird new R&B stuff – to explain what they were up to. "In the States, R&B is really the commercial music of the American Negro," Mann said. "We don't really pretend to play this.

FRIDAY (14th) 12-6
GEORGIE FAME
AND THE BLUE FLAMES
JOHN MAYALL'S
BLUES BREAKERS
SATURDAY (15th) 12-6
GEORGIE FAME
AND THE BLUE FLAMES
DICK MORRISSEY QT.
SUNDAY (16th) Afternoon
3-6 p.m.
ZOOT MONEY'S
BIG ROLL BAND
MONDAY (17th) 8-1
ZOOT MONEY'S
BIG ROLL BAND

CRAW DADDY
R & B CLUBS
EVERY SUNDAY
RICHMOND — R.A.A. GROUNDS
EVERY SATURDAY
CROYDON. — STAR HOTEL,
LONDON ROAD
WITH THE MOST BLUESWAILING
YARDBIRDS

THE SCENE
41 Gt. Windmill St., W.1
MONDAY
R&B RECORDS WITH

The most blueswailing Yardbirds blew up a storm at the Crawdaddy in Richmond, replacing the Stones as residents in late 1963.

All we are doing is playing a very basic sort of jazz, [placing] the accent very strongly on rhythm rather than harmony. Most of our stuff is 12-bar, but it is drawn from a wide field – from old Southern blues to Cannonball Adderley and Charlie Mingus. We find that if you get a lot of riffs going, the kids dancing can fasten their minds on the beat or the riff. In many cases I don't think they listen to the soloists, who are often playing straight modern-jazz. It really goes to show that if modern-jazz is presented right it could get a very big audience.[64]

In the summer of '63 the group also changed its name to Manfred Mann, continuing a marathon Monday-night Marquee residency for well over a year – by which time Tom McGuinness had come in on bass and the Manfreds had started to enjoy big pop hits.

Without doubt, 1963 had been the year in which R&B spread through London's clubs to offer a new sound among the existing trad- and modern-jazz. In the first half of the year the places to see R&B in central London included the Colyer Club at Studio 51, the Roaring 20s club, the Flamingo and the All-Nighter, the Marquee, and Gomelsky's Piccadilly Jazz Club at the old Cy Laurie premises in Great Windmill Street. To the west there were the Ealing Club, the Six Bells pub in Kings Road, Chelsea, the Crawdaddy and Eel Pie Island; to the north, the Refectory at Golders Green and the previously trad-only Manor House pub near Finsbury Park. During the year the Piccadilly became The Scene – run by Ronan O'Rahilly, of pirate radio fame – while north-London R&B fans gained Klooks Kleek at the Railway Hotel pub in West Hampstead. One writer at the time calculated that between mid-1963 and mid-1964 more than 280 trad-jazz clubs switched over wholly or partly to R&B.[65]

For a few brief months at the start of 1963 even Ronnie Scott's, the hallowed ground of modern-jazz, added R&B. They presented Alexis Korner's Blues Incorporated – now jazzier still with the inclusion of the great drummer Phil Seamen – as well as Hammond-organist Graham Bond and his band. Bond echoed Manfred Mann's disavowal: "I don't claim we play R&B at all," he told an interviewer. "Other people have given us the tag. I always have been and always will be predominantly a blues-rooted player. This [R&B] is really a new thing, an affiliation of modern-jazz with a beat – although nothing like soul-jazz. It is really a British thing."[66] By May, Ronnie's was back to what it did best: modern-jazz only. But trad-jazz venues were hardly immune. The Jazzshows Jazz Club at 100 Oxford Street had been a pure trad showcase for years, but even they felt the lure of R&B in '63, as the club's manager explained in October: "I don't think R&B is replacing trad, but you can't get away with seven nights a week of trad now. We are giving it a go with groups like the Graham Bond Quartet and we will give R&B a regular night in the new year."[67]

John Martin, an agent who handled several R&B bands, told *Melody Maker* at the end of 1963 how the scene had built rapidly, and explained that with the successful Stones now virtually priced out of the club circuit, the supply of groups was having trouble keeping up with the demand. "Trad got so polished and professional, and this new, raw music is like starting all over again," said Martin, neatly summarising a cyclical pop-music phenomenon. "[R&B] has got what trad had in the beginning: roughness and excitement."[68]

Back at the start of '63 a small-time west-London group, The Detours, were reconsidering their direction after supporting Johnny Kidd & The Pirates a few times at St Mary's Hall in Putney. The Detours decided to move away from the pop-cum-trad that had gained them little more than factory-party gigs, and streamlined themselves into a Pirates-style beat group: Peter Townshend on guitar, Roger Daltrey on vocals, John Entwistle on bass, and Doug Sandom on drums. St Mary's also saw the group supporting another eye-opening headliner that year, The

After organist Georgie Fame's success at the Flamingo, the Hammond organ seemed to become the instrument of choice for bandleaders hoping to gain ground at the Wardour Street club. Graham Bond (main picture) had played in Blues Incorporated, but formed his own Organisation in late 1963 with fellow escapees Jack Bruce, Ginger Baker and Dick Heckstall-Smith. They played regularly at the Flamingo in 1965. Zoot Money was another Hammond organist, and his Big Roll Band (seen here at the Flamingo, inset picture) included Andy Summers, later of The Police, on guitar (far left). The band recorded a live album, "Zoot!", at Klooks Kleek, a jazz and R&B club in north-west London, and later went psychedelic by turning into Dantalion's Chariot.

stereo

Zoot!

ZOOT MONEY'S BIG ROLL BAND

Rolling Stones. Townshend observed Keith Richard employing a slashing right-hand guitar action – a move he promptly copied, exaggerated and made his own. The Detours started to play more, including dates at their local Goldhawk Social Club in Shepherd's Bush, and frequent gigs at the Oldfield Hotel pub in Greenford. Their friend Richard Barnes wrote later about how the group's introductions at the Oldfield helped them change their name early in 1964 to The Who. "There was this [compère] and he loved to have a little joke when

introducing groups. He would say stuff like, 'And now I'd like to introduce The Detours – the who? Never heard of 'em,' and other assorted witticisms. I thought we could spike his guns."[69] It was also at the Oldfield that Keith Moon first played with the group. Sandom had left and part-timers filled in while a long-term replacement was sought. Moon later recalled for *Rolling Stone*:

> **When I heard their drummer had left, I laid plans to insinuate myself into the group. I went down and they had a session drummer sitting in with them. I got up on stage and said, 'I can do better than him.' They said go ahead, and I got behind this other guy's drums, and I did one song, 'Road Runner'. I'd had several drinks to get my courage up and when I got on stage I went arggGGHHHH on the drums, broke the bass-drum pedal and two skins, and got off.[70]**

It was around this time that The Who met up with out-and-out mod Pete Meaden. The mods had first come to light in the 1950s as "modernists", fans of modern-jazz. They dressed sharply in smart Italian fashion. But by 1963 mods had become a broader youth faction, popularly viewed as being in opposition to scruffier rockers and keen on little else than riding motor-scooters to clubs like the Flamingo and downing enough amphetamine pills to dance until dawn to very loud soul and R&B. Writer Stanley Cohen, in a rather more considered analysis, described the mod's "disdain for advancement at work, his air of distance, his manifest ingratitude for what society had given him… these were found more unsettling [by the establishment] than any simple conformity to the folklore image of the yob".[71]

Meaden secured gigs for the group at the main mod venue in central London, The Scene, and suggested changing their name, this time to the mod-friendly High Numbers – under which monicker they recorded their first single. By now their live sets were mixing R&B, Motown and soul covers, due in no small part to the influence of The Scene's resident DJ, Guy Stevens. Barnes again: "He had all the best records long before anybody else… I used to go along with Townshend to [Stevens's] flat in Regent's Park to hear records that the High Numbers might want to play on stage or record. He had hundreds of albums and singles from remote and unknown record companies. For a fee he'd tape the ones you wanted."[72]

In July film-maker Kit Lambert saw the group at the Bluesday club that Barnes ran at the Railway Hotel pub, by Harrow & Wealdstone tube station. The Railway had hosted a number of jazz clubs since the 1950s, and from 1962 an R&B club that regularly featured Cyril Davies and Long John Baldry. It was apparently at the Bluesday that Townshend first smashed his guitar into the ceiling above the stage and, sensing a good audience reaction, the group continued into further destructive routines. Lambert, son of British classical composer Constant Lambert, had dropped into the Railway during a search for a band to appear in a pop-music film that he and his partner Chris Stamp (brother of actor Terence) were planning. But such was Lambert's response to what he saw and heard that the pair decided instead to

65

Shepherd's Bush group in identity crisis: High Numbers or Who? Both for safety at Harrow in July 1964 ad (below); definitely The Who at the Marquee in March 1967 (left).

TUESDAY cont.

BLUESDAY R & B Club, The High Numbers. (Re The Who). "I'm the Face." Railway Hotel, Harrow, Wealdstone. 3/6d.

Pete Townshend named the Eel Pie publishing company he set up in the early 1980s after Eel Pie Island, a dancehall on an island in the Thames at Twickenham that hosted R&B and rock bands during the 1960s.

E.S.O.B.R.M.

HAPPY CHRISTMAS
from the
EEL PIE ISLAND JAZZ CLUB

manage the group. Within a few months The High Numbers were – permanently this time – The Who. Lambert and Stamp got them a contract with record producer Shel Talmy and secured an important residency at the Marquee that started in November 1964.

The Marquee had begun at Oxford Street as a jazz club back in 1958. By the time 1963 drew to a close the club was still presenting jazz four nights a week, with two nights each week devoted to R&B – the Cyril Davies All-Stars were in residence on Thursdays and Manfred Mann on Mondays. Marquee secretary John Gee wrote in the club's newsletter: "In the Siberian winter of 1963 it was 'house full' every Thursday night at the Marquee while Cyril blew and Long John Baldry and the Velvettes sang the blues to almost delirious fans."[73]

But tragedy struck Davies in January 1964. At the age of just 32 the great blues harmonica-player, singer, 12-string guitarist and R&B pioneer died from a heart ailment – which had not been helped by his continual heavy drinking. "I do not think that Britain will produce another bluesman of his stature," wrote a sorrowful Alexis Korner in an obituary of his one-time partner.[74] Davies's vocalist Long John Baldry took over the band and renamed it The Hoochie Coochie Men, retaining the Thursday-night Marquee residency. "A lot of people ask if I'm grateful to the Stones for everything," said Baldry a few months afterwards. "But of course if Cyril and Alex and I hadn't made it in the first place, the Stones would never have made it. The people I'm eternally grateful to are the people who helped me most, and they're Cyril and Alex."[75]

At the Marquee business was good, and the prospect of more visitors descending the steps to the basement under the Academy cinema in Oxford Street seemed certain. At the end of 1963, however, the Academy's owner had told Marquee boss Harold Pendleton that he was going to add a second cinema screen in the basement – where the Marquee was at present. The club had six months' notice to quit. Pendleton was devastated. "I started combing Soho for new club premises. But everyone had done this thousands of times, and I knew it was useless."[76] However, one day he happened by chance upon a large ground-floor premises in Wardour Street, previously used by Burberry the raincoat maker. "There was a tiny, narrow corridor, and when you got to the end it opened into a *huge* place, full of metal and glass partitions dividing it up into sections and rooms. Immediately I thought: get those partitions out and there's quite a bit of space."[77]

Pendleton was sure he had found his new Marquee, but... he had no capital. The trained accountant in him took over. Burberry was owned by Great Universal Stores; Pendleton went to their HQ in Tottenham Court Road. When he eventually got to see the estates manager, he found a fellow jazz fan. "They wanted £15,000 or so [about $24,000], with a 22-and-a-half-year-lease and no rent reviews. Think about that," Pendleton suggests. "This is 1964. Another 22-and-a-half years to go with no rent reviews whatsoever, and £15,000 for the lease. So I said, 'Will you lend me the money so I can buy it from you?' He said, 'Well, you've got a nerve. But the last person who sat in that chair wanted to open a chain of stores in Australia and wanted £70 billion. So I suppose we could scrape together £15,000 to loan to you.' I said thank you very much, and GUS lent me the money to buy their own premises. Talk about a piece of luck."[78]

Pendleton negotiated with Hoellering to take with him to the new location all the distinctive McBean-designed circus-theme decorations that had given the cinema basement such a distinctive atmosphere, planning effectively to replicate Marquee mark one in its new Wardour Street home – with the addition of wall-mirrors to open out the slightly smaller room. The

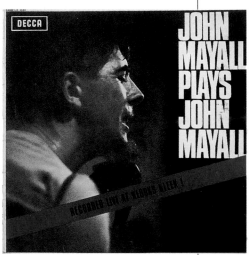

John Mayall's Bluesbreakers recorded their first album (above), released in 1965, live at Klooks Kleek club. Geno Washington & The Ram Jam Band played incessantly on the London club scene of the 1960s; here they are (opposite) performing at the National Jazz & Blues Festival in Richmond in 1965.

Marquee at Oxford Street closed on Sunday March 8th 1964 – the great jazz saxophonist Stan Getz headlined – and reopened at Wardour Street just five days later with Sonny Boy Williamson, The Yardbirds and Long John Baldry & The Hoochie Coochie Men. Pendleton couldn't resist defying his good luck by opening the new Marquee on Friday the 13th.

But everything went well, as secretary John Gee wrote in the club newsletter: "Thanks to the valiant efforts of builders, electricians, caterers and 101 other sundry characters, the New Marquee opened dead on time at 7.30pm on Friday March 13th. By that time an absolutely fantastic queue had assembled and most regretfully we had to turn some 600 away after the 'house full' notice went up. Sonny Boy Williamson really made Wardour Street wail that night and took his farewell bow in a magnificent fireman's helmet presented to him by Mr Coombs, our club manager, who was until his recent retirement Chief Fire Officer of Richmond. In April we hope to have the main club area completely finished."[79]

Visitors to the new Marquee during its first few months included The Alex Harvey Soul Band (fronted by the later Sensational Glaswegian), The Cheynes (with drummer Mick Fleetwood, later of Fleetwood Mac), John Mayall's Bluesbreakers (with the other half, John McVie, on bass), The Mark Leeman Five (with future Nice drummer Brian Davison) and The Moody Blues (playing some of their earliest London gigs). In November, The Who started their Tuesday-night residency which lasted until the following April. It did much to bolster the group's growing reputation amid the 'Maximum R&B' campaign launched by their new managers Lambert and Stamp, not least when a *Melody Maker* journalist visited the Marquee at the end of 1964 and gave the band its first press exposure.

R E V I E W

THE WHO

MARQUEE, **DECEMBER 29TH 1964**

"The Who, appearing each Tuesday at London's Marquee club, should be billed not only as 'Maximum R&B' but as 'Far-out R&B'. These four young musicians present their own brand of powerful, stinging rhythm-and-blues which, last Tuesday, quickly stimulated an enthusiastic audience. 'Heatwave' – the Martha & The Vandellas hit number – is given typically fiery Who treatment. Another of their outstanding numbers was an instrumental, '[You] Can't Sit Down'. This performance demonstrated the weird and effective techniques of guitarist [Pete] Townshend, who expertly uses speaker feedback to accompany many of his solos. The Who, spurred by a most exhilarating drummer and a tireless vocalist, must surely be one of the trendsetting groups of 1965."

NICK JONES, *MELODY MAKER*, **JANUARY 9TH 1965**

During the Marquee residency The Who played other London dates too: the Goldhawk and Ealing clubs, as well as the Red Lion in Leytonstone to the east and an all-nighter or two at Club Noreik in Tottenham to the north. But the Marquee was special, as Keith Moon confirmed some years later. "Playing the Marquee was the biggest thing ever for The Who, when we started," said Moon.

❝ Sure we used to get friends down to see us, but that was because Tuesday was a dead night, and we had to set the ball rolling. We gave free tickets for the Marquee to fans who came down to see us at the Goldhawk... The only place that had any influence, where the managers and promoters and press could see us, was at the Marquee. They had a very discerning audience there, and it helped us develop our musical ideas. We were finding our feet – and the Marquee put us on our feet.[80] **❞**

Eel Pie Island is in the River Thames at Twickenham. The Island is about a third of a mile long, a little over a mile upstream from Richmond, and has a relatively long history as a place of entertainment. As soon as a hotel and ballroom were built there in the 1830s, summer boating parties would regularly moor for willow-shaded revelry.

At the end of that decade Charles Dickens wrote in *Nicholas Nickleby*: "Miss Morleena Kenwigs had received an invitation to repair next day, per steamer from Westminster Bridge, unto the Eel-pie island at Twickenham; there to make merry upon a cold collation, bottled-beer, shrub, and shrimps, and to dance in the open air to the music of a locomotive band." Shrub, you will be pleased to hear, was a rum punch; as for the "locomotive band", the novelist was presumably making reference to a group of travelling players. As we shall see, such bands would flock to the Island through the years. Back in the 1840s, however, another visitor documented the Island's attractions and explained its name. "Upon this [islet] a house of entertainment has been erected; and here the river steamers are accustomed to land great numbers of holiday folks, desirous of the delights of pure air, and solicitous to banquet upon eel-pies, for which the tavern is famed."[81]

A little over 100 years later, Eel Pie Island had fallen into disrepair (notwithstanding a resurgence in the 1920s when it was popular for tea-dances). Arthur Chisnall was running a junkshop in Kingston, a few more miles upstream, and noticed a growing interest in jazz, skiffle and blues records among his student customers, especially those from the nearby art colleges in Kingston, Wimbledon and Twickenham. The enterprising Chisnall got to hear about the Island buildings, and in April 1956 held a jazz party there. Around 500 people turned up. Sensing a potentially useful venture, Chisnall started to host weekly events, turning the crumbling yet atmospheric ballroom into a trad-jazz club, sometimes called Eelpiland. During 1963 R&B bands started to play there too, with the Cyril Davies All-Stars and The Rollin' Stones among the first of many outfits to brave the dilapidated boards.

Jeff Beck was an early club member, and in 1964 formed his first band, The Tridents, who considered the Island virtually a home gig. "I used to play amid a wash of beer and smelly cigarettes," he later told an interviewer. "We used to have a really good time. It was our weekly job; the rest of the week we spent doing nothing. Then all of a sudden people started turning up in droves. There were 900 one week, which was apparently a record. It reached the stage where we were outdrawing The Yardbirds who were appearing at the Crawdaddy in Richmond."[82] Early in 1965 Beck would, of course, join The Yardbirds himself.

In order to reach the Island from Water Lane in Twickenham, on the north bank, a new footbridge with a toll of a few pence had replaced the old chain-ferry in 1957. "It was just wide enough to drive a Transit [van] over," wrote one club-goer, "provided all the band got out and mixed with the hoi polloi walking over. Getting the van stuck on the bridge was a weekly occasion that caused much merriment to the regulars and thoroughly annoyed the old lady in the hut who collected the toll."[83]

During the first few days of 1964 Cyril Davies played his final gig at the Island. His band's vocalist Long John Baldry wrote:

❝ Cyril had been ill for some months, that I knew, but the suddenness of his death threw me. Some days before, as we were crossing the footbridge from our old stamping ground Eel Pie Island, he said something that flashed back into my mind [when I was told that he was dead]. 'You know, John, I think this is the last time I'll walk on this bridge.' As it happened, that particular evening at the Island was to be his last public appearance.[84] ❞

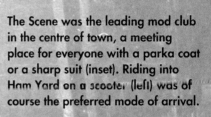

The Scene was the leading mod club in the centre of town, a meeting place for everyone with a parka coat or a sharp suit (inset). Riding into Ham Yard on a scooter (left) was of course the preferred mode of arrival.

Arthur Chisnall's club on Eel Pie Island had not been without problems, especially from local police who seemed to view it as a beatnik-infested vice den. Practical difficulties too arose: the buildings were in terminal decline, with enormous holes in the roof and decaying floors. On one notable summer night the electricity supply failed, and Long John Baldry led the Islanders out of the ballroom and played an acoustic set by the river.

It became obvious to a despairing Chisnall that he could not raise the huge amount of money needed in 1967 to make repairs and continue the club. When police raided, ostensibly over licensing arrangements, Chisnall decided at last to give up – after more than ten years of memorable events. Gigs did continue into 1970, but by this time the place was "pretty sleazy compared to the old club, and half the audience were police in long-haired wigs".[85] Squatters occupied the buildings but were evicted in 1971, and almost immediately afterwards the hotel and ballroom burned to the ground. The site is now occupied by up-market houses.

Another popular Island band was John Mayall's Bluesbreakers. Mayall had grown up in Manchester, but moved to London in 1962 at the suggestion of Alexis Korner. Early the following year Mayall formed his first Bluesbreakers, including John McVie on bass, and soon started playing R&B gigs such as the Ealing Club, the All-Nighter, the Six Bells and Studio 51. His first album, *John Mayall Plays John Mayall*, was a live recording made at Klooks Kleek in West Hampstead, north London, in December 1964. Mayall's label, Decca, had a recording studio a few doors away in Broadhurst Gardens, which made Klooks a handy location. A not-unbiased Alexis Korner described the record in its sleevenote as "one of the country's finest R&B artists recorded at one of London's leading R&B clubs", adding that "the odd words lost here and there don't really matter... what does matter is the compulsive power of the whole session". After the live LP's guitarist Roger Dean left Mayall in 1965, Eric Clapton joined, replaced the following year by Peter Green, in turn succeeded by Mick Taylor in 1967.

Dick Jordan had run the site of the Mayall recording, Klooks Kleek, as a jazz club above the Railway Hotel pub in West End Lane since 1961, "amidst decaying Victorian architecture in the seamier part of West Hampstead" according to his publicity. He'd named it after jazz drummer Kenny Clarke's 1956 LP *Klook's Clique*; Clarke's nicknames "klook" and "klook-mop" came from the sounds of his novel drum accents.

Jordan noted the change in musical taste during 1963 and in the summer added R&B groups to the club's attractions. But some big names were excluded. "The Rolling Stones wanted to play at Klooks, but I couldn't admit anyone under 18 because we were a pub," Jordan explained. "It was the same with The Yardbirds. Giorgio Gomelsky couldn't understand why I never booked them, but it was because they attracted what were the teenyboppers of the period."[86] Zoot Money, Hammond-organist and leader of The Big Roll Band, also made a live R&B record at Klooks: his fiery *Zoot!* album, with future Police guitarist Andy Summers on board, was recorded there in May 1966.

While R&B bands were having a ball in the clubs during the first half of the 1960s, a different kind of group was emerging in the pop charts. The Beatles relentlessly scored hit records after their first number-one single, *From Me To You*, in April 1963. Hundreds of beat-groups appeared in their wake.

The top beat-groups tended not to play much in London's clubs. Instead they slogged up and down the country on grinding tours of ballrooms, dancehalls, public baths, town halls and the like. Not that club work and hit records were mutually exclusive: Manfred Mann

played almost ceaseless club dates but also enjoyed pop hits like 'Do Wah Diddy Diddy'; The Animals moved down from Newcastle, played all the London clubs, and scored with 'House Of The Rising Sun'. But in general a distinction developed between R&B club bands on one hand, and hit beat-groups on the other.

Few bands of any persuasion were getting rich from all this work. A club date for The Graham Bond Organisation in 1964 at the renamed 100 Club (now enthusiastically geared to R&B) would net £15 ($24). While the average was nearer £35 [$55], after expenses for petrol, maintenance of a decrepit ex-ambulance, hotels, agency commission and instrument

The Small Faces (above) attempt a fast getaway in Richmond Mews from the back door of the Marquee. The fans have of course already removed the limousine's starter-motor. Inside the Marquee (inset picture) club regulars Manfred Mann, with Jack Bruce on bass, are joined in late 1965 by Eric Burdon alongside Mann vocalist Paul Jones.

accessories there was little left at the end of each week to be divided among organist Bond, saxman Dick Heckstall-Smith, bassist Jack Bruce and drummer Ginger Baker. "Even allowing for an inflation factor of five or six times since then, I still wonder how and why on earth the GBO kept going," a mystified Heckstall-Smith wrote later.[87]

Also in 1964, north-London group The Kinks were promoting their first hit 'You Really Got Me' by touring the country's ballrooms and civic halls in multi-group pop "packages". At the time the four-piece group was paid £250 a week ($400) for such industry, but as Ray Davies later explained:

> **Out of that we had to pay commission of 40 per cent to assorted managers and agents as well as our own bed and breakfast, which meant there was hardly any money left for us. But we were keen and ready for the big time which we thought was just around the corner, so the fact that we were making no money didn't bother us.[88]**

One of the first discotheques in London, La Discotheque in Wardour Street, was exclusively a place intended for dancing to records, but some discotheques did present live acts as well as playing records – for a while, at least. The Cromwellian in Earls Court, west London, was one of the best known of the new discos. Opened in 1965, "the Crom" as it was generally known offered name groups and pirate-station DJs in the basement, a big ground-floor bar, and gambling upstairs. Up-market nightclubs and suave discotheques like the Crom were just what some successful musicians were looking for: convivial hang-outs where, post-gig, one could drink and socialise into the early hours, with little risk of being mobbed.

One of the nightclubs favoured among the new pop elite was the Ad Lib in Leicester Place, just off Leicester Square, in the centre of London. The club was up at the top of a building which also housed the local council's street-cleaning and refuse-collection headquarters. A small lift was the only means to reach the penthouse niterie, where the visitor was greeted by fur-lined walls, mirrors everywhere, and tanks of piranha fish. Ad Lib manager Brian Morris said, "It belongs to the young people. We get all the young ones: young designers like Mary Quant or Jean Muir; the young actresses like Hayley Mills or Julie Christie; The Beatles."[89] George Melly noted: "Its great asset is a huge window looking down on London. For the pop stars, fashion photographers and young actors this must suggest a conquered world."[90]

The Beatles largely determined if a nightclub was in or not. Later the stamp of hipness would pass to the Scotch Of St James, and then the Speakeasy, but for a while the Ad Lib was definitely the place to be seen, and most decidedly in.

To Ringo Starr it was virtually a second home. Paul McCartney later recalled: "We started to get a bit of money and a bit of time, and that was the nightclub where the good music played, mainly black American. They had a black chef who used to come out at 11.30 and bang a tambourine and everyone would cheer and dance the conga. It was a shouty, lively scene."[91] John Lennon, said journalist Ray Coleman, "would get rather drunk after each concert and hold court at the Ad Lib, uttering unprintable things about other artists".[92] And the Ad Lib was, famously, one of the nightclubs that Lennon and Harrison went to with their wives in 1965 after innocently taking LSD for the first time. Psychedelia was about to enter the musical bloodstream.

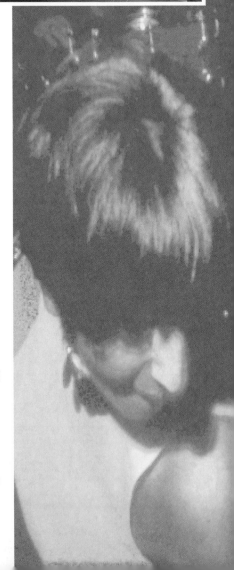

The Cromwellian discotheque in full flight during the 1960s (main picture). A three-floor fun factory in west London fashioned to allow the unrestrained festivities of the better-off reveller, it also offered gambling on the top deck (inset picture). Ray Davies later fondly remembered the Crom as somewhere one might "observe the almost endless supply of dolly girls parading in mini-skirts".

By the time this shot of The Yardbirds was taken in the first few months of 1966, British R&B's peak was in the past, and Jeff Beck (far right) had replaced Eric Clapton as the group's lead guitarist. Many of the bigger R&B groups had moved on from the small clubs in which they'd come to notice to tackle tours of bigger venues – like the Albert Hall on whose back-steps The Yardbirds pose here. The group did get to play at the great Victorian concert-hall later in '66 when they appeared there with the Stones and Ike & Tina Turner in the summer.

Cream appeared in summer 1966 when Eric Clapton from John Mayall's Bluesbreakers, Jack Bruce from Manfred Mann and Ginger Baker from The Graham Bond Organisation got together. In the first few weeks of their

marquee

90 Wardour Street   **London W.1**

Thursday, August 11th (7.30-11.0)
★ **THE MOVE**
★ BLUESOLOGY

Friday, August 12th (7.30-11.0)
★ **THE V.I.P.'s**
★ ROBERT STUCKEY TRIO

Saturday, August 13th (2.30-5.30)
★ **THE SATURDAY SHOW**
   Top of the Pops, live and on disc,
   introduced by guest D.J.s and
   featuring star personalities.

Saturday, August 13th (7.30-11.0)
★ SATURDAY NIGHT SOUL
★ **THE SOUL AGENTS**
★ THE GAME

Sunday, August 14th (7.30-10.45)
★ SUNDAY SPECIAL
★ **DIANE FERRAZ and**
   NICKY SCOTT
★ BO STREET RUNNERS

Monday, August 15th (7.30-11.0)
★ **JOHN MAYALL'S BLUES**
   BREAKERS
★ JAMES ROYAL SET

Tuesday, August 16th (7.30-11.0)
★ **THE CREAM**
   (Eric Clapton, Ginger Baker and
   Jack Bruce)
★ THE CLAYTON SQUARES

Wednesday, August 17th (7.30-11.0)
★ **ALEX CAMPBELL**
★ AND HIS SPECIAL GUESTS

marquee artists   Agency and Management
18 Carlisle Street, W.1 GER 6601

existence they played the Marquee (right; ad above), although their London debut was at Klooks Kleek.

PSYCHEDELIC AND SIXTIES VENUES map below

1 UFO
2 Tiles
3 Bag O'Nails
4 Marquee
5 Zebra
6 Saville Theatre
7 Temple
8 Happening 44
9 Middle Earth
10 The Lyceum

More info p144-145.

LIGHTSHOWS, PSYCHEDELIA AND JAMMING AT THE SPEAK

80

DURING 1965 BRITISH POP MUSIC seemed to be changing. The simple choice of being either an R&B band or a beat-group had apparently fractured as musicians listened more appreciatively to wider influences and absorbed sounds and styles from all manner of music. The prominent directors of this search, at least in the recording studio, were The Beatles. Their *Rubber Soul* LP – embracing folk and soul music, sitars, rockabilly and more – was that year's public touchstone of artful pop.

But there were still gigging bands in London who seemed barely aware that recording studios existed. For them the nightly slog of live music was all. Geno Washington & The Ram Jam Band played hundreds and hundreds of dates in the mid 1960s, and while they did make records and some of them did chart, that hardly seemed the point. One club even took its name from Washington's band. The Ram Jam in Brixton, south-west London, may have opened in February 1966 with The Animals but the music presented regularly there was largely black-oriented, reflecting the ethnic mix of the area.

Vocalist Washington, a black American serviceman who stayed in Britain after his discharge, often played at the Ram Jam, and his band's powerful brass-driven sound rendered soul classics in dynamic style as delirious crowds chanted for their hero: "Geno, Geno, Geno..." Washington usually bargained a percentage of the gate receipts with the clubs, and as he rarely failed to pack them he made good money. The Ram Jam Band regularly broke attendance records, and while they reportedly averaged a high £400 [$630] per gig, in 1966 they are said to have taken away an exceptional £800 [$1,260] from one north-London club date.

Washington's soul was light years away from the kind of music that a new four-piece London group, Pink Floyd, were making in the first few months of 1966. They had started to play at events organised by Bernard Stollman, a New Yorker who'd come to England and begun a casual Sunday-afternoon gathering of musicians, poets and artists at the Marquee which he called Spontaneous Underground. So casual, indeed, that the Marquee did not think it important enough to include in its regular weekly *Melody Maker* ad alongside The Move, the Spencer Davis Group, The Small Faces and the rest. Stollman instead put out his own distinctive flyers that promised "poets, pop singers, hoods, Americans, homosexuals ('because they make up ten per cent of the population'), 20 clowns, jazz musicians, 'one murderer', sculptors, politicians and some girls who defy description".[93]

Pop-folkie Donovan turned up too, accompanied by sitars and congas, as did Cornelius Cardew's uncompromising free-form improvising group AMM. Peter Jenner and Andrew King of Blackhill Enterprises first saw the Floyd here, and soon became the group's managers. At the Marquee they witnessed the Floyd revelling in the freedom, soaking up the do-what-you-like atmosphere, and indulging in protracted, clamorous jamming over the chords of Junior Walker and Chuck Berry songs. Often the group would grind to a halt in howls of echo and feedback as they set the controls for an early psychedelic experience. No doubt the hoods and sculptors and other architects of London's fledgling underground scene applauded themselves simply for being there as much as they acknowledged the group's well-intentioned meanderings.

In early 1966, as the Floyd were contributing to these jolly Sunday-afternoon japes, John "Hoppy" Hopkins was setting up the London Free School in Notting Hill, west London. This idealistic and largely theoretical "school" would supposedly offer alternative education to anyone fed up with the straight State variety. Hoppy and his cohorts also dabbled in a number of satellite activities, including the remarkably successful staging in summer 1966 of

the first Notting Hill carnival – during which a pantomime horse was arrested by wary police.

Floyd manager Peter Jenner became involved with the School and in October 1966, when a benefit to raise much-needed cash was proposed, he offered his group: Syd Barrett on guitar, Roger Waters on bass, Rick Wright on organ and Nick Mason on drums. The benefit took place at All Saints Hall in Powis Gardens, a few minutes away from the house in Powis Terrace that served as the School's HQ. At this first gig the Floyd's music was accompanied by a lightshow presented by Americans Joel and Tony Brown who set up some simple slide projectors to throw shapes and colours over and around the group.

R E V I E W

PINK FLOYD

ALL SAINTS HALL

OCTOBER 14TH 1966

"Last Friday the Pink Floyd, a new London group, embarked upon their first 'happening' – a pop dance incorporating psychedelic effects and mixed media – whatever that is! The slides were excellent – colourful, frightening, grotesque, beautiful – and the group's trip into outer-space sounds promised very interesting things to come. Unfortunately [it] all fell a bit flat in the cold reality of All Saints Hall... The Floyd need to write more of their own material – psychedelic versions of 'Louie Louie' won't come off – but if they can incorporate their electronic prowess with some melodic and lyrical songs, getting away from dated R&B things, they could well score in the near future."

NICK JONES, *MELODY MAKER*, OCTOBER 22ND 1966

Three years earlier, in the middle of 1963, the Marquee had hosted some of the first British multi-media experiments, including rudimentary lightshows. Poets Mike Horowitz and Pete Brown (later Cream's lyricist) organised a series of New Departures, including a motley crew of avant-garde and jazz musicians performed along with lights, slides and back-projections produced by artists Mark Boyle and Joan Hills. Brown said they aimed "to stimulate the jazz musicians into playing free music by giving them abstract coloured patterns to contend with".[94]

Pink Floyd also seem to have been involved in lighting experiments before the All Saints gigs. They'd provided music for Hornsey College of Art's Light-Sound Workshop in north London, probably in summer 1966 and again with Boyle, who was a lecturer at Hornsey. Boyle was the prime British lightshow pioneer, but the All Saints performances became regular events through October and into November 1966, and were attracting growing crowds to the tiny 300-capacity church hall, providing a new audience for the art of the lightshow. Jenner helped rig up the group's own elementary lightshow system, which was enhanced by the work of another Hornsey man, Joe Gannon (and later Peter Wynne Wilson).

By the following summer there were 23 lightshow specialists in and around London from whom equipment and operators could be hired.[95] Parallel events were taking place in the US, where lightshows had begun in San Francisco. Jenner said later:

 We thought we were doing what was happening on the West Coast – which we'd never heard. And it was totally different. Attempting to imitate when you don't actually know what you're imitating leads to genuine creativity, and I think that's what happened with the Floyd.[96]

Pink Floyd played at another significant event in October 1966, the launch party for *IT*. The underground paper was started by a group including Hoppy and Barry Miles (who ran the Indica alternative bookshop and gallery), and a party at the Roundhouse to celebrate *IT*'s

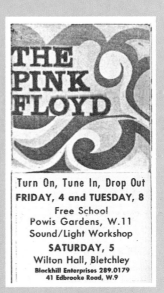

THE PINK FLOYD

Turn On, Tune In, Drop Out
FRIDAY, 4 and TUESDAY, 8
Free School
Powis Gardens, W.11
Sound/Light Workshop
SATURDAY, 5
Wilton Hall, Bletchley
Blackhill Enterprises 289.0179
41 Edbrooke Road, W.9

Roger Waters (far left) and Syd Barrett of Pink Floyd with psychedelic controls set and basic lightshow switched on at the All Saints Hall, Notting Hill, late in 1966. The church hall was used for these events by a local "Free School"; the ad (above) highlights dates there in November.

founding was suggested. The Roundhouse in Chalk Farm Road, north-west London, was indeed round; it was an old railway-turntable shed built in the 1840s that had been used since as a gin warehouse but was now in a poor state. Radical playwright Arnold Wesker ran a free-arts scheme called Centre 42, and in 1964 the Roundhouse had been donated to the scheme as a potential if derelict arts venue. Wesker apparently was pleased to hand over to the *IT* team the keys to the Roundhouse – which was still in dire need of refurbishment – and plans were made for the October 15th party. It was a Pop Op Costume Masque Drag Ball, no less. Posters were printed announcing music by Pink Floyd and Soft Machine, guaranteeing "Strip Trip, Happenings, Movies" and promising a "surprise" for "Shortest, Barest", a reference to a prize for the most minuscule dress rather than the decor at the Roundhouse.

On arrival at the Roundhouse guests were given sugar cubes (sans LSD, but a nice gesture) and entered the chilly expanse of the circular railway shed to see the Floyd emitting wild feedback while bathed in a pulsating wash of multicoloured lights. There was an enormous celebratory jelly, wallowed in and eaten at midnight by the fancy-dressed multitude. Soft Machine brought a motorcycle on-stage with the rest of their gear, wired it up with contact-mikes and broadcast its revving engine over their free-form rock. The building's two toilets quickly flooded, and the Floyd decelerated rapidly from 'Interstellar Overdrive' when the electricity failed. Celebrities like Paul McCartney (in Arabic outfit) fumbled in the dark along with 2,000 or so other revellers. Marianne Faithfull's nun costume secured her the "Shortest – Barest" prize once light had been restored, and a *Sunday Times* reporter scribbled "All apparently very psychedelic" in his notebook.

Three more events were staged at the Roundhouse, each an all-nighter. On December 3rd there was the Psychodelphia Versus Ian Smith Giant Freak Out, promising "screaming thousands, underground films, poets, happenings", music from Pink Floyd and the Ram Holder Messengers, and advice to bring one's own "ecstatogenic substances". (Ian Smith was prime minister of the detested regime in Rhodesia.) Later in the month the old engine shed hosted the Psychodelphia Double Giant Freak-Out Ball, starring on Friday night Geno Washington & The Ram Jam Band (Geno in a paisley shirt negotiating a cash deal with the hippies?), The Alan Bown Set, and Cream (who'd made their London debut in the summer at Klooks Kleek). On the wintry Saturday night, new year's eve, for 15/- a ticket (75p, about $1.20) it was Pink Floyd, The Who and The Move.

Doubtless it was the run of slapdash Roundhouse events – and a Freak Out Ethel gig at the Seymour Hall – that provoked an ad soon after in *Melody Maker*: "Freak Out-Schmeak Out. Turn Up, Shell Out, Get Lost. Keef Reef & The Curious Smokes, Willi Warmer's Giant Bingo, The Boring Mothers, Belle E Butons. Sporran jugglers. Underground Trains. Spot Prizes. Licensed fish bar (down the road). Moonlight. Constant running water. London Airport Runway Seven. Wot a carve-up!!!! (This space donated by the Pink Floyd and Blackhill Enterprises.)"

Nineteen-sixty-six had been a great year for Jimi Hendrix. He'd started it as the guitarist in King Curtis's band in New York. By June he'd formed his own group, The Blue Flames, and the following month was spotted playing with them in a club in Greenwich Village by Chas Chandler, who was on tour with The Animals. In September Jimi flew to London, having worked out a deal for Chandler to manage him, and almost the minute he arrived in town he had his first jam at a club – on this occasion the Scotch Of St James in Mason's Yard – and met his girlfriend-to-be Kathy Etchingham. Many years later she wrote: "When I walked in, I was aware of an incredible stillness in the atmosphere. Everyone in the club was listening intently to someone in the corner playing a guitar." Etchingham continued:

THE·SOFT·MACHINE TURNS·ON/AT·THE ZEBRA·EVRY SATDY GREEK ST. 10PM·BAR

The Zebra club took over the premises of Peter Cook's comedy club, The Establishment, in Greek Street, Soho, in 1966. This ad (above) from December heralds a residency at the Zebra by The Soft Machine, which at the time featured Kevin Ayers on bass, Robert Wyatt on drums, Daevid Allen on guitar and Mike Ratledge on keyboards.

R E V I E W

PINK FLOYD, THE WHO, THE MOVE

THE ROUNDHOUSE, CHALK FARM

DECEMBER 31ST 1966/

JANUARY 1ST 1967

"The Roundhouse was once called 'a derelict barn'. On Saturday it saw in the new year with little elevation of its stature... Despite the lack of facilities, the participants – ie the paying guests – adjusted as they always do. They blasphemed at the groups, got it together in the corners, and looned about to keep the circulation on the move... The Pink Floyd have a promising sound, and some very groovy picture slides which attract far more attention than the group, as they merge, blossom, burst, grow, divide and die. The Who almost succeeded in winning over the show with an immediate flurry of smoke bombs and sound-barrier smashing... After playing most of their new album tracks rather half-heartedly, Pete Townshend wheeled upon a fine pair of speakers and ground them with his shattered guitar into the stage. It was fair comment. The group had thrice been switched off as well as being constantly plunged into darkness by a team of lighting men – none of whom seemed to know where, in fact, the stage or The Who were positioned. The Move were more successful. Technically they had no hitches and their act came smoothly to a stage-shaking climax as TV sets with Hitler and Ian Smith pictures were swiped with iron bars, and a car was chopped up. Two girls were incensed enough to strip to the waist, and the remaining shivering crowds surged menacingly towards the stage, the demolished car, and the birds."

NICK JONES, *MELODY MAKER,* JANUARY 7TH 1967

" People were always getting up at the Scotch and jamming, but usually the club carried on around them, everyone talking and drinking. This was different; the whole place seemed mesmerised. Obviously something special was happening. It took a few moments for my eyes to adjust to the dark, and I couldn't see the guitarist as I made out Chas going up on to the stage and telling the guy to stop playing... 'I had to get him off,' [Chas said]. 'He's only got a seven-day visa and he's not supposed to be working, paid or unpaid.' I was instantly attracted [to Jimi]. I had never seen such an exotic man before. To my naive and unsophisticated eyes he seemed dangerous and exciting.[97] **"**

The Scotch had been opened in 1965 by Louis Brown and John Bloom in a small hemmed-in courtyard behind St James's Square, almost midway between Soho and Buckingham Palace. A few doors along in Mason's Yard was Barry Miles's Indica Gallery where John Lennon first met Yoko Ono at her art exhibition, two months after Jimi's jam. One of the pop-industry elite who frequented the Scotch – a favourite watering hole for the likes of The Beatles, Eric Burdon and Keith Moon – described it as "a split-level disco that had replaced the Ad Lib as the top spot, and came across with a touch more chic than the Cromwellian, which was number two".[98]

The Scotch, with its lurid Scottish-baronial decor, was "hidden away in the smart-set area so the groups can come here incognito," as co-owner Louis Brown put it at the time. "Nobody bothers them. This is more than a club to the pop world," he boasted, "it's a home."[99] However, as George Melly pointed out, "The table reserved for the top groups was on a little platform slightly above the level of the rest of the floor; it was also corralled off. The top groups were not to be bothered, perhaps, but their presence was not allowed to pass unnoticed. [The Scotch] has struck a clever balance between privacy and adulation on their behalf."[100]

Over the coming months Jimi was to be seen regularly on the London club scene, jamming

THE JIMI HENDRIX EXPERIENCE

BLAISES

DECEMBER 21ST 1966

"Jimi Hendrix, a fantastic American guitarist, blew the minds of the star-packed crowd who went to see him at Blaises on Wednesday. Among those in the audience were Pete Townshend, Roger Daltrey, John Entwistle, Chas Chandler and Jeff Beck. They heard Jimi's trio blast through some beautiful sounds like 'Rock Me Baby', 'Third Stone From The Sun', 'Hey Joe' and even an unusual version of The Troggs 'Wild Thing'. Jimi has great stage presence and an exceptional guitar technique which involved playing with his teeth on occasions and no hands at all on others! Jimi looks like becoming one of the big club names of '67."

CHRIS WELCH, *MELODY MAKER*, DECEMBER 31ST 1966

with anyone and willing to play anything available: he'd get up with Brian Auger at Blaises, or with Cream at the Central London Polytechnic. A band had been formed around him – Mitch Mitchell on drums and Noel Redding on bass – and The Jimi Hendrix Experience played short spells in France and Germany. At the end of November they hosted a press launch in London at the revived Bag O'Nails club in Kingly Street. *Record Mirror* was the first to publish an interview with Jimi after the Bag do, and when the reporter asked for a definition of the Experience's music, Jimi explained: "We don't want to be classed in any category. If it must have a tag, I'd like it to be called 'free feeling'. It's a mixture of rock, freak-out, blues and rave music."[101]

Beck later recalled the December gig at Blaises: "I heard this sound blasting up the road. I got out the cab, went in and there was Jimi. I just couldn't believe it. He was singing 'Like A Rolling Stone'. I knew the tune, but the way he treated it was something else. He was going crazy and the people were going crazy. After that everyone was blown away. I have been ever since."[102] Blaises was another of London's mid-1960s up-market clubs, "a more sultry disco than the Crom",[103] situated in the basement of the Imperial Hotel in Queen's Gate, Knightsbridge (and demolished in 1992).

It was clear to many of the onlookers that Hendrix was a star in the making, and as 1967 got underway the guitarist began slowly to make the transition from clubs to concert halls. At the end of March his first UK tour commenced, another of the mixed-bag "packages", this one including The Walker Brothers, Cat Stevens, Engelbert Humperdinck and others. The first night

Jimi Hendrix at the Marquee early in 1967 (main picture). Boxer Billy Walker opened his Upper Cut club in east London in December 1966, and during the first week (ad, right) included "Jimmy Hendrix" on boxing-day afternoon for 5/- (25p, about 40¢). Jimi's lowly status at the time is evident by the fact that everyone else commands entrance charges of at least twice that. Jimi is alleged to have written 'Purple Haze' in the dressing room here. The Upper Cut was closed a year later.

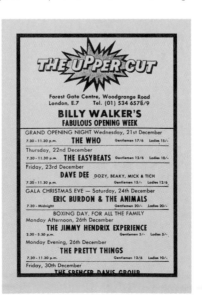

88

Sundays in '67 meant the Saville Theatre in Shaftesbury Avenue and concerts promoted by Brian Epstein. Jimi Hendrix, a Saville regular, relaxes in the theatre's dressing room (right) while Pink Floyd (below: Wright, Waters, Mason, Barrett) pose against a Saville mural.

SUNDAYS at the SAVILLE
A NEMS PRESENTATION
OCTOBER 1st*
PINK FLOYD
TOMORROW
Featuring KEITH WEST
GUEST STAR TIM ROSE
*Presented in association with Brian Morrison Agency
OCTOBER 8th
JIMI HENDRIX EXPERIENCE
OCTOBER 15th*
JR. WALKER ALL STARS
*Presented in association with Rik and John Gunnell
OCTOBER 22nd
THE WHO
OCTOBER 29th
THE CREAM
BOOK: TEM 4011

was at the Finsbury Park Astoria (which would later be renamed The Rainbow Theatre). *NME* writer Keith Altham recalled a significant decision made in the dressing-room before the show:

> **Various things were being discussed about what they could actually do that night to grab some of the headlines and capture people's attention. I think [simply] because I had a variflame lighter, I said, 'What would happen if we set light to his guitar?' I kind of said it as a joke and Chas said, 'That's not a bad idea.' I said [that a solidbody guitar] would take 15 minutes to catch. And Chas said, 'Well, if we use lighter fuel [the fuel will burn rather than] the actual guitar.' So we tried a few experimental runs in the dressing-room and it worked.[104]**

This and other visual stunts that audiences came to expect from him would try the patience of Hendrix the serious musician during his rise to fame over the coming months and years. Meanwhile the early gigs continued. In May '67, after that first British tour, Hendrix made his debut at the Saville Theatre in Shaftesbury Avenue. The Saville had been a working theatre since it opened in 1931, and then in 1965 Beatles' manager Brian Epstein took over the licence with the intention of staging rock concerts on a regular basis. With a capacity of just over 1,200 it was large enough to suggest importance, but small enough to retain an almost club-like intimacy. The Saville's Sunday evening concerts that began at the end of 1966, overseen by Epstein himself, became a popular draw on the London scene. The Beatles were regular visitors – their boss could wangle them free tickets – and McCartney later recalled an especially memorable Hendrix date in June 1967:

> **Jimi opened, the curtains flew back and he came forward, playing 'Sgt Pepper' – and it had only been released on the Thursday, so that was like the ultimate compliment... To think that that album had meant so much to him as to actually do it by the Sunday night, three days after the release... I put that down as one of the great honours in my career.[105]**

Hendrix was one of many of the newly popular acts that played the Saville on Sundays: Cream appeared here, Fairport Convention, the Incredible String Band, Bluesology (with a young Elton John), The Who, Tomorrow, Pink Floyd, Jeff Beck, US visitors such as Little Richard, and the British debuts of bands like The Bee Gees and Steve Winwood's Traffic. "It was like another rehearsal, only this time with an audience," admitted Traffic's drummer Jim Capaldi, underlining the growing feeling among many bands that they could just jam and generally find their way in public. "They were very receptive," Capaldi said of the Saville audience, "and we managed to work a few things out."[106]

But not everything worked out. In summer '67 Brian Epstein, the man who ran The Beatles and The Saville, died. Three years later The Beatles split; three years later The Saville would be converted to a cinema, its role as a rock theatre finished.

"I was at the Saville watching Jimi Hendrix [on August 27th] when the announcement was made," wrote journalist Ray Coleman some years later. "The crowd was told, 'The promoter of this show and a man we all owe much to, Brian Epstein, has died.' Hendrix had fittingly – for that's what Eppy would have wanted – blown our minds with a show that he never eclipsed. But it was bad outside the theatre that night when beads and bells denoting peace jangled, but some lousy, stinking, thoughtless, heartless 'fans' revolted against the decision to

The Queen Elizabeth Hall was part of the South Bank complex at Waterloo that also included the Royal Festival Hall. It was another medium-size venue put to use during the late 1960s for rock concerts such as this 1967 date by hippie-folk outfit The Incredible String Band.

A majestic lightshow at UFO, the psychedelic club that began in Tottenham Court Road in December 1966. Early publicity (ad for two opening nights, December 23rd and 30th 1966, below) highlighted the club's all-night operation. Negative press reports and ever-growing crowds forced UFO to move to The Roundhouse in Chalk Farm in August 1967, where the club lasted until its final show in October.

Look out for
U.F.O.'s
Nite Tripper
Dec. 23rd - 30th
All night

cancel the second Hendrix performance as a mark of respect for Epstein. 'We paid money for the show – get the show on. Who was Brian Epstein anyway?' That was the tone of the anger as the crowd going out met the throngs milling outside."[107]

If the Saville was the main big-stage gig on London's underground scene, then its key club was the relatively shortlived UFO. The success of the Floyd's gigs at the small All Saints Hall and the unsuitability of the drafty Roundhouse had led Hoppy the hippie and Joe Boyd, an American who'd just been sacked as Elektra Records' UK representative, to look for premises in the centre of town in which to hold a new club. The Blarney was an Irish club complete with polished dancefloor in a 600-capacity basement in Tottenham Court Road, just along from Oxford Street, and its owner was delighted to get £15 ($24) and the soft-drinks income in exchange for letting it out to Hoppy and Boyd on Friday nights.

In December 1966 UFO opened there. Originally it was viewed with caution, as an experiment, and just two Fridays were initially booked from the Blarney, the 23rd and the 30th. But success came quickly. The premises used for UFO had hosted a number of clubs since it had first been used as Rector's back in 1920 (see page 11). It was known in the 1930s as the Carlton Dancehall. But the basement had witnessed nothing like the scenes that would develop at UFO's highly successful all-nighters over the coming months.

From the outset, UFO was intended to be the psychedelic epitome of hipness – and strictly, *strictly* underground. At the slightest hint of any kind of commercial interest the kaftan-clad inner circle would throw up a fragrant smokescreen, making it clear that capitalist straights were most certainly not welcome, man. And the place would be a trip for all the senses: the multi-media of New Departures, Spontaneous Underground and All Saints was stepped up a notch at UFO, the visitor assaulted as much by the musical delights as the visual treats. Also on hand were erotic plays, poetry readings, bad-trip counselling, underground magazine sales, theatre groups, juggling acts, movies and definitely no alcohol. It was a "trippy adventure playground" said Paul McCartney.[108]

The lightshows were an especially important part of the UFO experience. Floyd's lighting man Peter Wynne Wilson recalled: "UFO was where we all developed our ideas – the group musically, and me designing the lighting – because it was such a responsive situation. We used to put lighting all over the club."[109] Wilson and Russell Page would cover one area, while Mark Boyle and Jack Braceland worked on others. The effect was dazzling and impressive. "You were pounded with sound as well as images," recalls Steve Howe of UFO regulars Tomorrow. "There was a massed wall of bubbling, oozing oil chopped up with movie clips – maybe an upside-down *Laurel And Hardy* or some sensuous cartoon – plus perhaps a film of a triangle changing into a square and then a circle. It was all psyching you out," he laughs. "The idea was that the mind would not be able to think straight."[110]

For a while Pink Floyd were virtually the house band at UFO; theirs was a perfect concoction of now rhythmic, now ethereal music with which to entertain the gentle, laidback folk who populated the club. "Their sound fitted that period," UFO club-goer Pete Townshend said later, "with echo on all the instruments.

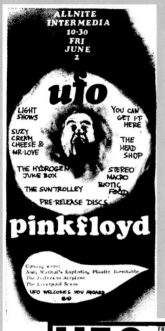

UFO tried to make promo items reflect the multi-media vibe of the club, and their visual flair contrasted with the plain listings seen in most of the rest of the music press in 1967.

❝ I once got Eric Clapton to come down because I thought what Syd was doing was very interesting. We both enjoyed him, although you could never quite hear what he was up to... [His echo units formed] a kind of sound field, a textural wash of sound that wasn't always melodically or harmonically correct but always very interesting and satisfying."[111] ❞

A number of bands became UFO favourites as the club progressed through the first half of 1967. Beyond the ubiquitous Pink Floyd and Soft Machine one might catch Procol Harum celebrating their number-one 45 'Whiter Shade Of Pale', Arthur Brown as ever with blazing bonnet, or Tomorrow generally freaking out. Steve Howe describes the band coming upon UFO as "like meeting the perfect wave". He continues:

❝ UFO was in the capital, and it was the capital of the movement, a sort of psychedelic haven. If you didn't watch out in the dressing room they'd put acid in your Coca-Cola – that was a hazard. You'd see people acting it up a bit, thinking they were in a movie, which was the LSD thing. What was good was that you lost all sense of class distinction: if you were a hippie you were a hippie, aristocracy or east-end. I would find myself playing guitar solos for ten minutes, left alone to exploit my improvisations. There was space for these new things. Meanwhile Twink [John Alder] would usually carry on and then fall over his drums, Keith [West] would wander around screaming a bit, and bassist Junior [John Wood] would be dancing with Suzy Creamcheese. Apparently there were many Suzy Creamcheeses – maybe this one really was the original Zappa girl, I don't know.[112] ❞

Another club-goer, Peter Fryer, wrote at the time about how the enormity of sound often limited other activities. "Those who enjoy UFO speak warmly of the empathy and non-verbal communication attained there with people of like mind," he said. "Verbal communication is scarcely possible, so loud is the music. The visitor sees a collection of charming but withdrawn individuals, smiling vaguely at friends, jerked at times by the music's rhythms, but ultimately quite self-sufficient and self-absorbed as each intently explores his private world and savours his private visions."[113]

One UFO regular who we can assume was already having to deal with more than his fair share of private visions was Floyd guitarist Syd Barrett. Joe Boyd told of an occasion when the Floyd, returning to the club victorious from exterior successes, went by him on their way to the stage. Boyd greeted his old chums. "The last one was Syd, and the great thing about Syd was that he had a twinkle in his eye... he had this impish look about him, this mischievous glint. He came by and I said, 'Hi, Syd.' He just kind of looked at me. I looked right in his eye

DOUBLE
GIANT FREAK - OUT BALL
ROUNDHOUSE, CHALK FARM RD., N.W.1
FRI., 30th DEC., 10 p.m. onwards
GENO WASHINGTON and the RAMJAM BAND
THE CREAM • ALAN BOWN SET
and Supporting Groups
PSYCHODELPHIA
SATURDAY, 31st DECEMBER, 10 p.m. onwards
NEW YEAR'S EVE — ALL NIGHT RAVE
THE WHO THE MOVE Supporting Groups
Late licensed bars   Central Heating   New improved entrance
facilities   Psychedelic lighting affects   Tickets 15/- each show,
available at: Indica Books, Housmans, Better Books, Collets,
Dobells and Biba's Boutique. Postal application, S.A.E.
Postal Order to: U.M.L., 235 Camden Road, N.7.
Make sure of your ticket now to avoid disappointment.

UFO's move from Tottenham Court Road to The Roundhouse in summer 1967 was not an entirely happy one. The cold expanse of the Roundhouse had been criticised before when it hosted the Psychodelphia events (December 1966 ad, above). UFO closed for good in October 1967.

R E V I E W

PINK FLOYD

UFO, JULY 28TH 1967

"In a cacophony of sound played to a background of multi-coloured projected lights the Pink Floyd proved they are Britain's top psychedelic group before the hip audience at UFO on Friday night. In two powerful sets they drew nearly every conceivable note from their instruments but ignored their two hit singles. They included 'Pow R Toc H' and a number which received its first hearing called 'Reaction In G' which they say was a reaction against their Scottish tour when they had to do 'See Emily Play'. Bass player Roger Waters gave the group a powerful depth and the lights played on to them set an impressive scene. Many of the audience found the Floyd's music too much to sit down to and in more subdued parts of the act the sound of jingling bells from their dancing masters joined in. It is clear that the Floyd prefer playing to UFO-type audiences rather than provincial ones and are at their best in an atmosphere more acceptable to them."

ROGER SIMPSON, *MELODY MAKER*, AUGUST 5TH 1967

The 14-Hour Technicolor Dream was held overnight on April 29th 1967 at Alexandra Palace in north London. So vast was its cathedral-like Great Hall that a stage was set up at each end with different attractions. Members of the crowd (estimated at around 10,000; see main picture) would move around as new "scenes" developed and the full multi-media nature of the event revealed itself. Over 40 bands were expected to play at the event, but some of those booked failed to appear. The inset picture (right) shows Ginger Johnson's African Drummers providing a keen rhythmic pulse at one end of the hall. Other acts appearing included Pink Floyd, The Move and The Social Deviants.

Chill-out zone at Ally Pally's April '67 Technicolor Dream. A "Love-In Festival" (ad below) followed in July.

and there was no twinkle, no glint. It was like somebody had pulled the blinds. You know: nobody home. It was a real shock. Very, very sad."[114]

UFO at Tottenham Court Road did not last. In June 1967 Hoppy was imprisoned for drug offences. The *News Of The World* got wind of the story and published their usual truth-seeking investigation, a two-parter headlined: "The Psychedelic Experience: Pop Stars and Drugs". One thing led to another: the police became interested in the club's activities and put pressure on The Blarney's owner; he lost his nerve and in August withdrew UFO's rental agreement.

UFO events continued in name back at the dreaded Roundhouse. "We realise that many members and friends had come to love the premises at 31 Tottenham Court Road, but we were unfortunately unable to accommodate all the people that wanted to come in," the UFO

London's own hip newspaper
INTERNATIONAL TIMES
presents

14-HOUR TECHNICOLOR DREAM

Giant Benefit Against
★ **FUZZ ACTION** ★

30 GROUPS

including:

**MOVE ★ PINK FLOYD
PETER TOWNSHEND**

many beautiful people

FESTIVAL OF LIGHT MACHINES

Tickets £1 in Advance Only

From all sources, or:
DAVE CURTIS, 57 Greek Street, W.1

**APRIL 29th, 8 p.m.
ALEXANDRA PALACE, N.22**

Look for the Technicolor Poster

THIS SATURDAY ALL NIGHT LOVING!
ALEXANDRA PALACE 9 P.M. TILL 9 A.M.

ERIC BURDON THE ANIMALS

LOVE IN FESTIVAL

TICKETS £1-0-0

organisers said in an August '67 release. "We also realise that to many of our friends 'Roundhouse' means a cold, uncomfortable place which has been the site of some unsuccessful 'freak out' promotions in the past. It is, however, now vastly improved in comfort and we tried it out with a private party for members only this past Friday night and consensus was that it was one of the best UFOs ever."[115] UFO presented some regulars from Tottenham Court Road at the Roundhouse, as well as psychedelic recruits such as Dantalion's Chariot, who were really Zoot Money's Big Roll Band in newly flowered and somewhat ill-fitting

packaging. However, by the middle of October 1967 UFO was gone from the Roundhouse and, indeed, gone for good.

Earlier that year The 14-Hour Technicolor Dream took place. It was a benefit for *IT*, conceived after the underground paper's offices had been raided by police. This "free speech benefit", with tickets priced at £1 ($1.60), would be an all-nighter staged at Alexandra Palace in April 1967.

"Ally Pally", as many Londoners call Alexandra Palace, was a large gothic building in the grounds of Alexandra Park, between Muswell Hill and Wood Green in north London. It was re-opened in 1875 after the original structure burnt to the ground two weeks after first opening in 1873, and included a concert hall, theatre and offices. From the 1930s to the 1950s part of the building was used by the BBC as a TV studio (and was the site of the Corporation's historic first TV broadcast in August 1936).

For the Technicolor Dream in 1967, dozens of acts, musical and otherwise, were slated to appear. They would perform on one of two simultaneously working stages, combining to create a programme designed to catch the imagination of audiences used to UFO's carefree, multi-media shows. UFO stalwarts Pink Floyd and Soft Machine were booked, of course, as were The Pretty Things, The Creation, The Move, The Social Deviants, The Purple Gang and many more.

When it came to the night the crowds were certainly there – maybe as many as 10,000, many taking advantage of the shuttle bus service from the nearby tube stations. However, a good number of the bands were not so fortunate in their transport arrangements. In fact, they may not even have known they were supposed to be playing at the event, such was the lackadaisical "organisation". Pink Floyd did at least turn up – even if it was gone three o'clock in the morning. The first light of dawn rather suited the band. It was a shame about the no-show bands, but there were plenty of other distractions – films and slides, a fibreglass igloo, masses of joss sticks, a helter-skelter, chanting sessions, lightshows, even stoned idiots trying acrobatics on the scaffolding. "Alexandra Palace isn't the best place for acoustics," said one reporter who attended the event. "Most often the sound echoed up into the huge dome and away."[116]

Barry Miles observed: "I just couldn't believe it. Outside, the straights of Wood Green were watching their tellies, and inside this time-machine there were thousands of stoned, tripping, mad, friendly, festive hippies. Talk about two different worlds!"[117] The *Sunday Mirror* reflected: "The whole thing was rather like the last struggle of a doomed tribe trying to save itself from extinction." And Russell Hunter, who may or may not have been in The Social Deviants, said much, much later: "The 14-Hour Technicolor Dream was one of the first hippie things I went to. People have told me that I did play at it, but I don't believe them."[118]

Despite the loose attitude to organisation and the shambolic nature of some of the evening's entertainment, there was no doubting the crowds that such an event could draw, and another Alexandra Palace all-nighter was scheduled for July. It was called the International Love-In Festival.

"Boot-in would have been a better name," suggested a tongue-in-cheek if rattled *Melody Maker* afterwards. "The full casualty list has yet to be announced, including the missing, and those who died of exposure during the long wait to get in." Arthur Brown was apparently stopped from returning to the hall in order to play his second set, and several people were hurt in a number of separate skirmishes. "The amplification, allied to the monstrous acoustics of the hall, made it impossible to hear any announcements or the singers, while the groups all sounded like a stereo set with one speaker on the blink."[119] This general atmosphere could not

Pink Floyd's 1967 concert at the 850-seater Queen Elizabeth Hall (ad, above) witnessed one of the band's first attempts at surround-sound. "New material has been specially written and will be given for the first time, including some specially prepared four-way stereo tapes," said a news release. "Sadly we are not allowed to throw lighting effects as planned on to the external surfaces of the hall, nor even the foyer, but inside should be enough!" The *Financial Times* reviewer wrote: "The audience which filled the hall was beautiful, if strangely subdued, and to enjoy them was alone worth the price of a ticket. When you add an irrepressible Pink Floyd and a free authentic daffodil to take home, your cup of experience overflows."

44 Gerrard Street in Soho housed many basement clubs: the Star in 1931, Phoenix in '54, 44 Skiffle in 1956, a 2-Is off-shoot in '57, and Happening 44 (ad, below) in '67.

The Electric Garden (ad, above) was the shortlived forerunner to Middle Earth. Both were set in the large basement of an old house in Covent Garden, a building also used as a fruit-and-vegetable warehouse.

have helped Pink Floyd, but they had a bigger problem to contend with. Syd Barrett had been playing with his chemistry set. At first he couldn't be found, and the audience grew restless as the Floyd were announced but nothing happened. Barrett was finally discovered. His guitar was plugged in, and his stoned person carefully propped in front of the microphone. At last the Floyd set commenced. But it didn't last long. June Child, secretary at Floyd's management operation (and later married to Marc Bolan), remembered: "Suddenly [Syd] put his hands on the guitar and we thought great, he's actually going to do it. And he stood there, he just stood there, tripping out of his mind. They did three, maybe four numbers, and we got him off."[120] Barrett was reported the following week as "suffering from nervous exhaustion" and the group withdrew from further engagements. He just about lasted with the Floyd until early the following year, and was replaced by David Gilmour.

The last of the big psychedelic all-nighters, Christmas On Earth Continued, was put on in December 1967 at a chilly, vast Victorian hangar, Olympia in west London. The attractions included Jimi Hendrix, Eric Burdon & The Animals, Tomorrow, Pink Floyd with a still remote Barrett, and an impressive in-the-round lightshow.

During 1967 UFO didn't only inspire people to put on bigger events, but to copy the idea of the psychedelic multi-media club. That summer – "the summer of love" as some like to call it now – saw two such ventures opened: Happening 44, started by lighting man Jack Braceland in the much-clubbed basement of 44 Gerrard Street ("UFO members admitted; bring your card"); and The Electric Garden, soon to become Middle Earth, launched in the basement of the 17th century building in King Street, Covent Garden, that 120 years earlier had housed Evans's Music-And-Supper Rooms (see page 10).

For a few months after opening in May 1967 the Electric Garden put on acts (including familiar UFO artists like Arthur Brown and Tomorrow) during all-nighters on Fridays and Saturdays as well as a 6pm-to-11pm slot on Sundays. But when UFO closed its doors in Tottenham Court Road in August it seemed to spark a minor coup in Covent Garden. The Electric Garden had committed a number of unforgivable "straight" sins, not least the selling of alcohol, and so was placed in the hands of the underground. Or something like that, anyway. Oz magazine's Richard Neville explained later that the "bad vibrations" sensed by Yoko Ono on the Electric Garden's opening night came from rival underground entrepreneurs. The operation was, he said, soon annexed by "less commercial elements".[121] A release from the as-yet-unnamed new venture read: "Everyone can come in free during the day to do their own thing, whatever it is. We'll be having sounds; groups can practice. London's first digger shop will be opening with free clothes, washing machines for use, food, so please bring anything you don't want.

❝ Remember that this is your club; if you want it to happen then we'd like your help. At night there will be groups, films, events and a few completely unpredictable things, which will blow your minds. Profits from the evenings will go to organisations on the scene, like [drug-legalisation pressure group] SOMA and [drug-offenders rights organisation] Release. The Club will be closed on Friday nights, in deference to UFO [at the Roundhouse]. Watch IT for further news. This Saturday, 19 August, come and choose a name for this environmental space. Votes will take place often. Peace and love.[122] ❞

The voters dipped into their well-thumbed copies of *Lord Of The Rings* to come up with the club's new name: Middle Earth. The operation's hippie frontman was Dave Howson, who had been one of the co-organisers of the 14-Hour Technicolor Dream, and he was backed in the running of Middle Earth by businessman Brian Waldman, manager of Edinburgh band Writing On The Wall, and Waldman's brother Paul.

Covent Garden was at that time still a working fruit-and-vegetable market – it lasted there until 1974 – and the market-workers were often less than appreciative of what they perceived as weird goings-on at 43 King Street. "Middle Earth took your breath away," remembered a club-goer. "You'd go through these desolate, wet streets into this basement in King Street, just near the Opera House, into this great space filled with music and incense and drugs, this

In July 1968 Middle Earth was forced to move from its original Covent Garden basement to The Roundhouse. Its big achievement was to present Jefferson Airplane and The Doors there in September.

During its tenure in King Street, Covent Garden, Middle Earth put on a stream of good bands. This ad (inset) from one week in September 1967 alone has a tempting line-up, but the club also witnessed the occasional US visitor, including the UK debut of Captain Beefheart.

great huge warehouse with pineapples and bananas."[123] On one occasion a team of market porters armed with hammers and other weapons apparently tried to storm the Middle Earth basement after being told that the high-spirited revellers inside had been sacrificing children in the course of their entertainments. The porters were misinformed, but inflicted some damage anyway as a precaution.

Middle Earth had some distinct advantages over UFO, not least that it had permanent premises. The large basement consisted of a long series of connected rooms, perfectly mysterious and ideally suited to confounding the stoned visitor. In the main band room, which was long, low and painted black, there was a DJ's booth beneath the stage – Jeff Dexter and John Peel were regulars – and a lighting gantry along one wall. In other rooms there'd be acoustic strumming, perhaps Marc Bolan and Tyrannosaurus Rex, films would be shown, poetry read, bodies painted. From all reports the lightshows at Middle Earth were the best yet, with the American system employed by Zoot Money's psychedelic incarnation, Dantalion's Chariot, deemed especially good. It was said that they had brought operators over from San Francisco who had worked in the US with Eric Burdon & The Animals.

The main band tended to come on about 3am. This may have been an exotic experience for the visitors, but wasn't quite so alluring for the bands themselves. Charlie Whitney, then guitarist of Middle Earth regulars Family, recalls:

> **For the all-nighters we'd get to Middle Earth about 8pm, set the gear up. About 10pm all these freaks would walk in to this big, big place. Over the sound system they'd be playing classical music. Fantastic atmosphere, really surreal in a way: they'd be walking around in long kaftans all night. The organisers expected us to play about 3 or 4 in the morning. So... you just had to keep yourself together while all these other people were out of their minds. I remember in particular that they used to use the strobe-light all the time, and that would just about finish you off. Playing an hour's set at 4 in the morning with the strobe on ain't a good idea.[124]**

Middle Earth had slightly better staying power than UFO, but it too suffered from police intervention, and in July 1968 the club was forced to move out of King Street. The drafty old Roundhouse again came into use, and Middle Earth re-opened there on July 27th with Traffic headlining. They lasted until early 1969 when a Commissioner at the Old Bailey refused Paul Waldman a licence to continue "pop music" after midnight, ordering him to stop promoting. And that was the end of Middle Earth.

The Roundhouse went on into the 1970s to host Sunday afternoon-and-evening multi-band gigs called Implosion. Hundreds of groups appeared over the years, from Quintessence and Mighty Baby in September 1969 to Elton John and Brinsley Schwarz by April 1972. But Middle Earth's greatest coup there had come in September 1968 when they presented two phenomenal American bands, The Doors and Jefferson Airplane (see review overleaf).

When The Speakeasy was opened by Roy Flynn around the end of 1966 in Margaret Street, just north of Soho, the rock elite soon discovered a handy new watering hole, a prime early-hours jamming post, and an altogether useful hanging-out kind of place. By May 1967 an *NME* reporter was enjoying a drink or two there. "Pop people in their off-duty hours often strike me as being similar to migratory birds," he jotted down. "For about six months they settle in one club and then suddenly – whoosh, they all flock to another. At the moment their present nesting ground appears to be The Speakeasy. I have watched these rare birds

Tiles club opened in Oxford Street in April 1966. Despite much promotion the club is remembered by many who played there as lacking in atmosphere. Among the faceless dance bands some big names such as The Animals and The Who did appear before Tiles closed at the end of 1967. Pink Floyd played in June that year on the same day 'See Emily Play' came out (ad, above).

fluttering from the Ad Lib to the Scotch, to the Cromwellian, the In Place, Sybilla's, Dolly's and the Bag O'Nails. Some of these clubs have prospered, some have faded and a few have disappeared, such is the fickleness of the club-going public. The Speakeasy, however, has an excellent chance of success."[125]

Visitors to the Speak had first to get into the place. It became legendary as the club to which entrance was easy only for those with at least one hit record that week. "Hard to get

into? No, nearly impossible if you are not a member," wrote Penny Valentine in *Disc*, "and even harder to become one because it's so full. Therefore try to latch on to a happy-hippie-scenegoer who belongs."[126] Once okayed, the lucky clubber would enter through the mirrored door of a wardrobe, having paused briefly at the wreathed-coffin cash desk. Why not have a drink at the very long bar? A large portrait of Al Capone looked down on the assembled guzzlers. On a good night he might see you nursing a glass next to The Bee Gees, Jeff Beck, or The Who.

A stream of good bands performed at the Speak. Hendrix's Experience was among the first, in January 1967. Marianne Faithfull said that when she went here to see the great guitarist with Mick Jagger, Mr Jimi tried to seduce her, whispering: "What are you doing with this jerk, anyway?" Cream appeared in August, just before jetting off for their first US tour, with compère Frank Zappa introducing them as a "dandy little combo". One folk reviewer admitted difficulties trying to pay attention to Roy Harper and his acoustic guitar sandwiched between a Mae West film and the resounding Spooky Tooth. Joe Boyd took an unknown Joni Mitchell to the Speak when she came to London looking for a publishing deal; she ended up

---

R E V I E W

THE DOORS, JEFFERSON AIRPLANE

MIDDLE EARTH, ROUNDHOUSE, SEPTEMBER 6TH 1968

"The stage lights went up and John Densmore, Ray Manzarek and Robbie Krieger launched into 'Back Door Man' to herald the arrival of the front Doors man, Jim Morrison. He walked majestically on stage clad in a tight black leather suit, white shirt and brown shoes. The crowd applauded him and Morrison, taking up a stance at the mike, smiled briefly and belted into his first song... For the ritualistic 'The End' Morrison asked for the lights to be put out. Eventually after pleading, and finally shouting, he got the lights off and The Doors became shadowy figures... The song began and a dramatic effect was building up when a spotlight suddenly came on, killing the whole thing. Understandably Morrison walked off but the group kept on playing. The light went out and Morrison returned to finish the song.

During 'Light My Fire' he leapt down into the fenced-off space between the stage and the audience... This caused confusion, with the cameraman [there] becoming tied up in Morrison's mike wire. Morrison screamed into the mike and then held it into the audience for girls to scream into... The six-strong Jefferson Airplane's presentation is looser and more casual, but any lack in visual effect was more than made up by their amazing lightshow... Two guitars, bass and drums built up layers of sounds against the hard vocal work of Grace Slick, Marty Balin and Paul Kantner. Lead guitarist Jorma Kaukonen plays thoughtful, well-constructed solos and doesn't rely on speed for effect... It's been said that it is impossible to get The Doors and Jefferson Airplane together on the same stage in the USA. Last weekend, Middle Earth achieved the impossible."

TONY WILSON, *MELODY MAKER*,
SEPTEMBER 14TH 1968

NO EXIT

NO EXIT

The bar at The Speakeasy became a social centre for London's music industry from the late 1960s. The bar (main picture; the dancefloor and stage were to the right) became the place to meet, swap gossip, even hire and fire. As a desperate measure, record company execs might even watch one of the fine bands appearing. Often, early-hours shows would culiminate in all-star jams; Hendrix was an enthusiastic jam-session regular at the Speak. Co-managers Roy Flynn and Mike Carey are overseen here (inset picture) by Al Capone, no doubt amused by the legal sale of drinks in this particular Speakeasy.

playing at the club, in effect opening for the Incredible String Band. Speak owner Roy Flynn, first manager of Yes, had his group audition for Atlantic there. And in April '69 King Crimson joined a long list of bands who used it for their press launch; Thin Lizzy, for example, made it the site for their English debut in December 1970.

The Speakeasy was also a key place to go to if you fancied a jam. "There was a lot of blowing at the Speak," Charlie Whitney of Family agrees. "People like Ritchie Blackmore would just get up. Hendrix was always blowing there. Couldn't get him off! He didn't care what he played, either: guitar, bass, anything, he'd be there. And with anybody. It was definitely *the* after-hours musician's place."[127] Chris Welch from *Melody Maker* had another theory for the Speakeasy's popularity. "[It was] probably because of the tireless patience of the head waiter and the staff, who did not seem to mind too much when Mr Moon appeared naked letting off fire extinguishers, or Ginger Baker hurled the odd dinner at some rival who had displeased him."[128] For some, however, it was all a bit too much. Soft Machine's Robert Wyatt, for example: "Rock groups meeting in expensive clubs that are difficult to get into? What's all that crap?"[129]

During the first years of The Speakeasy's existence, other clubs were still catching up with the psychedelic craze. The Flamingo and its offshoot The All-Nighter, down in Wardour Street, underwent a rather desperate transformation in August 1967 when they became The Pink Flamingo. The ceiling was covered in flowers, psychedelic paintings adorned the walls and – an odd touch – above the audience lurked stuffed pigeons. Or perhaps they were baby flamingos? Eric Burdon & The Animals opened the newly-attired club on a stage decorated with flowers, beads and jewels. One reporter noted that there were few hippies in evidence on the opening night.

New management took over in November 1969 and the premises were given another fresh name. This time 33-37 Wardour Street became The Temple. "The new underground," the owners suggested. "Non-plastic, just a nice place to groove with nice head sounds and lights." The likes of Steamhammer, East Of Eden and Van Der Graaf Generator played The Temple, the venue lasting until the end of 1971.

Meanwhile, further up Wardour Street, the Marquee continued to present bands every night, and a wonderfully mixed bag it was. In December 1966 David Bowie was here with his backing band The Buzz, while in the following month alone the club could offer big new names like Pink Floyd, Jimi Hendrix and Cream, pop groups such as The Herd (with Peter Frampton) and Marmalade, folk-rock from Al Stewart or The Bunch (Fairports on leave), reggae from Jimmy Cliff, and dues-paying from Timebox (most of which became Patto) and Syn (with Chris Squire and Pete Banks, later of Yes). With this kind of variety, the Marquee had no need for psychedelic renaming or other pretensions, even if DJ John Peel did try a couple of Perfumed Garden events based on his pirate-radio programme.

And the blues was alive and well. Still in that single month of January 1967, the Marquee presented homegrown blues artists such as The Artwoods (Jon Lord on organ, Keef Hartley on drums) and John Mayall, as well as the real thing from Freddy King and Champion Jack Dupree. Maybe the beat/R&B divide did survive after all. The beat-groups of the early 1960s were not averse to psychedelia and had little trouble finding a home in the so-called "progressive" era, while musicians who felt at ease in the earlier R&B bands were well positioned for this "blues boom" of the later 1960s that resonated around bands such as Fleetwood Mac, Led Zeppelin, Chicken Shack and Free.

The Lyceum theatre, just off The Strand near Waterloo Bridge, had opened in 1904 and was the sixth building on the site to present entertainment, the original dating back to the

1760s. By the mid 1950s The Lyceum was run by leisure group Mecca which owned many ballrooms around the UK, and toward the end of the 1960s Harold Pendleton from the Marquee started to promote Midnight Court events there, all-nighters that the Marquee's respectable hours did not allow.

Thus in April 1969 a late-night Lyceum visitor could have dozed between sets by Jeff Beck, Caravan, Al Stewart and Ron Geesin. But other independent promoters staged rock gigs at The Lyceum too, one of the best-known being the charity show for UNICEF in December that featured at its climax the Plastic Ono Supergroup with John Lennon, George Harrison, Eric Clapton, Keith Moon and others. This was the first time that Lennon and Harrison had appeared on a British concert stage together since The Beatles' final NME Pollwinners bash at the Wembley Empire Pool three years earlier.

R E V I E W

TEN YEAR AFTER

MARQUEE, OCTOBER 6TH 1967

"Ten Years After are currently drawing huge applause and crowds at London's Marquee club on Friday nights, and it is not difficult to see why. Here is a group that eschew flower power and thus appeal to those among us who refer to themselves as 'dedicated blues fans'. And here is hard blues in any language, played with skill and feeling. Lead guitarist Alvin Lee, with Clapton hairstyle and vast speed, can gain applause in mid-solo, and his brother on drums, Ric, has great skill at constructing logical solos. The group are completed by Chick [Churchill] on organ and Leo Lyons on bass. With explosions like a 12-and-a-half-minute version of 'Help Me', here is a group being taken to heart by serious group fans, and bringing about one of those 'events' on the scene that the Marquee so frequently produces."

CHRIS WELCH, MELODY MAKER, OCTOBER 21ST 1967

In July 1970 the West Hampstead club Klooks Kleek started a series of Klooks At The Lyceum concerts, blessed on the opening night by the first rolling back of the Lyceum's exciting new sliding roof, through which passers-by could enjoy the strains of Black Sabbath, Yes (with ex-Tomorrow man Steve Howe publicly filling the band's guitar vacant spot for the first time) and Uriah Heep.

In September 1970 the great soul-rock band Sly & The Family Stone came over from the States and played The Lyceum. Eric Clapton had arranged to meet Jimi Hendrix at this gig, on the 16th. Clapton himself had appeared at The Lyceum a few months earlier with his new group, Derek & The Dominos. One account of Jimi's final days that September has Clapton and Hendrix seeing each other at The Lyceum, but able only to wave from one box to another. When Hendrix failed to show at a jam organised for Sly Stone later that night at The Speakeasy, some thought it strange. Jimi was a resolute jam-sessioneer, especially at the Speak. A day or so later, during the morning of the 18th, Hendrix was dead.

Many groups who had come up through the London clubs during the 1960s found that success inexorably led to concerts at larger and larger venues, beyond even the middle-size halls like The Lyceum. London's two main concert halls at the time, the Albert Hall and the Royal Festival Hall, had occasionally been used for pop music since the 1950s, but the demand from rock promoters for suitable larger venues saw these halls in greater demand through the late 1960s and into the 1970s. At the 3,000-seat Festival Hall, which had been built at a Thames-side site for the 1951 Festival Of Britain, Pink Floyd unveiled in April 1969 what they called their Azimuth Co-ordinator, an improved version of the quadraphonic "surround" sound system that the group and their helpers had been working on for some time. In fact the Festival Hall

PSYCHEDELIA

106

The chilly expanses of the Roundhouse, an old railway-engine turning shed in Chalk Farm, north-west London, had been used for rock concerts since December 1966 when the dilapidated building hosted the launch party for the underground paper, *IT*. Despite shortcomings as far as the comfort and warmth of its visitors were concerned (see typical shivering guests, inset picture below) Roundhouse events continued, including University gigs (1968 Brunel ad, inset above) plus UFO and Middle Earth shows. In the main picture, projectors are prepared on a makeshift lightshow platform in the middle of a Roundhouse audience for a concert in the late 1960s.

PSYCHEDELIA

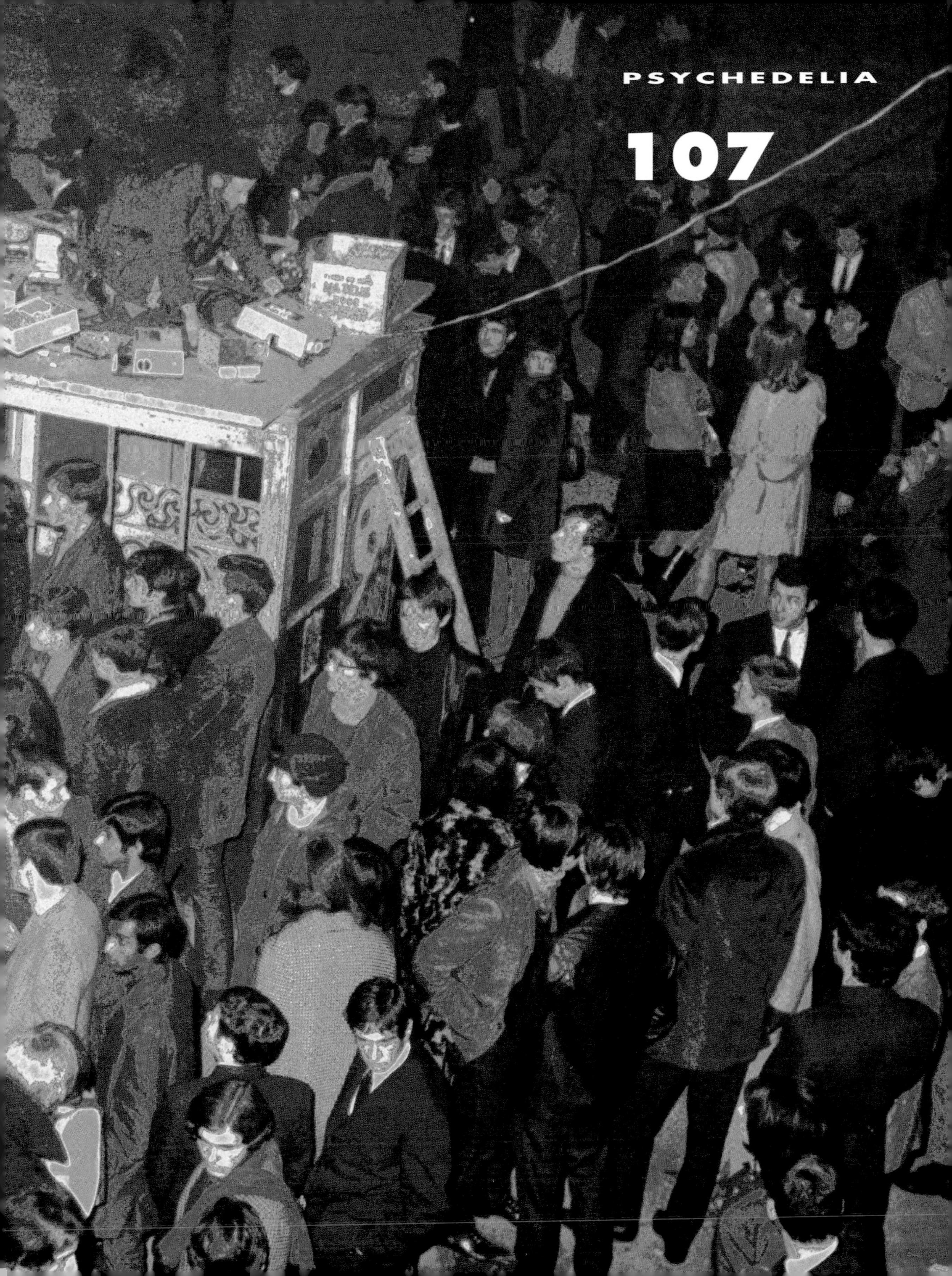

itself had in its first few years of existence needed no fewer than 168 microphones and speakers installed at various points around the auditorium to improve its sound.

In September 1969 Family presented An Evening Of Family Entertainment at the Festival Hall. They had devised a novel first half that featured not the usual support bands but a troupe of variety acts. What larks! There was Rex Roper, the world champion whip-strip artist, Olly Grey "who will attempt a new world plate-spinning record", Sholomir & Yasmin, apparently masters of "the mystic arts", the mysterious Mr Lee Stevens, described as "the bird with the feathers", and a juggler or two. The audience, amused at first, grew increasingly bored as this "entertainment" ground on. One reviewer called it "mixed mediocrity". No doubt it had all seemed like a good idea in the van on the way back from a gig. Family did not repeat the event.

The 5,000-seat Albert Hall, in Kensington Gore, near the south side of Hyde Park, was first opened in 1871 as part of a memorial to Queen Victoria's husband Prince Albert. The circular hall soon suffered from its infamous sound problems, notably unhelpful echoes. The conductor Sir Thomas Beecham remarked with customary wit that a musical work receiving its first performance at the Albert Hall was immediately assured of a second. To attend to these deficiencies, the hall's hollow dome was stuffed in 1949, while the hanging of plastic discs from the ceiling in 1968 proved a more suitable sonic improvement. Despite this tinkering, at its best the Albert Hall retains a magical atmosphere that transcends its size and has the power to lift a good performance into a great one.

A good Albert Hall year was 1966: Dylan and The Hawks plugged in their amplifiers on its stage in May; the Stones recorded some tracks for Got Live If You Want It in September; and the following month Eric Clapton became very excited at a concert by the great Mississippi-born blues guitarist Otis Rush. "Judging by Clapton's behaviour," one audience member observed, "he must be one of Rush's most ardent followers. His voice could be heard above all others requesting in no uncertain manner that Otis should stay on stage rather than make way for other artists to do their spots."[130] Clapton himself played here two years later during the London dates of Cream's farewell concerts, and in much later in his illustrious career would virtually live at the place for extended periods of time.

DEEP PURPLE
SPEAKEASY
MARCH 20th
Last appearance before
2nd USA tour
48 Margaret St. London W1

Despite occasional prestige events in small clubs like The Speakeasy, many newly successful bands were by the late 1960s seeking bigger venues and lucrative overseas tours.

R E V I E W

GENESIS
THE LYCEUM, APRIL 9TH 1971

"Rock mogul Tony Stratton-Smith scored a singular success with his Easter concerts. At London's Lyceum he put on a parade of bands at sessions on Friday and Sunday… Genesis proved both absorbing and entertaining. A fine new band, they have improved greatly on their early days and have an asset in their showman flute player and singer, Peter Gabriel, noted for amusing announcements and a finale on the 'The Knife' in which he hurled an ancient bass drum aloft and demolished quantities of sound equipment. Phil Collins played excellent drums and Steve Hackett (guitar), Mike Rutherford (bass) and Tony Banks (organ) obtained a bright, clear sound."

CHRIS WELCH, *MELODY MAKER*, ARPIL 17TH 1971

The Albert Hall's classical heritage has not been lost on some rock performers, most conspicuously when Deep Purple recorded their *Concerto For Group And Orchestra* in September 1969 with the Royal Philharmonic Orchestra. A few months later at a more conventional concert there Deep Purple tripped the decibel meter to register as the world's

loudest rock group. There is one seat in the Hall where the last note of that performance still reverberates to this day. During the following summer Soft Machine became the first rock act to play at the Albert Hall's annual Prom concerts, which had been strictly classical since moving there in 1941. However, equipment problems plagued the Softs' performance, prompting Robert Wyatt to improvise a chorus of "Abandon! Abandon!" to one of the group's otherwise largely instrumental pieces.

An important source of gigs for bands in the early 1970s was the expanding college and university circuit, The Who famously underlining its significance when they recorded their *Live At Leeds* LP in February 1970 at Leeds University. Presenting live music certainly wasn't anything new for further-education establishments – an example among many would be Northampton College in Finsbury, north London, hosting Long John Baldry, Rod Stewart and Graham Bond back in 1964 – but it was becoming more important. Key London venues in the late 1960s and early 1970s included the Central London Polytechnic, Imperial College, City University and the London School Of Economics.

"Among the bands on the rock circuit," said *Melody Maker* in 1970, "it is generally agreed that the college/university scene is both the most lucrative to work and, in many places, by far the most satisfying from the point of view of audience participation and understanding."[131] Among the firm favourites of the college/university circuit was Family, and at this time one survey placed them as the highest-paid college group, going out for £1,000 ($1,600) a night. Today Charlie Whitney, then the group's guitarist, reflects on the implications. "We went from playing maybe five clubs a week to perhaps one university a week, which I didn't think was good for the band," he says. "I felt we were better when we were working all the time. But the agent would say well, they're not going out for less than this – and that then puts many of the other venues out of the frame. I don't think that was a good move. I think we priced ourselves out and the band suffered for it. When you don't play regularly your machine isn't so well-oiled."[132]

By the early 1970s Pink Floyd too had reached the position where the concert fees they could attract had increased dramatically since the £15 ($24) they were paid to appear at the *IT* launch in late 1966. But keyboardist Rick Wright put their elevated income in perspective for a 1971 interviewer. "In the papers there has been a lot of talk about us charging £2,000 [$3,150] for each concert," he said, "but we have gone out recently for as little as £400 [$630].

If a university can only fit 1,000 into the concert, then we will only charge £400. Universities have put it around that we charge £1,800 [$2,800], and [they] are frightened to approach us because they think they won't be able to afford the group. We want to keep tickets down to around £1 [$1.60] at the maximum. The money we live on comes from record royalties and the gig money is almost all spent on the upkeep of the band. This past 12 months we have just about broken even as far as income from gigs and expenditure on putting them on is concerned. We have a huge amount of equipment to keep up to scratch and have just bought a new mixer for £2,000.[133]

As the 1970s proceeded Floyd and some of the other newly successful "progressive" outfits – Emerson Lake & Palmer, Yes, King Crimson, and later ELO and Queen – would be vilified in some quarters as an out-of-touch elite who by their very presence were provoking another pop music revolution. Of course, it wasn't quite as simple as that.

Led Zeppelin, formed by Jimmy Page of The Yardbirds, played their first British gig at the Marquee in October 1968 (pictured, right). It was a pity that the club's ad for the gig (above) omitted the word "New" in "The Yardbirds". Melody Maker's reviewer at the gig said, "The re-grouped Yardbirds... are now very much a heavy group, with singer Robert Plant leading and ably holding his own against a powerful backing trio... One of the best numbers of the set was 'Dazed And Confused' featuring interesting interplay of Plant's voice and Page's guitar on which he used a violin bow, creating an unusual effect... Generally there appears to be a need for Led Zeppelin to cut down on volume a bit."

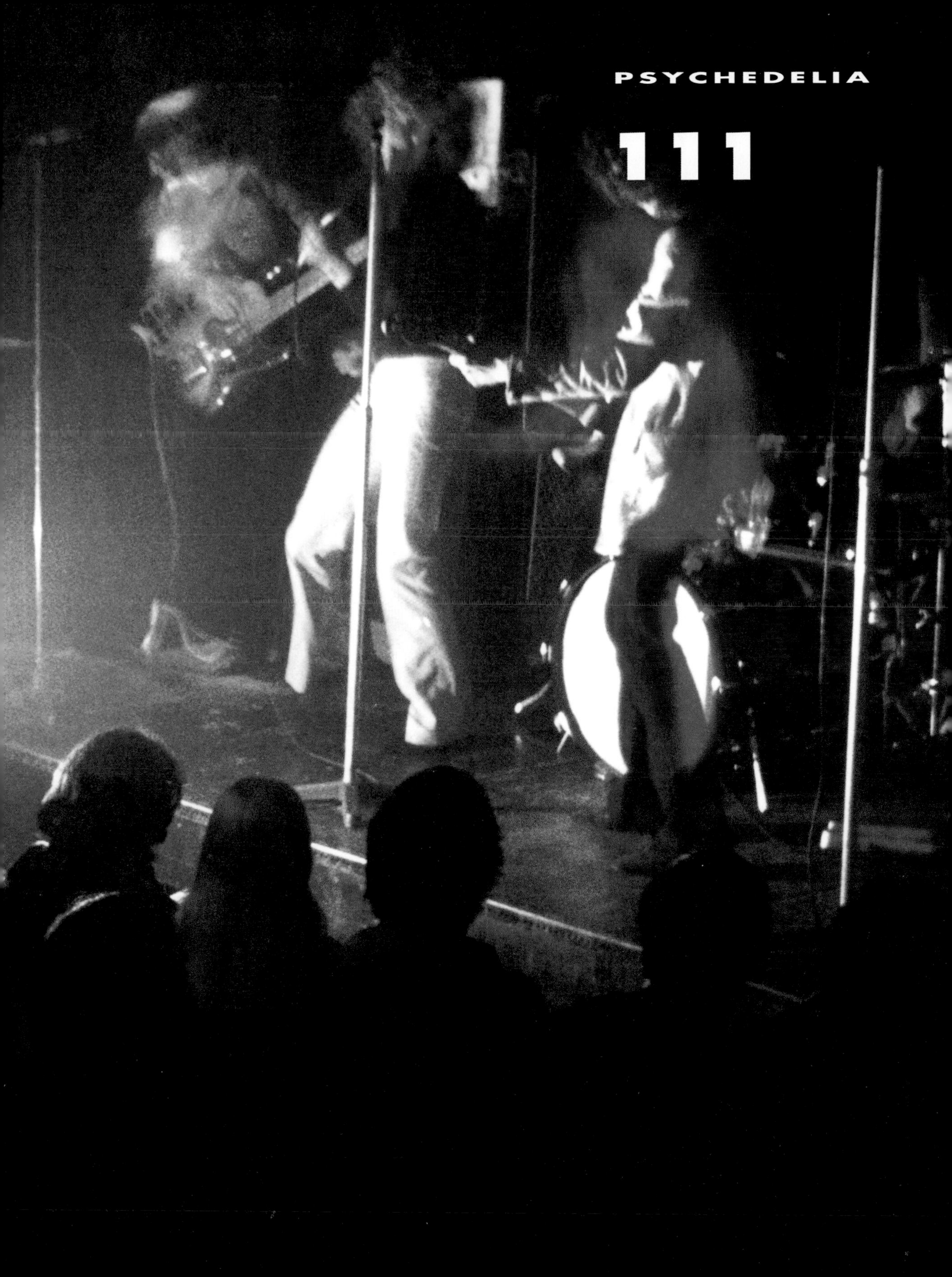

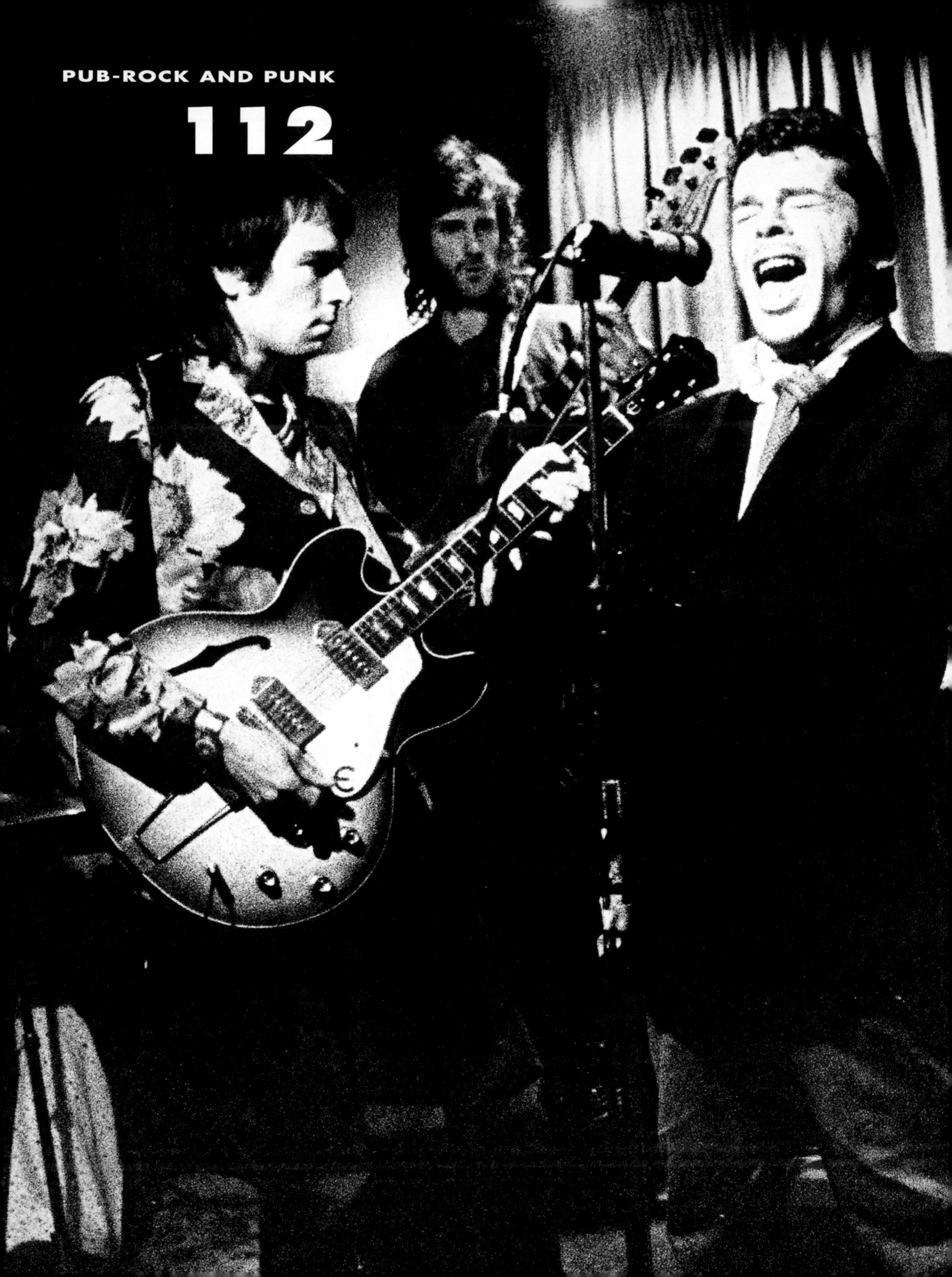

GOOD-TIME MUSIC IN THE PUBLIC BAR TONIGHT

IT WAS 1972, AND THE MUSIC PRESS suddenly said, "Ah-ha, the new thing is pub-rock!" Hold on, said everyone else in London, we've been going to see bands in pubs for years. This was true. Indeed the phenomenon dated back to a time before even amplification or lager had been invented. The music-hall of the Victorian and Edwardian eras certainly had its roots in music performed in pubs, but for years, decades, even centuries before that, taverns and inns had attracted and amused the thirsty customer or weary traveller by hiring a few musicians to bash out some popular songs.

During the early 1970s a realisation began to dawn that top bands' concerts were simply too vast, and that these elevated artists were becoming increasingly remote from their audience. Some thought they were raking in too much money, as well. "Big groups charge appalling prices for gigs," DJ Bob Harris said in 1971. "So many rock musicians have lost sight of the people."[134]

Economics had also affected many of the middle-league bands, sending them away from regular club dates to numerically fewer but individually more lucrative university gigs. If rock music was to continue to flourish, then injections of new talent had to be found... somewhere. All of which led to this new focus on the bands that were playing in pubs. And, more specifically, in London pubs.

During 1971 some of the pubs that would later become part of the "new" circuit were already presenting bands. Toward the end of that year, for example, the music-loving beer-drinker with a selective ear might have enjoyed Vinegar Joe or the Sensational Alex Harvey Band at The Torrington in North Finchley, and Slowbone or Spreadeagle at The Pied Bull in Islington, both in north London, or to the west of town could have taken in Quiver or Uriah Heep at Fulham's Greyhound – which at the time was one of the few pubs that was presenting rock music seven nights a week. And there were plenty more bands playing at these and other pubs all across town.

It's difficult to discern any kind of link between those acts – largely because there is none, other than that they all played in pubs at the time. But by 1972 elements of the weekly pop press were seeking a contrast to the glam-laden charts that were full of Slade and Sweet and

Ian Dury with Kilburn & The High Roads at The Kensington (left), one of the London pubs that became part of the so-called pub-rock circuit. Pictured with vocalist Dury are guitarist Keith Lucas, bassist Charlie Hart and saxman Davey Payne (pianist Russell Hardy and drummer David Rohoman were out of shot). The ad (right) includes among much jazz the Kilburns gig in February 1973 at which this photo was taken.

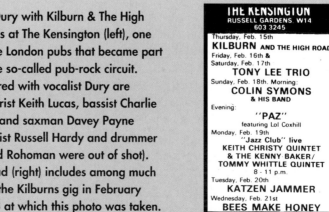

THE KENSINGTON
RUSSELL GARDENS, W14
603 3245

Thursday, Feb. 15th
KILBURN AND THE HIGH ROAD
Friday, Feb. 16th &
Saturday, Feb. 17th
TONY LEE TRIO
Sunday, Feb. 18th. Morning:
COLIN SYMONS
& HIS BAND
Evening:
"PAZ"
featuring Lol Coxhill
Monday, Feb. 19th
"Jazz Club" live
KEITH CHRISTY QUINTET
& THE KENNY BAKER/
TOMMY WHITTLE QUINTET
8 - 11 p.m.
Tuesday, Feb. 20th
KATZEN JAMMER
Wednesday, Feb. 21st
BEES MAKE HONEY

114

The pub-rock scene lasted from 1971 to 1975 and involved bands such as Brinsley Schwarz, Chilli Willi & The Red Hot Peppers and Bees Make Honey. They built up a following for their unpretentious, good-time music performed at pubs throughout the city. One of the best-known of the pub venues was The Hope & Anchor in Islington, north London. It also housed a simple studio and saw the beginnings of the Stiff record label, one of the first of an outburst of small British indies that followed.

116

The Hope & Anchor saw all the best-known pub-rock acts on its stage, including Ducks Deluxe (April 1973 ad, above). In later years, Joy Division played an early London date there in 1978, and the following year a youthful U2 gigged at the Hope, apparently to an audience of no more than nine.

R E V I E W

ACE, *THE KENSINGTON,* **SEPTEMBER 6TH 1973**

"Ace are quite definitely living up to their name. Paul Carrack's Hammond playing was to the fore [while] Alan King plays rhythm guitar and plays it good. King listens to what's happening around him and his light finger-picking style gives that sound fullness but doesn't clutter the excellent, bluesy lead work of Phil Harris. Vocals aren't particularly distinguished though the three-part harmonies of Carrack, King and Harris are fine. They gain confidence and support from weight of numbers. The first set was low-key but 'Six Days On The Road' (now something of a pub standard) was good. The second set, however, was a stormer. Any band that plays The Four Tops 'Loving You Is Sweeter Than Ever' has me won over right from the start. A very fair jam session... on a slow blues and then on Tommy Tucker's 'Hi Heel Sneakers' lifted the band and the crowd. 'Twenty-four Hours' and 'Time Ain't Long' were the last two songs, but the names weren't important. The atmosphere was rampant, the band was Ace and drummer Steve Witherington was a bitch!" **GEOFF BROWN,** *MELODY MAKER,* **SEPTEMBER 15TH 1973**

Gary Glitter and T.Rex, and caught hold of the best of the no-nonsense pub acts. These became the so-called "pub-rock bands", and while this was by its very nature a necessarily loose tag, it did come to be attached relatively firmly to bands such as Brinsley Schwarz, Ducks Deluxe, Chilli Willi & The Red Hot Peppers, Bees Make Honey, Kilburn & The High Roads, and Ace.

Minus later guitarist Ian Gomm, Brinsley Schwarz (the band) had come infamously to public attention in 1970 when their management company chartered an aircraft to take the band and a planeload of music-biz and press to see them play at the Fillmore East in New York. It certainly did bring the Brinsleys to notice – but gained them accusations of hype in the process. Surviving that, and acquiring a record deal, the band continued to produce pleasant country-flavoured rock. When bassist Nick Lowe was asked a couple of years later if they had invented pub-rock, he denied the charge.

We were I suppose the first name band to be involved with it. We used to live near Kentish Town [in north London], near The Tally Ho pub. There was an American set-up called Eggs Over Easy and they had asked the [landlord] if they could play three or four nights a week. At first few people came to hear them and then numbers grew, and for a time people didn't come to pose, they came to hear some good, unpretentious music, music which often grew on the spot, of which people were part. The other band had to go so we stepped in.[135]

One of the requirements of pub-rock was this general unpretentiousness to which Lowe alludes, a good-time attitude to music that could incorporate elements of the best dance-oriented pop picked from a broad range of sources – rock'n'roll to country-rock, Motown to R&B. The shrewd band might also include enough self-penned numbers in a similar vein to prick the ears of the audience – and any record-company people or press reviewers who might drop by.

As pub-rock's popularity peaked in 1973 and 1974 more pubs hosted music. Added to the circuit were venues like The Lord Nelson in Holloway and The Brecknock in Camden Town in north London; The Newlands Tavern in Brockley to the south; The Nashville Room in West Kensington and The Golden Lion in Fulham, to the west; and The Bridge House in Canning Town to the east. One of the best-known was The Hope & Anchor in Islington, north

London, where landlord Fred Granger oversaw the appearance of every pub-rock band worth the tag – and a few more besides.

Also on the premises at the Hope was a rudimentary if effective studio run by Dave Robinson, who later with Jake Riviera formed Stiff Records. It was at the Hope that the finest band to appear from pub-rock was formed when Bob Andrews (keyboards) of Brinsley Schwarz, Martin Belmont and Brinsley Schwarz (guitars) lately of Ducks Deluxe, and Andrew Bodnar (bass) and Steve Goulding (drums) of Bontemps Roulez became The Rumour.

Then in summer 1975 The Rumour joined forces with Graham Parker, a singer-songwriter making demos at the Hope's studio who needed a good band. And he certainly got one. But by this time a new sound was threatening to be heard in London's pubs and clubs. The punks were about to be unleashed.

Ducks Deluxe at home (left) awaiting the daily delivery of the sealed envelope from their agent which would reveal the name and location of that particular night's pub gig. Often during the wait the band would, as here, work on the hilarious comedy routines that they employed on-stage as a foil to their heady musical mix of country, rock'n'roll and soul.

R E V I E W

DUCKS DELUXE, *100 CLUB,* **JULY 1ST 1975**

"The Ducks' last gig was no farewell, but the celebration of a passing era. The Ducks, augmented by Brinsley Schwarz and Billy Rankin, were joined in the celebration by Bob Andrews and Nick Lowe (the Brinsleys), Lee Brilleaux (Dr Feelgood) and Martin Stone (Chilli Willi) who relit the fuse and exploded into a debris of R&B and rock'n'roll that threatened to rip the joint as if the late summer of 1973 was going to stay with us for ever more. From the opening chords of 'Fireball' on Sean Tyla's battered guitar through 'Coast To Coast', 'Brown Sugar' and 'Route 66' he and Martin Belmont proved once more that, while they may not be the metropolis's best musicians, they certainly know how to pull it all together. Subtlety was never a trademark of Sean and Martin, but subtlety was never what their audiences came for – just energy and feeling a-plenty. It's saddening that the music business seems to have too little time for a British band like Ducks Deluxe. Perhaps The Tyla Gang and Brinsley Schwarz's new venture with Bob Andrews and Martin Belmont [The Rumour] will have more success than the fine outfits that have gone under in the last few months."

CHAS DE WHALLEY, *LET IT ROCK,* **AUGUST 1975**

Eddie & The Hot Rods (right) secured their first gig at The Kensington pub through Dr Feelgood, another high-energy band from Essex. Both outfits seemed to inhabit a space somewhere between pub and punk, playing in a gutsy, no-nonsense style. The Hot Rods played London pub-circuit venues such as The Red Cow, The Newlands Tavern and The Nashville Room, and were signed to Island Records after an A&R man spotted them at the Nashville. They made a *Live At The Marquee* EP before their first LP (above) which, at least visually, indicated the band's punk leanings.

Eddie & The Hot Rods seen live at The Greyhound in Fulham, west London (above) in 1976. The Greyhound had started presenting bands in 1971 and, unusually for the time, began offering music seven nights a week. By the following year several other pubs had joined The Greyhound on the London "circuit" of venues, the number of which increased dramatically as the 1970s progressed. By the time punk took hold in 1976 and 1977 pub-rock itself had expired, but bands of all kinds had continued to appear in pubs, and it was natural that punk precursors such as Eddie & The Hot Rods, Dr Feelgood, The 101ers and Kilburn & The High Roads should tread early musical steps in pubs.

The New York Dolls (main picture) in 1973 playing at the launch of the Rainbow Room (ad, above) at the Biba store in Kensington. They were Malcolm McLaren's first choice as punks worth managing.

122

In September 1976 at The 100 Club in Oxford Street, sandwiched between the venue's customary trad-jazz acts like George Melly and Ken Colyer, punk's first "festival" (ad above) blasted out thanks to the efforts of Siouxsie & The Banshees, The Damned, The Clash, The Buzzcocks, The Sex Pistols and others. The Pistols also appeared that November at the Notre Dame Hall (main picture, right) near Leicester Square.

IF THERE WAS ONE MONTH WHEN PUNK could be said to have arrived on the London gig scene, it was September 1976. On the 20th and 21st the 100 Club hosted the Punk Rock Festival, two nights of mayhem, skirmish and injury as The Sex Pistols, The Clash, Siouxsie & The Banshees, The Damned, The Buzzcocks and others went about their raucous business in the Oxford Street basement. These two uproarious sessions – one club-goer lost an eye in the process – amounted to what a music-press observer declared as "indisputable evidence that a new decade in rock is about to begin".[136]

If this really was a beginning, then punk had been in a state of readiness for some time. Pub-rock had been symbolically buried the previous summer when Ducks Deluxe played their farewell gig, also at the 100 Club. Yet there were similarities to punk in the way that the pub bands appeared largely to ignore the standard music-biz routines, even if on the surface at least the musical substance was rather different. Pistols vocalist Johnny Rotten had been to see Kilburn & The High Roads a number of times and had clearly studied frontman Ian Dury's stage manner. But there was one band in particular which at the time straddled the stylistic gap between pub and punk: Dr Feelgood.

The Feelgoods' name alone summed up the spirit of pub-rock. Their music too was a fiery concoction that mixed old-style R&B in the shape of singer/harp-player Lee Brilleaux with a thoroughly modern brutality supplied by manic guitarist Wilko Johnson. Here was a sweat-soaked role model for any band who wanted to learn how to harness raw power on stage. "On a good night," said Brilleaux, "you come off purged of all that anger and frustration. To me, that's what rock'n'roll's about – working frustrations out."[137] Punks in almost everything but name and sartorial style, Dr Feelgood achieved their peak of success in October 1976 when their third album, the live *Stupidity*, topped the album charts.

There had been an uneasy mood among music-makers and music-business people during the years leading up to punk's British birth. The nation's economy was in recession, and the super-flash mega-concerts still prevalent appeared to some onlookers as at least vulgar, at most redundant. But surely those involved were immune to such thoughts? Not necessarily. Harvey Goldsmith promoted many of the larger concerts at the time, and yet he revealed genuine concern when asked to comment on the live music scene for a *Melody Maker* investigation into The State Of Rock, published in summer 1975. "We're now in a position similar to that of America a year ago," said Goldsmith. "Too many big acts on the road and not enough punters – and even then they can hardly afford to see the big ones.

❝ How many promoters are taking risks these days? How many of them are trying to break new artists? Look at all the big shows: how many new acts are on the bills? Everybody's fighting over the same few big acts, and there's no risk-taking. The situation is going to get worse; people are killing off the market.[138] ❞

Goldsmith agreed that the small club and "village-hall" scene was now virtually redundant as a success ladder for new artists, who needed greater financial backing and tended to be started off at a higher level. And colleges, said Goldsmith, at one time in the early 1970s seen as saviours of the live-music scene, were losing money because of what he described as a sharp rise in bands' fees. The London pub-rock scene had died through the gradual accumulation of small debts; most agents only seemed interested in booking acts that they

could put out for £500 ($800) and more a night, preferring to make bigger money for less work rather than deal with several groups at £20 and £50 ($30 and $80) a night.

Peter Jenner, Pink Floyd's old manager at Blackhill Enterprises and still active in band promotion, blamed concert-goers for the state of live music in 1975. "It's not some huge conspiracy to keep good bands down," he clarified.

> **The public gets the music they deserve. And if they don't want to go and see groovy, exciting new bands who're just starting out rather than go see Yes, then that's going to be reflected in the number of gigs and the amounts of money available for groovy little bands. It doesn't seem as if our culture can support that any more... You've got these monster bands who've built up over the last ten years who are just sucking all the money from the market. Which obviously affects the future of new bands who might turn out to be another Floyd or another Yes or another whoever. What we need is for a lot of bands to go absolutely down the drain and be forgotten about. I think that then something much more within the nature of the times will emerge.[139]**

An all-nighter – in true spirit-of-67 style, despite the punks' supposed detestation of hippies – was staged in August 1976 at The Screen On The Green, a cinema in Islington, north London. Also on the bill were The Clash (the band's public debut) and The Buzzcocks. The handbill (above) was the first designed for the group by Jamie Reid, executed in an early version of his "cut-up" style.

How did Yes and Floyd and ELP and all Jenner's other "monsters" feel about this damage that they were apparently inflicting on the music? Rick Wakeman had played keyboards with Yes since 1972 and, silver cape flying and keyboards stacked around him, was often seen as a symbol of the excesses of the early-1970s rock elite. And yet Wakeman, speaking in 1974 just a few months before leaving Yes, expressed what to some seemed surprisingly sympathetic views. "There is an incredible gap in music at the moment, because there's no influx of exciting new bands coming up," he complained. "The music business has got incredibly into money – and promoters, agents and managers aren't all that interested in promoting new talent when they've got established bands."[140]

Greg Lake was the bass-playing L of ELP, a group which had come to require no less than one giant tour truck for each member of the group. Almost the whole point of the band seemed to be technological overkill. Lake maintained the image of the "monsters" when boasting to an interviewer in summer 1974 about the way in which the band's on-the-road operation had worked up to that time. "Our basic idea was to perfect our own atmosphere and recreate it each night. It was a good idea but the problems involved were immense," he explained, adding, apparently without irony, "We had 100 road managers at one point, so you can see the cost. And yet we could justify each roadie, until we had a different system designed. It was really down to fatigue among the guys putting up the equipment." The interviewer could not help but ask Lake how many roadies they'd used when ELP had started in 1970. "Three," replied Lake. "No, was it four?"[141]

As well as the pub-rock scene, there were other signs in the early 1970s that alternatives might exist to the "monsters". Some British visitors to New York were noticing a newer, brasher type of group emerging on the club scene there. "There are dozens of immature, young bands playing in scruffy late-night places in Greenwich and the Bowery every evening," wrote *Melody Maker*'s Chris Charlesworth in 1974, "creating a similar atmosphere to that which existed in London in the early 1960s. Excitement, sweat, crude and simple music, and a 'take-it-or-leave-it' attitude mingle together in this new generation of bands."[142] He described the work of some of these "barely competent musicians... and their shameless

punk rock", including Wayne County ("in full drag"), Television ("another whose expertise is overshadowed by enthusiasm"), and The New York Dolls ("no newcomers these days… they set the bandwagon rolling in the first place").

The New York Dolls had formed in 1972, and that year 22-year-old singer David Johansen summed up their stance for *Rolling Stone*: "We like to look 16 and bored shitless." They'd come to Britain for the first time in October 1972. At home they'd been used to those small club audiences, but on their opening night in London they were somehow booked to play to 13,000 people, on the bill at a charity bash in the enormous Wembley Arena with headliners Rod Stewart and The Faces. A critic said that the Dolls played one of the worst sets he'd ever seen, a slipshod mix of alarmingly sleazy visuals, garage-rock blundering and tired old guitar licks.

A few days later the Dolls' drummer, Billy Murcia, died in "unknown circumstances" after a binge at The Speakeasy (although David Bowie's later song 'Time' suggests it involved a quantity of Quaalude sedatives and red wine). With some time on their hands before heading back to New York, the surviving members of the band visited the King's Road in Chelsea, the correct place to shop for would-be pop-star clothes. One of the stores they dropped by was Let It Rock, which specialised in 1950s rock'n'roll outfits, though their own taste centred on women's clothes and make-up. The shop's co-owner, Malcolm McLaren, wasn't in at the time.

McLaren had grown up in Stoke Newington, north London, then attended art school, and in 1971 at the age of 25 opened the Let It Rock shop in King's Road with his girlfriend, Vivienne Westwood. Two years later they changed the shop's name (and presumably hired a skilled signwriter) to Too Fast To Live, Too Young To Die, and visited New York to exhibit designs at the city's National Boutique Show. McLaren hooked up with the Dolls; besotted, he followed the band everywhere, soaking up the New York club atmosphere and eyeing the newer bands on show. Back in England, McLaren saw the Dolls again on their return visit in November 1973 when they played the opening of the Rainbow Room above the trendy Biba store in Kensington, west London, and virtually managed them for a period in '74. He then set about revamping his shop, and during 1975 McLaren and Vivienne Westwood changed its name to Sex, and they now set about offering a modern, brasher style of clothing including leather, rubber and bondage wear. Some of the individuals hanging around the place started to form a group.

Paul Cook and Steve Jones had grown up together in Shepherd's Bush, west London, and formed an early makeshift group with guitarist Warwick "Wally" Nightingale around 1973. They went regularly to the King's Road in search of clothes like those worn by their hero Rod Stewart, and often popped into Sex. McLaren suggested another couple of shop regulars join them and, after some rearranging, Glen Matlock (bass) and John Lydon (vocals) started rehearsing in various London locations with Cook (drums) and Jones (guitar) as The Sex Pistols. Toward the end of 1975 McLaren rented for them an attic and ground-floor rehearsal room in Denmark Street, off Charing Cross Road in central London. Most of the band lived there and they worked regularly on developing their own material as well as charging through various covers of favourite Who and Small Faces songs.

The Sex Pistols played their first gig in November 1975 at St Martin's School Of Art, just down the road from their new hideaway. In fact it was so close that they carried their gear to the gig – where they supported Bazooka Joe, an early outfit of Adam Ant's. It was by all reports a ramshackle affair. Lydon, now dubbed Johnny Rotten thanks to his dental display, sported a Pink Floyd T-shirt with "I hate" scrawled above, and stared at the small audience

ENDALE PRESENTS **CLASH** THE WHITE RIOT 1977 TOUR

plus:— BUZZ-COCKS, **JAM**, Subway Sect, AND THE PREFECTS

All tickets £2.20 inc VAT available from Box Office, London Theatre Bookings and usual agents : Tel. 01-263 3148

at the *Rainbow* MONDAY, MAY 9th 7.30 pm

The Clash on their May 1977 White Riot tour (main picture) soundchecking for a performance at The Rainbow. On a smaller scale, two months earlier they'd played the Coliseum, a bingo-hall in Harlesden, north London (right).

128

THE SEX PISTOLS, *MARQUEE*, FEBRUARY 12TH 1976

"'Hurry up, they're having an orgy on stage,' said the bloke on the door as he tore the tickets up. I waded to the front and straightway sighted a chair arching gracefully through the air, skidding across the stage and thudding contentedly into the PA system, to the obvious nonchalance of the bass, drums and guitar. Well, I didn't think they sounded *that* bad on first earful – then I saw it was the singer who'd done the throwing. He was stalking round the front rows, apparently scuffing over the litter on the floor between baring his teeth at the audience and stopping to chat to members of the group's retinue. He's called Johnny Rotten and the monicker fits. [They are] a quartet of spiky teenage misfits from the wrong end of various London roads, playing 60s-styled white punk rock as unself-consciously as it's possible to play it these days, ie self-consciously… I'm told the Pistols' repertoire includes lesser-known Dave Berry and Small Faces numbers (check out early Kinks' B-sides leads), besides an Iggy & The Stooges item and several self-penned numbers like the moronic 'I'm Pretty Vacant', a meandering power-chord job that produced the chair-throwing incident. No one asked for an encore but they did one anyway: 'We're going to play Substitute.' 'You can't play,' heckled an irate French punter. 'So what?' countered the bassman, jutting his chin in the direction of the bewildered Frog. That's how it is with the Pistols – a musical experience with the emphasis on Experience. 'Actually, we're not into music,' one of the Pistols confided afterwards. Wot then? 'We're into chaos.'"

NEIL SPENCER, *NME*, FEBRUARY 19TH 1976

between the five songs the group managed to play before the plug was pulled. The group, fired up by this first live burst, continued to play through November and December and into the new year, mainly at art colleges.

In February of 1976 they played their first major London gig, at the still prestigious Marquee. They were supporting Eddie & The Hot Rods, another raw R&B group that, like Dr Feelgood, straddled pub-rock and punk. Neither Marquee nor Hot Rods were impressed by the Pistols. The Rods said that the punks had smashed up their gear, driven out their audience and pelted them with bottles.[143] The Marquee did not invite the Pistols back. But Rotten and band had obtained something much more valuable from that gig: it gained them their first review in the pop press, published in the following week's *NME* alongside a picture and under the arresting headline: "Don't look over your shoulder, but the Sex Pistols are coming."[144]

The first hints that the group might have difficulty finding enough places willing to stage their kind of anarchic music came with the Marquee's check on further dates. But in April McLaren did manage to secure a gig at the premises of a strip club called El Paradise in Brewer Street, at the heart of Soho's red-light district. He thought that it might prove an ideally seedy location for a regular club for the group, but this scheme faltered and the group seem only to have played there once. McLaren explained at the time that the band weren't appearing at too many pubs because pub bands played what the crowd wanted rather than following their own inclinations. Paul Cook said: "We didn't want anything to do with [pub-rock]. We wanted to break out and be better and bigger. We didn't like that 'please like us and have a good time' attitude. We also didn't want to play in pubs for the rest of our lives."[145] As it was clear that El Paradise was not viable as a regular haunt, McLaren intended to obtain the old UFO premises in Tottenham Court Road to "create a scene and a lot of bands".

He said: "The trouble with the pubs is that they're free, and people come for that reason.

THE BRECKNOCK 227 Camden Rd. NW1

		Admission Free
Thurs., Mar. 31st	SLOWBONE	
Fri., Apr. 1st	THE MOTORS	
Sat., Apr. 2nd	HOMBRE	
Sun., Apr. 3rd	SCARECROW	
Mon., Apr. 4th	URCHIN	
Tues., Apr. 5th	GODZILLA	
Wed., Apr. 6th	CHAMPION	–

Mick Jones at The Brecknock in August 1977 (right). The occasion was the second-ever gig by The Rich Kids, formed by ex-Pistols bassist Glen Matlock. As Matlock had once depped for a missing Clash-person, Jones filled in tonight for Matlock's new group who were still short of the final Kid. He arrived two months later in the shape of Midge Ure.

marquee

| 90 Wardour St., W1 | 01-437 6603 |

OPEN EVERY NIGHT FROM 7.00 p.m. to 11.00 p.m.
REDUCED ADMISSION FOR STUDENTS AND MEMBERS

Thurs 30th June (adm. 95p)

ULTRAVOX!
The Stukas & Ian Fleming
Please come early

Fri. 1st July (Adm. 70p)

NO DICE
Plus Support & Ian Fleming

Sat. 2nd July (Adm. 70p)
Free admission with this ad. before 8 pm

GLORIA MUNDI
Neo & Ian Fleming

Sun. 3rd July (Adm. £1.25)

THE DAMNED
Rings & Nick Leigh

Mon. 4th July (Adm. £1.25)

THE DAMNED
Johnny Moped & Jerry Floyd

Tues. 5th July (Adm. £1.25)

THE DAMNED
Plus support & Jerry Floyd

Wed. 6th July (Adm. £1.25)

THE DAMNED
The Adverts & Ian Fleming

Thurs. 7th July
SEE PANEL BELOW

Fri. 8th July (Adm. 70p)

GIGGLES
Easy & Ian Fleming

Hamburgers and other hot and cold snacks are available

The Damned's vocalist Dave Vanian (main picture) brought a touch of theatricality to the sometimes po-faced world of punk. The inset shot shows the band in 1977 at one of their many dates at central-London punk club The Roxy. The band were (left to right): Captain Sensible (bass), Vanian, Rat Scabies (drums) and Brian James (guitar).

Ronnie Scott's in Soho has a reputation as one of the leading jazz clubs in town, but in 1970 opened a more broad-minded adjunct called Upstairs. The indulgence stretched to punk-related acts, and during one week in September 1976 (ad, above) those taking the stairs might have enjoyed Squeeze on Tuesday followed by The Jam the following night. Downstairs, for those fed up with four-four, Genesis drummer Phil Collins's jazz-rock group Brand X were on every night.

If you're at a Sex Pistols gig you wanted to go, because you spent money to get in. I opened my shop because I wanted people to make a certain statement if they wore my clothes. The Sex Pistols are another extension of that."[146] McLaren's plan for the UFO premises also came to nothing. A pity: it would have made an interesting spectacle if the punks had moved into the old hippie playground: spiky hair replacing flowing locks, bondage trousers for kaftans, amphetamines in place of LSD.

Other bands began to emerge proclaiming the punk ethic. Quite a few had their roots in an outfit of wildly varying line-ups called London SS, started in 1975 by Tony James (later of Chelsea, Generation X and Sigue Sigue Sputnik) and Mick Jones (later of The Clash), but at various times also including guitarist Brian James (later of The Damned), and two more proto-Clash men, drummer Terry Chimes and bassist Paul Simonon.

It was during the summer of 1976 that Mick Jones formed The Clash with his old art-school chum Simonon, joined by Chimes, guitarist Keith Levene, plus Joe Strummer who'd been bashing out fine R&B with The 101ers for a couple of years. After rehearsing for some months at a studio in Chalk Farm, north-west London, The Clash held a press launch there in August 1976, and later the same month made their public debut when they appeared with the Pistols and Manchester band The Buzzcocks at a "Midnight Special" concert held at The Screen On The Green, a cinema in Islington, north London.

Pistols aide Nils Stevenson recalled the Midnight Special as "a marvellous event". But, he said, "It was very hippie in a way. Malcolm and I had carte blanche to do what we wanted, and both being from that arty scene we came up with a very 1967 type of event. All the artistic people who picked up on it and could be some help were old hippies who had cut their hair."[147] Few forget to mention the appearance at the Screen of Suzi Dallion, soon better

known as Siouxsie. She and some friends – the "Bromley Contingent" as they became known – had started to go to every Pistols gig, and she stood out at the Screen thanks to fishnet stockings, black cupless bra, swastika armband and little else. This was pure punk chic, apparently. Buzzcocks' manager Richard Boon also remembered the visual emphasis at the Screen. "There was a sense of people competing for copyright on presenting ideas," he said. "The Clash went out into the alleyway to get dressed so that no one could see that they were wearing slogans and paint-spatter. There was that urge to secure their turf."[148]

In September came the 100 Club's Punk Rock Festival. The Oxford Street club was one of London's longest-running live music dives, having started as a jazz club in the 1940s. The next decade had seen it hosting primarily trad-jazz, but in the early 1960s the 100 had shifted to presenting fashionable rhythm-and-blues bands. By the mid 1970s the club was back to jazz, but with a rock act one night each week. The Pistols had first appeared there in March 1976, supporting Plummet Airlines, and began something of a mini-residency in May, playing twice that month, once each in June and July, and twice in August.

Caroline Coon was at both nights of the "Festival" – Monday 20th and Tuesday 21st September – to cover the event for *Melody Maker*. "'Do It Yourself' could be the motto down at the 100 Club," she wrote, buoyed up by the boisterous enthusiasm of the audience, many of whom had queued for hours to get in. "Everyone wants to get in on the act. Everyone can."[149] Subway Sect were first on, playing their first-ever gig, and guitarist Paul Smith certainly underlined the DIY ethic: he'd only been playing for five weeks. Teams of record-company execs, TV and radio personalities, musicians, press and "punk-scene regulars" swapped opinions at the bar.

Suzi & The Banshees came on next, apparently having decided their line-up only hours before. Suzi sang, Steve Bailey ("Steve Havoc", later Steve Severin) was playing a borrowed bass, Sid Vicious ("Johnny Rotten's friend and inventor of the pogo dance") was on drums, and "mature gent" Marco Pirroni played guitar. They did a wild improvisation based on The Lord's Prayer; the audience wondered how much longer this appalling racket was going to continue. The prototype Banshees ground to a halt. "If the punk rock scene has anything to offer," suggested Coon, "then it's the opportunity to get up and experience the reality of their wildest, stage-struck dreams." As long as it's only for 20 minutes. As a contrast, The Clash then previewed their new four-man line-up, now minus guitarist Levene.

[The Clash] pitched like rockets, powering through their first number, 'White Riot'. The audience is instantly approving. The band is fast, tough and lyrical, and they've mastered the way of dovetailing Joe's mellow approach with Mick's spiky aggression. They blaze through 'London's Burning'… The sound, though disciplined, is bursting forth. They'll be a cornerstone for the developing punk rock scene.[150]

Finally, the band everyone wanted to see. Coon noted: "Not everyone is happy about the Pistols' growing success and notoriety. The private party is over; the band are public property. It had to happen." The Sex Pistols closed this first night of the 100 Club Festival with a raucous hour-and-a-bit of crowd-pleasing punk, Rotten and Jones at least looking like pop stars in the making.

The second night was inevitably an anti-climax after the highs of Monday. The months-old Damned had evolved from London SS members Chris Miller (drums, soon called Rat Scabies) and Brian James (guitar). They'd invited old school pal Ray Burns (bass, soon Captain

The Rock Garden opened in Covent Garden, just along from Middle Earth's old building in King Street, in 1976. Their ads were often stuffed with reviews and comments, like this example from summer 1977 that includes XTC ("And you've never heard of them! Shame!") and post-pubbers The Tyla Gang ("damn fine music"). It was almost as if someone at the Rock Garden loved music.

Sensible) to join, and the band was completed when they met Dave Letts (vocals, soon Dave Vanian) at The Nashville Room. Meanwhile, at the 100 Club they suffered from poor sound and a stupid glass-throwing incident in the audience, and by the time The Vibrators took to the stage, jamming with guitarist Chris Spedding, there were police wading through the crowd. Last on were The Buzzcocks and, according to Coon, the Mancunians couldn't quite bring the evening back to life. "[Howard] Devoto insists that he is only in a rock band temporarily," she reported, "and his self-consciousness impedes them coming across."[151]

One could never accuse McLaren of self-consciousness. As 1976 continued he had the Pistols begin their task of fleecing a succession of record companies. In December, manager and group wallowed in the national outrage caused when a taunted Steve Jones accurately called a TV presenter a "fucking rotter" live on-air. Bassist Matlock was replaced by the witless Sid Vicious in February 1977. However, by the end of that year the Pistols had virtually fizzled out.

McLaren had regularly called on his art-school background to dress up his commercial activities in "Situationist theory" and all the rest. From the outside it looked more like an astute manager sensing the right time for another of pop music's reinvigorations, acting quickly and, thanks to the required application of shock, drawing maximum attention to his boys. Probably McLaren and the Pistols' most valuable contribution was in clearing a path for more new bands, attracting record companies and other music-biz types by showing them that there was indeed worthy action about. It was a resounding reply to all the complaints of earlier years that the music scene was caught in a rut. Major labels and a fresh crop of independents enlisted punks and punk-pretenders alike: at the sharp end, The Clash signed to the mighty CBS and The Jam were picked up by Polydor; on a humbler level, ex-pub-rock hustlers Dave Robinson and Jake Riviera snaffled The Damned for their new Stiff label that had been started with the help of a £400 loan ($630) from Dr Feelgood's Lee Brilleaux.

Several of the acts illuminated by the newly trained spotlight would prove to have greater musical potential than the narrow simplicity of punk at first allowed. "This a chord," said an

THE RED COW

Thursday, August 4
WINDOW
Adm. Free
Friday, August 5
JOHNNY DUCANN BAND
(ex Atomic Rooster)
Adm. Free
Saturday, August 6
THE POLICE
Adm. 60p
Sunday, August 7
HEAD OVER HEELS
Adm. Free
Wednesday, August 10
PRAIRIE OYSTER
Adm. Free
Hammersmith Road, W 6

Fun with trios in 1977: The Jam at The Roxy club (opposite); The Police at The Red Cow pub (ad, above).

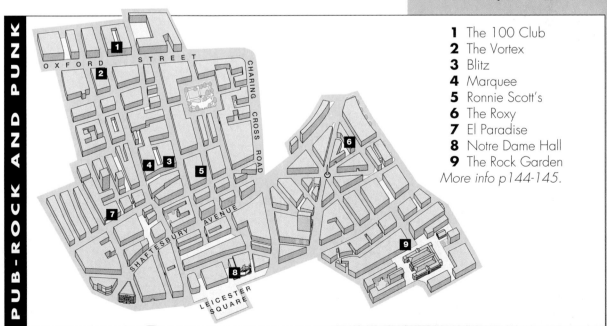

PUB-ROCK AND PUNK

OXFORD STREET

CHARING CROSS ROAD

SHAFTESBURY AVENUE

LEICESTER SQUARE

1 The 100 Club
2 The Vortex
3 Blitz
4 Marquee
5 Ronnie Scott's
6 The Roxy
7 El Paradise
8 Notre Dame Hall
9 The Rock Garden
More info p144-145.

Down at The Roxy in Covent Garden a young person's fancy oft turned to jumping about to the rhythm of a punk-rock combo. This was known as pogoing, and is demonstrated for us here by The Roxy Formation Team (main picture). The Roxy had opened in a basement in Neal Street at the end of 1976 and was run by Andy Czezowski, who also managed Generation X. That's his boys at The Roxy (below, left to right): Tony James (bass), Billy Idol (vocals), Mark Laff (drums) and Bob Andrews (guitar). Tony Parsons in *NME* praised their combination of "songs with lyrics about change and revolution but melodies cute enough for 'boy meets girl'."

THE JAM

THE ROUNDHOUSE, APRIL 17TH 1977

"The Jam [are] great. Simple as that. Any 18-year-old kid who takes pride in playing an old bright red six-string Rickenbacker (a pox on all yer Telecasters and Les Pauls, now this is a *guitar*) and plays it well, even ringing out various feedback squeals at the end of every number, is more than all right in my code of rock lore. In fact, The Jam impress me enough for me [to envisage them] taking over where the Feelgoods left off (not that The Jam are The 'Goods, by the way) substituting youthful exuberance for some of that band's more idiosyncratically successful stunts. The Jam, anyway, are superbly tight at virtually all times, each member juxtaposing his instrumental drive against the others for maximum effect, everything strictly in tune, harmonies always right on pitch. 'In The City', their single, is still the best number in their repertoire; sometimes in their usurping of old numbers, specifically 'Ride Your Pony' and 'Sweet Soul Music', they forfeit too much of the song's real power in the name of speed. But I'd rather see The Jam any day than any number of attitude fetishists, if only because they've bothered to put the music first – and as such they will survive long after the 'I'm So Bored With...' merchants have scurried back to their parents' houses in Wanstead."

NICK KENT, *NME*, APRIL 24TH 1977

issue of a punk fanzine alongside a series of diagrams. "This is another. Here is a third. Now form a band."152 XTC and Squeeze were among the bands that benefited from punk but evidently had a number of more elaborate chords to hand.

Squeeze, suggested one reviewer after he'd seen the south-Londoners at the Marquee in summer 1977, were like a kitsch 1960s soundtrack. "Singer Glenn Tilbrook doesn't actually

Adam & The Ants formed in 1977, and vocalist Jordan, who made the average punk's spiky hair look like a workaday perm, joined the band later that year, playing The Roundhouse (right) in May 1978 .

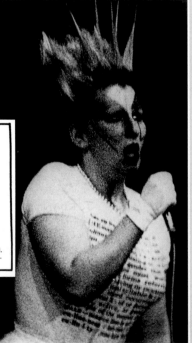

Adam Ant started life as Stuart Goddard and, once he'd been through bands like Bazooka Joe and The B-Sides, he put together his first Adam & The Ants early in 1977, debuting at The Roxy (main picture) in April. At first the band suffered at the hands of the pop press. "Negative pop to corrupt the innocent," said the *NME* with its customary cheeky humour. Despite legions of followers who dressed in Ant fashions, it would not be until 1980 that the newly piratical Adam would sweep the charts. Adam would be assisted by guitarist Marco Pirroni, who'd first appeared as a distorted drone-maker at Siouxsie & The Banshees debut at The 100 Club's Punk Rock Festival in 1976.

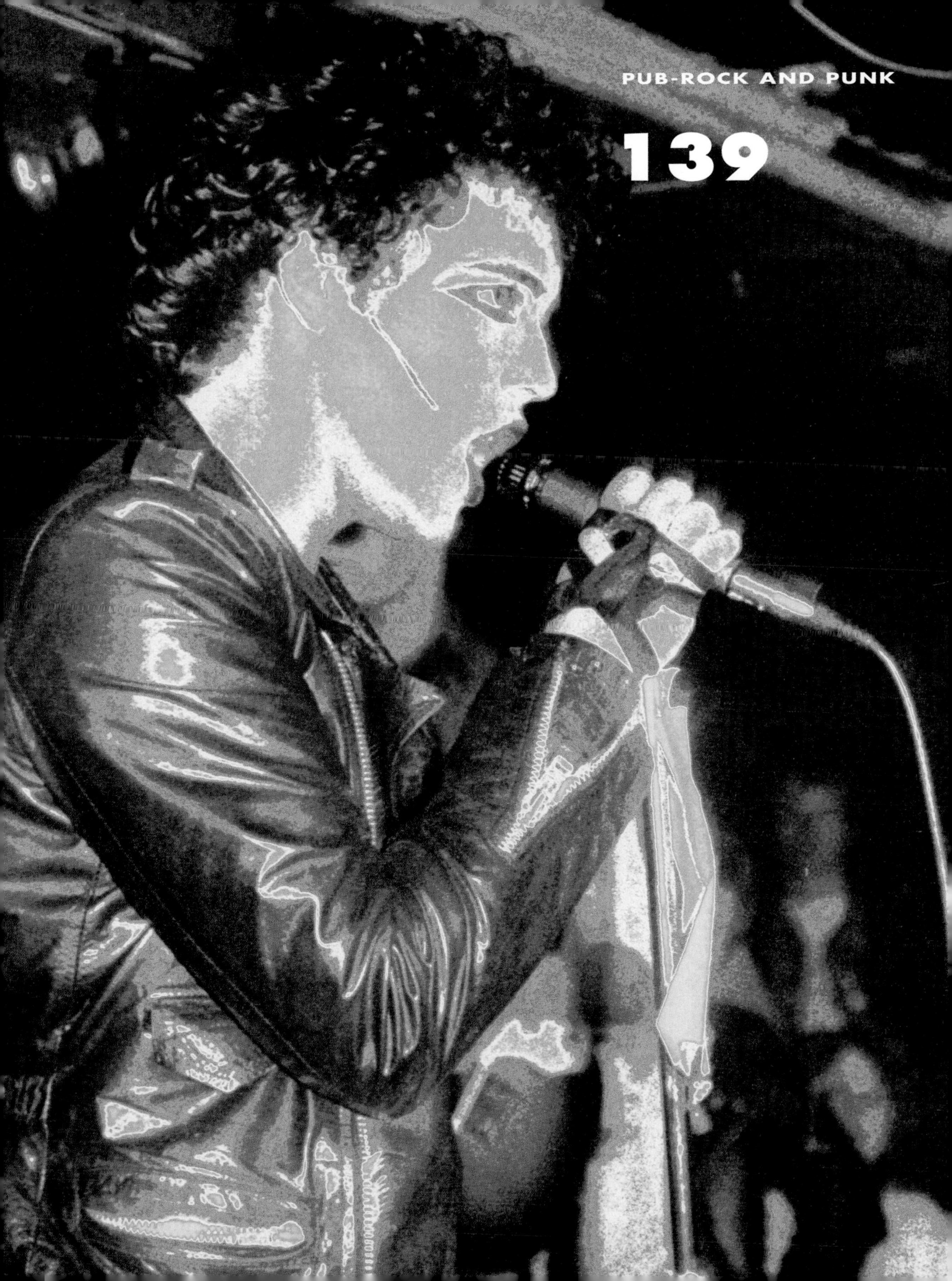

sound like Terry Dene (or so I'm assured) but he sure as hell sounds like *someone* from that pre-Beatles era," wrote the baffled *NME* man, uncertain whether the musical skills on offer aligned with the current fashion diktat.[153]

XTC were similarly equipped to go beyond mere punk. Their roadie Steve Warren kept diaries relating to many of the west-country band's formative gigs in London during 1977 – mostly in pubs which were by now reaping benefits from the fresh interest in bands following the punk surge. Warren himself was of course well aware that XTC were different from the rabble. "Andy [Partridge, vocalist] looks really menacing," he wrote after a gig at The Golden Lion in Fulham, west London. "I'm sure he looks a bit like Johnny Rotten. Never mind."

XTC also played at The Roxy, a new punk venue in central London. "Place gets heavier by the minute," noted Warren, "with lots of leather, chains and various other strange clothes. Heaviest guy is one with glasses, short hair, no teeth, an arm-band, studded gloves, leather trousers and jackboots... Colin [Moulding, bassist] gets hit by glass. Band leaves stage after 29 minutes, thank God... Lots of trouble when the place closes."[154] Toward the end of 1976 it had begun to look as if some hardline punk bands might be left with nowhere to play. The Sex Pistols were busy causing havoc, and their Anarchy tour of Britain with The Clash ended up virtually gig-less as frightened local authorities cancelled bookings. London venues like The Marquee and the 100 Club were also shying away from punks. And so the city acquired a few new specialist punk clubs, just as McLaren had intended.

The Roxy opened in Neal Street, Covent Garden, at the very end of 1976. The premises had housed Chaguaramas Club, open since 1971 when it began to present progressive acts such as Egg and Stackridge, while more recently it had been known as a gay club. Andy Czezowski, once Vivienne Westwood's accountant, had come across the place when looking for a suitable venue for his proposed punk club, and persuaded owner Rene Albert to lease him the small basement and tiny upstairs bar. The club opened with a "preview night" on December 21st with Siouxsie & The Banshees and Generation X, a band managed by Czezowski. On new year's day 1977 The Clash played at The Roxy, and with its central London location the club quickly established itself as a suitably scruffy hang-out.

After a few gigs-worth of punk treatment the club's ceiling had been torn down, intensifying the bomb-site ambience. One aspect that couldn't be modified was its size: despite the capacity of 250 being constantly exceeded, the basement was small. Promoter Miles Copeland, working with McLaren to try to create bookings for the largely gig-free Pistols, told a reporter in January 1977: "We can't put the Pistols on at places the size of The Roxy because the band are just too big for a place that small. There would be more people outside than in the actual club."[155] And anyway, ran the subtext, why should McLaren help someone who'd nicked his idea for a punk club?

The Damned became regular attractions in the early months of The Roxy's existence. "[Czezowski] either made or destroyed the punk scene when he opened The Roxy," Damned guitarist Brian James recalled later. "It was my favourite gig for a while, but it became a snobby scene... Once the clothes, the uniform, started becoming more important than the audience, the punk scene went out of the window."[156] Drummer Rat Scabies said:

❝ The Roxy was run the right way. Andy [Czezowski] used to say, 'It's your club, smash the toilets up, it's down to you, but it only means you won't have anywhere to piss next week.' They used to smash them up anyway. People were sweating and pogoing about, but I never saw any real trouble among the punters. They never bothered to have bouncers at The Roxy.[157] ❞

VORTEX
AT CRACKERS 203 WARDOUR ST LONDON W1
MONDAY JULY 11
Siouxsie and the Banshee's
Slits
Ants
+ D.J. NIC LEE
——————
Licensed Bars 2 a.m. — Admission £1

Siouxsie considers the means of production (opposite) at The Roxy. Her band The Banshees were regulars at both of the new punk hang-outs, The Roxy and The Vortex.

A future beyond punk was clear to Allan Jones of *Melody Maker* when he reviewed Elvis Costello & The Attractions at Dingwalls in Camden Town in July 1977 (Elvis is pictured at the soundcheck, right). "The joint is so packed you couldn't squeeze in a greased monkey after 10pm," Jones reported. "The Attractions pick their way through the glare behind Costello. Pete Thomas, the former rhythm merchant with Chilli Willi, settles in behind the traps, Bruce Thomas (ex-Quiver) eases in on bass, and Steven Young [later Naive] sneaks in behind the keyboards. Elvis straps on his Fender and the action starts with 'Welcome To The Working Week'. They then play the most startling set I've experienced since Television pinned me to the deck in Glasgow. This combo is so damned hot they could reduce the Post Office Tower to a mess of molten metal in 60 seconds flat. The sound is naked and aggressive – only 'Alison' offers a respite from the intensity – dominated by El's wonderfully spare guitar style... Young's keyboards sparkle with a sinister shine, while Thomas and Thomas punch out the rhythm with emphatic panache. The songs [from the first LP *My Aim Is True*, released that week] were whacked out with an extraordinary force, fierce expressions of frustration, rage and revenge: 'End Of The World' was alarmingly violent, climaxing with a chilling scream of 'Dear LORD...' and trailing into silence... And then (as if a boy could stand any more!) there was a song called 'Watching The Detectives': simply the best new song I've heard this year... Elvis vanished after the gig, less than enamoured of Dingwalls' general vibe, apparently."

Czezowski was ousted from The Roxy in a dispute in April 1977, but the club soldiered on into the early months of the following year, presenting a series of acts in its shabby confines and generating a couple of *Live At...* compilation albums. "The club still books punk acts," reported *NME* in summer 1977, "but most of the 'elite' bands have shunned it, or grown out of it."[158]

A second punk club appeared in central London in July 1977 when The Vortex was opened by the management of Crackers disco at their premises in Wardour Street, near the corner of Oxford Street. Standard Crackers fare was a Bowie Night on Wednesdays, a cock-and-hen night on Thursdays, plus "weekend spectaculars". A year earlier, when the Pistols were playing the 100 Club, Malcolm McLaren had said, "Half the audience we were attracting were kids who normally would've been down the road at Crackers. These were young kids – mostly in the 16 to 18 bracket – who'd been into Bowie and Roxy Music [but had been left behind] because those acts just got too big, too distant."[159]

The new Vortex was much bigger than The Roxy, with a capacity of some 850, and on the opening Monday night presented two Manchester bands, The Buzzcocks and The Fall, plus ex-New York Dolls guitarist Johnny Thunders and his Heartbreakers. The following week it was Adam & The Ants, The Slits, and Siouxsie & The Banshees. More acts followed, but with punk well past its first flush The Vortex came to a halt along with The Roxy in the opening months of 1978. At least The Vortex lives on in song, as Paul Weller sings affectionately of the club's special atmosphere in The Jam's 'A Bomb In Wardour Street': "I'm stranded on the Vortex floor, my head's been kicked in and blood's starting to pour..."

Other new and revamped London venues appeared during the 1970s, including The Rock Garden, which opened in 1976 at the corner of James Street and King Street in Covent Garden, and Dingwalls Dance Hall at Camden Lock, north-west London, opened in June 1973. Camden Town in effect became the Soho of the later 1970s, developing an important live music scene. The Music Machine in Camden High Street was the prime large venue. The building had first opened as The Camden Theatre back in December 1900, hosted variety acts throughout the 1920s and acted as a BBC studio during the 1950s and 1960s. Siouxsie & The Banshees and Johnny Thunders' Heartbreakers were among the first acts to play the newly-named Music Machine in May 1977, and two months later guitarist Andy Summers played his first gig with The Police there. In 1982 it would become The Camden Palace. Another new Camden High Street venue of the 1970s was The Electric Ballroom, opened in summer 1978.

The Damned played their "goodbye bash" at The Rainbow Theatre in April 1978. The Rainbow had first appeared in 1971 in the same building as the old Finsbury Park Astoria in north London where Hendrix had sautéed his Stratocaster in 1967 and, hosting plenty of rock acts through the years, it was a popular if drafty large venue. At the very end of the 1970s another new musical faction loomed when Spandau Ballet played their first public gig at the Blitz club in Great Queen Street, central London.

In a timeless phrase George Melly once suggested that "each successive pop music explosion has come roaring out of the clubs in which it was born like an angry young bull".[160] Melly then ran with the metaphor to make a good point about the entertainment establishment only allowing new music a public existence when it ceases to be dangerous. Our requirement of the angry young bull is simpler. In more recent years, among drum'n'bass, tech house and more, live bands seem to have far fewer places in which to rage around, as London's live-music clubs – their natural breeding grounds – have diminished. It always seems so pointless and such a pity when a rich, eventful life is allowed to decline in solitude and neglect.

THE GREYHOUND
175 FULHAM PALACE RD., W.6

Thurs April 3	**MOON**
Fri April 4	**PONGE**
Sat April 5	**TOKUMBO**
Sun April 6	**THE EQUALS**
Mon April 7	**FAST EDDY**
Tues April 8	**FLIP CITY**
Wed April 9	**CONSORTIUM**

ADMISSION FREE

Costello's band before he turned into Elvis was the busy Flip City. They played regular gigs on London's pub circuit, including this date (ad, above) at Fulham's Greyhound in April 1975.

This directory lists all the clubs mentioned in the book, with addresses, active periods and musical descriptions.

A

Academic Prince of Wales, Hammersmith; 1956, jazz club.
Ad Lib 7 Leicester Place WC2; 1963-66, nightclub.
Albert Hall Kensington Gore SW7; 1871-current, concert hall.
Alexandra Palace The Avenue N10; 1875-1980, 1982-current, hall.
All Nighter 33-37 Wardour Street W1; 1959-66, jazz/R&B club.
All Saints Hall Powis Gardens, W11; 1966, church hall; demolished.
Annabel's 44 Berkeley Square W1; 1961-current, nightclub.
l'Auberge Richmond; 1950s, coffee bar.

B

Bag O'Nails 9 Kingly Street W1; 1930-74, club.
Baker Street Jive Club 15 Baker Street W1; 1956, skiffle/rock'n'roll club.
Ballads & Blues various locations inc: ACTT, Soho Square W1; Black Horse pub, Rathbone Place W1; Princess Louise pub, 208-209 High Holborn W1; Sevendown pub, 7 Carlisle Street W1; 1954-65, folk club.
Bar Of Music 37 Oxford Street W1; 1955-56, jazz club.
Beat City 79 Oxford Street W1; 1964-65, pop club.
Bedford College Regent's Park NW1; rock 1968-70, college.
Bedsitter 120 Holland Park Road W11; 1964-65, pop club.
Blaises Imperial Hotel, 121 Queen's Gate SW7; 1965-68, nightclub; demolished 1992.
Blitz 4 Great Queen Street WC2; 1979-83, "new romantic" club.
Blue Boar M1 motorway; egg and chips and a slice.
Blue Gardenia St Anne's Court W1; 1961, club.
Blue Horizon Nag's Head pub, 205 York Road SW11; 1967-68, blues club.
Blue Opera see Cooks Ferry Inn.
Bluesday Railway Hotel, Railway Approach, Harrow; 1964, R&B club.
Blues & Barrelhouse Round House, 83-85 Wardour Street W1; 1957-61, pub.
Blues City El Toro Club, 251 Finchley Road NW2 1962; blues/pop club.

Blue Room 16 Garrick Street WC2; 1953, jazz club.
Boathouse Kew Bridge, Kew & Brentford; 1958, skiffle club.
Bread Basket 65 Cleveland Street W1; 1955-64, skiffle coffee bar; demolished.
Brecknock 227 Camden Road NW1; rock 1974-, pub.
Bridge House 23 Barking Road E16; rock 1974-, pub.
Buffalo 184 Camden High Street NW1; 1960s, ballroom.
Bumpers 7-14 Coventry Street W1; 1971, rock club; demolished.
Bunjies 27 Litchfield Street WC2; 1954-current, folk club.

C

Café de Paris 3 Coventry Street W1; 1920s-current, nightclub.
Café des Artistes 266 Fulham Road SW10; 1957-75, club.
Cat's Whisker 1 Kingly Street W1; 1955-57, coffee bar.
Cave 44 Gerrard Street W1; 1956, skiffle club.
The Cellar 2 Regent's Park Road NW1; 1961, folk club.
Chez Red Lion, 640 Leytonstone High Road E11; Chestnut Tree, Lea Bridge Road E17; 1970-73, rock pub.
Chiquito's 32 Hanway Street W1; 1957-62, skiffle coffee bar.
Club Americana Mapleton Hotel, 39 Coventry Street W1; 1955-56, jazz club.
Club Basie various locations inc: Tavistock Restaurant, 18 Charing Cross Road WC2; Mapleton Hotel, Coventry Street W1; Doric Ballroom, 10 Brewer Street W1; 1956-59, jazz club.
Club Haley Tavistock Restaurant, 18 Charing Cross Road WC2; 1956, rock'n'roll club.
Club M Mapleton Hotel, 39 Coventry Street W1; 1957-58, jazz club.
Club Noreik 834 Seven Sisters Road N15; 1963-66, pop club all-nighters.
Club 11 41 Great Windmill Street W1; 50 Carnaby Street W1; 1948-50, jazz club.
Coliseum Harlesden; punk 1977, bingo hall.
Cooks Ferry Inn Angel Road N18; music 1948-75, jazz, pop, rock.
Copacabana 50 Carnaby Street W1; 1950, jazz.
Country Club 210A Haverstock Hill NW3; 1963-74, pop/rock club.
Les Cousins 49 Greek Street W1; 1965-74, folk club.
Crawdaddy Station Hotel, 1 Kew Road, Richmond (now Bull & Bush pub); Richmond Athletic Association clubhouse, Twickenham Road,

Richmond; Star Hotel, Croydon; Edwina's Club 133 Seven Sisters Road N7; 1963-65, R&B club.
Cromwellian 3 Cromwell Road SW7; 1965-77, nightclub.
Cy Laurie's Jazz Club 41 Great Windmill Street W1; 1950-60, jazz club.

D

Dankworth 79 Oxford Street W1; 1955, jazz club.
Delta 6 New Compton Street WC2; 44 Gerrard Street W1; 1950-52, jazz club.
Dingwalls Dance Hall Camden Lock NW1; 1973-current, rock club.
La Discotheque 17 Wardour Street W1; 1961-65, music club.
Dominion Theatre Tottenham Court Road W1; pop 1957-65, theatre.
Double D 372 Mare Street E8; 1964, R&B club.
007 52 Baker Street W1; 1965, pop club.
Dublin Castle 94 Parkway NW1; music 1974-80s, pub.

E

Ealing Club 42A The Broadway, Ealing W5; 1959-65, jazz/R&B club.
Eel Pie Island Water Lane, Twickenham; 1956-71, music club; demolished.
Electric Ballroom 184 Camden High Street NW1; 1978-current, club.
El Condor 17 Wardour Street W1; 1957-61, music club.
El Paradise 24 Brewer Street W1; punk 1976, strip club.
Embassy 6-8 Old Bond Street W1; 1921-80s, nightclub.

F

Factory 28 Leicester Square WC2; 1970, rock club.
Feldman Swing Club 100 Oxford Street W1; 1942-54, jazz club.
Finsbury Park Astoria 232-236 Seven Sisters Road N4; pop/rock 1963-69, cinema.
Fishmongers Arms High Road N22; music 1950s-80s, pub.
Flamingo various locations inc: Mapleton Hotel, 39 Coventry Street W1; Cafe Anglais, Leicester Square WC2; Doric Rooms, 10 Brewer Street W1; Pigalle Restaurant, 190 Piccadilly W1; 33-37 Wardour Street W1 (best known); 1952-76, jazz/R&B club.
Florida various locations inc: Benelux Restaurant, 13 Wardour Street W1; Cafe Anglais, Leicester

Square WC2; 1954-58, jazz club.
44 Skiffle Club 44 Gerrard Street W1; 1955-56, skiffle club.
Freight Train 44 Berwick Street W1; 1957-66, skiffle coffee bar.

G

Gallion 12 Little Newport Street WC2; 1948-51, jazz club.
Gaumont State Cinema 195-199 Kilburn High Road NW6; 1930s-current, theatre/cinema.
Global Village The Arches, Villiers Street WC2, 1973, rock club.
Golden Lion 490 Fulham Rd, SW6; rock 1973-79, pub.
Goldhawk Road Social Club 205 Goldhawk Road W6; 1960s, pop/R&B club.
Good Earth 44 Gerrard Street W1; 1968, rock club.
Good Earth various locations inc: 16-17 Gerrard Street W1; 41 Great Windmill Street W1; 1952-57, jazz club.
Greyhound 175 Fulham Palace Road W6; rock 1971-80s, pub.
Gyre & Gimble 31 John Adam St WC2; 1955-63, skiffle coffee bar.

H

Half Moon 93 Lower Richmond Rd SW15; 1964-current, folk club.
Hammersmith Palais Shepherd's Bush Road W6; 1919-current, ballroom.
Happening 44 44 Gerrard Street W1; 1967-68, rock club.
Heaven & Hell 57 Old Compton Street W1; 1956-65, skiffle coffee bar.
Hippodrome Charing Cross Road WC2; 1910s-current, ballroom.
Hope & Anchor 207 Upper Street N1; rock 1972-80s, pub.
Hornsey College of Art 77 Crouch End Hill N8; rock 1966, college; now union building.
Horseshoe Hotel 264-267 Tottenham Court Road W1; 1967-69, folk club.
Humphrey Lyttleton 100 Oxford Street W1; 1951-59, jazz club.
100 Club 100 Oxford Street W1; 1964-current, music club.

I

Imperial College SW7; rock 1969-70, college.
Implosion Roundhouse, 100 Chalk Farm Road NW1; 1969-73, rock club.

J

Jack of Clubs 10 Brewer Street W1; 1964, R&B club.
Jazzshows 100 Oxford Street W1; 1959-64, jazz club.
Jigs 124-126 Wardour Street W1; 1930-1942, jazz club.

K

Kaleidoscope 20 Gerrard Street W1; 1956-69, jazz coffee bar.
Ken Colyer (New Orleans) 10-11 Great Newport St WC2; 1954-70, music club.
Kensington Russell Gardens W14; rock 1971-80s, pub.
King Sound King's Cross Cinema, Caledonian Road N1; 1972-76, cinema.
Klooks Kleek Railway Hotel, 100 West End Lane NW6; 1961-72, jazz/rock club.

L

London Jazz Centre 14 Greek Street W1; 1956, jazz club.
London Jazz Club 100 Oxford Street W1; 34 Bryanston Street W1; 1950-1954, jazz/skiffle club.
London Palladium 7-8 Argyll Street W1; 1910-current, theatre.
Lord Nelson 100 Holloway Rd N7; rock 1972-80s, pub.
Lord Palmerston 648 Kings Rd SW6; rock 1973-79, pub.
Lyceum Wellington St WC2; 1904-current, ballroom.

M

Le Macabre 23 Meard St W1 1957-74, skiffle coffee bar.
Mandrake 4 Meard Street W1; 1952-75, jazz/rock club.
Manor House 316 Green Lanes N4; music 1955-70, pub.
Marquee (mark one) 165 Oxford Street W1; 1958-64, music club; demolished.
Marquee (mark two) 90 Wardour Street W1; 1964-88, music club; demolished.
Marquee (mark three) 105 Charing Cross Road WC2; 1988-96, rock club.
Metronome Mapleton Hotel, 39 Coventry Street W1; 1956, jazz club.
Middle Earth 43 King St WC2; Roundhouse, 100 Chalk Farm Road NW1; Royalty Theatre, Lancaster Road W11; 1967-69, rock club.
Mitre Tunnel Approach SE10; rock 1970-75, pub.
Modern Music 5 Gerrard Street W1; 1957, jazz club.
Mojo 1 Dean Street W1; 1963-

64, music club.
Music Machine 1A Camden High St NW1; 1976-81, rock club.

N

Nashville (Room) 171 North End Road W14; rock 1975-80s, pub.
New Birdland Mapleton Hotel, 39 Coventry Street W1; 1955, jazz club.
Newlands Tavern Stuart Road SE15; rock 1972-78, pub.
Night Angel 21 Hanway Place W1; 1970, rock club.
Northern Polytechnic Holloway Road N7, rock 1969-72, college
Northampton College St John's St E1; pop 1964, college.
Notre Dame Hall 5 Leicester Place WC2; music 1961-current, hall.
Nucleus 9-11 Monmouth Street WC2; 1958-63, music coffee bar.

O

Oldfield Hotel Oldfield Lane, Greenford; music 1960s, pub.
Olympia Hammersmith Road W6; music 1960s, hall.

P

Pad Two 72A Berwick Street W1; 1960-61, jazz club.
Partisan 7 Carlisle Street W1; 1959-63, music coffee bar.
Pheasantry King's Road SW6; music 1968-70, rock club.
Phoenix 44 Gerrard Street W1; 1954-55, jazz club.
Piccadilly 5-7 Denman Street W1; 1957-58, jazz club.
Piccadilly Jazz Club 41 Gt Windmill Street WC2; 1961-63, jazz/R&B club.
Pickwick 15-16 Gt Newport Street WC2; 1963-72, nightclub.
Pied Bull Liverpool Road N1; jazz/rock 1950-80s, pub.
Pigalle 196 Piccadilly W1; 1960s, nightclub.
Pink Flamingo 33-37 Wardour Street W1; 1967-68, rock club.
Playground at Hatchetts 67 Piccadilly W1; 1967-70, rock club.
Pontiac Zeeta House, 200 Upper Richmond Road SW15; 1965-66, pop club.

Q

Quartet 44 Gerrard Street W1; 1954-55, jazz club.
Queen Elizabeth Hall Belvedere Roadd SE1; 1967-current, theatre.

R

Railway Hotel Railway Approach, Harrow; 1962-63, R&B club.
Rainbow 232 Seven Sisters Road N4; 1971-85, theatre.
Rainbow Room Biba, Kensington High Street W8; 1973-79, club.
Ram Jam 390 Brixton Road SW9; 1966-69, music club.
Red Cow 157 Hammersmith Rd W6; rock 1974-80s, pub.
Refectory 911 Finchley Road NW11; 1964-70s, pub.
Revolution 14-16 Bruton Place W1; 1967-76, nightclub.
Roaring 20s 50 Carnaby Street W1; 1960-74, jazz/R&B club.
Rochester 145 Stoke Newington High Street N16; rock 1975-80s, pub.
Rock Garden 6-7 The Piazza WC2; 1976-current, rock club.
Ronnie Scott's 39 Gerrard Street W1; 47 Frith Street W1; 1959-current, jazz club.
Round House 83-85 Wardour Street W1; skiffle/folk/R&B 1955-64, pub.
Roundhouse 100 Chalk Farm Road NW1; music 1966-85, hall.
Roxy 41-43 Neal St WC2; 1976-78, punk club.
Royal Festival Hall Belvedere Road SE1; 1951-current; concert hall.

S

St Mary's Hall Hotham Road SW15; 1960-66, R&B/rock club.
Sam Widges 9 D'Arblay St W1, 1958-61, music coffee bar.
Saville Theatre 135-149 Shaftesbury Avenue WC2; music 1966-70, theatre; now cinema.
Scene 41 Great Windmill Street WC2 (also accessible from Ham Yard WC2); 1963-65, pop/R&B club.
Scotch of St James 13 Masons Yard SW1; 1965-72, nightclub.
Scot's Hoose 38 Romilly Street W1; folk 1961-69, pub.
Screen On The Green 83 Upper Street N1; music 1976, cinema.
Seymour Hall Bryanston Place W1; music 1967, hall.
Shakespeare's Head Carnaby Street; folk 1970s, pub.
Singers Club various locations inc: Enterprise pub, Long Acre WC2; Horseshoe Hotel pub, 264-267 Tottenham Court Road W1; New Merlin's Cave pub, Marjorie St W1; Pindar of Wakefield pub, Gray's Inn Road W1; The Plough, 27 Museum Street, W1; Union Tavern pub, Lloyd Baker Street W1;

1959-79, folk club.
Sisters 834 Seven Sisters Road N15; 1970-74, rock club.
Six Bells King's Road SW3; music 1930s-60s, pub.
Skiffle & Blues Round House, 83-85 Wardour Street W1; 1955-57, pub.
Skiffle Cellar 49 Greek Street W1; 1957-60, skiffle club.
Soul Station 134 Wardour Street W1; 1960-66, music club.
Speakeasy 48 Margaret Street W1; 1966-78, rock club.
Stork Room 99 Regent Street W1; music 1950s, nightclub.
Studio 51 10-11 Great Newport St WC2; 1951-82, music club.
Surrey Rooms The Oval SE11; music 1969-76, pub.
Swan Hammersmith Broadway W6; music 1970s, pub.

T

Tally Ho Fortress Road NW5; music 1961-80s, pub.
Temple 33-37 Wardour Street W1; 1969-72, rock club.
Thames Polytechnic Calderwood Street SE18; rock 1972-7/3, college.
Tiles 79 Oxford Street W1; 1966-67, pop/rock club.
Top Ten 9 D'Arblay St W1; 1957 rock'n'roll club.
Top Ten 50 Carnaby Street W1; 1963, R&B club.
Torrington 811 High Road N12; music 1971-80s, pub.
Troubadour 265 Old Brompton Rd SW5; folk 1960-current, coffee bar/club.
2-Is 59 Old Compton Street W1; 44 Gerrard Street W1 (briefly); 1956-70, music coffee bar.

U

UFO 31 Tottenham Court Road W1 (demolished); Roundhouse, 100 Chalk Farm Road NW1; 1966-67, rock club.
Upper Cut Woodgrange Road, E7; 1966-67, pop/rock club.

V

Venue 160 Victoria Street SW1; 1979-80s, rock club.
Vortex 203 Wardour St W1; 1977-78, punk club.

Z

Zebra 18 Greek Street W1; 1966-67, rock club.

MARQUEE LOCATIONS
165 Oxford St 1958-64
90 Wardour St 1964-88
105 Charing Cross Rd 1988-96

LIVE AT THE MARQUEE

From here to page 189 we detail all the pop bands that played at The Marquee from April 1962 to December 1979. Why the Marquee? The club was the first to host R&B regularly in the early 1960s – hence the start date – and from that time on proved to be an accurate barometer of all the trends swirling around London's fiery music scene. Up to page 163 is an A-to-Z listing of all the bands involved, indicating the dates they played the club and their total number of appearances, with occasional notes dropped in to enhance your enjoyment. A chronological log follows from page 164. The data was obtained from the Marquee's regular advertising, and so on rare occasions a band listed may not have actually played, or a substitute act may have appeared. We have also omitted pure jazz bands. This unique inventory is a fascinating microcosm of British rock music across two explosive decades, and reveals the crucial importance of a healthy live music scene to the creation and development of excellent music.

A

A1 (5 appearances) 19-01-77, 11-08-77, 15-09-77, 24-09-77, 07-10-77
Aardvark (1 appearance) 22-09-70
Mick Abrahams Band (16 appearances) 11-02-69, 18-04-69, 29-04-69, 27-06-69, 13-11-70, 20-04-71, 23-11-71, 11-07-72, 03-09-72, 22-09-72, 04-01-73, 12-02-73, 23-10-75, 08-01-76, 05-02-76, 13-05-76
Post-Blodwyn Pig band for Mick.
AC/DC (11 appearances) 11-05-76, 12-05-76, 04-06-76, 26-07-76, 02-08-76, 09-08-76, 16-08-76, 23-08-76, 24-08-76, 07-09-76, 08-09-76
The Accelerators (1 appearance) 23-01-79
Accrington Stanley (2 appearances) 27-04-71 25-05-71
Ace (10 appearances) 29-05-73, 02-07-73, 01-10-73, 08-10-73, 15-10-73, 22-10-73, 22-11-73, 06-12-73, 04-03-74, 18-03-74
The Acres (1 appearance) 23-06-79
The Action (25 appearances) 14-12-65, 24-12-65, 30-12-65, 04-01-66, 18-01-66, 28-01-66, 08-02-66, 15-02-66, 29-03-66, 05-04-66, 26-04-66, 19-05-66, 30-06-66, 12-07-66, 23-08-66, 06-09-66, 23-09-66, 18-10-66, 22-11-66, 03-02-67, 04-04-67, 13-06-67, 01-08-67, 03-10-67, 23-10-67
Actress (1 appearance) 06-05-70
Adam & The Ants (15 appearances) 12-11-77, 26-11-77, 11-12-77, 05-01-78, 12-01-78, 19-01-78, 26-01-78, 27-03-78, 14-04-78, 24-06-78, 13-07-78, 05-09-78, 06-09-78, 28-11-78, 29-11-78
Adam's Recital (1 appearance) 13-08-67
Adolphus Rebirth (1 appearance) 26-05-70
Advertising (3 appearances) 11-07-77, 22-10-77, 10-01-79
The Adverts (6 appearances) 06-07-77, 02-09-77, 26-07-78, 27-07-78, 23-10-79, 24-10-79
Affinity (7 appearances) 23-08-69, 08-11-69, 15-11-69, 16-01-70, 22-05-70, 28-10-70, 07-08-72
AFT (4 appearances) 15-11-76, 29-11-76, 13-12-76, 03-01-77
After The Fire (11 appearances) 28-02-77, 23-06-77, 20-02-78, 17-04-78, 17-05-78, 20-06-78, 20-09-78, 15-12-78, 15-02-79, 30-03-79, 23-05-79
Agnes Strange (2 appearances) 19-07-75, 26-01-76
Charlie Ainley Band (1 appearance) 05-04-78
Air Fiesta (1 appearance) 12-02-72
Airforce (1 appearance) 27-10-70
Laurel Aitken (1 appearance) 26-03-67
Akido (1 appearances) 09-03-72
Alberto Y Lost Trios Paranoias (12 appearances) 10-10-74, 24-10-74, 19-01-75, 07-02-75, 14-04-75, 11-06-75, 03-09-75, 22-10-75, 22-12-76, 27-12-76, 27-12-77, 28-12-77
The Albertos were a wonderful team of pranksters who created a searing sonic satire on the denim-clad three-chord-trickstery of Status Quo in their 'Heads Down No Nonsense Mindless Boogie' 45 that nudged the Top-50 in 1978.
Alfalpha (3 appearances) 18-10-76, 19-10-76, 21-04-77
Alkatraz (2 appearances) 13-10-75, 10-12-75
Alquin (3 appearances) 01-05-73, 13-

08-73, 19-03-74
Alternative TV (1 appearance) 20-06-77
Amazing Blondel (9 appearances) 28-06-70, 30-08-70, 21-06-71, 01-10-71, 09-08-74, 20-09-74, 29-12-74, 03-07-75, 07-08-75
Amazorblades (1 appearance) 17-06-77
Amberband (3 appearances) 24-07-76, 05-09-76, 26-09-76
The Amboy Dukes (6 appearances) 16-06-66, 28-03-67, 18-07-67, 17-10-67, 07-12-67, 28-12-67
Amen Corner (3 appearances) 26-12-66, 29-08-67, 21-11-67
America (2 appearances) 08-01-71, 20-10-71
Amity (2 appearances) 02-12-73, 29-05-75
Amon Duul II (1 appearance) 20-06-72
Amory Kane (1 appearance) 01-06-70
Andy Anderson (1 appearance) 22-03-72
Doris Anderson (1 appearance) 30-06-74
John Andrews (1 appearance) 21-10-66
Andromeda (7 appearances) 07-11-68, 14-12-68, 14-01-69, 23-01-69, 22-02-69, 02-07-69, 11-07-69
Andwella's Dream (3 appearances) 19-09-69, 24-01-70, 11-12-70
Ange (7 appearances) 16-04-73, 24-08-73, 26-10-73, 12-07-74, 19-02-75, 26-03-75, 11-02-76
A French prog band that made some headway in London in the early 1970s.
Angelic Upstarts (1 appearance) 29-01-79
Angletrax (2 appearances) 07-04-79, 11-05-79
The Animals (5 appearances) 05-07-65, 03-11-65, 13-12-66, 08-08-67, 19-12-67
That Marquee debut for the Newcastle group in July 1965 broke every existing box office record at the club – a record that would be broken again just four months later by The Who.
Ankh (1 appearance) 10-11-72
Anna Purna (1 appearance) 19-12-71
Anno Domini (9 appearances) 03-03-70, 28-08-70, 21-11-70, 24-12-70, 05-01-71, 26-02-71, 12-03-71, 28-05-71, 02-11-71
Dave Anthony (2 appearances) 02-02-66, 17-11-66
Anything Acoustic (7 appearances) 11-02-70, 18-02-70, 25-02-70, 04-03-70, 11-03-70, 18-03-70, 25-03-70
Apostrophe (1 appearance) 08-07-78
Arbre (1 appearance) 04-04-76
Arc (1 appearance) 02-03-71
Arcadium (6 appearances) 18-10-69, 03-11-69, 01-12-69, 29-12-69, 26-01-70, 16-09-70
Argent (4 appearances) 01-06-70, 12-02-71, 01-04-71, 24-05-71
Ariel (6 appearances) 04-11-74, 29-11-74, 17-04-75, 09-05-75, 25-05-75, 12-06-75
Armada (18 appearances) 15-01-70, 14-03-70, 30-03-70, 24-04-70, 06-08-70, 20-08-70, 10-09-70, 17-09-70, 07-10-71, 14-10-71, 21-10-71, 28-10-71, 05-01-72, 19-01-72, 26-01-72, 06-03-72, 20-04-72, 18-05-72
Joan Armatrading (1 appearance) 30-06-74
The Artwoods (5 appearances) 22-08-66, 03-10-66, 07-11-66, 05-12-66, 12-01-67
With Jon Lord (keys) and Ron Wood (guitar)

alongside singer Art Wood.

Asaph (1 appearance) 08-10-76
Asfalto (1 appearance) 20-10-78
Asgard (1 appearance) 13-10-72
Ashcan (1 appearance) 06-12-69
Ashman Reynolds (1 appearance) 08-02-72
Ashton, Gardner & Dyke (7 appearances) 10-10-68, 11-11-68, 16-03-71, 27-04-71, 25-05-71, 05-08-71, 17-09-71
An amalgamation of two ex-Remo Four members – Tony Ashton (keys) and Roy Dyke (perc) – plus one ex-Creation chap, Kim Gardner (bass). Ashton went on to bash keys for the final line-up of Family.
Asrail (1 appearance) 19-12-70
Assagai (3 appearances) 26-07-71, 04-04-72, 13-04-72
Asylum (6 appearances) 30-04-75, 14-02-76, 07-03-76, 14-03-76, 21-03-76, 28-03-76
Atlantis (1 appearance) 28-03-73
Atomic Rooster (8 appearances) 12-09-69, 16-10-69, 04-11-69, 31-03-70, 26-06-70, 09-10-70, 18-12-70, 13-04-71
Organist Vincent Crane here perched by drummer Carl Palmer, later the P of ELP.
The Attack (2 appearances) 27-02-68, 11-03-68
Audience (21 appearances) 14-06-69, 16-06-69, 16-10-69, 27-10-69, 28-10-69, 19-12-69, 31-12-69, 12-01-70, 26-04-70, 17-05-70, 28-06-70, 19-07-70, 16-08-70, 25-10-70, 08-01-71, 16-04-71, 08-07-71, 16-08-71, 19-10-71, 23-05-72, 09-08-72
Brian Auger (24 appearances) 13-08-63, 10-11-63, 23-11-63, 29-12-63, 26-01-64, 23-02-64, 12-02-64, 09-12-64, 16-12-64, 23-12-64, 30-12-64, 06-01-65, 15-01-65, 27-01-65, 20-02-65, 24-10-66, 21-11-66, 26-12-66, 29-10-68, 29-07-69, 14-10-69, 29-01-71, 05-10-73
Keyboardist Auger's Trinity began early at the Marquee, but hit the big time in 1968 when with vocalist Julie Driscoll they scored a hit with Dylan's 'This Wheel's On Fire'.
The Authentics (16 appearances) 01-05-64, 08-05-64, 15-05-64, 22-05-64, 29-05-64, 05-06-64, 12-06-64, 19-06-64, 26-06-64, 03-07-64, 10-07-64, 17-07-64, 24-07-64, 29-07-64, 14-08-64, 28-08-64,
The Autographs (2 appearances) 07-10-78, 09-12-78
Automatic Man (4 appearances) 22-06-76, 23-06-76, 15-07-76, 16-07-76
The Automatics (12 appearances) 04-03-78, 18-04-78, 07-04-78, 21-04-78, 04-05-78, 18-05-78, 01-06-78, 08-06-78, 15-06-78, 22-06-78, 29-06-78, 19-10-78
Autumn (1 appearance) 13-11-70
The Average White Band (8 appearances) 25-10-72, 22-02-73, 29-03-73, 10-05-73, 31-05-73, 23-08-73, 08-01-74, 2-01-75
Axiom (1 appearance) 13-02-71
Axis (3 appearances) 06-07-73, 27-07-73, 20-08-73
Axis Point (1 appearance) 18-09-79
Kevin Ayers (1 appearance) 10-05-70

B

Babe Ruth (24 appearances) 25-07-72, 15-12-72, 27-12-72, 11-01-73, 29-01-73, 21-02-73, 05-03-73, 02-04-73, 01-05-73, 03-07-73, 14-12-73, 16-01-74, 20-03-74, 03-07-74, 20-11-74, 21-01-75, 08-07-75, 19-08-75, 18-12-75, 17-04-76, 25-10-76, 19-11-76, 20-01-77, 13-04-77
Baby (1 appearance) 27-02-75
Babylon (4 appearances) 03-07-69, 16-08-69, 28-08-69, 08-09-69
Back Door (10 appearances) 03-03-75, 27-06-75, 20-02-76, 12-04-76, 25-05-76, 21-07-76, 04-08-76, 15-09-76, 29-09-76, 3-10-76
With the magnificent bassist Colin Hodgkinson on board, this outfit played a fine mix of jazz-rock and blues-rock. A year earlier than their Marquee debut they'd played the Empire Pool, Wembley, during a tour supporting leading pomp-rockers ELP.
Back Street Crawler (2 appearances) 11-05-76, 12-05-76
Guitarist Paul Kossoff's band after Free.
Back To Front (1 appearance) 14-03-77
Back To Zero (3 appearances) 17-06-79, 15-07-79, 20-10-79
Backbeats The (1 appearance) 03-05-78
Bacon Fat (1 appearance) 06-11-70
Mo Bacon (1 appearance) 15-09-73
Badger (2 appearances) 16-01-73, 06-03-74
Bag O' Blues (1 appearance) 14-12-67
Ginger Baker (1 appearance) 19-07-71
Bakerloo (5 appearances) 06-02-69, 28-02-69, 11-03-69, 09-05-69, 14-05-70
Blues-prog band with Clem Clempson on guitar. After the inevitable split Clempson joined Colosseum and – much, much later – fat wads of cash were exchanged for the Bakerloo LP on the Harvest label, ideally in unplayed condition inside original HMV bag and with unfolded till receipt.
Bakerloo Blues Line (3 appearances) 26-11-68, 12-12-68, 10-01-69
Long John Baldry (77 appearances) 06-02-64, 13-02-64, 20-02-64, 27-02-64, 05-03-64, 13-03-64, 19-03-64, 26-03-64, 02-04-64, 09-04-64, 16-04-64, 23-04-64, 30-04-64, 21-05-64, 28-05-64, 04-06-64, 11-06-64, 18-06-64, 25-06-64, 02-07-64, 09-07-64, 16-07-64, 06-08-64, 13-08-64, 20-08-64, 10-09-64, 17-09-64, 01-10-64, 15-10-64, 22-10-64, 29-10-64, 05-11-64, 12-11-64, 19-11-64, 26-11-64, 03-12-64, 24-12-64, 30-12-64, 07-01-65, 04-02-65, 11-02-65, 25-02-65, 04-03-65, 11-03-65, 01-04-65, 08-04-65, 15-04-65, 22-04-65, 29-04-65, 06-05-65, 13-05-65, 20-05-65, 27-05-65, 03-06-65, 10-06-65, 17-06-65, 24-06-65, 04-08-65, 18-08-65, 02-11-65, 30-12-65, 08-03-67, 17-03-67, 21-04-67, 09-06-67, 28-07-67, 14-08-67, 15-09-67, 19-10-67, 23-11-67, 30-04-68, 13-05-70, 15-07-70, 08-02-72, 18-09-72, 04-10-74, 24-11-75
Up to June '65 these dates are for Baldry's Hoochie Coochie Men, a fine outfit renamed after Cyril Davies's early death had deprived the All-Stars of its great leader. The HCM added Rod Stewart to a shifting line-up, proving to be one of the great gigging R&B bands of the early 60s.
Russ Ballard (1 appearance) 07-05-76
The ex-Argent guitar chap.
Balloon & Banana (4 appearances) 14-03-71, 04-04-71, 11-04-71, 18-04-71
Banco (1 appearance) 08-12-75
A Band Called O (9 appearances) 23-03-75, 04-06-75, 29-7-75, 27-10-75, 30-12-75, 22-03-76, 14-07-76, 30-08-76, 15-12-76
Bandana (2 appearances) 28-01-77, 15-03-77
Bandit (1 appearance) 18-03-77
Bank Of England Brass (2 appearances) 07-06-76, 08-06-76
The Banned (3 appearances) 30-04-78, 25-06-78, 30-07-78
The Banshees (1 appearance) 08-11-65
Not, of course, the Siouxsie mob in a time machine, but R&Bers from Newcastle.
Barabbas (1 appearance) 06-12-71
The Barbarians (1 appearance) 25-09-64
Bill Barclay (2 appearances) 18-06-73, 11-08-74
Barclay James Harvest (2 appearances) 29-10-70, 05-02-71
Mark Barry (3 appearances) 22-10-66, 17-12-66, 27-01-67
Peter Baughen (1 appearance) 30-04-67
Bauhaus (1 appearance) 03-11-79
Bazooka (1 appearance) 14-05-77
Bazooka Joe (2 appearances) 19-03-77, 08-10-77
Bazoomis (3 appearances) 01-11-77, 03-11-77, 19-11-77
BB Blunder (1 appearance) 27-08-71
Be-Bop Deluxe (2 appearances) 30-03-74, 01-10-74
George Bean (1 appearance) 21-02-67
Bearded Lady (18 appearances) 14-02-74, 28-02-74, 29-11-75, 21-02-76, 10-04-76, 22-05-76, 12-06-76, 10-07-76, 07-08-76, 25-09-76, 23-10-76, 27-11-76, 04-12-76, 22-01-77, 06-02-77, 13-02-77, 20-02-77, 27-02-77
The Beatstalkers (10 appearances) 02-04-68, 27-04-68, 29-06-68, 09-07-68, 11-07-68, 25-07-68, 01-08-68, 15-08-68, 29-08-68, 25-01-69
Jeff Beck (9 appearances) 11-04-67, 06-06-67, 26-09-67, 12-12-67, 20-02-68, 09-04-68, 24-09-68, 14-01-69, 06-06-69
Beckett (13 appearances) 06-08-72, 15-01-73, 27-05-73, 05-07-73, 05-08-73, 17-09-73, 08-11-73, 21-01-74, 25-02-74, 18-07-74, 22-08-74, 03-10-74, 19-12-74
Bedlam (5 appearances) 31-07-73, 10-09-73, 21-11-73, 09-12-73, 20-01-74
Bees Make Honey (3 appearances) 20-05-74, 03-12-74, 04-12-74
The Bees (2 appearances) 26-03-67, 09-05-67
Beggars Death (1 appearance) 08-11-71
Beggars Opera (10 appearances) 19-09-71, 09-12-71, 03-02-72, 17-02-72, 15-11-72, 07-02-73, 09-05-73, 16-05-73, 27-09-73, 02-11-73
One of those prog-rock bands of the time that made an album on Vertigo, the swirly label that almost guaranteed prog content.
Bell And Arc (2 appearances) 07-07-71, 16-11-71
Eric Bell (5 appearances) 16-07-78, 15-10-78, 17-01-79, 14-02-79, 28-02-79
Graham Bell (6 appearances) 22-07-66, 06-09-66, 14-10-66, 17-10-75, 09-01-76, 15-03-76
Ben (2 appearances) 23-11-70, 30-12-71
Benefit (2 appearances) 12-07-75, 04-10-75
Nigel Benjamin (1 appearance) 06-04-77
Cliff Bennett (3 appearances) 25-10-66, 15-11-66, 16-09-71
Duster Bennett (13 appearances) 24-05-68, 14-06-68, 12-07-68, 22-07-68, 13-08-68, 23-08-68, 18-09-68, 02-10-68, 21-10-68, 17-08-70, 29-10-70, 28-01-72, 19-05-72
Berlin & The Jerks (1 appearance) 27-02-78
Bethnal (14 appearances) 15-09-76, 16-12-76, 03-01-78, 10-01-78, 17-01-78, 24-01-78, 31-01-78, 07-02-78, 14-02-78, 21-02-78, 28-02-78, 24-08-78, 25-11-79, 26-11-79
London rockers grateful to be swept along in the wake of punk, they embraced the movement by giving away copies of their live 'The Fiddler' in '77; the bowman in question was violinist George Csapo.
Jon Betmead (1 appearance) 28-12-69
Better Looking (1 appearance) 09-04-78
Biffo (1 appearance) 09-08-75
Big Finger (2 appearances) 01-10-69, 13-10-69
The Big Fir (1 appearance) 08-12-69
Big Toe (1 appearance) 31-03-70
Biggles (1 appearance) 19-10-72
Theodore Bikel (1 appearance) 18-12-66
Trevor Billmuss (3 appearances) 10-02-70, 23-08-70, 27-08-70
The Birds' Birds (1 appearance) 20-02-67
Birth (1 appearance) 23-04-70
Birth Control (2 appearances) 07-07-71, 11-10-73
Bitch (3 appearances) 20-04-72, 23-08-72, 03-10-73
Black August (2 appearances) 20-04-70, 16-08-70
Black Cat Bones (15 appearances) 06-10-67, 11-11-67, 24-11-67, 31-12-67, 12-01-68, 09-02-68, 06-04-68, 26-04-68, 18-06-68, 08-07-68, 26-07-68, 09-08-68, 02-09-68, 16-09-68, 11-11-68
Guitarist Paul Kossoff was a member of this band before he joined Free.
Black Sabbath (6 appearances) 13-02-69, 14-11-69, 16-03-70, 14-05-70, 08-07-70, 15-09-70
Black Slate (2 appearances) 25-04-79, 08-08-79
Black Velvet (2 appearances) 16-02-69, 04-03-73
Black Widow (2 appearances) 16-07-70, 10-12-71
Blackfoot Sue (3 appearances) 08-11-74, 24-02-75, 07-04-75, 28-05-75
Blank Cheque (1 appearance) 19-09-78
Blast Furnace (2 appearances) 10-11-78, 19-12-78
Blast Furnace & The Heatwaves (1 appearance) 22-07-78
Blaze (4 appearances) 20-07-74, 14-09-74, 07-12-74, 13-06-76
Blazer Blazer (5 appearances) 28-08-78, 29-08-78, 30-08-78, 28-10-78, 08-12-78
Blend (1 appearance) 04-09-70
Blitz (1 appearance) 13-07-78
Blitzkids (1 appearance) 07-01-78
Blitzkrieg (4 appearances) 17-08-70, 09-10-70, 26-04-71, 25-04-72
Blodwyn Pig (18 appearances) 18-04-69, 29-04-69, 20-05-69, 30-05-69, 27-06-69, 19-11-69, 25-07-69, 15-08-69, 29-08-69, 30-09-69, 10-02-70, 03-06-70, 18-09-70, 15-12-70, 22-03-74, 23-04-74, 16-07-74, 23-08-74
Formed after guitarist Mick Abrahams decided that Jethro Tull were veering too far away from the blues and left the group. By the December 1970 gig here Abrahams had ceased Pigging and ex-Yes man Pete Banks – a busy Marquee man – joined.
Blonde on Blonde (2 appearances) 08-08-71, 14-11-71
Blondel (1 appearance) 19-01-71

Blood Donor (1 appearance) 06-06-79

Bloodson (1 appearance) 08-12-70

Blossom (2 appearances) 10-08-67, 28-02-68

Blossom Toes (4 appearances) 23-09-69, 13-10-69, 25-11-69, 09-12-69

Jim Cregan on guitar, who would later play that lovely acoustic solo on Cockney Rebel's 'Make Me Smile' hit in '75.

Ken Bloxham (1 appearance) 06-05-75

Blue Angel (1 appearance) 13-10-76

The Blue Beats (5 appearances) 02-06-64, 09-06-64, 16-06-64, 23-06-64, 30-06-64

Blue Max (1 appearance) 31-08-78

The Blue Monks (1 appearance) 30-09-66

Blue Screaming (1 appearance) 16-10-78

The Bluebirds (6 appearances) 07-05-64, 14-05-64, 01-06-64, 11-06-64, 18-06-64, 25-06-64

Blues By Six (9 appearances) 07-01-63, 14-01-63, 21-01-63, 28-01-63, 04-11-62-63, 18-02-63, 25-02-63, 04-03-63

Blues City Shakedown (1 appearance) 27-04-67

Blues Incorporated (40 appearances) 10-05-62, 17-05-62, 24-05-62, 31-05-62, 07-06-62, 14-06-62, 21-06-62, 28-06-62, 05-07-62, 12-07-62, 19-07-62, 26-07-62, 02-08-62, 09-08-62, 16-08-62, 23-08-62, 30-08-62, 06-09-62, 13-09-62, 20-09-62, 27-09-62, 04-10-62, 11-10-62, 18-10-62, 25-10-62, 01-11-62, 08-11-62, 15-11-62, 22-11-62, 29-11-62, 03-12-62, 06-12-62, 10-12-62, 13-12-62, 17-12-62, 20-12-62, 24-12-62, 27-12-62, 31-12-62, 11-09-66

Highly volatile line-ups; hugely influential group. The first R&B band to play regularly in Britain, and the Marquee became its home for seven months after now-famous experiments at the Ealing Club.

The Blues Roots (1 appearance) 22-10-65

Blues Syndicate (1 appearance) 02-05-66

The Blues Train (1 appearance) 01-10-65

Bluesology (16 appearances) 16-12-65, 22-02-66, 12-04-66, 22-04-66, 25-06-66, 08-07-66, 14-07-66, 06-08-66, 11-08-66, 26-09-66, 07-10-66, 20-10-66, 29-10-66, 12-11-66, 30-12-66, 17-03-67

Reg Dwight aka Elton John on the joanna.

The Bluesyard (1 appearance) 27-05-67

Colin Blunstone (1 appearance) 30-10-72

Bo Street Runners (8 appearances) 16-09-65, 15-02-66, 30-03-66, 21-04-66, 16-05-66, 26-05-66, 14-08-66, 15-09-66

On bail were Mick Fleetwood (drums), Mike Patto (vox) and Tim Hinkley (keys). The group's eponymous 1964 EP is now a gilt-edged collectable on Oak Records, a label run by R.G. Jones who had a well-used recording studio in south London.

Bobbie McGee and Me (1 appearance) 25-06-74

The Boilerhouse (4 appearances) 04-12-67, 26-12-67, 29-12-67, 16-04-68

Bond & Brown (3 appearances) 17-03-72, 25-08-72, 06-10-72

Graham Bond (26 appearances) 03-12-62, 10-12-62, 17-12-62, 13-04-63, 20-05-63, 08-07-65, 29-07-65, 12-08-65, 26-08-65, 09-09-65, 23-09-65, 07-10-65, 21-10-65, 04-11-65, 18-11-65,

02-12-65, 07-03-66, 02-05-66, 06-06-66, 04-07-66, 08-08-66, 01-12-66, 31-10-69, 06-01-70, 24-02-70, 29-03-71

Check out the dates for appearances by Bond as an interval organist with Blues Incorporated as well as with his own bands: Organisation, and Initiation.

Bono (2 appearances) 18-05-72, 6-07-72

The Bonzo Dog Doo-Dah Band (6 appearances) 19-02-67, 19-03-67, 07-05-67, 16-07-67, 03-09-67, 15-04-68

Five years ago I was a four-stone apology; today, I am two separate gorillas.

Boogie Woogie Red and Baby Boy Warren (1 appearance) 26-05-72

The Books (1 appearance) 03-11-79

Boomtown Rats (5 appearances) 03-06-77, 15-07-77, 03-08-77, 18-08-77, 14-09-77

Pre-knighthood employment for Mr Geldof.

The Boots (2 appearances) 10-08-68, 31-08-68

Kevin Borich (1 appearance) 10-10-79

Boris & Teargas (1 appearance) 26-10-70

Bouncer (5 appearances) 18-10-75, 12-06-76, 26-06-76, 02-10-76, 14-11-76

David Bowie (20 appearances) 08-10-65, 05-11-65, 19-11-65, 11-02-66, 10-04-66, 17-04-66, 24-04-66, 01-05-66, 08-05-66, 15-05-66, 22-05-66, 29-05-66, 05-06-66, 12-06-66, 03-07-66, 21-08-66, 28-08-66, 13-11-66, 15-06-69, 03-02-70

The earliest dates here are Mr Jones with his Lower Third, but by the April '66 gig he'd switched to Sundays and "Bowie Showboat" events with The Buzz. "David Bowie sweated away for years on a Sunday with nobody, repeat nobody, coming to see him," says Marquee boss Harold Pendleton. "We were always nice to him and he loved us, and when he was a star he came back and did things like videos at the Marquee." On the 1969 gig Dave and a new American singer-songwriter called James Taylor were supporting The Strawbs.

Alan Bown (19 appearances) 28-04-66, 07-06-66, 30-06-66, 29-08-66, 05-09-66, 19-09-66, 10-10-66, 31-10-66, 14-11-66, 28-11-66, 19-12-66, 28-02-67, 02-05-67, 04-07-67, 22-08-67, 10-10-67, 06-05-69, 19-12-69, 02-11-70

Bown's Set had Robert Palmer singing.

Boxer (1 appearance) 24-10-75

Boy Bastin (1 appearance) 23-07-77

Eddie Boyd (2 appearances) 16-01-68, 09-02-68

The Boyfriends (7 appearances) 18-02-78, 08-03-78, 03-05-78, 12-04-78, 19-04-78, 26-04-78, 17-08-78

The Boys (10 appearances) 24-10-73, 05-12-65, 23-05-77, 08-08-77, 02-11-77, 03-11-77, 02-01-78, 27-02-78, 11-12-78, 19-12-79

Boz (9 appearances) 16-08-65, 26-08-65, 02-09-65, 09-09-65, 23-09-65, 04-10-65, 14-10-65, 02-12-65, 21-03-66

Later on in his varied career Boz Burrell played bass with King Crimson (Fripp taught the vocalist the rudiments of the four-string thing) and then Bad Company.

Howard Bragen (1 appearance) 22-07-77

Brainbox (1 appearance) 26-06-69

Brainchild (2 appearances) 07-07-77, 19-07-77

The Brakemen (1 appearance) 07-08-64

The Brakes (7 appearances) 23-04-78, 22-05-78, 07-07-78, 17-09-79, 24-09-79, 08-10-79, 15-10-79

Bram Stoker (2 appearances) 28-09-70, 04-07-71

Brand X (6 appearances) 22-12-75, 30-07-76, 26-08-76, 23-04-77, 13-03-68, 22-04-72

Phil Collins drumming in 13/8.

The Breakthru (5 appearances) 11-01-68, 06-05-68, 27-06-68, 08-08-69, 18-08-69

Bobby Breen (3 appearances) 03-11-64, 10-11-64, 17-11-64

Brethren (2 appearances) 07-06-70, 09-08-70

Paul Brett (5 appearances) 25-02-71, 04-03-71, 11-03-71, 06-04-71, 25-03-73

Brewers Droop (10 appearances) 07-03-71, 29-10-71, 21-01-72, 24-03-72, 05-05-72, 04-08-72, 20-10-72, 22-11-72, 22-06-73, 07-11-73

Brewster (4 appearances) 18-12-75, 10-01-72, 24-01-75, 18-03-75

Derek Brimstone (1 appearance) 11-03-70

Bronco (1 appearance) 30-09-70

Bronx Cheer (7 appearances) 20-04-73, 28-05-73, 29-06-73, 12-10-73, 27-12-73, 06-04-74, 29-06-74

Elkie Brooks (1 appearance) 07-05-65

Edgar Broughton (8 appearances) 23-07-70, 27-03-73, 25-09-73, 30-12-73, 29-04-75, 11-04-77, 11-08-77, 11-08-77

Always handy to have Edgar around if you need some demons exorcised.

Andy Brown (1 appearance) 17-07-73

Arthur Brown (10 appearances) 05-11-66, 21-08-67, 04-09-67, 11-09-67, 18-09-67, 13-04-68, 06-08-68, 27-03-70, 29-05-70, 27-05-71

Jimmy Brown (1 appearance) 11-07-66

Joe Brown (2 appearances) 31-12-71, 07-06-73

Maxine Brown (2 appearances) 24-02-67, 05-10-67

Pete Brown (4 appearances) 14-09-69, 19-06-70, 22-08-71, 07-11-71

Roscoe Brown (10 appearances) 01-11-65, 13-12-65, 24-12-65, 08-02-66, 15-04-66, 19-11-66, 24-11-66, 13-01-67, 27-02-67, 12-05-67

Steve Brown (4 appearances) 01-06-74, 18-07-74, 23-11-74, 12-04-75

Victor Brox (3 appearances) 03-09-66, 24-10-66, 28-04-72

Brunning Hall (19 appearances) 03-03-72, 12-05-72, 19-05-72, 26-05-72, 02-06-72, 09-06-72, 16-06-72, 30-06-72, 14-07-72, 21-07-72, 28-07-72, 04-08-72, 25-08-72, 01-09-72, 15-09-72, 22-09-72, 06-10-72, 20-10-72, 27-10-72

Bruno AD (1 appearance) 09-07-72

Brush (5 appearances) 06-09-72, 02-10-72, 06-11-72, 15-12-72, 02-03-73

John Bryant (1 appearance) 08-03-72

Callum Bryce (2 appearances) 17-07-71, 28-08-71

Bubastis (5 appearances) 24-11-70, 09-05-71, 23-05-71, 27-05-71, 22-08-71

Roy Buchanan (1 appearance) 08-05-73

Buckley (1 appearance) 27-07-73

Budgie (6 appearances) 14-12-70, 21-05-73, 11-02-74, 09-06-74, 30-03-75, 31-03-75

Budlipp Springer (1 appearance) 16-07-74

Bullitt (1 appearance) 16-02-72

The Bunch (6 appearances) 08-10-66, 01-12-66, 31-12-66, 09-01-67, 21-01-67, 02-03-69

Various Fairport Conventioneers in somewhat thin disguise as The Bunch.

Bunny (1 appearance) 01-12-75

Eric Burdon (3 appearances) 02-08-73, 03-08-73, 04-08-73

Burglar Bill (1 appearance) 15-11-75

Solomon Burke (2 appearances) 14-06-65, 18-07-66

Burlesque (1 appearance) 23-11-75

Eddie Burns (1 appearance) 14-01-72

Burnt Oak (14 appearances) 07-10-71, 14-10-71, 21-10-71, 28-10-71, 12-11-71, 26-01-72, 19-04-72, 25-05-72, 28-05-72, 26-06-72, 25-04-73, 27-05-73, 23-06-73, 22-07-73

Business (10 appearances) 16-04-70, 05-06-70, 22-07-78, 12-08-78, 16-09-78, 24-10-78, 07-11-78, 21-11-78, 23-01-79, 10-10-79

Paul Butterfield (1 appearance) 10-11-66

The Buzzards (1 appearance) 21-08-79

This band were guitar-maintenance experts.

The Buzzcocks (4 appearances) 04-08-77, 04-10-77, 21-11-77, 22-11-77

Byzantium (4 appearances) 16-05-71, 18-01-72, 18-09-72, 29-11-72

Keysman Chaz Jankel later joined Ian Dury's Blockheads. After a solo turntable hit in '81 with 'Ai No Corrida' Jankel enjoyed America's biggest dance hit of '82 with 'Glad To Know You', co-written with Dury.

C

C Gas 5 (2 appearances) 27-11-78, 09-01-79

C Jam Blues (3 appearances) 25-03-67, 15-04-67, 09-06-67

Cado Belle (3 appearances) 01-06-77, 29-07-77, 25-10-78

An assured bunch of Scottish songsters with fine vocalist Maggie Reilly.

John Cale (1 appearance) 02-05-77

Caledonia (2 appearances) 03-06-76, 17-03-77

The Callies (1 appearance) 22-03-72

Camel (12 appearances) 27-04-72, 18-07-72, 03-09-73, 15-11-73, 28-12-73, 17-01-74, 08-02-74, 14-03-74, 30-05-74, 20-06-74, 18-08-74, 29-10-74

Cameras (1 appearance) 22-05-79

Jimmy Campbell (1 appearance) 12-10-70

Canned Heat (1 appearance) 30-09-68

Canton Trig (2 appearances) 08-10-73, 15-10-73

Capability Brown (14 appearances) 24-05-72, 21-09-72, 16-10-72, 18-12-72, 12-03-73, 23-05-73, 22-08-73, 06-09-73, 05-11-73, 04-01-74, 08-03-74, 29-03-74, 24-04-74, 14-06-74

Tony Capstick (1 appearance) 22-03-72

Captain Clapham (1 appearance) 23-05-76

Captain Cook's Dog (2 appearances) 11-07-76, 20-09-76

Caravan (16 appearances) 05-02-69, 18-02-69, 05-03-70, 02-04-70, 28-05-70, 18-06-70, 02-07-70, 30-07-70, 05-09-71, 17-12-71, 28-03-72, 17-10-72, 09-01-73, 23-04-73, 25-06-73, 24-07-73

This lot loved tricky time sigs and had that big, thick Canterbury organ sound to the fore, just like their chums Soft Machine.

Cardboard Orchestra (1 appearance) 28-02-70

Caribou (1 appearance) 14-02-77

Paul Carmen (1 appearance) 16-10-74

Carpettes (2 appearances) 14-11-79, 28-11-79

Carrots Rock Workshop (1

appearance) 25-06-72

Martin Carter (1 appearance) 01-03-74

Casablanca (2 appearances) 07-07-74, 09-03-75

Casey (1 appearance) 07-10-70

Cast Iron (1 appearance) 30-03-72

Castle Farm (1 appearance) 06-07-70

Cat Iron (6 appearances) 29-05-72, 06-06-72, 26-07-72, 15-08-72, 21-08-72, 29-03-73

The Cat's Pajamas (1 appearance) 13-01-68

Catch 22 (1 appearances) 10-01-67

Champion (2 appearances) 28-06-78, 21-09-78

Chance Of A Lifetime (1 appearance) 23-04-75

Chango (1 appearance) 25-07-71

Michael Chapman (12 appearances) 21-05-74, 26-07-74, 24-07-75, 24-03-77, 08-04-77, 09-04-77, 13-08-77, 14-08-77, 19-10-77, 20-10-77, 01-08-78, 02-08-78

Chapman-Whitney Streetwalkers (3 appearances) 11-08-75, 12-08-75, 13-08-75

"Three nights in a heatwave," recalls guitarist Charlie Whitney. "The band ended up playing almost nude: it was definitely shorts and singlets. But they were three really great nights, among the best ever."

Dick Charlesworth's Big Blues (20 appearances) 07-07-64, 14-07-64, 21-07-64, 28-07-64, 04-08-64, 11-08-64, 18-08-64, 25-08-64, 01-09-64, 08-09-64, 15-09-64, 22-09-64, 29-09-64, 06-10-64, 13-10-64, 20-10-64, 27-10-64, 03-11-64, 10-11-64, 17-11-64

Jazz-tinted R&B man Charlesworth gave up a Tuesday-night residency in November 1964 to make way for The Who.

Charlie (4 appearances) 27-01-73, 30-11-76, 08-02-77, 22-03-77

Charlie & The Wide Boys (4 appearances) 15-01-74, 18-02-74, 31-03-74, 16-09-74

Charon (1 appearance) 02-08-71

Chas & Dave (1 appearance) 10-12-78

Cheap Stars (1 appearance) 14-02-78

Checkmate (1 appearance) 06-01-78

Cheeks (1 appearance) 04-08-75

The Cheese (2 appearances) 25-06-68, 29-06-68

Chelsea (11 appearances) 04-06-77, 10-08-77, 21-12-77, 18-01-78, 23-05-78, 16-06-78, 28-07-78, 17-10-78, 14-11-78, 18-07-79, 29-08-79

Cherry Vanilla (2 appearances) 03-10-77, 16-05-78

The Cheynes (10 appearances) 03-02-64, 10-02-64, 17-02-64, 24-02-64, 02-03-64, 16-03-64, 23-03-64, 30-03-64, 07-05-64, 14-05-64

Featured Mick Fleetwood, later of Fleetwood Mac, on drums, and keyboard-player Pete Bardens, later of Shotgun Express and Camel among many others.

Chicago Blues Band (2 appearances) 09-09-68, 27-09-68

The Chicago Line (1 appearance) 10-03-67

Chicken Shack (25 appearances) 15-08-67, 13-10-67, 31-10-67, 20-11-67, 04-12-67, 01-03-68, 27-12-68, 14-03-69, 11-04-69, 13-06-69, 22-07-69, 27-01-70, 26-05-70, 16-02-71, 13-07-71, 10-10-72, 14-12-72, 12-12-72, 23-01-73, 06-03-73, 11-04-73, 28-05-73, 26-06-73, 07-09-73, 12-10-73

Guitarist-vocalist Stan Webb was the guiding light of this revered blues-rock band which started work at the Marquee during the blues boom of 1967.

Child (1 appearance) 05-04-75

Childe Rolande (4 appearances) 01-07-70, 19-08-70, 04-11-70, 15-02-71

Sonny Childe (4 appearances) 17-10-66, 12-12-66, 20-01-67, 10-02-67

The Children (1 appearance) 31-03-67

Chilli Willi & The Red Hot Peppers (6 appearances) 23-01-74, 06-02-74, 20-02-74, 08-04-74, 01-08-74, 30-08-74

China Street & Cygnets (1 appearance) 02-05-79

The Chords (9 appearances) 15-06-79, 17-06-79, 16-07-79, 30-07-79, 19-08-79, 10-09-79, 25-09-79, 10-11-79, 11-11-79

Keith Christmas (5 appearances) 17-06-70, 07-02-74, 08-02-74, 06-12-74, 24-01-75

Cigarette & Burning Boots (1 appearance) 29-07-71

Circus (32 appearances) 27-01-68, 19-05-68, 05-03-69, 15-03-69, 18-04-69, 13-05-69, 26-05-69, 01-06-69, 10-06-69, 20-06-69, 08-07-69, 18-07-69, 25-07-69, 29-07-69, 01-08-69, 06-08-69, 13-08-69, 20-08-69, 27-08-69, 03-09-69, 10-09-69, 17-09-69, 24-09-69, 01-10-69, 08-10-69, 15-10-69, 22-10-69, 24-10-69, 05-11-69, 12-11-69, 19-11-69, 26-11-69

Circus saxist Mel Collins went on to King Crimson among dozens of other sessions.

Cirkus (2 appearances) 15-03-76, 15-05-76

City Boy (2 appearances) 06-12-75, 28-06-77

City Waites (1 appearance) 04-11-71

Clancy (5 appearances) 05-09-75, 09-10-75, 02-02-76, 12-03-76, 17-06-76

John Cooper Clark (1 appearance) 04-04-79

Clark Hutchinson (1 appearances) 12-06-70

Class (1 appearance) 31-10-69

Clayson and the Argonauts (2 appearances) 07-01-78, 20-05-78

Obie Clayton (1 appearance) 01-07-76

The Clayton Squares (13 appearances) 15-03-66, 26-04-66, 03-05-66, 17-05-66, 24-05-66, 31-05-66, 21-06-66, 26-07-66, 02-08-66, 09-08-66, 16-08-66, 23-08-66, 30-08-66

Guitarist Andy Roberts went on to work with Scaffold, The Liverpool Scene and Plainsong, and was one of the voice-over artists contributing to the satirical TV puppet series Spitting Image.

Clear Blue Sky (1 appearance) 12-10-70

The Cleavers (1 appearance) 13-12-78

Clemen Pull (14 appearances) 19-04-75, 14-07-75, 09-07-75, 14-09-75, 21-09-75, 28-09-75, 07-12-75, 14-12-75, 21-12-75, 28-12-75, 08-05-76, 21-8-76, 20-11-76, 22-11-76

Jimmy Cliff (8 appearances) 23-12-65, 10-02-66, 24-02-66, 08-03-66, 10-05-66, 14-06-66, 26-01-67, 05-03-68

Climax (17 appearances) 22-06-70, 24-08-70, 14-10-70, 24-06-71, 07-01-72, 14-07-72, 09-10-72, 11-12-72, 05-01-73, 28-02-73, 18-03-73, 21-07-73, 08-09-73, 28-09-73, 27-03-74, 25-10-79, 26-10-79

The Clique (1 appearance) 18-09-64

Clouds (25 appearances) 21-12-67, 12-02-68, 11-05-68, 07-08-68, 28-08-68, 14-11-68, 16-11-68, 19-12-68, 04-01-69, 21-01-69, 29-01-69, 26-02-69, 06-03-69, 19-03-69, 25-03-69, 23-04-69, 01-05-69, 21-08-69, 28-08-69, 08-09-69, 22-09-69, 27-10-69, 20-11-69, 11-12-69

CMB (1 appearance) 30-05-79

Coast Road Drive (2 appearances) 11-10-73, 06-05-74

Cochise (3 appearances) 04-08-70, 15-03-71, 20-07-71

Cock Sparrow (5 appearances) 19-02-76, 04-05-76, 14-10-76, 02-10-77, 09-10-77

Cock-A-Hoop (7 appearances) 16-02-67, 12-03-67, 20-03-67, 20-04-67, 29-05-67, 07-08-67, 08-12-67

Joe Cocker (16 appearances) 16-05-68, 25-06-68, 10-07-68, 17-07-68, 24-07-68, 31-07-68, 14-08-68, 21-08-68, 28-08-68, 06-09-68, 12-09-68, 26-09-68, 14-11-68, 05-12-68, 19-12-68, 23-01-69

Cockney Rebel (1 appearance) 16-03-73

Cold River lady (2 appearances) 21-07-73, 06-06-73

Collusion (1 appearance) 06-07-72

Colosseum (11 appearances) 01-11-68, 03-01-69, 14-02-69, 18-03-69, 24-04-69, 26-05-69, 01-07-69, 01-08-69, 28-10-69, 23-12-69, 17-03-70

Colosseum II (5 appearances) 22-04-76, 23-04-76, 16-06-76, 04-10-76, 05-10-76

Comus (7 appearances) 11-10-70, 25-11-70, 04-02-71, 11-02-71, 18-02-71, 25-02-71, 04-03-71

Conny Condell (1 appearance) 05-03-75

The Condors (1 appearance) 17-02-67

Consortium (8 appearances) 07-03-70, 28-05-75, 09-08-75, 06-09-75, 11-10-75, 01-11-75, 02-12-76, 12-02-77

Continuum (2 appearances) 18-03-70, 13-04-72

Contraband (1 appearance) 04-02-74

Mike Cooper (1 appearance) 27-08-74

Peter Cooper (1 appearances) 14-05-69

Copperfield (1 appearance) 20-07-72

Copra (9 appearances) 14-05-68, 23-07-68, 19-08-68, 07-09-68, 09-11-68, 18-06-77, 17-08-77, 14-12-77, 01-10-78

Cosmetix (2 appearances) 06-07-74, 02-11-74

Cosmos (1 appearance) 28-12-69

Cosmosis (2 appearances) 09-07-71, 12-07-71

Mike Cotton Sound (9 appearances) 03-08-64, 08-10-64, 18-03-65, 07-05-65, 14-06-65, 05-08-65, 17-12-65, 28-03-66, 19-05-67

Another example of a jazzman turning to R&B when it became fashionable in the early 1960s. On this occasion virtually the whole band went R&B with leader Cotton.

Cottonwood (5 appearances) 26-04-72, 25-05-72, 20-08-72, 26-09-72, 04-01-73

Jonathon Coudrille (1 appearance) 03-05-71

Johnny Cougar (2 appearances) 06-04-78, 02-05-78

John Coughlan (3 appearances) 06-10-76, 28-09-79, 29-09-79

Count Bishops (5 appearances) 09-03-76, 02-04-76, 26-06-76, 04-09-76, 18-05-77

Country Joe and the Fish (1 appearance) 29-03-69

Five months later Joe would be leading the mud-soaked crowds at Woodstock in his rousing Fish Cheer: "Give me an F...."

Country Jug (1 appearance) 16-10-71

The Counts (1 appearance) 04-06-68

Courtesan (1 appearance) 10-05-75

Julian Covey (2 appearances) 04-05-65, 23-09-66

Cowboy International (2 appearances) 13-09-79, 16-11-79

Kevin Coyne (3 appearances) 22-07-74, 29-08-74, 24-11-74

The Crabs (2 appearances) 30-11-77, 08-02-78

The Cramps (1 appearance) 05-06-79

Crawler (1 appearance) 18-09-78

Crazy Mabel (1 appearance) 10-06-71

Cream (7 appearances) 16-08-66, 27-09-66, 08-11-66, 10-01-67, 21-03-67, 23-05-67, 28-11-67

The Creation (5 appearances) 12-07-66, 05-05-67, 23-06-67, 07-07-67, 04-08-67

Creation's guitarist Eddie Phillips was ahead of the pack in many of the effects he employed. Sometimes he played his instrument with an avant-Page violin bow.

Tony Crerar (1 appearance) 22-06-69

Cressida (5 appearances) 04-08-69, 05-11-69, 05-12-69, 20-12-69, 11-05-70

Jason Crest (1 appearance) 27-04-69

Crew (10 appearances) 30-01-71, 06-03-71, 20-03-71, 05-06-71, 13-11-71, 05-02-72, 04-03-72, 15-04-72, 13-05-72, 24-06-72

The Criminals (1 appearance) 10-09-77

Crocodile (2 appearances) 17-06-71, 26-10-71

The Crooks (2 appearances) 07-10-78, 30-06-79

The Crow (5 appearances) 27-03-72, 05-11-73, 07-05-65, 25-06-65, 23-07-65

The Crowd (3 appearances) 06-09-65, 24-09-65, 05-10-65

Cruiser (2 appearances) 21-05-76, 15-08-77

Cuby's Blues Band (2 appearances) 09-08-69, 02-12-69

The Cure (5 appearances) 27-01-79, 04-03-79, 11-03-79, 18-03-79, 25-03-79

Early days for three imaginative boys.

Curly (5 appearances) 16-05-74, 05-02-75, 28-04-75, 23-06-75, 30-04-76

Custer's Track (23 appearances) 04-07-70, 03-08-70, 08-07-70, 12-09-70, 19-09-70, 10-10-70, 24-10-70, 14-11-70, 28-11-70, 31-12-70, 06-02-71, 20-02-71, 10-04-71, 08-05-71, 03-07-71, 24-04-71, 31-07-71, 21-08-71, 25-09-71, 27-11-71, 15-01-72, 19-02-72, 25-03-72

Cyanide (1 appearance) 22-05-79

Cyko & The Red Devils (4 appearances) 05-05-64, 12-05-64, 19-05-64, 26-05-64

The Cymbaline (1 appearance) 08-04-69

Czar (1 appearance) 10-08-70

D

D Dancer (1 appearance) 06-03-76

D'Abo Band (1 appearance) 01-11-72

Da Da (3 appearances) 02-06-70, 19-07-70, 18-05-71

Robert Palmer, Elkie Brooks and Pete Gage thinking about forming Vinegar Joe.

Daddy Longlegs (5 appearances) 29-01-70, 31-05-70, 12-01-71, 19-01-73, 19-09-74

Daga Band (3 appearances) 29-03-75, 28-06-75, 20-09-75

The Damned (5 appearances) 03-07-77, 04-07-77, 05-07-77, 06-07-77

Damp Savannah (1 appearance) 03-09-72

John Danbrough (1 appearance) 17-01-72

The Dandies (1 appearance) 31-03-78

Dando Shaft (1 appearance) 29-03-72
Dandy & The Wypp Dancers (1 appearance) 26-03-67
Danta (2 appearances) 14-03-71, 09-02-72
Darien Spirit (2 appearances) 08-03-74, 29-03-74
Dark Star (10 appearances) 29-04-73, 16-06-73, 09-08-73, 25-08-73, 06-10-73, 03-11-73, 15-12-73, 05-01-74, 09-02-74, 20-04-74
Darlings (4 appearances) 02-05-67, 20-05-67, 17-07-67, 29-07-67
The Darts (1 appearance) 02-08-77
Dave Dee, Dozy, Beaky, Mick & Tich (1 appearance) 25-07-67
Cyril Davies (58 appearances) 11-04-62, 03-01-63, 10-01-63, 17-01-63, 24-01-63, 31-01-63, 07-02-63, 14-02-63, 21-02-63, 28-02-63, 07-03-63, 14-03-63, 21-03-63, 28-03-63, 04-04-63, 11-04-63, 18-04-63, 25-04-63, 02-05-63, 09-05-63, 16-05-63, 23-05-63, 30-05-63, 06-06-63, 13-06-63, 27-06-63, 30-06-63, 04-07-63, 11-07-63, 18-07-63, 25-07-63, 01-08-63, 08-08-63, 15-08-63, 22-08-63, 29-08-63, 05-09-63, 12-09-63, 19-09-63, 26-09-63, 03-10-63, 10-10-63, 17-10-63, 24-10-63, 31-10-63, 07-11-63, 14-11-63, 21-11-63, 28-11-63, 05-12-63, 12-12-63, 19-12-63, 24-12-63, 02-01-64, 09-01-64, 16-01-64, 23-01-64, 30-01-64
Apart from the 1962 date, these are appearances by Davies with his excellent group the R&B All-Stars. They were still billed as Davies's band for four gigs after his tragic death in January 1964, but the outfit was soon relabelled as vocalist Long John Baldry's Hoochie Coochie Men.
Davies & Murrell (1 appearance) 10-01-74
Spencer Davis (30 appearances) 01-03-65, 04-05-65, 15-06-65, 29-06-65, 20-07-65, 03-08-65, 16-09-65, 21-09-65, 19-10-65, 09-11-65, 16-11-65, 07-12-65, 11-01-66, 22-02-66, 08-03-66, 10-05-66, 14-06-66, 19-07-66, 20-09-66, 01-11-66, 20-12-66, 07-02-67, 30-05-67, 10-09-68, 25-02-70, 03-04-73, 02-05-73, 26-07-73, 28-01-74, 19-04-74
Lester Dawson (7 appearances) 03-03-64, 17-03-64, 24-03-64, 31-03-64, 07-04-64, 21-04-64, 28-04-64
Daylight Robbery (2 appearances) 14-11-74, 27-03-79
Dead Fingers Talk (4 appearances) 20-10-76, 14-05-78, 19-07-78, 12-09-78
Deaf School (2 appearances) 21-07-77, 18-12-77
Dear Mr Tyme (1 appearance) 09-11-70
Decameron (1 appearance) 21-10-74
The Decoys (2 appearances) 23-10-79, 24-10-79
Kiki Dee (2 appearances) 02-05-74, 13-02-75
The Deep Feeling Band (2 appearances) 23-12-66, 02-02-67
Deep Joy (2 appearances) 26-06-70, 21-07-70, 14-08-70, 06-10-70, 17-10-70, 23-10-70, 27-10-70
Deep Purple (1 appearance) 09-09-69
Stephen Delft (6 appearances) 01-07-70, 19-08-70, 09-09-70, 07-10-70, 04-11-70, 06-01-71
Folk singer and guitar expert whose partner Judith Pieppe was instrumental in furthering the early careers of players such as Paul Simon and Al Stewart.
Dell (2 appearances) 30-04-72, 14-05-72

Demick & Armstrong (3 appearances) 23-02-71, 12-03-71, 19-03-71
Demon Fuzz (2 appearances) 25-11-70, 06-06-71
The Depressions (2 appearances) 05-11-77, 28-01-78
Derek & The Dominos (1 appearance) 11-08-70
Andy Desmond (1 appearance) 29-07-77
Big Pete Deuchar's Country Blues (21 appearances) 07-01-63, 14-01-63, 21-01-63, 28-01-63, 04-02-63, 11-02-63, 18-02-63, 25-02-63, 04-03-63, 1-03-63, 18-03-63, 25-03-63, 01-04-63, 08-04-63, 22-04-63, 29-04-63, 06-05-63, 13-05-63, 20-05-63, 27-05-63, 03-06-63
One of the earliest bands to exploit the taste for the new British R&B music, jazzer Deuchar's Country Blues outfit played an influential residency at the Marquee during the first half of 1963.
Diable Coxhill (1 appearance) 03-06-71
Diabolus (1 appearance) 25-07-71
Dick & The Firemen (2 appearances) 11-05-73, 23-04-75
Most of Patto in a different uniform.
The Dickies (1 appearance) 04-12-79
Errol Dickson (2 appearances) 07-01-72, 21-04-72
Dinner At The Ritz (1 appearance) 28-06-77
Dire Straits (6 appearances) 14-03-78, 21-03-78, 28-03-78, 11-04-78, 05-07-78, 06-07-78
Dirty Tricks (5 appearances) 28-11-75, 05-12-75, 14-01-76, 05-08-76, 05-11-76
The Dissatisfieds (3 appearance) 04-09-64, 02-10-64, 09-10-64
Jim Distant (2 appearances) 20-01-71, 22-02-71
The Diversions (1 appearance) 07-01-76
Dixie (1 appearance) 12-01-74
Dizzy (3 appearances) 25-07-73, 25-04-74, 08-05-74
Dockyard (1 appearance) 25-06-72
Dr Feelgood (3 appearances) 07-10-74, 02-12-74, 02-01-75
Dr K's Blues Band (3 appearances) 06-02-68, 16-10-68, 30-10-68
Doctor Marigold (1 appearance) 07-11-72
Doctor Ross (1 appearance) 02-06-72
An earlier small-run pressing of their song 'The Flying Eagle' on Blue Horizon from the 1960s is now a valuable collectable.
Doctors of Madness (9 appearances) 30-03-76, 13-07-76, 03-08-77, 02-06-77, 26-07-77, 16-08-77, 02-04-78, 10-04-78, 16-04-78
The Dodgers (2 appearances) 30-08-76, 07-09-78
Dog Feet (1 appearance) 11-12-70
Dog Soldier (1 appearance) 14-01-75
The Dog That Bit People (1 appearance) 15-09-70
Dogs (3 appearance) 10-05-75, 31-05-75, 04-10-75
Dogwatch (2 appearances) 09-10-76, 06-11-76
Dole Queue (1 appearance) 06-10-77
Doll By Doll (5 appearances) 02-12-77, 07-02-79, 10-04-79, 18-04-79, 21-12-79
The Doll (5 appearances) 11-02-78, 12-02-78, 13-02-78, 28-02-78, 09-05-79
Dolphins (1 appearance) 27-10-74
The Donkeys (4 appearances) 01-08-79, 02-08-79, 03-08-79, 04-08-79
John Dowie (1 appearance) 28-06-76

Bob Downes (1 appearance) 13-07-70
Dragon Fly (1 appearance) 11-07-75
Dragons (1 appearance) 12-04-77
Simon Drake (1 appearance) 07-02-77
Barry Dransfield (1 appearance) 21-11-73
Dream Police (24 appearances) 11-07-68, 29-08-68, 14-09-68, 21-09-68, 28-09-68, 05-10-68, 12-10-68, 19-10-68, 02-11-68, 09-11-68, 16-11-68, 23-11-68, 30-11-68, 07-12-68, 14-12-68, 21-12-68, 28-12-68, 15-07-69, 18-07-70, 29-08-70, 01-10-70, 15-10-70, 26-11-70, 10-12-70
A Glaswegian band that featured Onnie McIntyre and Hamish Stuart. These two went on to provide the twin-guitar thrust of funk chiefs The Average White Band (whose Marquee debut was in October '72) while in the late 1980s Stuart would join Paul McCartney's band.
The Dream (6 appearances) 26-08-67, 02-09-67, 09-09-67, 16-09-67, 23-09-67, 30-09-67
Julie Driscoll (1 appearance) 29-10-68
The Drones (4 appearances) 14-11-77, 10-10-78, 11-01-79, 22-08-79
Drug Addix (1 appearance) 06-05-78
Druid (8 appearances) 27-02-76, 11-04-76, 03-05-76, 10-05-76, 17-05-76, 24-05-76, 31-05-76, 03-12-76
Dry Ice (1 appearance) 16-12-69
Ducks Deluxe (5 appearances) 17-01-75, 28-02-75, 21-03-75, 19-05-75, 20-06-75
Duffy (3 appearances) 04-12-70, 01-06-73, 12-02-77
Duke, Duke & the Dukes (1 appearance) 14-10-75
John Dummer (14 appearances) 07-02-68, 07-11-68, 22-11-68, 24-12-68, 02-01-69, 04-03-69, 14-03-69, 07-04-69, 15-04-69, 29-05-69, 27-12-69, 10-01-70, 21-07-72, 14-05-73
Aynsley Dunbar (20 appearances) 20-11-67, 15-12-67, 12-01-68, 16-01-68, 26-01-68, 23-02-68, 15-03-68, 12-04-68, 10-05-68, 12-07-68, 13-09-68, 29-11-68, 24-12-68, 07-01-69, 20-02-69, 03-06-69, 02-09-69, 11-11-69, 20-01-70, 13-02-70
Leslie Duncan (1 appearance) 15-12-71
Champion Jack Dupre (5 appearances) 03-05-64, 29-05-66, 15-01-67, 01-03-67, 27-10-72
Simon Dupree (2 appearances) 11-12-67, 02-01-68, 02-07-68
Dusky Ruth (1 appearance) 14-03-71
Dynaflow Blues Band (1 appearance) 19-07-68
Dynamite Day (2 appearances) 08-01-78, 04-04-78

E

Earth (4 appearances) 03-01-69, 06-02-69, 28-02-69, 11-03-69
East of Eden (23 appearances) 06-08-68, 22-08-68, 03-09-68, 17-09-68, 31-10-68, 06-11-68, 20-11-68, 12-12-68, 26-12-68, 05-05-70, 02-10-70, 05-11-70, 19-11-70, 03-04-72, 25-07-72, 05-09-72, 29-05-73, 07-08-73, 16-10-73, 30-01-75, 13-05-75, 31-07-75, 04-09-75
Easy (1 appearance) 08-07-77
Eater (1 appearance) 03-01-79
Echo Bravo (1 appearance) 03-12-79
Eclection (11 appearances) 04-09-68, 11-09-68, 23-10-68, 06-11-68, 07-07-69, 21-07-69, 04-08-69, 25-08-69, 29-

09-69, 01-02-71, 13-04-71
At various times featured Trevor Lucas, later of Fotheringay, and Poli Palmer, one of rock's few vibes players and later of Family.
Eddie & The Hot Rods (12 appearances) 25-04-76, 12-02-76, 09-07-76, 10-08-76, 03-09-76, 17-09-76, 21-09-76, 21-09-77, 22-08-77, 23-08-77, 24-08-77, 25-08-77
The Edge (4 appearances) 09-10-78, 08-11-78, 04-01-79, 27-02-79
Edison Lighthouse (1 appearance) 31-12-73
Egg (2 appearances) 31-01-70, 22-04-71
Cracking instrumental prog band: Dave Stewart (keys) later formed Hatfield & The North (certainly not to be confused with Kilburn & The High Roads).
Eggs Over Easy (1 appearance) 15-06-71
Egypt (3 appearances) 21-12-70, 25-03-71, 24-05-71
Eire Apparent (1 appearance) 19-12-67
The Elastic Band (5 appearances) 01-03-69, 09-04-69, 29-04-69, 11-09-69, 20-10-69
Elder Kindred (1 appearance) 24-11-72
Electric Chair (1 appearance) 25-05-77
Electric Chairs (1 appearance) 25-04-78
The Electric Prunes (1 appearance) 05-12-67
Eliokafanati (1 appearance) 20-10-67
Eliot (1 appearance) 13-01-71
David Elliot (1 appearance) 23-11-71
Ellis (3 appearances) 14-06-73, 09-08-73, 03-12-73
Dave Ellis (2 appearances) 31-08-73, 29-11-73
Elrick (2 appearances) 19-07-73, 14-10-73
Elyse (1 appearance) 02-12-70
Elysium (1 appearance) 01-04-74
Emanon (1 appearance) 13-05-69
Embers West (2 appearances) 06-10-66, 07-11-66
The Emeralds (1 appearance) 05-05-66
Emily Muff (2 appearances) 07-10-69, 31-12-69
English Assassins (1 appearance) 16-11-77
The Enid (20 appearances) 24-02-76, 25-03-76, 16-04-76, 25-06-76, 08-07-76, 20-08-76, 24-09-76, 12-10-76, 02-11-76, 22-07-77, 29-08-77, 24-12-77, 03-08-78, 04-08-78, 05-08-78, 23-12-78, 25-07-79, 26-07-79, 27-07-79, 24-12-79
Enter (1 appearance) 27-05-78
Entire Sioux Nation (2 appearances) 16-04-69, 18-09-69
The Epics (1 appearance) 01-06-67
Episode Six (8 appearances) 27-08-66, 17-09-66, 11-10-66, 18-10-66, 25-10-66, 01-11-66, 15-11-66, 22-11-66
The Equals (1 appearance) 02-02-75
Equinox (1 appearance) 05-06-75
Equity (1 appearance) 29-07-72
The Erection (1 appearance) 30-06-67
Esperanto (8 appearances) 01-05-74, 05-06-74, 17-06-74, 08-07-74, 19-07-74, 08-08-74, 09-09-74, 30-10-74
David Essex (1 appearance) 28-05-72
John Evan Smash (2 appearances) 19-06-67, 04-08-67
Proto-Jethro Tull band with Ian Anderson, Glenn Cornick (bass) and later Tullites John Evan (keys) and Barriemore Barlow (drums).
Evensong (1 appearance) 09-02-72
Roy Everett (2 appearances) 06-02-69, 11-03-69

Every Which Way (1 appearance) 13-10-70

Everyone (1 appearance) 30-10-70

The Exception (6 appearances) 18-03-68, 25-04-68, 13-05-68, 01-06-68, 22-06-68, 26-01-69

The Exotics (3 appearances) 02-09-64, 10-09-64, 23-09-64

The Explosives (2 appearances) 05-01-69, 19-01-69

The Extras (6 appearances) 06-02-79, 20-02-79, 09-03-79, 20-03-79, 23-04-79, 20-07-79

Extremist (1 appearance) 01-12-79

Eyes (1 appearance) 24-01-79

Eyes of Blue (9 appearances) 05-01-67, 04-02-69, 20-02-69, 28-03-69, 11-04-69, 19-04-69, 30-04-69, 31-05-69, 25-10-69

The Welsh West-Coast sound; keyboardist Phil Ryan later joined Man.

F

Fable (3 appearances) 02-01-74, 24-01-74, 23-02-74

Fabulous Poodles (9 appearances) 15-08-76, 11-10-76, 01-11-76, 04-02-77, 29-04-77, 16-09-77, 29-12-77, 01-07-79, 24-11-78

The Faces (3 appearances) 25-09-70, 20-11-70, 01-02-71

Factotum (1 appearance) 07-08-66

Fagin (2 appearances) 02-10-70, 19-11-70

Fail Safe (1 appearance) 25-09-70

Fairfield Parlour (2 appearances) 11-05-70, 19-04-71

Fairport Convention (7 appearances) 29-01-68, 24-04-68, 18-09-68, 25-09-68, 02-10-68, 09-10-68, 30-10-68

The Fall (4 appearances) 08-09-78, 17-12-78, 29-07-79, 18-11-79

Fame (7 appearances) 03-10-78, 25-11-78, 24-01-79, 01-04-79, 29-04-79, 24-06-79, 17-07-79

Georgie Fame (7 appearances) 13-02-66, 24-04-66, 12-10-67, 18-10-76, 19-10-76, 17-02-77, 18-02-77

Family (16 appearances) 21-03-67, 24-04-67, 16-05-67, 23-05-67, 16-06-67, 10-07-67, 07-08-67, 11-06-68, 09-07-68, 17-09-68, 22-10-68, 03-12-68, 17-06-69, 05-08-69, 07-10-69, 31-12-69

On that first date, Leicester group Family supported Cream, and Eric Clapton offered to buy Charlie Whitney's distinctive double-neck Gibson guitar. Whitney declined, but allowed Clapton to play it during Cream's set when it sounded "very sweet".

The Famous Jug Band (1 appearance) 25-03-70

The Fancy Bred (3 appearances) 23-03-67, 06-04-67, 11-05-67

Lee Farden (1 appearance) 31-03-79

Chris Farlowe (5 appearances) 29-07-63, 18-04-67, 28-07-75, 14-09-79, 27-12-79

Farm (1 appearance) 26-04-70

Gary Farr (2 appearances) 17-06-70, 05-10-70

Better known as vocalist with his T-Bones.

Fashion (2 appearances) 11-03-79, 10-05-79

Fastbuck (2 appearances) 19-12-75, 27-04-76

Fat Daughter (1 appearance) 12-12-69

Fat Matress (5 appearances) 26-08-69, 21-04-70, 14-08-70, 23-10-70, 27-11-70

Stuffed by ex-Jimi bassist Noel Redding.

Fay Bill (1 appearance) 13-09-71

FBI (11 appearances) 03-08-75, 10-08-75, 17-08-75, 31-08-75, 19-09-75, 08-10-75, 24-12-75, 30-01-76, 16-03-76, 23-07-76, 06-08-76

Feather (2 appearances) 28-05-71, 31-05-71

FELA (1 appearance) 19-07-71

Felder's Orioles (1 appearance) 20-01-67

Felix (1 appearance) 04-04-76

Julie Felix (1 appearance) 17-07-66

Rod Felton (3 appearances) 06-04-74, 01-07-74, 02-07-74

Fenmen (1 appearance) 02-12-66

Fernhill (1 appearance) 08-11-71

Ferris Wheel (1 appearance) 09-01-68

This band boasted a very good vocalist, one Linda Lewis.

FF&Z (1 appearance) 30-08-72

57 Men (1 appearance) 16-07-79

Fingerprintz (1 appearance) 13-10-79

Fireweed (1 appearance) 03-10-71

Fischer Z (2 appearances) 05-12-78, 16-05-79

Patrick Fitzgerald (2 appearances) 08-05-78, 09-05-78

Five Hand Reel (7 appearances) 06-06-75, 02-07-75, 07-04-76, 19-07-76, 13-06-77, 09-11-77, 01-12-77

The Five Proud Walkers (1 appearance) 08-05-67

Flame (1 appearance) 05-12-70

Flare (1 appearance) 28-10-70

Flash (4 appearances) 22-02-72, 09-05-72, 06-06-72, 24-10-72

Post-Yes haven for guitarist Pete Banks and keyboardist Tony Kaye.

Fleetwood Mac (9 appearances) 15-08-67, 05-09-67, 29-09-67, 27-10-67, 24-11-67, 29-12-67, 29-03-68, 30-08-71, 31-08-71

Flesh (19 appearances) 15-07-72, 12-08-72, 19-08-72, 04-11-72, 23-03-73, 19-05-73, 23-06-73, 28-07-73, 11-08-73, 25-08-73, 01-09-73, 15-09-73, 22-09-73, 30-09-73, 27-10-73, 10-11-73, 24-11-73, 08-12-73, 24-12-73

Fleur De Lys (1 appearance) 10-04-67

Highly rated in hindsight, the group's first two singles were produced by Jimmy Page, the second with strong guitar work from Phil Sawyer, ex-Cheynes and Shotgun Express.

The Flies (2 appearances) 21-11-77, 22-11-77

Flux (1 appearance) 25-04-74

Flying Aces (2 appearances) 17-11-76, 13-01-77

Flying Hat Band (2 appearances) 23-09-71, 07-03-72

The Flys (2 appearances) 17-02-79, 08-05-79

Focus (2 appearances) 08-03-72, 11-08-72

Fogg (1 appearance) 03-01-76

Food (1 appearance) 06-12-68

Food Band (1 appearance) 02-01-79

The Footprints (1 appearance) 01-04-67

Forum (1 appearance) 22-01-70

The Foster Brothers (7 appearances) 05-09-76, 12-09-76, 19-09-76, 26-09-76, 14-11-76, 11-10-76, 02-12-77

The Foundations (2 appearances) 02-04-68, 28-02-70

Andy Fraser Band (1 appearance) 04-11-75

Free (15 appearances) 21-06-68, 07-10-68, 14-10-68, 21-10-68, 28-10-68, 04-11-68, 12-11-68, 18-11-68, 25-11-68, 02-12-68, 09-12-68, 16-12-68, 23-12-68, 16-01-69, 13-02-69

Free At Last (4 appearances) 02-10-66, 03-11-66, 20-11-66, 15-12-66

Freedom (1 appearance) 24-11-71

Freight (1 appearance) 06-05-72

Fresh (1 appearance) 12-06-77

Fresh Maggots (1 appearance) 10-10-71

Friends (1 appearance) 08-01-78

Fritz & The Blue Beats (4 appearances) 05-05-64, 12-05-64, 19-05-64, 26-05-64

Raymond Froggatt (2 appearances) 13-06-72, 27-10-74

Frogmorton (1 appearance) 15-12-75

Fruup (10 appearances) 23-07-71, 10-05-72, 18-06-72, 02-07-72, 30-07-72, 15-02-73, 10-10-73, 26-05-75, 06-04-76, 14-04-76

Belfast prog-rockers resident in London.

Jesse Fuller (1 appearance) 30-04-67

Lowell Fulson (1 appearance) 11-05-69

Fumble (22 appearances) 17-05-72, 31-10-72, 21-06-73, 14-07-73, 04-10-73, 31-12-73, 12-02-74, 12-04-74, 28-05-74, 31-07-74, 17-09-74, 07-11-74, 16-01-75, 08-04-75, 15-07-75, 23-09-75, 24-12-75, 03-02-76, 16-04-76, 20-06-76, 12-08-76, 14-04-77

Fury (4 appearances) 30-05-77, 15-06-77, 17-11-77, 21-01-78

Michael Fury (1 appearance) 22-09-76

Fusion Orchestra (12 appearances) 05-09-71, 17-08-72, 12-10-72, 20-11-72, 03-02-73, 26-03-73, 15-07-73, 25-10-73, 13-02-74, 22-04-74, 21-06-74, 26-08-74, 25-09-74, 18-11-74, 22-12-74, 06-02-75, 27-02-75, 20-03-75, 01-05-75

G

Rory Gallagher (9 appearances) 18-05-71, 20-07-71, 04-10-71, 05-10-71, 09-04-72, 03-05-74, 04-05-74, 05-05-74, 15-01-79

The Game (1 appearance) 13-08-66

Elmer Gantry (2 appearances) 10-04-69, 24-04-69

Gantry's Velvet Opera had Strawbs rhythm section Richard Hudson and John Ford.

Gasworks (4 appearances) 16-08-75, 25-10-75, 22-11-75, 03-04-76

Ron Geesin (1 appearance) 18-05-69

Eccentric instrumentalist whose avant-garde ramblings influenced Pink Floyd around the time of this show for the studio-recorded tracks of the "Ummagumma" LP. Geesin would also collaborate with the group on their later "Atom Heart Mother" album.

Generation X (8 appearances) 31-03-77, 20-07-77, 12-08-77, 06-09-77, 13-09-77, 20-09-77, 27-09-77, 20-06-79

Genesis (10 appearances) 04-02-70, 19-02-70, 14-06-70, 12-07-70, 30-08-70, 04-10-70, 10-11-70, 06-05-71, 09-07-71, 19-09-72

Geno & The Sharks (1 appearance) 02-12-79

Gentle Giant (3 appearances) 15-07-70, 14-09-70, 24-11-71

Simon Dupree & The Prog Sound.

Gentlemen (1 appearance) 19-02-77

Geordie (3 appearances) 18-10-72, 12-09-73, 23-07-74

Giant Marrowfat (1 appearance) 07-06-68

Giants (1 appearance) 24-04-79

Gibbons Steve (8 appearances) 09-04-75, 13-06-76, 30-06-76, 14-10-76, 10-12-76, 18-01-77, 20-12-78, 1-12-78

Giggles (21 appearances) 08-11-75, 27-12-75, 10-01-76, 17-01-76, 24-01-76, 31-01-76, 28-02-76, 13-03-76, 02-05-76, 09-05-76, 16-05-76, 23-05-76, 30-05-76, 27-06-76, 11-07-76, 08-08-76, 20-09-76, 12-11-76, 06-12-76, 08-07-77, 29-09-77

Gilberto Gil (7 appearances) 14-03-71, 19-03-71, 11-04-71, 18-04-71, 25-04-71, 02-05-71, 16-05-71

Ian Gillan (11 appearances) 12-06-78, 13-06-78, 14-06-78, 28-09-78, 29-09-78, 27-12-78, 28-12-78, 29-12-78, 10-07-79, 11-07-79, 12-07-79

Dana Gillespie (2 appearances) 13-02-76, 09-04-76

Gordon Giltrap (3 appearances) 02-02-71, 10-02-75, 01-04-76

Gimme Hope (1 appearance) 03-12-75

Gin House (1 appearance) 05-07-70

Ginger (1 appearance) 12-11-70

Girl (3 appearances) 05-12-79, 12-12-79, 28-12-79

The Glass Menagerie (17 appearances) 02-03-68, 01-04-68, 29-04-68, 07-05-68, 22-06-68, 03-07-68, 15-07-68, 31-07-68, 08-08-68, 20-08-68, 24-07-69, 26-08-69, 13-09-69, 25-09-69, 09-10-69, 23-10-69, 21-11-69

Glencoe (7 appearances) 24-08-71, 23-05-72, 15-06-72, 01-08-72, 19-02-73, 30-07-73, 13-09-73

Global Village Trucking Company (3 appearances) 23-05-74, 23-02-75, 30-06-75

Gloria Mundi (22 appearances) 20-11-76, 22-11-76, 21-01-77, 22-02-77, 26-02-77, 31-03-77, 15-04-77, 30-04-77, 14-05-77, 02-07-77, 01-09-77, 25-09-77, 14-10-77, 28-10-77, 11-11-77, 25-11-77, 22-02-78, 03-03-78, 15-03-78, 31-03-78, 16-11-78, 05-01-79, 07-09-79

Gnasher (1 appearance) 04-04-74

Gnidrolog (5 appearances) 11-05-71, 27-07-71, 03-11-71, 12-04-72, 08-11-72

Gnome Sweet Gnome (6 appearances) 02-04-71, 25-04-71, 13-07-71, 06-08-71, 02-09-71, 08-10-71

The Gods (15 appearances) 08-09-67, 07-10-67, 13-01-68, 20-01-68, 27-01-68, 10-02-68, 17-02-68, 24-02-68, 02-03-68, 16-03-68, 23-03-68, 30-03-68, 29-04-68, 09-05-68, 30-05-68

Herbie Goins & The Night-Timers (4 appearances) 06-01-67, 26-01-67, 09-02-67, 23-02-67

Soul-infused singer big in clubs and low on recordings, though he did wax a few tracks, including one or two when with Blues Incorporated in the mid 1960s.

Golden Earring (1 appearance) 24-09-73

Gollum (1 appearance) 30-05-71

Gong (4 appearances) 12-06-73, 08-09-75, 09-09-75, 10-09-75

Gonzales (8 appearances) 14-08-71, 25-01-72, 21-05-75, 17-09-75, 19-11-75, 23-01-76, 25-02-76, 05-04-76

The loosely defined line-ups of this fine funk outfit at times included Mick Eve (ex-Georgie Fame's Blue Flames) and Rosko Gee (the talented bassman who went on to play with Traffic).

Gooch (1 appearance) 07-12-66

Good Habit (10 appearances) 13-05-71, 06-01-72, 21-03-72, 24-05-73, 04-06-73, 12-04-74, 23-05-75, 18-07-75, 15-08-75, 06-10-75

Good Stuff (1 appearance) 27-04-77

The Good-Goods (3 appearances) 17-09-66, 27-10-66, 30-12-66

Philip Goodhand-Tait (6 appearances) 13-02-67, 13-03-67, 10-11-71, 01-03-74, 06-07-75, 10-02-67

The Goodtime Band (1 appearance) 28-04-67

Sam Gopal (1 appearance) 03-01-70
Pre-Hawkwind psychedelia from Lemmy.
Gorman Ghost (1 appearance) 24-01-70
Grace (1 appearance) 26-04-72
Gracious (11 appearances) 27-09-69, 13-02-70, 30-04-70, 17-05-70, 08-06-70, 29-06-70, 31-08-70, 21-09-70, 19-10-70, 14-12-70, 06-04-72
Grail (18 appearances) 08-05-69, 20-05-69, 17-06-69, 01-07-69, 07-07-69, 14-07-69, 21-07-69, 15-08-69, 04-09-69, 15-09-69, 26-09-69, 06-10-69, 17-10-69, 07-11-69, 25-11-69, 10-02-70, 26-03-70, 31-07-70
Grand Hotel (8 appearances) 17-09-77, 02-10-77, 09-10-77, 16-10-77, 23-10-77, 30-10-77, 04-12-77, 20-11-78
Grand Slam (10 appearances) 23-03-74, 27-07-74, 21-09-74, 19-10-74, 14-12-74, 18-01-75, 23-01-75, 01-02-75, 15-02-75, 01-03-75
Granny's Intentions (13 appearances) 22-01-68, 07-03-68, 28-03-68, 18-04-68, 09-05-68, 16-05-68, 23-05-68, 11-06-68, 01-07-68, 24-07-68, 30-07-68, 26-09-68, 15-05-70
Gary Moore played briefly with this lot, who kept it in the family by turning into...
Granny's New Intentions (11 appearances) 22-05-70, 25-06-70, 22-07-70, 06-08-70, 13-08-70, 20-08-70, 27-08-70, 03-09-70, 10-09-70, 17-09-70, 24-09-70
Grapefruit (1 appearance) 16-09-69
Grass (1 appearance) 16-11-71
Gravy Train (2 appearances) 19-09-71, 14-09-74
Grease Band (1 appearance) 09-09-71
Greasy Bear (1 appearance) 10-09-71
The Grebbels (8 appearances) 04-06-64, 02-07-64, 09-07-64, 16-07-64, 23-07-64, 06-08-64, 13-08-64, 20-08-64
Peter Green (1 appearance) 24-06-70
Greenslade (10 appearances) 28-11-72, 09-03-73, 06-04-73, 03-05-73, 22-05-73, 29-06-73, 19-07-73, 23-10-73, 09-04-74, 28-08-74
Greep (3 appearances) 11-01-74, 03-08-74, 08-02-75
Griffin (3 appearances) 31-08-69, 05-03-70, 17-04-72
John Grimaldi (1 appearance) 13-04-76
Carol Grimes (6 appearances) 21-06-71, 13-01-72, 02-02-72, 12-01-76, 01-07-76, 23-09-76
Gringo (2 appearances) 17-08-71, 20-01-72
Grisby Dyke (1 appearance) 16-03-70
Grizelda (1 appearance) 08-10-70
The Groop (2 appearances) 20-07-68, 01-08-68
Grope (1 appearance) 15-12-69
Groundhogs (30 appearances) 13-08-65, 30-08-65, 25-10-65, 04-11-65, 07-02-69, 04-05-69, 13-06-69, 27-06-69, 04-07-69, 22-07-69, 19-08-69, 02-09-69, 16-09-69, 30-09-69, 24-10-69, 06-11-69, 18-12-69, 29-01-70, 13-03-70, 21-05-70, 25-06-70, 24-07-70, 29-09-70, 22-12-70, 11-05-74, 26-11-74, 12-03-75, 26-10-76, 27-10-76, 28-10-76
The 1965 dates saw the blues group billed as John Lee's Groundhogs when they backed John Lee Hooker, but later outings were advertised as Tony McPhee & The Groundhogs. This reflected the arrival of the band's new leader and a gradual move toward heavier rock.
Gruppo Sportivo (2 appearances) 02-06-78, 12-10-78
Gryphon (10 appearances) 22-08-73, 12-11-73, 20-01-76, 04-03-76, 24-04-

76, 18-06-76, 17-08-76, 09-03-77, 23-03-77, 27-04-77
Isaac Guillory (3 appearances) 02-03-75, 22-11-76, 23-11-76
Guinever (1 appearance) 27-07-75
Gully Foyle (1 appearance) 03-02-72
Gun (5 appearances) 13-06-68, 06-07-68, 17-07-68, 27-08-68, 18-02-69
Buddy Guy (1 appearance) 25-02-65
Gwenyway (7 appearances) 10-04-72, 17-04-72, 23-04-72, 30-04-72, 07-05-72, 14-05-72, 21-05-72
Gygafo (1 appearance) 01-03-78
Gygato (1 appearance) 12-10-74
Gypp (8 appearances) 17-04-78, 12-09-69, 29-09-69, 21-10-69, 21-04-70, 27-10-71, 29-07-74

H

Jenny Haan (4 appearances) 03-02-77, 11-05-77, 24-07-77, 15-08-77
The Habits (1 appearance) 19-07-66
Hackensack (7 appearances) 18-10-70, 11-04-71, 18-04-71, 25-04-71, 07-10-73, 25-11-73, 28-03-74
Halcyon (1 appearance) 13-07-74
Half Human Band (1 appearance) 10-08-74
Halfbreed (4 appearances) 29-05-71, 15-01-7, 29-01-76, 03-03-76
Bob Hall (1 appearance) 27-11-69
Claire Hamill (1 appearance) 01-10-71
Hammer (1 appearance) 18-09-70
Peter Hammill (1 appearance) 20-09-72
Handbag (1 appearance) 02-09-76
Happy Days (1 appearance) 28-07-71
Hard Meat (11 appearances) 03-04-69, 24-04-69, 16-05-69, 22-05-69, 09-07-69, 30-09-69, 13-01-70, 06-02-70, 20-02-70, 27-02-70, 24-03-70
Tim Hardin (5 appearances) 17-12-73, 04-07-75, 26-08-75, 06-02-76, 14-05-76
Hardin & York (22 appearances) 31-08-69, 18-09-69, 17-10-69, 14-11-69, 28-11-69, 05-12-69, 12-12-69, 24-03-70, 19-05-70, 30-06-70, 28-07-70, 04-09-70, 29-12-7, 23-02-71, 12-04-71, 15-06-71, 03-08-71, 24-09-71, 27-12-71, 29-02-72, 26-02-74, 14-08-75
Hardin & York & Fenwick (1 appearance) 15-09-72
Harlot (7 appearances) 09-05-75, 22-06-75, 29-06-75, 06-07-75, 13-07-75, 20-07-75, 27-07-75
Harlow (1 appearance) 10-07-78
Harmony Grass (7 appearances) 08-04-69, 12-08-69, 30-12-69, 11-04-70, 16-05-70, 13-06-70, 15-08-70
Featuring former members of Tony Rivers & The Castaways. Rivers was a talented singer and appeared over a long period providing keen backing vocals for many artists, not least Sir Cliff Richard.
Harp (1 appearance) 01-02-75
Harpoon (1 appearance) 13-05-76
Bobby Harrison (1 appearance) 06-07-76
Lalla Harrison (1 appearance) 09-04-76
Mike Harrison (1 appearance) 02-12-75
Harry The Horse (1 appearance) 08-07-70
Harsh Reality (1 appearance) 02-04-69
Mike Hart (3 appearances) 23-09-69, 21-11-69, 12-12-69
Keef Hartley (24 appearances) 12-08-68, 30-08-68, 04-09-68, 23-09-68, 30-

09-68, 08-10-68, 15-11-68, 18-07-69, 03-10-69, 24-12-69, 04-02-70, 12-05-70, 16-06-70, 14-07-70, 22-09-70, 17-11-70, 18-03-71, 08-06-71, 13-06-71, 14-06-71, 21-09-71, 21-12-71, 15-11-74, 02-12-75
Alex Harvey (35 appearances) 14-01-65, 04-03-65, 11-03-65, 01-04-65, 08-04-65, 15-04-65, 22-04-65, 29-04-65, 06-05-65, 13-05-65, 20-05-65, 27-05-65, 03-06-65, 10-06-65, 17-06-65, 24-06-65, 01-07-65, 15-07-65, 07-12-65, 11-01-66, 29-03-70, 23-02-72, 01-03-72, 05-04-72, 05-06-72, 11-10-72, 04-12-72, 18-01-73, 07-03-73, 17-04-73, 15-05-73, 20-06-73, 18-09-73, 23-02-77, 24-02-77
Harvey's datelist here covers a number of different bands that the Glaswegian headed through the years. At first it was The Alex Harvey Soul Band, later The Sensational Alex Harvey Band, and the March 1970 date was billed as The Alex Harvey Hair Band. A proud recipient of the Marquee Long Service Medal, Harvey died in 1982 at the age of just 46.
George Hatcher (9 appearances) 05-01-77, 19-01-77, 09-02-77, 07-03-77, 27-06-77, 25-07-77, 30-08-77, 19-09-77, 17-11-77
Hate (2 appearances) 28-09-70, 02-11-70
Lee Hawkins (1 appearance) 13-03-68
Hawkwind (2 appearances) 24-11-69, 26-01-71
Tony Hazzard (1 appearance) 03-01-72
Head Waiter (1 appearance) 03-04-78
Headboys (3 appearances) 15-05-79, 29-05-79, 13-06-79
Heads Hands & Feet (7 appearances) 20-07-70, 21-09-70, 01-12-70, 30-03-71, 21-07-71, 18-04-72, 16-05-72
Early Tele-bending from Albert Lee, one of the few to play lead guitar for Eric Clapton.
Headstone (2 appearances) 25-11-74, 13-01-75
Heartbreaker (10 appearances) 08-04-76, 08-04-76, 05-07-76, 24-07-76, 22-08-76, 11-09-76, 21-09-76, 02-10-76, 25-10-76, 30-10-76, 12-03-77
Hearts 'n' Souls (2 appearances) 03-04-68, 08-05-68
Heavy Heart (5 appearances) 17-10-73, 31-10-73, 14-11-73, 28-11-73, 12-12-73
Heavy Jelly (1 appearance) 11-06-70
Heavy Metal Kids (16 appearances) 18-08-73, 29-12-73, 17-02-74, 05-04-74, 29-04-74, 29-05-74, 05-07-74, 16-08-74, 06-09-74, 05-11-74, 31-12-74, 15-02-75, 31-12-75, 22-09-77, 23-09-77, 20-03-78
Dick Heckstall-Smith Band (2 appearances) 29-09-72, 23-02-73
Saxman from Blues Incorporated, Graham Bond Organisation, Colosseum et cetera.
Hedgehog High (1 appearance) 22-03-72
Hedgehog Pie (2 appearances) 07-04-76, 12-07-76
Helfer (1 appearance) 10-03-72
Hellraiser (1 appearance) 02-02-74
Hemlock (1 appearance) 04-01-73
Jimi Hendrix (2 appearances) 24-01-67, 24-10-67
Bobby Henry (1 appearance) 28-04-79
Bruce Henry (2 appearances) 25-11-79, 26-11-79
Richard Henry (1 appearance) 16-01-67
Herbal Mixture (5 appearances) 09-09-67, 07-10-67, 06-11-67, 25-11-67, 16-12-67

The Herd (41 appearances) 25-04-66, 19-05-66, 27-06-66, 28-07-66, 22-08-66, 01-09-66, 10-09-66, 27-09-66, 01-10-66, 15-10-66, 22-10-66, 29-10-66, 05-11-66, 12-11-66, 19-11-66, 26-11-66, 03-12-66, 10-12-66, 17-12-66, 24-12-66, 02-01-67, 09-01-67, 16-01-67, 23-01-67, 06-02-67, 13-02-67, 27-02-67, 06-03-67, 13-03-67, 03-04-67, 10-04-67, 17-04-67, 24-04-67, 01-05-67, 15-05-67, 05-06-67, 19-06-67, 03-07-67, 31-07-67, 07-11-67, 30-07-68
Heron (2 appearances) 25-11-70, 01-12-71
Heron (6 appearances) 29-03-77, 26-04-77, 27-05-77, 29-06-77, 28-07-77, 07-10-77
Mike Heron's Reputation (5 appearances) 14-07-75, 27-08-75, 06-11-75, 26-02-76, 24-03-76
Incredible String Band mainman goes rockier in solo mode.
Carolyn Hester (1 appearance) 06-03-68
Hi-Fi (6 appearances) 19-03-78, 27-05-78, 25-09-78, 16-10-78, 23-10-78, 06-11-78
High Broom (1 appearance) 16-06-70
Highly Inflammable (1 appearance) 12-04-71
Highway (3 appearances) 20-09-73, 05-10-73, 07-07-74
Roy Hill (1 appearance) 22-09-78
Steve Hillage (2 appearances) 07-08-78, 08-08-78
Hinkley's Heroes (2 appearances) 22-11-76, 23-11-76
Chris Hinze (1 appearance) 03-05-75
Robert Hirst (9 appearances) 07-01-67, 11-02-67, 25-02-67, 27-03-67, 27-06-67, 11-08-67, 01-09-67, 25-09-67, 09-10-67
Jon Hiseman's Tempest (3 appearances) 02-10-73, 11-12-73, 30-04-74
Drummer Hiseman twixt Colosseums; this version had ex-Patto Ollie Halsall on guitar.
Hobo (5 appearances) 05-10-75, 12-10-75, 19-10-75, 26-10-75, 09-02-76
James Hogg (1 appearance) 05-06-73
Hogsnort Rupert (1 appearance) 14-10-63
Wendy Hoile (3 appearances) 10-04-72, 17-04-72, 07-05-72
Hok Cottage (1 appearance) 19-01-72
Hokus Poke (1 appearance) 14-05-71
Ram Holder (3 appearances) 15-12-66, 09-06-71, 21-07-71
Gary Holton's Gems (1 appearance) 26-04-79
Post-Heavy Metal Kids and pre-Wayne, vocalist Holton formed the shortlived Gems.
Hooker (2 appearances) 21-02-76, 09-05-77
John Lee Hooker (2 appearances) 09-05-66, 20-06-67
Hookfoot (5 appearances) 14-04-70, 10-11-71, 16-12-73, 07-01-74, 10-03-74
Hot Rock (1 appearance) 22-03-75
Hous Hin (1 appearance) 29-07-73
House of Lords (30 appearances) 28-04-68, 30-06-68, 04-07-68, 14-07-68, 21-07-68, 18-08-68, 25-08-68, 01-09-68, 08-09-68, 15-09-68, 22-09-68, 29-09-68, 06-10-68, 13-10-68, 20-10-68, 27-10-68, 03-11-68, 10-11-68, 17-11-68, 24-11-68, 01-12-68, 22-12-68, 12-01-69, 02-02-69, 23-02-69, 02-03-69, 09-03-69, 16-03-69, 30-03-69, 06-04-69
Howl (1 appearance) 30-10-70
Howlin' Wolf (3 appearances) 26-11-64, 29-05-69, 06-11-69

I (continued, column 1)

Mike Hugg (1 appearance) 12-11-74

Alan Hull (1 appearance) 18-03-70

Human Instinct (2 appearances) 08-01-68, 14-02-68

Human League (2 appearances) 21-06-79, 22-06-79

Humble Pie (5 appearances) 17-04-70, 02-06-70, 04-08-70, 09-02-71, 11-03-71

Hummingbird (1 appearance) 13-12-73

Hungry Horse (7 appearances) 22-11-75, 15-04-76, 29-04-76, 18-11-76, 15-01-77, 05-02-77, 05-03-77

Hunter Muskett (4 appearances) 11-02-70, 18-02-70, 25-02-70, 25-03-73

Hurricane (1 appearance) 27-09-71

Hush (1 appearance) 13-07-74

Hustler (16 appearances) 26-01-74, 21-02-74, 03-03-74, 21-03-74, 13-04-74, 24-05-74, 10-06-74, 27-06-74, 28-07-74, 14-08-74, 14-09-74, 23-10-74, 21-11-74, 06-01-75, 08-05-75, 25-06-75

J.B. Hutto (2 appearances) 04-02-7, 18-02-72

I

Idle Race (1 appearance) 20-10-70
Jeff Lynne had left in January for The Move; the Idlers needed two to fill the gap: Dave Walker (vox) and Mike Hopkins (guitar).

The Idols (1 appearance) 18-11-78

If (8 appearances) 24-05-70, 09-03-71, 25-06-71, 28-12-71, 15-06-72, 23-08-72, 08-03-73, 29-11-73
Big brassy jazz-rock mob that shilled some air around the Wardour Street club.

Igginbottom (2 appearances) 01-11-69, 11-11-69

Iguana (2 appearances) 08-03-72, 13-02-73

Illusion (5 appearances) 10-05-77, 31-08-77, 13-10-77, 06-11-77, 13-11-77

The Illusions (1 appearance) 21-07-67

Imagination (2 appearances) 26-07-69, 13-09-69

Impact Blues (1 appearance) 12-08-67

Imperial Show Band (2 appearances) 10-06-77, 24-07-77

The Impulsions (3 appearances) 03-04-64, 10-04-64, 17-04-64

The In Crowd (3 appearances) 10-12-65, 09-02-67, 23-02-67
Shortly after this last date the In Crowd became the psychedelically-inclined Tomorrow, with Steve Howe on guitar and Keith West on vocal.

Incandescant Mantle (2 appearances) 01-10-69, 08-10-69

Indigo (1 appearance) 05-08-72

Infant (1 appearance) 18-11-71

Ingoes (1 appearance) 01-01-65

Initiation (1 appearance) 31-10-69

Inner Circle (2 appearances) 22-03-79, 23-03-79

Neil Innes (2 appearances) 02-08-70, 20-10-75
An old Bonzo Dogger, Innes later starred as Lennonalike Ron Nasty in The Rutles incisive movie "All You Need Is Cash".

Inside Out (2 appearances) 23-09-72, 21-10-72

The Intellectuals (2 appearances) 26-10-78, 09-11-78

Interns (1 appearance) 03-09-70

Interview (1 appearance) 28-08-79

Invaders (2 appearances) 29-01-79, 09-08-79

IPOH (1 appearance) 26-07-75

Iron Maiden (2 appearances) 19-10-79, 09-12-79

Iron Prophet (1 appearance) 01-10-70

Ironside (1 appearance) 24-03-74

Isis (1 appearance) 01-04-73

The Iveys (12 appearances) 21-11-66, 09-12-66, 22-12-66, 20-07-67, 24-08-67, 16-09-67, 14-10-67, 30-11-67, 25-01-68, 03-02-68, 23-03-68, 13-07-68

Ivor Biggun (1 appearance) 12-12-78

The Ivy League (1 appearance) 14-05-65

The Ivys (1 appearance) 06-01-68

J

Jab Jab (1 appearance) 18-01-79

The Jab (1 appearance) 29-10-76

Jack The Lad (14 appearances) 10-07-73, 28-08-73, 19-11-73, 09-01-74, 23-01-74, 06-02-74, 20-02-74, 18-04-74, 15-05-74, 12-06-74, 26-06-74, 09-07-75, 10-11-75, 26-05-76

Jackal (3 appearances) 27-10-71, 05-11-71, 27-01-72

Jackson Heights (6 appearances) 25-08-70, 10-11-70, 08-07-71, 07-08-72, 27-11-72, 05-02-73

J.J. Jackson (1 appearance) 20-06-69

Joe Jackson (1 appearance) 09-02-79

Jade (1 appearance) 28-02-73

Jade Hexagram (1 appearance) 03-04-68

Jade Warrior (3 appearances) 17-02-72, 14-08-72, 29-11-72

The Jags (7 appearances) 17-03-79, 06-05-79, 13-05-79, 20-05-79, 27-05-79, 18-08-79, 09-11-79
Towards the end of our period some bands were tagged "power pop": sort of punky energy but with the melodic sensibilities of pop. Such were The Jags, driven by Nick Watkinson (vox) and John Alder (guitar).

Jailbait (5 appearances) 06-07-74, 15-03-75, 26-04-75, 27-09-75, 20-03-76

The Jam (3 appearances) 22-01-77, 24-02-78, 25-02-78

Brian James (1 appearance) 28-05-79

Buster James (2 appearances) 02-09-77, 13-05-78

Jimmy James (57 appearances) 18-05-65, 31-05-65, 07-06-65, 14-06-65, 21-06-65, 28-06-65, 05-07-65, 12-07-65, 19-07-65, 26-07-65, 02-08-65, 09-08-65, 16-08-65, 23-08-65, 30-08-65, 06-09-65, 13-09-65, 20-09-65, 27-09-65, 04-10-65, 11-10-65, 18-10-65, 25-10-65, 01-11-65, 08-11-65, 15-11-65, 22-11-65, 29-11-65, 13-12-65, 20-12-65, 10-01-66, 17-01-66, 24-01-66, 31-01-66, 14-02-66, 21-02-66, 03-03-66, 21-03-66, 04-04-66, 12-05-66, 13-06-66, 11-07-66, 30-08-66, 13-09-66, 26-09-66, 11-10-66, 18-11-66, 06-12-66, 31-12-66, 31-01-67, 25-04-67, 05-03-68, 15-10-68, 18-04-70, 20-06-70
Most of the earlier dates feature James's hard-working soul band The Vagabonds.

Kelly James (1 appearance) 24-05-70

Nicky James (1 appearance) 11-09-71

Jan Dukes De Grey (2 appearances) 12-04-70, 19-04-70

Bert Jansch (9 appearances) 07-12-76, 14-12-76, 28-12-76, 11-01-77, 15-02-77, 05-04-77, 31-05-77, 12-09-77, 14-12-78

Janus (1 appearance) 01-03-75

Japan (1 appearance) 17-09-77

Jasper (1 appearance) 30-08-69

Peter Jay (6 appearances) 03-03-67, 24-03-67, 26-05-67, 30-06-67, 21-07-67, 25-08-67

Jellybread (8 appearances) 18-12-69,

27-01-70, 06-07-70, 29-09-70, 05-12-71, 25-02-72, 07-04-72, 23-06-72

Jerico Jones (3 appearances) 20-06-71, 29-06-71, 12-01-72

Jerry The Ferret (5 appearances) 08-08-76, 18-09-76, 24-11-76, 10-12-76, 19-03-77

Jessop & Co (1 appearance) 16-01-71

Jet (1 appearance) 01-08-75

Jethro Tull (19 appearances) 02-02-68, 09-02-68, 16-02-68, 15-03-68, 29-03-68, 15-04-68, 03-05-68, 17-05-68, 31-05-68, 14-06-68, 28-06-68, 05-07-68, 19-07-68, 26-07-68, 09-08-68, 23-08-68, 20-09-68, 11-10-68, 26-11-68

The J.J. Sound (1 appearance) 08-02-68

Jo'Burg Hawk (3 appearances) 21-03-73, 18-04-73, 03-03-74

David John (2 appearances) 21-08-64, 11-12-64

Elton John (1 appearance) 05-06-70

John's Boys (1 appearance) 02-11-79

John's Children (1 appearance) 03-12-66
Marc Bolan joined a few months later.

Johnny Curious & The Strangers (1 appearance) 20-09-77

Johnny Moped (3 appearances) 04-07-77, 06-05-79, 17-07-78

Ginger Johnson (5 appearances) 18-05-70, 24-06-70, 30-12-70, 25-04-71, 14-07-71

Linton Kwesi Johnson (2 appearances) 10-06-79, 11-06-79

Wilko Johnson (12 appearances) 10-05-78, 11-05-78, 10-08-78, 11-08-78, 12-04-79, 13-04-79, 14-04-79, 15-04-79, 15-08-79, 16-08-79, 17-08-79, 10-12-79

Joint (2 appearances) 12-06-69, 21-06-69

Jolt (4 appearances) 06-09-77, 26-10-77, 27-01-78, 03-09-78

Jon (3 appearances) 09-10-67, 11-12-67, 01-02-68

Clive Jones (1 appearance) 31-10-75

Paul Jones (2 appearances) 25-01-72, 21-03-72

Ronnie Jones (4 appearances) 11-10-62, 18-10-62, 21-06-65, 06-12-65

Jonesy (13 appearances) 16-04-72, 4-04-72, 19-06-72, 13-07-72, 26-10-72, 17-12-72, 03-01-73, 12-01-73, 09-02-73, 16-02-73, 30-03-73, 30-04-73, 25-05-73

Jopal (1 appearance) 10-02-72

Paul Joses (1 appearance) 14-11-75

Journey (1 appearance) 16-04-71

Joy Division (1 appearance) 04-03-79
The Mancunian grumpies turned up at the Marquee for this early London showing, five months before the release of their first LP.

JSD Band (9 appearances) 20-12-71, 13-03-72, 23-03-72, 04-05-72, 08-06-73, 18-06-73, 19-12-73, 02-08-74, 16-12-74

Judas Jump (2 appearances) 23-06-70, 20-10-70

Judas Priest (11 appearances) 05-10-72, 11-02-74, 09-06-74, 19-09-74, 01-11-74, 02-04-75, 30-04-75, 16-05-75, 13-06-75, 02-09-75, 05-11-75

Jugglers (2 appearances) 08-02-75, 15-03-75

Juicy Lucy (3 appearances) 18-11-69, 07-04-70, 04-09-72

Julian's Treatment (8 appearances) 04-10-69, 16-02-70, 23-02-70, 02-03-70, 09-03-70, 23-03-70, 20-04-70, 28-12-70

July (2 appearances) 24-08-68, 12-09-68

Junco Partners (4 appearances) 07-05-

69, 23-05-69, 06-11-69, 14-06-70

Junior's Eyes (4 appearances) 30-05-68, 27-02-69, 23-06-69, 03-02-70
On that last date they backed David Bowie; Eyes guitarists Mick Wayne and Tim Renwick had already played on Bowie's 'Man Of Words' LP, and Wayne had contributed to the previous summer's 'Space Oddity' single too.

Junkyard Angel (2 appearances) 15-01-71, 18-04-72

Just William (1 appearance) 28-12-68

Justine (3 appearances) 25-05-70, 27-07-70, 31-08-70

K

Kahn (1 appearance) 02-07-71

Kahva Jute (1 appearance) 22-10-71

Kala (1 appearance) 25-03-73

Karakorum (3 appearances) 17-12-70, 14-01-71, 09-03-71

Karass (1 appearance) 03-02-74

Billy Karloff (1 appearance) 20-12-79

Woody Kearn (3 appearances) 02-12-68, 09-01-69, 24-01-69

Jo Ann Kelly (7 appearances) 30-04-67, 10-09-69, 07-09-69, 21-09-69, 27-11-69, 10-01-70, 30-06-74

Jonathan Kelly (2 appearances) 03-09-71, 16-12-71

Jonathan Kelly's Outside (7 appearances) 31-01-74, 04-07-74, 12-09-74, 26-09-74, 06-10-74, 03-11-74, 11-12-74

Tony Kelly (1 appearance) 19-08-74

Kenny (1 appearance) 04-05-79

Kent PC (1 appearance) 10-03-70

Richard Kent (2 appearances) 24-03-67, 24-07-67

Key Largo (1 appearance) 17-07-70

Khan (2 appearances) 28-09-71, 17-12-71

Greg Kihn (2 appearances) 07-12-77, 21-05-79

Kilburn & The High Roads (5 appearances) 10-01-75, 18-02-75, 24-03-75, 18-02-76, 29-04-76
Ian Dury demolished the Roads in summer '76, forming The Blockheads a year later.

Killer (5 appearances) 16-04-77, 28-05-77, 12-06-78, 13-06-78, 14-06-78

Killing Floor (7 appearances) 28-01-69, 12-03-69, 19-06-69, 23-05-71, 22-12-71, 04-02-72, 17-03-72,

The Killjoys (3 appearances) 21-10-77, 30-01-78, 23-06-78

Kinane (1 appearance) 14-10-72

Ben E King (2 appearances) 31-05-66, 30-10-67

King Biscuit Boy (1 appearance) 29-10-71

King Crimson (17 appearances) 16-05-69, 25-05-69, 01-06-69, 08-06-69, 29-06-69, 06-07-69, 13-07-69, 20-07-69, 27-07-69, 03-08-69, 10-08-69, 17-08-69, 24-08-69, 09-08-71, 10-08-71, 10-02-73, 11-02-73

King Earle Boogie Band (2 appearances) 04-04-72, 12-05-72

Freddy King (4 appearances) 04-03-69, 19-06-69, 13-11-69

Ray King (1 appearance) 21-09-67

Kingfish (1 appearance) 19-08-77

Kippington Lodge (9 appearances) 21-09-68, 05-10-68, 17-10-68, 26-10-68, 07-06-69, 05-07-69, 16-07-69, 3-12-69, 20-12-69

Kircus (2 appearances) 16-12-75, 17-12-75

Kiss (3 appearances) 11-11-70, 22-01-71, 09-11-74

Kites (1 appearance) 06-04-77
Kleptomania (1 appearance) 09-02-75
The Klubs (2 appearances) 14-03-68, 03-05-69
The Knack (2 appearances) 25-05-79, 14-06-79
Tony Knight (1 appearance) 03-04-67
Krysia Kogan (3 appearances) 06-11-77, 09-11-77, 13-11-77
Korda Paul (1 appearance) 01-03-71
Korner Alexis (1 appearance) 06-04-62
Though it began in January, this was the only billed appearance of Korner and Cyril Davies's ground-breaking R&B interval act with Chris Barber's band. Previously, the Marquee had been strictly jazz-only.
Lee Kosmin (5 appearances) 11-11-76, 31-01-77, 06-03-77, 13-03-77, 08-05-77
Kraan (1 appearance) 29-10-75
Krakatoa (1 appearance) 05-05-76
Krazy Kat (4 appearances) 01-04-76, 16-02-77, 06-05-77, 01-03-78
Kripple Vision (2 appearances) 20-07-70, 21-10-70
Sonja Kristina (1 appearance) 12-07-78
David Kubinec (2 appearances) 16-12-78, 26-01-79
Kursaal Flyers (6 appearances) 10-03-75, 09-06-75, 21-07-75, 22-09-7, 15-10-75, 13-01-76
Kursaals (2 appearances) 03-05-77, 04-05-77
KY & The Kays (1 appearance) 01-12-79

L

LA (1 appearance) 07-09-70
Patti La Belle (1 appearance) 17-05-66
Lace (1 appearance) 09-01-70
Denny Laine & His Electric String Band (2 appearances) 08-06-67, 08-09-67
Laine had left The Moody Blues to form this novel amplified-strings band (well before ELO). He later joined McCartney's Wings.
Lake (1 appearance) 19-05-77
Lambrettas (1 appearance) 22-09-79
Lancaster (2 appearances) 02-04-71, 20-05-71
Land (1 appearance) 14-09-72
Ronnie Lane (2 appearances) 03-12-74, 04-12-74
The Late Show (2 appearances) 14-01-78, 22-04-78
Reg Law (1 appearance) 28-07-79
Paul Layton (1 appearance) 30-04-67
Le Gay (2 appearances) 16-06-67, 24-02-68
Leaf Hound (1 appearance) 10-05-71
Their classic heavy-rock Decca LP of that year, "Growers Of Mushroom", is a record-collector's dream these days.
Led Zeppelin (4 appearances) 18-10-68, 10-12-68, 28-03-69, 23-03-71
That first date was billed (see p110) as "The British debut of The Yardbirds" but someone had left out the word "New". Soon they were plain old Led Zeppelin. The '71 date was a "let's go back to the small clubs" scheme. Bloody crowded, they say.
Barry Lee (1 appearance) 15-10-66
Freddie Lee (1 appearance) 27-09-71
Robert Lee (1 appearance) 19-11-71
The Mark Leeman Five (74 appearances) 13-04-64, 01-06-64, 08-06-64, 15-06-64, 22-06-64, 29-06-64, 06-07-64, 31-08-64, 02-11-64, 09-11-64, 16-11-64, 07-12-64, 14-12-64, 21-

12-64, 28-12-64, 04-01-65, 11-01-65, 18-01-65, 25-01-65, 01-02-65, 22-02-65, 01-03-65, 08-03-65, 15-03-65, 22-03-65, 29-03-65, 19-04-65, 26-04-65, 03-05-65, 11-05-65, 18-05-65, 25-05-65, 08-06-65, 15-06-65, 29-06-65, 06-07-65, 13-07-65, 20-07-65, 03-08-65, 10-08-65, 17-08-65, 24-08-65, 31-08-65, 07-09-65, 4-09-65, 21-09-65, 27-09-65, 12-10-65, 19-10-65, 26-10-65, 02-11-65, 09-11-65, 16-11-65, 09-12-65, 14-12-65, 21-12-65, 28-12-65, 31-12-65, 03-01-66, 10-01-66, 24-01-66, 14-02-66, 21-02-66, 28-02-66, 10-03-66, 17-03-66, 24-03-66, 30-03-66, 07-04-66, 14-04-66, 21-04-66, 28-04-66, 05-05-66, 16-05-66
Well in the Top 10 for most-appearances-at-the-Marquee, the MLF played a popular jazz-flavoured R&B. The band continued in name after Leeman (John Ardrey) was killed in a car smash in 1965.
Eric Leese (1 appearance) 16-07-70
Legend (2 appearances) 09-11-70, 07-03-71
Les E'Lite (1 appearance) 16-06-79
Les Flambeaux (1 appearance) 12-06-71
Levi & The Rockats (1 appearance) 25-04-78
Leviathan (5 appearances) 15-05-69, 18-06-69, 12-07-69, 23-07-69, 07-08-69
Levinsky (1 appearance) 15-03-73
Dave Lewis (5 appearances) 15-04-78, 03-11-78, 19-01-79, 02-02-79, 23-02-79
Lew Lewis Reformer (5 appearances) 08-04-79, 30-04-79, 30-08-79, 31-08-79, 31-12-79
Ex-Eddie & The Hot Rods R&B harp-man.
Linda Lewis (1 appearance) 20-10-71
Leyton Buzzards (1 appearance) 27-03-79
Life Blud (1 appearance) 28-03-72
Lifetime (1 appearance) 06-10-70
Drummer Tony Williams; bassist Jack Bruce; guitarist John McLaughlin; wonderfully wild.
Lightnin' Slim (2 appearances) 25-02-72, 09-06-72
Lightning Raiders (1 appearance) 23-06-79
Lindisfarne (5 appearances) 20-09-70, 13-10-70, 03-11-70, 05-07-71, 0-09-71
Lionheart (1 appearance) 02-09-78
Listen (3 appearances) 23-04-72, 11-06-72, 5-06-72
Little Acre (1 appearance) 07-10-76
Little Big Band (1 appearance) 11-09-73
Little Bo Bitch (8 appearances) 18-11-78, 08-01-79, 04-02-79, 11-02-79, 18-02-79, 25-02-79, 06-07-79, 06-11-79
Little Bob Story (5 appearances) 02-04-76, 10-06-76, 26-11-76, 01-03-77, 11-07-77
Little Free Rock (12 appearances) 08-01-70, 18-05-70, 24-06-70, 16-12-70, 30-12-70, 20-01-71, 07-03-71, 21-03-71, 28-03-71, 04-04-71, 11-04-71, 18-04-71
Little River Band (1 appearance) 08-10-76
Little Rooster (2 appearances) 16-06-79, 31-12-79
Little Walter (1 appearance) 01-10-64
Live Wire (2 appearances) 28-08-79, 29-12-79
Liverpool Scene (4 appearances) 14-07-69, 28-07-69, 10-03-70, 14-04-70
Focusing on the poetry of Adrian Henri, the Scene also included musicians such as saxman Mike Evans, who later became the Musicians Union's first Rock Organiser.

Ian Lloyd (3 appearances) 22-09-67, 13-10-67, 27-10-67
Local Operator (1 appearance) 18-03-79
Lockjaw (1 appearance) 27-02-71
Gerry Lockran (2 appearances) 16-11-66, 07-12-66
Locomotive (2 appearances) 06-02-69, 11-03-69
Locomotive GT (1 appearance) 08-06-74
Locus (1 appearance) 21-01-76
Jackie Lomax (1 appearance) 11-06-70
Apple Records signing Lomax had an LP out the previous year that featured three Beatles and a Clapton. Did any of them turn up to this Marquee gig, perchance?
London (2 appearances) 26-02-68, 08-12-77
London, live...
London Zoo (1 appearance) 30-11-79
Long Vehicle (1 appearance) 01-12-74
The Longboatmen (1 appearance) 29-11-66
Longdancer (2 appearances) 09-11-73, 07-06-74
The Look (7 appearances) 06-02-78, 08-04-78, 18-04-78, 05-05-78, 12-05-78, 18-05-78, 26-05-78
Loose Ends (3 appearances) 29-03-66, 26-05-66, 09-09-66
Lots (1 appearance) 13-09-68
The Love Affair (14 appearances) 18-02-67, 08-04-67, 03-06-67, 17-06-67, 08-07-67, 27-07-67, 17-08-67, 31-08-67, 14-09-67, 28-09-67, 26-10-67, 16-11-67, 21-11-67, 17-07-70
Love Sculpture (10 appearances) 20-09-68, 01-10-68, 16-10-68, 22-10-68, 13-11-68, 20-11-68, 06-12-68, 04-02-69, 01-04-69, 19-08-69
Lovin' Spoonful (1 appearance) 18-04-66
Loving Awareness (7 appearances) 02-09-76, 22-09-76, 01-10-76, 29-10-76, 11-11-76, 08-12-76, 24-12-76
Lulu & The Luvvers (1 appearance) 24-08-65
The Lurkers (12 appearances) 24-06-77, 29-07-77, 03-11-77, 05-02-78, 19-02-78, 20-04-78, 28-05-78, 29-05-78, 07-11-79, 14-11-79, 21-11-79, 28-11-79
Don Lusher (1 appearance) 26-06-68
Luv Machine (1 appearance) 10-06-70
Jackie Lynton (7 appearances) 08-10-74, 31-01-75, 06-03-75, 30-09-76, 19-04-77, 07-06-77, 01-09-78

M

Mabel Greer's Toyshop (4 appearances) 09-12-67, 01-01-68, 20-01-68, 02-05-68
Anderson, Banks and Squire formed Yes a month after this last date.
The Maddening Crowd (3 appearances) 06-05-69, 24-05-69, 28-05-69
Made In Sweden (2 appearances) 18-11-69, 05-08-70
The Magazine (1 appearance) 02-06-71
Maggot (1 appearance) 16-11-70
Magic (1 appearance) 05-10-74
Magma (2 appearances) 05-12-73, 17-03-74
Magna Carta (11 appearances) 12-10-69, 28-12-69, 04-01-70, 11-01-70, 18-02-70, 15-04-70, 14-03-75, 10-04-75, 30-05-75, 22-01-76, 17-03-76

Magnets (1 appearance) 20-01-79
Magnum (1 appearance) 15-12-79
The Magnums (1 appearance) 22-04-79
Mahatma (22 appearances) 24-02-73, 03-03-73, 10-03-73, 07-04-73, 12-05-73, 26-05-73, 02-06-73, 16-06-73, 09-07-73, 16-07-73, 23-07-73, 12-08-73, 02-09-73, 09-09-73, 01-11-73, 18-11-73, 06-01-74, 19-01-74, 15-02-74, 27-02-74, 24-03-74, 19-04-74
Mahatma Kane Jeeves (27 appearances) 25-04-72, 01-06-72, 22-06-72, 06-07-72, 20-07-72, 27-07-72, 03-08-72, 10-08-72, 17-08-72, 31-08-72, 07-09-72, 14-09-72, 28-09-72, 05-10-72, 19-10-72, 11-11-72, 18-11-72, 25-11-72, 09-12-72, 16-12-72, 23-12-72, 30-12-72, 06-01-73, 13-01-73, 20-01-73, 27-01-73, 17-02-73
Mahjun (1 appearance) 01-05-76
Main Horse Airline (2 appearances) 15-12-79, 02-04-72
Major Bull (1 appearance) 14-08-76
Major Wiley (2 appearances) 07-07-72, 09-08-77
Majority (3 appearances) 15-07-66, 02-12-66, 20-02-67
Man (7 appearances) 05-06-69, 11-08-69, 05-09-69, 26-12-69, 28-01-71, 27-08-71, 24-07-72
Mandragon (2 appearances) 02-07-70, 02-09-70
Mandrake (3 appearances) 30-12-69, 27-01-71, 21-03-71
At one time featured vocalist Robert Palmer.
Mandrake Paddlesteamer (2 appearances) 10-05-69, 25-06-69
Manfred Mann (102 appearances) 09-12-62, 18-03-63, 25-03-63, 01-04-63, 08-04-63, 15-04-63, 22-04-63, 29-04-63, 06-05-63, 13-05-63, 27-05-63, 03-06-63, 10-06-63, 17-06-63, 24-06-63, 01-07-63, 08-07-63, 15-07-63, 22-07-63, 29-07-63, 05-08-63, 12-08-63, 19-08-63, 19-08-63, 26-08-63, 26-08-63, 02-09-63, 09-09-63, 16-09-63, 23-09-63, 30-09-63, 07-10-63, 14-10-63, 21-10-63, 28-10-63, 04-11-63, 11-11-63, 18-11-63, 25-11-63, 02-12-63, 09-12-63, 16-12-63, 23-12-63, 30-12-63, 06-01-64, 13-01-64, 20-01-64, 27-01-64, 10-02-64, 30-03-64, 06-04-64, 13-04-64, 20-04-64, 04-05-64, 11-05-64, 18-05-64, 08-06-64, 15-06-64, 22-06-64, 29-06-64, 06-07-64, 20-07-64, 27-07-64, 10-08-64, 17-08-64, 24-08-64, 31-08-64, 07-09-64, 14-09-64, 21-09-64, 28-09-64, 05-10-64, 12-10-64, 19-10-64, 26-10-64, 02-11-64, 09-11-64, 16-11-64, 30-11-64, 28-12-64, 15-03-65, 05-04-65, 12-04-65, 11-05-65, 24-05-65, 19-07-65, 17-08-65, 14-09-65, 26-10-65, 28-12-65, 25-01-66, 01-03-66, 12-04-66, 07-06-66, 29-11-66, 07-05-68, 12-10-71, 07-12-71, 18-12-73, 19-04-76, 20-04-76, 21-04-76
The later dates are for his Earthband, but however you count it that Mr Mann is according to our calculations well in the lead for most-appearances-at-the-Marquee.
Mankind (1 appearance) 24-04-79
Mantis (6 appearances) 21-04-75, 13-03-76, 08-05-76, 10-07-76, 11-09-76, 25-09-76
Maran Mark (3 appearances) 18-09-73, 29-09-72, 25-02-74
March Hare (5 appearances) 27-12-71, 29-02-72, 14-10-72, 02-12-72, 05-05-73
Marmalade (42 appearances) 19-01-67, 03-02-67, 16-03-67, 23-03-67, 30-03-67, 06-04-67, 13-04-67, 04-05-67, 11-05-67, 18-05-67, 01-06-67, 15-06-

67, 29-06-67, 06-07-67, 13-07-67, 20-07-67, 27-07-67, 03-08-67, 10-08-67, 17-08-67, 24-08-67, 31-08-67, 14-09-67, 21-09-67, 28-09-67, 26-10-67, 30-11-67, 31-12-67, 11-01-68, 01-02-68, 29-02-68, 21-03-68, 18-04-68, 23-05-68, 13-06-68, 27-06-68, 27-08-68, 21-01-69, 15-07-69, 02-05-72, 06-08-73, 29-10-73

Marseilles (1 appearance) 05-04-78
John Martyn (2 appearances) 07-09-77, 08-09-77
Brett Marvin (14 appearances) 07-09-69, 21-09-69, 11-02-72, 31-03-72, 30-06-72, 28-07-72, 27-04-73, 21-09-73, 18-01-74, 04-04-74, 17-05-74, 21-07-74, 22-09-74, 31-10-74
Mason Alley (2 appearances) 25-01-72, 21-03-72
Masterswitch (2 appearances) 26-03-77, 09-07-77
Matt Black Sunday (1 appearance) 10-04-76
Al Matthews (5 appearances) 10-07-72, 28-08-72, 23-12-72, 20-02-73, 25-09-73
Matthews Southern Comfort (1 appearance) 28-03-70
This was two months after Ian Matthews' post-Fairport group released its first LP, with Gordon Huntley on pedal-steel guitar.
May Blitz (3 appearances) 31-01-70, 13-07-70, 11-10-70
John Mayall's Bluesbreakers (42 appearances) 04-11-63, 18-11-63, 02-12-63, 16-12-63, 30-12-63, 03-02-64, 17-02-64, 24-02-64, 23-03-64, 06-04-64, 27-04-64, 11-05-64, 18-05-64, 10-08-64, 11-04-66, 30-05-66, 11-06-66, 25-07-66, 15-08-66, 03-09-66, 04-10-66, 11-11-66, 08-12-66, 27-12-66, 30-01-67, 16-02-67, 12-03-67, 27-04-67, 16-05-67, 26-06-67, 28-08-67, 31-10-67, 26-12-67, 13-02-68, 26-03-68, 16-04-68, 28-05-68, 18-06-68, 13-08-68, 02-01-69, 30-06-69
The British School Of Bluesbreaking. The first date here had Mayall plus John McVie on bass, Bernie Watson on guitar and Martin Hunt on drums. You'd have seen drummer Hughie Flint and Clapton by the April '66 gig; Peter Green and Aynsley Dunbar on board from the later summer '66 dates; and Mick Taylor and Keef Hartley from summer '67 — along with loads of other chaps coming and going, of course.
Mayfields Mule (1 appearance) 19-06-70
MC5 (1 appearance) 31-07-70
John McCoy (1 appearance) 24-09-66
Country Joe McDonald (1 appearance) 10-11-74
Shelagh McDonald (1 appearance) 23-09-70
McGuinness Flint (6 appearances) 20-03-73, 21-04-73, 13-07-73, 19-09-73, 22-05-74, 15-12-74
McKenna Mendelson Mainline (1 appearance) 29-05-69
Andy McKinley (5 appearances) 02-04-64, 09-04-64, 16-04-64, 24-04-64, 30-04-64
Sandy McLelland (3 appearances) 05-07-78, 06-07-78, 17-09-78
Meal Ticket (9 appearances) 28-11-76, 29-12-76, 16-03-77, 07-04-77, 07-04-77, 06-06-77, 09-03-78, 10-03-78, 09-07-78
Mean Street (2 appearances) 03-09-77, 05-11-77
Media (1 appearance) 16-09-78
Medicine Hat (1 appearance) 29-11-69
Medicine Head (26 appearances) 06-07-70, 21-12-70, 19-02-71, 21-05-71,

22-06-71, 17-08-71, 01-09-72, 03-10-72, 13-04-73, 01-06-73, 14-04-74, 15-04-74, 20-12-74, 28-01-75, 14-04-75, 10-06-75, 22-07-75, 11-09-75, 11-09-75, 21-10-75, 17-12-75, 04-05-76, 14-09-76, 04-01-77, 03-02-77, 17-05-77
The Mekons (1 appearance) 09-10-79
The Members (8 appearances) 22-10-77, 27-11-77, 21-02-78, 16-05-78, 02-03-79, 03-03-79, 20-09-79, 21-09-79
Included drummer Adrian Lillywhite, brother of producer Steve Lillywhite who made great records with XTC, Peter Gabriel, The Psychedelic Furs, Talking Heads and more.
Memphis Slim (3 appearances) 21-05-64, 23-05-64, 27-05-65
Menace (1 appearance) 21-12-77
Meridian (2 appearances) 10-12-71, 08-01-77
Merlin (1 appearance) 09-12-71
Max Merritt (4 appearances) 30-05-71, 22-10-71, 02-12-71, 08-08-75
Merton Parkas (7 appearances) 31-07-79, 29-08-79, 2-09-79, 9-09-79, 27-09-79, 07-12-79, 08-12-79
Metro (2 appearances) 05-02-77, 02-12-79
MI-Five (3 appearances) 08-09-66, 03-10-66, 14-11-66
Michigan Rag (2 appearances) 07-04-72, 23-06-72
Migil Five (2 appearances) 27-04-64, 25-05-64
Miller Brothers (1 appearance) 03-06-71
Steve Miller's Delivery (3 appearances) 09-12-68, 21-12-68, 11-05-69
Keysman Miller went on to Caravan, drummer Pip Pyle to Hatfield & The North.
Million (3 appearances) 04-10-71, 05-10-71, 08-02-72
A Million People (1 appearance) 17-02-73
Probably not.
The Mirage (1 appearance) 04-02-67
Mirrors (3 appearances) 22-06-70, 24-08-70, 14-10-70
Mr Big (5 appearances) 16-03-74, 10-02-76, 11-06-76, 26-01-77, 07-07-77
Mr Fox (1 appearance) 19-08-70
Mr Moses Schoolband (1 appearance) 31-10-71
Mr Proud (1 appearance) 27-11-70
Sammy Mitchell (1 appearance) 21-07-76
Mixed Media (16 appearances) 01-10-69, 08-10-69, 15-10-69, 22-10-69, 29-10-69, 05-11-69, 11-11-69, 18-11-69, 25-11-69, 03-12-69, 10-12-69, 17-12-69, 07-01-70, 14-01-70, 21-01-70, 28-01-70
Mobile (1 appearance) 22-11-79
The Mods (1 appearance) 15-06-79
Zoot Money (5 appearances) 25-11-63, 23-12-63, 16-03-64, 17-01-67, 28-01-72, 17-11-74, 08-01-78
One of the R&B organ chiefs who, with the Big Roll Band earlier on, spent more of his time at the Flamingo than here.
Albert Monk (1 appearance) 02-09-71
Mono (1 appearance) 05-05-78
The Monopoly (1 appearance) 15-07-67
Monotone (1 appearance) 30-11-77
Montana Red (3 appearances) 28-05-76, 20-06-76, 28-05-77
The Mooche (5 appearances) 17-07-69, 21-08-69, 06-09-69, 09-10-69, 15-11-69
The Moody Blues (19 appearances) 03-09-64, 11-09-64, 24-09-64, 04-10-64, 23-11-64, 07-12-64, 14-12-64, 21-12-64, 04-01-65, 08-02-65, 22-02-65,

22-03-65, 19-04-65, 10-05-65, 01-06-65, 23-07-65, 31-08-65, 28-09-65, 08-10-68
The Brum boys recorded their first hit, 'Go Now', in the recently opened Marquee studio around the back of the club.
Moon (8 appearances) 10-03-76, 29-06-76, 20-07-76, 27-08-76, 13-09-76, 21-12-76, 01-02-77, 24-05-77
Moon Martin (2 appearances) 23-11-79, 24-11-79
Moonrider (3 appearances) 12-12-74, 08-08-75, 16-10-75
Gary Moore (9 appearances) 28-02-72, 08-05-72, 22-05-72, 17-07-72, 31-07-72, 19-07-73, 23-09-73, 14-10-73, 30-12-73
G.T. Moore (4 appearances) 05-08-74, 14-10-74, 06-04-75, 29-05-75
Morgan (23 appearances) 03-09-71, 11-10-71, 25-10-71, 04-11-71, 11-11-71, 18-11-71, 25-11-71, 16-12-71, 30-12-71, 13-01-72, 27-01-72, 02-02-72, 21-02-72, 02-03-72, 23-03-72, 06-04-72, 15-05-72, 12-06-72, 09-11-72, 16-11-72, 23-11-72, 30-11-72, 07-12-72
John Morgan (36 appearances) 11-11-67, 19-01-68, 16-02-68, 08-03-68, 12-04-68, 04-05-68, 31-05-68, 11-10-68, 25-10-68, 22-11-68, 13-12-68, 28-11-68, 13-12-68, 27-12-68, 14-02-69, 19-02-69, 25-02-69, 18-03-69, 07-04-69, 17-04-69, 01-05-69, 21-05-69, 04-06-69, 18-06-69, 26-06-69, 03-07-69, 10-07-69, 17-07-69, 31-07-69, 08-08-69, 22-08-69, 11-09-69, 02-12-69, 15-01-70, 30-03-70, 15-04-70
The very first date was keyboardist/vocalist John Morgan's Blues Band; thereafter it was mostly The Spirit Of John Morgan, a strongly blues-based outfit popular at the Marquee — as this datelist testifies.
Morning (2 appearances) 12-03-70, 17-04-70
Dick Morrisey (2 appearances) 11-05-68, 21-05-68
Mortimer (1 appearance) 30-01-69
The Motels (1 appearance) 12-10-79
Mother Sun (3 appearances) 10-05-74, 17-08-74, 05-10-74
Mother Superior (1 appearance) 11-11-75
Mothers Pride (3 appearances) 30-03-74, 18-05-74, 16-11-74
The Motivation (2 appearances) 06-02-67, 06-03-67
Motorhead (5 appearances) 21-08-75, 12-11-75, 18-11-76, 28-01-77, 01-04-77
The Motors (10 appearances) 07-03-77, 22-07-77, 09-05-77, 21-09-77, 28-09-77, 05-10-77, 12-10-77, 22-12-77, 23-12-77, 25-08-78
Mott The Hoople (2 appearances) 30-09-70, 19-01-71
Mount (1 appearance) 16-04-77
Mountain Ash (1 appearance) 19-06-76
Mouse & The Traps (1 appearance) 20-04-69
The Move (27 appearances) 01-04-66, 07-04-66, 13-05-66, 20-05-66, 20-06-66, 23-06-66, 07-07-66, 14-07-66, 21-07-66, 28-07-66, 04-08-66, 11-08-66, 18-08-66, 25-08-66, 08-09-66, 15-09-66, 22-09-66, 29-09-66, 06-10-66, 13-10-66, 20-10-66, 27-10-66, 17-11-66, 24-11-66, 11-07-67, 19-09-67, 27-02-68
The Movies (5 appearances) 20-02-75, 04-07-78, 15-08-78, 27-10-78, 26-03-79
The Moving People (1 appearance) 05-03-67

Mox & John LaMont (1 appearance) 30-08-67
Mucky Duck (3 appearances) 03-10-70, 31-10-70, 07-11-70
Mud (5 appearances) 25-08-67, 23-09-67, 30-12-67, 30-03-68, 12-06-68
Early appearances by Les Gray's pop group which later had a series of hits, notably 'Tiger Feet' in 1974.
Muddy Waters (2 appearances) 12-11-68, 19-11-68
Curtis Muldoon (3 appearances) 05-08-71, 17-09-71, 16-02-72
Muleskinners (5 appearances) 12-11-64, 23-11-64, 04-12-64, 08-01-65, 01-06-65
If you picked up a copy of their privately-pressed "Muleskinners" EP on that last date, you'd have a valuable item today. Pianist Ian McLagan went on to join The Small Faces in summer 1965.
Mumma Bear (1 appearance) 22-05-71
Mungo Jerry (5 appearances) 27-04-70, 06-04-71, 29-06-71, 05-06-77, 28-11-77
Muscles (5 appearances) 20-05-72, 10-01-77, 17-01-77, 24-01-77, 31-01-77
The Mushrooms (2 appearances) 15-05-68, 16-06-68
Music (1 appearance) 08-06-72
My Cake (2 appearances) 16-02-70, 27-05-70
My Dear Watson (1 appearance) 26-04-69
The Mylton Rhode (1 appearance) 17-02-68
Mynd (2 appearances) 07-06-75, 05-07-75
Mythica (1 appearance) 06-05-71

N

Napoleon (2 appearances) 02-05-70, 11-07-70
Nashville Teens (2 appearances) 05-09-70, 28-04-76
Nasty Pop (3 appearances) 27-01-77, 10-03-77, 20-04-77
National Anthem (1 appearance) 19-04-71
National Flag (20 appearances) 02-04-75, 24-04-75, 25-04-75, 24-05-75, 22-06-75, 29-06-75, 06-07-75, 13-07-75, 20-07-75, 22-08-75, 18-09-75, 10-10-75, 27-11-75, 11-12-75, 16-01-76, 19-02-76, 05-03-76, 26-03-76, 30-04-76, 28-05-76
National Head Band (1 appearance) 20-10-71
Natural Acoustic Band (3 appearances) 17-11-71, 12-04-72, 22-11-72
Navy Blue (1 appearance) 16-01-68
Nazareth (11 appearances) 21-09-71, 12-11-71, 18-01-72, 03-05-72, 05-06-72, 14-08-72, 21-11-72, 19-12-72, 25-01-73, 14-03-73, 10-04-73
The Neat Change (40 appearances) 10-12-66, 24-12-66, 31-12-66, 07-01-67, 14-01-67, 21-01-67, 28-01-67, 04-02-67, 11-02-67, 18-02-67, 25-02-67, 02-03-67, 31-03-67, 08-05-67, 22-05-67, 22-06-67, 14-10-67, 21-10-67, 28-10-67, 04-11-67, 11-11-67, 18-11-67, 25-11-67, 02-12-67, 09-12-67, 16-12-67, 23-12-67, 30-12-67, 25-01-68, 05-02-68, 19-02-68, 13-05-68, 08-06-68, 06-07-68, 13-07-68, 20-07-68, 27-07-68, 03-08-68, 10-08-68, 17-08-68
Guitarist Pete Banks, later of Yes, was a Neat Changer at one point.

Nelson (1 appearance) 18-08-71

Neo (4 appearances) 02-07-77, 14-07-77, 02-11-77, 24-04-78

Neon Hearts (1 appearance) 13-01-79

The Neutrons (1 appearance) 22-05-75

The New Hearts (10 appearances) 16-08-77, 17-10-77, 14-11-77, 23-01-78, 10-02-78, 13-04-78, 28-04-78, 27-06-78, 14-07-78, 09-08-78

The New Nadir (7 appearances) 22-12-67, 13-02-68, 04-03-68, 22-03-68, 09-04-68, 19-04-68, 03-05-68

New Paths (14 appearances) 25-05-69, 01-06-69, 08-06-69, 06-07-69, 13-07-69, 20-07-69, 27-07-69, 06-08-69, 13-08-69, 20-08-69, 03-09-69, 10-09-69, 17-09-69, 24-09-69

The New Songs (9 appearances) 07-06-67, 14-06-67, 21-06-67, 28-06-67, 05-07-67, 12-07-67, 19-07-67, 26-07-67, 02-08-67

The News (7 appearances) 26-04-78, 29-04-78, 15-06-78, 22-06-78, 15-07-78, 30-09-78, 06-10-79

Next (1 appearance) 02-06-78

The Nice (32 appearances) 02-10-67, 16-10-67, 24-10-67, 06-11-67, 13-11-67, 27-11-67, 18-12-67, 01-01-68, 08-01-68, 15-01-68, 22-01-68, 26-02-68, 04-03-68, 11-03-68, 18-03-68, 25-03-68, 01-04-68, 11-04-68, 26-04-68, 02-05-68, 21-05-68, 06-06-68, 20-06-68, 04-07-68, 18-07-68, 08-08-68, 22-08-68, 05-09-68, 19-09-68, 05-11-68, 28-01-69, 10-06-69

Barely a month old on their Marquee debut, The Nice had previously acted as backing group to singer P.P. Arnold, but now Keith Emerson (keys), Brian Davison (perc), Lee Jackson (bass) and David O'list (gtr) set their own course. O'List was out by the September '68 dates and they continued as a trio, with Emerson becoming increasingly unfriendly toward his organ.

Nichelson (1 appearance) 04-05-72

Nico (2 appearances) 08-05-78, 09-05-78

Nicol & Marsh (1 appearance) 11-05-75

Nicol & Marsh Easy Street (1 appearance) 26-01-75

Nigger (3 appearances) 02-05-71, 16-05-71, 30-05-71

The Night Shift (7 appearances) 03-08-64, 03-09-64, 24-09-64, 08-10-64, 16-10-64, 30-10-64, 19-11-64

Nighthawks (2 appearances) 21-01-72, 24-03-72

Nimbo (1 appearance) 05-03-71

Nimbus (1 appearance) 06-11-71

999 (9 appearances) 09-09-77, 31-05-79, 01-06-79, 02-06-79, 01-10-79, 02-10-79, 03-10-79, 04-10-79, 05-10-79

9.30 Fly (2 appearances) 20-06-71, 17-10-71

The Nips (1 appearance) 02-11-79

The Nite People (32 appearances) 05-12-66, 23-12-66, 01-01-67, 16-03-67, 13-04-67, 15-05-67, 22-05-67, 06-06-67, 04-07-67, 13-07-67, 25-07-67, 19-08-67, 11-09-67, 02-10-67, 23-10-67, 07-11-67, 13-11-67, 12-12-67, 31-12-67, 02-01-68, 29-01-68, 20-02-68, 07-03-68, 08-04-68, 22-04-68, 06-05-68, 20-05-68, 10-06-68, 01-07-68, 15-07-68, 05-08-68, 19-08-68

No Dice (11 appearances) 22-05-76, 21-04-77, 01-07-77, 15-09-77, 12-12-77, 06-01-78, 09-02-78, 30-11-78, 30-12-78, 06-03-79, 11-10-79

Noakes Rab (1 appearance) 20-09-72

Noir (1 appearance) 23-07-70

Nothineverappens (1 appearance) 17-10-71

Nova (5 appearances) 04-01-76, 11-01-76, 18-01-76, 25-01-76, 11-03-77

Nova Carmina (1 appearance) 01-07-70

November (1 appearance) 24-02-72

Nucleus (12 appearances) 23-01-70, 30-01-70, 06-03-70, 14-03-70, 21-03-70, 03-04-70, 24-04-70, 01-05-70, 30-04-71, 16-12-73, 07-11-75, 04-02-76

Nutz (16 appearances) 17-10-74, 22-01-75, 21-02-75, 24-04-75, 24-07-75, 29-08-75, 30-09-75, 28-10-75, 27-01-76, 17-02-76, 05-07-76, 22-10-76, 02-12-76, 12-04-77, 07-06-77, 12-07-77

NW10 (2 appearances) 22-02-78, 11-12-78

O

Object (1 appearance) 08-04-72

The Objects (5 appearances) 17-03-66, 14-04-66, 29-04-66, 03-06-66, 29-07-66

The Occasional Word (1 appearance) 01-10-69

Phil Ochs (1 appearance) 08-12-65
Rare UK appearance by the great American folk-singer who probably sang songs like 'Draft Dodger Rag' at this date. In 1976 Ochs commited suicide in New York at the age of 36.

Octopus (7 appearances) 30-11-68, 01-01-69, 18-01-69, 12-02-69, 15-02-69, 12-04-69, 28-06-69

Odd Fox (1 appearance) 20-11-71

Old Nick (1 appearance) 11-11-71

David O'List (2 appearances) 21-01-71, 29-01-71

On (2 appearances) 04-06-71, 26-09-71

One Night Stand (1 appearance) 22-07-72

The One (3 appearances) 29-03-75, 11-04-75, 25-04-75

1-2-3 (7 appearances) 11-03-67, 18-03-67, 25-03-67, 07-04-67, 28-04-67, 12-05-67, 25-05-67

The Only Ones (2 appearances) 01-10-77, 13-03-78

Opal Butterfly (1 appearance) 24-09-71

The Open Mind (19 appearances) 21-10-67, 04-11-67, 13-11-67, 05-12-67, 23-12-67, 06-01-68, 15-01-68, 03-02-68, 19-02-68, 09-03-68, 21-03-68, 22-04-68, 27-07-68, 15-08-68, 21-08-68, 31-08-68, 14-09-68, 01-09-69, 25-09-69

Open Road (1 appearance) 15-10-71

Oppo (6 appearances) 09-09-76, 03-10-76, 25-10-76, 25-11-76, 11-12-76, 24-12-76

The Opposition (1 appearance) 19-06-79

Orange (5 appearances) 28-09-74, 30-11-74, 25-01-75, 19-04-75, 28-06-75

Orange Bicycle (1 appearance) 24-09-67

Orange Blossom (1 appearance) 01-04-70

Origin (3 appearances) 04-07-71, 15-07-71, 26-09-71

Original Mirrors (2 appearances) 01-11-79, 15-11-79

Orme (1 appearance) 11-11-73

Orphan (2 appearances) 24-08-72, 03-02-73

The Orphans (1 appearance) 02-05-78

Osborne's Greep (2 appearances) 02-03-74, 10-05-74

Oscar (1 appearance) 28-01-76

Osibisa (1 appearance) 12-07-70

John Otway (1 appearance) 08-06-77

Out Of Nowhere (1 appearance) 12-09-78

The Outpatients (1 appearance) 12-08-79

The Outsiders (1 appearance) 07-03-69

Overtown (7 appearances) 24-12-74, 15-01-75, 29-01-75, 12-02-75, 26-02-75, 13-04-75, 27-04-75

Oxo Whitney (1 appearance) 28-06-73

Ozo (1 appearance) 15-04-78

P

Pacific Drift (1 appearance) 29-05-70

Pacific Eardrum (2 appearances) 12-03-78, 16-08-78

Palm Beach Express (12 appearances) 25-01-75, 22-03-75, 17-05-75, 05-07-75, 30-08-75, 13-09-75, 01-02-76, 08-02-76, 15-02-76, 22-02-76, 29-02-76, 07-07-76

Palomino (1 appearance) 02-09-72

Panama Scandal (12 appearances) 12-09-76, 19-09-76, 09-11-76, 27-11-76, 13-12-76, 15-01-77, 06-02-77, 13-02-77, 20-02-77, 27-02-77, 11-04-77, 21-05-77

Pandemonium (2 appearances) 24-09-67, 27-04-68

Panties (1 appearance) 03-12-78

Paper Bubble (1 appearance) 22-06-69

Paradise (1 appearance) 08-06-75

Paris (1 appearance) 23-02-79

Bobby Parker (2 appearances) 19-11-68, 29-11-68

Graham Parker & The Rumour (2 appearances) 07-06-76, 08-06-76

The Parking Lot (1 appearance) 28-01-67

Patriarch of Glastonbury's Band (7 appearances) 15-02-71, 01-03-71, 05-04-71, 03-05-71, 07-06-71, 02-08-71, 06-09-71

Patto (21 appearances) 19-03-70, 07-04-70, 01-05-70, 09-06-70, 18-06-70, 21-08-70, 07-01-71, 15-03-71, 11-06-71, 30-07-71, 20-08-71, 05-09-71, 19-11-71, 01-05-72, 08-06-72, 20-08-72, 13-11-72, 22-12-72, 22-01-73, 04-02-73, 14-02-73
These dates span the life of Patto, a band that evolved from Timebox and included Mike Patto (vox) and Ollie Halsall (guitar).

The Paupers (1 appearance) 28-12-69

Peaches (2 appearances) 09-03-74, 25-05-74

Pegasus (17 appearances) 04-10-68, 23-10-68, 01-11-68, 08-11-68, 15-11-68, 25-11-68, 23-12-68, 17-01-69, 13-02-69, 21-02-69, 01-04-69, 19-04-69, 25-04-69, 17-05-69, 04-06-69, 24-06-69, 02-08-69

Penance Rock Mission (1 appearance) 04-09-71

Pendulum (1 appearance) 22-01-72

Penetration (4 appearances) 30-07-77, 31-07-77, 01-08-77, 21-06-78

Percy's Package (1 appearance) 29-01-79

Pere Ubu (2 appearances) 08-05-78, 09-05-78

Christine Perfect (1 appearance) 20-03-70

Perigeo (1 appearance) 17-03-75

Philharmonic Rock Duo (1 appearance) 03-08-72

Phoenix (1 appearance) 07-10-76

The Photos (2 appearances) 08-11-79, 29-11-79

Picadilly Line (17 appearances) 07-06-67, 14-06-67, 21-06-67, 28-06-67, 05-07-67, 12-07-67, 19-07-67, 26-07-67, 02-08-67, 09-08-67, 16-08-67, 23-08-67, 30-08-67, 06-09-67, 13-09-67, 20-09-67, 27-09-67
Yes, we know, but apparently that's how they spelled it.

Nick Pickett (19 appearances) 18-06-71, 30-08-71, 31-08-71, 14-09-71, 01-11-71, 13-12-71, 07-02-72, 14-02-72, 28-02-72, 22-05-72, 17-07-72, 31-07-72, 23-02-73, 13-04-73, 21-04-73, 29-10-74, 07-07-76, 10-05-77, 23-10-78

Pieces Fit (4 appearances) 01-04-72, 03-06-72, 08-07-72, 26-08-72

Piggy (1 appearance) 29-06-74

Pink Fairies (17 appearances) 03-07-70, 10-07-70, 26-01-71, 03-08-71, 23-07-71, 23-08-71, 23-12-71, 27-12-73, 07-02-74, 30-10-75, 29-12-75, 08-03-76, 09-03-76, 03-08-76, 10-02-77, 11-02-77

Pink Floyd (5 appearances) 22-12-66, 29-12-66, 05-01-67, 19-01-67, 09-03-67
These are the five billed Marquee shows given by the group, but earlier in 1966 they had also appeared at some private Sunday-afternoon multimedia events called Spontaneous Underground. For more details see page 80.

Pinpoint (4 appearances) 31-05-79, 01-06-79, 02-06-79, 17-11-79

The Piranhas (3 appearances) 28-01-78, 11-08-79, 30-10-79

The Pirates (11 appearances) 16-05-77, 15-12-77, 11-01-78, 24-03-78, 25-03-78, 28-08-78, 29-08-78, 30-08-78, 25-06-79, 26-06-79, 27-06-79

The Plague (1 appearance) 22-02-68

Plaincover (1 appearance) 30-04-72

Robert Plant (2 appearances) 08-02-68, 23-02-68

Planxty (1 appearance) 13-02-73

Plastix (1 appearance) 08-02-78

Playground (4 appearances) 02-07-67, 30-07-67, 27-08-67, 12-08-69

Martin Plum (1 appearance) 27-07-74

Plummet Airlines (9 appearances) 21-01-77, 20-03-77, 27-03-77, 03-04-77, 10-04-77, 17-04-77, 24-04-77, 17-06-77, 19-11-77

Pluto (1 appearance) 08-04-71

Poem (1 appearance) 25-09-72

Polecat (1 appearance) 15-08-76

The Police (4 appearances) 25-05-77, 24-06-77, 22-01-78, 09-09-78

Poodles (13 appearances) 03-05-75, 17-05-75, 26-07-75, 18-10-75, 02-11-75, 09-11-75, 16-11-75, 23-11-75, 30-11-75, 05-01-76, 01-03-76, 21-06-76, 18-07-76

Poor Son (1 appearance) 25-03-71

Poor Souls (1 appearance) 02-07-65

Pop Group (1 appearance) 17-08-77

John Potter (1 appearance) 19-12-78

Cozy Powell (2 appearances) 09-01-75, 15-05-75

Jimmy Powell & The Five Dimensions (4 appearances) 17-12-64, 21-01-65, 18-02-65, 14-08-67
Briefly in an earlier line-up was Rod Stewart before the wee lad was snaffled by Long John Baldry for his Hoochie Coochie Men.

Duffy Power (2 appearances) 04-11-66, 28-04-72
Tireless blues singer-guitarist-harpist.

Praeger & Rye (1 appearance) 03-03-72

Prairie Dog (1 appearance) 16-10-77

Praying Mantis (2 appearances) 19-10-79, 09-12-79

Prelude (1 appearance) 10-10-73

The Press (1 appearance) 05-05-79

The Pretenders (8 appearances) 02-04-79, 03-04-79, 22-10-79, 29-10-79, 05-11-79, 12-11-79, 22-12-79, 23-12-79

Pretty Things (1 appearance) 24-08-72

Alan Price (11 appearances) 05-10-65, 11-11-65, 25-11-65, 09-12-65, 16-12-65, 04-01-66, 20-01-66, 17-02-66, 24-05-66, 05-07-66, 20-09-66

Price Red (4 appearances) 04-02-64, 11-02-64, 18-02-64, 25-02-64

Pride & Joy Buzz Band (4 appearances) 15-02-68, 07-12-67, 04-01-68, 18-01-68

The Prime Apples (1 appearance) 13-06-67

Prince Buster (1 appearance) 09-05-67

Principal Edwards (2 appearances) 14-09-69, 26-11-73

Procession (21 appearances) 15-01-69, 08-02-69, 22-03-69, 26-03-69, 05-04-69, 12-04-69, 10-05-69, 17-05-69, 24-05-69, 31-05-69, 07-06-69, 14-06-69, 16-06-69, 21-06-69, 28-06-69, 16-02-74, 16-03-74, 27-04-74, 22-06-74, 28-06-74, 24-08-74

This popular Marquee band included guitarist Mick Rogers, who later worked with Manfred Mann in the Earthband.

Procol Harum (2 appearances) 12-06-67, 12-03-68

The Prxxx Pirates (1 appearance) 27-08-79

PTO (1 appearance) 20-02-78

Public Foot The Roman (1 appearance) 07-08-73

Puckless Blend (8 appearances) 08-02-71, 28-03-71

Pugmaho (2 appearances) 05-12-71, 27-06-72

Pulsar (1 appearance) 05-03-75

Pumphouse Gang (2 appearances) 24-10-76, 04-12-76

Punchin' Judy (1 appearance) 11-01-75

Punishment Of Luxury (5 appearances) 03-10-78, 13-02-79, 07-05-79, 23-08-79, 31-10-79

Pure Wing (2 appearances) 28-03-71, 02-05-71

Purple Hearts (3 appearances) 16-06-79, 13-07-79, 24-07-79

The Pyramid (1 appearance) 08-06-67

A few months later vocalist Ian Matthews joined Fairport Convetion.

Q

Q (1 appearance) 26-01-73

The Q Set (2 appearances) 24-02-67, 05-10-67

Quadrille (12 appearances) 10-06-71, 31-08-72, 18-11-73, 08-12-73, 24-12-73, 03-01-74, 12-01-74, 25-01-74, 14-02-74, 28-02-74, 26-04-74, 23-09-74

Quantum Jump (2 appearances) 18-07-77, 27-10-77

Quatermass (2 appearances) 06-12-69, 21-05-70

Terri Quaye (1 appearance) 16-06-71

Queen (2 appearances) 09-04-73, 23-07-73

That first date by Mercury's lads was a headliner. Three months later, on the release of their debut single 'Keep Yourself Alive' and eponymous first album, they were in a support slot. Not for long.

Tommy Quickly (1 appearance) 20-06-65

Quicksand (2 appearances) 23-07-72, 19-05-74

The Quik (1 appearance) 02-11-67

Quiver (4 appearances) 10-05-70, 11-06-69, 23-04-73, 02-07-73

Quiverland Brothers (1 appearance) 05-04-73

Another appellation for the combined efforts of The Sutherland Brothers and Quiver.

R

The Race (6 appearances) 04-09-66, 04-10-66, 08-11-66, 20-11-66, 08-12-66, 27-12-66

Racing Cars (11 appearances) 26-04-76, 03-11-76, 01-12-76, 06-01-77, 07-02-77, 05-12-77, 06-12-77, 06-06-78, 06-08-78, 27-09-78, 18-12-78

Racoon (1 appearance) 24-10-72

Radha Krishna Temple (1 appearance) 28-09-69

Radiators From Space (2 appearances) 15-10-77, 07-03-78

Radio Birdman (1 appearance) 24-04-78

Radio Stars (7 appearances) 05-08-77, 05-09-77, 30-09-77, 20-07-78, 21-07-78, 31-12-78, 13-03-79

Rage (1 appearance) 03-10-77

Rainbow Reflection (1 appearance) 04-04-88

Rainbows (4 appearances) 27-02-69, 26-03-69, 16-04-69, 23-04-69

Rambling Strip (3 appearances) 01-04-78, 15-11-77, 26-09-79

Ramrod (4 appearances) 26-06-78, 10-07-78, 18-08-78, 19-04-79

Random Hold (3 appearances) 14-10-79, 28-10-79, 13-11-79

Randy (2 appearances) 25-01-74, 28-04-74

Randy Pie (1 appearance) 15-06-74

Raped (1 appearance) 13-01-79

Rare Bird (17 appearances) 23-10-69, 09-12-69, 08-01-70, 22-01-70, 05-02-70, 19-02-70, 19-03-70, 09-04-70, 23-04-70, 06-05-70, 01-09-70, 08-12-70, 10-07-72, 20-02-73, 22-11-74, 18-12-74, 04-02-75

Rasputin (1 appearance) 02-08-75

Rat (3 appearances) 22-07-70, 23-09-72, 12-10-72

Raven (1 appearance) 07-06-70

The Ravens (2 appearances) 23-11-79, 24-11-79

Raw Material (3 appearances) 01-06-71, 03-11-71, 08-12-71

Razorback (15 appearances) 07-02-76, 04-07-76, 17-07-76, 05-08-76, 13-08-76, 8-08-76, 23-09-76, 16-10-76, 21-11-76, 08-11-75, 20-03-76, 03-04-76, 29-05-76, 18-06-76, 03-09-76

Reaction (3 appearances) 29-11-77, 12-08-78, 11-11-78

With later Talk Talk mainman Mark Hollis.

The Reaction (1 appearance) 21-07-68

The Records (3 appearances) 31-01-79, 28-06-79, 29-06-79

Red (2 appearances) 17-11-76, 14-01-77

Red Dirt (1 appearance) 15-02-72

The Red Light District (8 appearances) 06-06-68, 17-06-68, 24-06-68, 10-07-68, 18-07-68, 05-09-68, 24-09-68, 14-10-68

Red Star (2 appearances) 26-06-68, 26-02-70

Noel Redding (2 appearances) 01-06-76, 02-06-76

Reds Whites & Blues (2 appearances) 29-07-75, 22-10-75

Redwing (2 appearances) 05-11-71, 09-10-73

Redwood (1 appearance) 05-12-78

David Rees (1 appearance) 24-06-71

Tony Reeves (1 appearance) 16-07-75

Refuge (1 appearance) 01-10-73

Refugee (3 appearances) 11-03-74, 11-04-74, 18-06-74

Regeneration (1 appearance) 03-06-73

Reggae Regular (1 appearance) 26-02-79

Regulation Control (1 appearance) 12-03-78

Terry Reid (24 appearances) 26-05-67, 30-06-67, 21-07-67, 25-08-67, 10-09-68, 06-03-69, 13-03-69, 20-03-69, 27-03-69, 03-04-69, 15-04-69, 08-05-69, 15-05-69, 16-05-69, 22-05-69, 05-06-69, 12-06-69, 22-01-71, 05-03-71, 11-05-71, 27-07-71, 26-10-71, 10-06-73, 11-06-73

Reign (1 appearance) 23-11-73

Reinhardt Boogie Band (1 appearance) 03-07-77

Remo Four (5 appearances) 20-06-65, 15-09-67, 14-11-67, 28-11-67, 14-12-67

Remus Down Boulevard (5 appearances) 30-09-76, 08-11-76, 25-01-77, 19-04-77, 21-06-77

Renaissance (15 appearances) 11-08-69, 18-08-69, 01-09-69, 15-09-69, 06-10-69, 20-10-69, 07-11-69, 19-02-71, 23-04-71, 04-06-71, 24-08-71, 29-09-71, 11-01-72, 26-07-72, 15-08-72

Renia (1 appearance) 27-07-72

Requiem (2 appearances) 20-03-70, 26-10-70

The Rezillos (4 appearances) 26-02-78, 09-06-78, 12-11-78, 13-11-78

Rhode Island Red (1 appearance) 16-02-78

Rhythm Traps (1 appearance) 06-09-76

Rich & Grimes with Babylon (1 appearance) 27-05-69

The Rick 'n' Beckers (2 appearances) 12-02-67, 26-02-67

Rico (3 appearances) 9-08-77, 10-06-79, 11-06-79

Ricotti & Albuquerque (2 appearances) 06-11-70, 18-12-70

Riff Raff (2 appearances) 16-07-73, 07-10-73

The Rift (1 appearance) 23-06-66

Rikki & The Last Days Of Earth (2 appearances) 04-11-77, 01-05-78

Rimmington (1 appearance) 27-11-72

The Ring of Truth (1 appearance) 04-12-69

Rings (1 appearance) 03-07-77

The Riot Squad (1 appearance) 05-06-68

Rippa (1 appearance) 18-07-76

Rising Sun (1 appearance) 28-12-71

Ritzi (1 appearance) 10-04-78

Ritzy (1 appearance) 07-08-76

Rivers Blue (18 appearances) 07-01-68, 14-01-68, 21-01-68, 28-01-68, 18-02-68, 25-02-68, 03-03-68, 10-03-68, 17-03-68, 24-03-68, 31-03-68, 07-04-68, 14-04-68, 21-04-68, 28-04-68, 05-05-68, 08-12-68, 15-12-68

Rivers Invitation (2 appearances) 20-05-68, 27-05-68

Tony Rivers (9 appearances) 09-06-66, 07-08-66, 03-01-67, 14-02-67, 07-03-67, 14-04-67, 18-08-67, 23-07-68, 20-08-68

Riviera Feedback (1 appearance) 09-07-76

Ro Ro (2 appearances) 02-01-73, 16-01-73

Andy Roberts (1 appearance) 23-09-70

Tom Robinson Band (3 appearances) 11-09-77, 10-10-77, 24-10-77

Three appearances either side of the October release of TRB's smash hit single '2-4-6-8 Motorway'.

Rock Rebellion (2 appearances) 23-06-74, 05-09-74

Rock Rebellion & Dr. Marigold (1 appearance) 07-11-72

Rock Workshop (2 appearances) 23-06-74, 05-09-74

Rocking Chair (1 appearance) 03-08-70

Rococo (2 appearances) 02-12-73, 27-03-76

Jess Roden Band (5 appearances) 30-09-74, 10-12-74, 18-05-76, 19-05-76, 20-05-76

Roden was one of Alan Bown's vocalists.

Roger The Cat (1 appearance) 19-09-78

Ronji Southern Band (1 appearance) 11-06-76

The Rolling Stones (4 appearances) 10-01-63, 17-01-63, 24-01-63, 31-01-63

These are the four billed dates the Stones played at the Marquee, but they had completed some earlier interval slots during the previous summer. The interval was the point when the main bands slipped out to the pub, because the Marquee was still unlicensed at this time.

Roogalator (15 appearances) 06-05-76, 21-05-76, 25-07-76, 18-08-76, 10-09-76, 27-09-76, 15-10-76, 05-12-76, 12-01-77, 21-02-77, 13-05-77, 04-09-77, 08-11-77, 29-11-77, 29-01-78

Room (1 appearance) 23-11-70

The Roosters (1 appearance) 15-07-63

Guitarist Eric Clapton was in The Yardbirds three months later; bassist Tom McGuinness joined Manfred Mann the following year.

Tim Rose (3 appearances) 23-02-60, 16-07-68, 20-02-75

Ross Stag (1 appearance) 13-12-74

Rossocks (1 appearance) 19-08-73

Rough Diamond (1 appearance) 28-04-77

Rowan Oak (1 appearance) 04-04-72

Rowdies (1 appearance) 04-08-74

Roxette (1 appearance) 17-07-79

Roxy Music (1 appearance) 31-05-72

Just a week or two before their fine first album burst forth, Bryan Ferry (vox) and Eno (stuff) played the Marquee with Andy Mackay (sax), Paul Thompson (drums) and Graham Simpson (bass).

Royal James (5 appearances) 11-04-66, 05-07-66, 15-08-66, 20-08-66, 19-09-66

Rubber Rhino (1 appearance) 17-10-75

The Rubinoos (4 appearances) 30-06-78, 01-07-78, 02-07-78, 03-07-78

Ruby (4 appearances) 21-05-73, 30-06-73, 27-08-73, 10-09-73

Rule The Roost (1 appearance) 10-03-79

The Rumble Band (1 appearance) 05-03-67

Rumble Strip (1 appearance) 29-07-78

Rumpelstiltskin (1 appearance) 05-07-70

Running Man (2 appearances) 08-12-71, 29-03-72

Tom Rush (1 appearance) 22-05-68

Rushwood (6 appearances) 03-02-73, 07-03-73, 14-03-73, 31-03-73, 14-04-73, 28-04-73

Ray Russell (1 appearance) 20-05-71

Rusty Butler (2 appearances) 06-11-73, 20-11-73

The Ruts (5 appearances) 19-07-79, 13-08-79, 14-08-79, 17-12-79, 18-12-79

Saffron (1 appearance) 02-08-71
Saffron & Friends (1 appearance) 02-12-70
Sailor (1 appearance) 26-01-75
The Saints (6 appearances) 11-06-77, 13-07-77, 31-10-77, 01-11-77, 27-01-78, 26-03-78
Salamander (1 appearance) 01-09-70
Salford Jets (1 appearance) 04-11-78
Salt (18 appearances) 29-05-76, 17-07-76, 14-08-76, 18-09-76, 16-01-77, 23-01-77, 30-01-77, 22-04-77, 19-06-77, 26-06-77, 10-07-77, 17-07-77, 18-10-77, 13-12-77, 25-01-78, 01-02-78, 23-02-78, 19-03-78
Salt 'n' Pepper (1 appearance) 09-04-70
Salt Of The Earth (1 appearance) 02-01-71
Sam Apple Pie (8 appearances) 11-05-69, 21-05-69, 30-05-69, 05-09-74, 08-12-74, 11-03-76, 04-07-76, 22-08-76
Sammy (3 appearances) 11-10-72, 05-12-72, 07-02-73
Samson (13 appearances) 10-07-69, 19-07-69, 05-08-69, 14-08-69, 29-08-69, 09-09-69, 22-09-69, 02-10-69, 14-10-69, 30-10-69, 04-11-69, 23-06-70, 16-12-70
Sandgate (6 appearances) 17-10-72, 09-01-73, 23-08-73, 03-04-74, 04-04-75, 18-05-75
Sandhams Village (18 appearances) 07-03-71, 14-03-71, 21-03-71, 28-03-71, 04-04-71, 11-04-71, 18-04-71, 25-04-71, 02-05-71, 09-05-71, 16-05-71, 23-05-71, 30-05-71, 06-06-71, 20-06-71, 04-07-71, 11-07-71, 18-07-71
Sands (22 appearances) 08-04-66, 22-04-66, 06-05-66, 13-05-66, 23-05-66, 27-05-66, 20-06-66, 28-06-66, 07-07-66, 04-08-66, 18-08-66, 01-10-66, 13-10-66, 28-10-66, 04-11-66, 25-11-66, 09-12-66, 16-12-66, 13-01-67, 27-01-67, 17-02-67, 02-06-67
Sarolta With The Turnstile (1 appearance) 26-04-69
Sarsparilla (1 appearance) 23-11-68
Sarstedt Peter (1 appearance) 11-05-72
Sassafras (12 appearances) 21-08-73, 01-12-74, 08-01-75, 13-03-75, 02-06-75, 23-07-75, 25-11-75, 18-03-76, 11-08-76, 30-12-76, 14-06-77, 06-10-78
Satisfaction (4 appearances) 27-05-70, 18-11-70, 01-04-71, 17-06-71
Sattva (3 appearances) 06-08-71, 08-10-71, 11-10-71
Saturnalia (2 appearances) 04-10-72, 13-03-73
Savage Derek (1 appearance) 03-07-67
Savoy Brown (28 appearances) 11-11-66, 15-01-67, 19-02-67, 20-03-67, 20-04-67, 29-05-67, 20-06-67, 01-12-67, 02-02-68, 01-03-68, 19-04-68, 02-08-68, 01-10-68, 17-01-69, 23-05-69, 10-10-69, 16-12-69, 04-10-72, 30-01-73, 20-04-73, 22-01-74, 01-07-74, 02-07-74, 04-03-75, 15-04-75, 03-06-75, 10-07-75, 16-02-76
Guitarist Kim Simmonds was the driving force behind this resilient British blues-rock band, and would regularly bring them back to the Marquee after Euro and US tours.
Leo Sayer (1 appearance) 11-07-73
Scapa Flow (1 appearance) 06-06-71
Scarecrow (6 appearances) 19-06-76, 28-06-76, 18-09-76, 26-03-77, 27-08-77, 26-08-78
Scarlet Strange (1 appearance) 07-01-

77
Scars (1 appearance) 25-03-79
The Scenery (1 appearance) 26-03-67
Henry Schifter (1 appearance) 30-11-72
Schunge (1 appearance) 18-10-72
Schy (1 appearance) 13-11-72
Scooter (1 appearance) 25-08-79
Scorpions (3 appearances) 11-11-75, 29-03-76, 21-11-76
Colin Scott (2 appearances) 11-02-70, 15-04-70
Kerry Scott (4 appearances) 02-10-72, 26-10-72, 06-11-72, 07-06-74
Pete Scott (1 appearance) 22-03-72
Scrapyard (1 appearance) 25-05-76
Scratch (1 appearance) 05-01-70
Scream (1 appearance) 20-11-79
Screaming Lord Sutch (1 appearance) 07-11-72
Screemer (4 appearances) 08-01-77, 04-03-77, 04-04-77, 15-05-77
Screens (1 appearance) 10-02-79, 01-05-79, 07-07-79
Screwdriver (1 appearance) 04-06-77
Scylla (1 appearance) 24-05-75
Second Avenue (1 appearance) 12-03-77
Secret Affair (5 appearances) 12-05-79, 26-05-79, 08-07-79, 15-07-79, 22-07-79
Second Front (1 appearance) 22-02-75
Marianne Segal (1 appearance) 10-11-71
Selofane (1 appearance) 04-06-68
The Senate (1 appearance) 30-10-67
The Sensory Armada (2 appearances) 18-11-67, 27-11-67
747 (1 appearance) 14-08-73
Seventh Heaven (1 appearance) 17-06-76
Seventh Wave (8 appearances) 19-06-74, 10-09-74, 27-09-74, 22-10-74, 03-01-75, 07-10-75, 23-12-75, 02-01-76
The Sex Pistols (1 appearance) 12-02-76
The group apparently damaged some gear owned by headline group Eddie & The Hot Rods, leading to a ban from the Marquee. But they also got their first press notice, in the NME, so weren't too troubled.
The Seychelles (1 appearance) 26-05-67
SF2 (2 appearances) 21-09-75, 29-09-75
Shacklock (4 appearances) 25-11-71, 04-01-72, 01-02-72, 03-04-72
Shades (6 appearances) 03-10-69, 01-11-69, 13-11-69, 29-11-69, 16-12-69, 18-07-71
Shake (2 appearances) 04-09-79, 11-09-79
Chris Shakespear (1 appearance) 25-09-67
Shakey Vic's (4 appearances) 17-11-67, 15-12-67, 16-01-69
Sham 69 (1 appearance) 21-10-77
Shanghai (3 appearances) 27-01-75, 19-06-75, 26-09-75
Shango (1 appearance) 12-09-71
Shangoe (1 appearance) 09-06-73
Shape Of The Rain (1 appearance) 17-11-71
Sharks (7 appearances) 14-08-73, 09-10-73, 04-12-73, 15-01-74, 12-03-74, 30-07-74, 24-09-74
The Sharrons (3 appearances) 29-05-68, 16-06-68, 19-06-68
Allan Lee Shaw (1 appearance) 19-01-73
Sheerwater (2 appearances) 30-11-74, 14-06-75
Sheffields (1 appearance) 10-12-64
Brush Sheils & Skid Row (1 appearance) 05-03-79

Shepstone & Dibbens (1 appearance) 12-02-74
Tony Sheridan (1 appearance) 03-12-75
Shide & Acorn (1 appearance) 26-02-71
Shirts (1 appearance) 24-07-78
The Shoo String Band (2 appearances) 08-03-69, 05-04-69
Shotgun Express (1 appearance) 20-06-66
One month old, this edition of the Express included Rod Stewart (vocals), Peter Green (guitar), Mick Fleetwood (drums) and Pete Bardens (keyboards).
Showbiz Kids (6 appearances) 23-09-78, 06-01-79, 03-02-79, 21-04-79, 19-05-79, 14-07-79
Sidewinder (2 appearances) 28-04-73, 03-06-77
The Sidewinders (2 appearances) 20-09-65, 07-02-66
Silas (3 appearances) 07-03-70, 13-03-70, 28-03-70
Silent Sister (2 appearances) 23-10-76, 04-02-77
The Silkie (1 appearance) 22-09-65
Mike Silver (1 appearance) 24-09-73
Silverhead (2 appearances) 19-08-73, 20-12-73
Simon & Garfunkel (1 appearance) 10-07-66
Remarkable, on reflection... but there they were, cooing away on material drawn from the "Sound Of Silence" LP that had been released four months earlier.
Simon's Fancy (4 appearances) 30-07-73, 06-08-73, 12-08-73, 20-08-73
Simple Minds (4 appearances) 03-07-79, 07-08-79, 13-12-79, 14-12-79
Sin (1 appearance) 16-11-70
The Sinceros (4 appearances) 14-05-79, 04-06-79, 18-06-79, 02-07-79
Skeater (1 appearance) 03-02-77
Skid Row (22 appearances) 07-09-70, 18-06-71, 14-09-71, 01-11-71, 15-11-71, 22-11-71, 29-11-71, 13-12-71, 07-02-72, 14-02-72, 02-04-72, 16-04-72, 24-04-72, 10-05-72, 04-06-72, 18-06-72, 02-07-72, 16-07-72, 30-07-72, 14-05-75
The Skids (4 appearances) 01-11-78, 08-02-79, 28-03-79, 29-03-79
Stuart Adamson later formed Big Country, Richard Jobson later the Armoury Show.
Skin Alley (10 appearances) 17-11-69, 02-01-70, 12-02-70, 04-05-70, 05-10-70, 15-03-71, 22-04-71, 09-03-72, 17-05-73, 01-11-73
Skinny Cat (1 appearance) 25-10-70
Skip Bifferty (11 appearances) 11-03-67, 29-04-67, 01-05-67, 04-01-68, 18-01-68, 15-02-68, 22-02-68, 14-03-68, 28-03-68, 04-04-68, 25-04-68
Skunks (1 appearance) 11-11-77
Sky (1 appearance) 05-10-75
Skye Wine (2 appearances) 05-01-68, 26-01-68
Skyfield (1 appearance) 14-06-75
Slack Alice (8 appearances) 08-07-73, 14-11-74, 03-02-75, 21-04-75, 07-07-75, 12-09-75, 12-09-75, 21-04-75
Slade (11 appearances) 27-03-70, 10-04-70, 08-05-70, 12-06-70, 15-07-70, 12-08-70, 08-10-70, 22-07-71, 18-09-71, 24-12-71, 29-08-72
Slam Creepers (1 appearance) 05-12-68
Slaughter & The Dogs (3 appearances) 09-01-78, 30-03-78, 03-09-79
Sleaz Band (2 appearances) 01-03-72, 05-06-72
Sleepy (2 appearances) 18-10-68, 07-

12-68
Slider (1 appearance) 28-10-72
Slowhand (1 appearance) 03-12-73
Slump (1 appearance) 07-05-72
The Small Faces (2 appearances) 22-03-66, 28-06-66
Small Hour (3 appearances) 31-07-79, 05-09-79, 12-09-79
The Smiggs Band (1 appearance) 03-07-76
Smile (1 appearance) 13-12-69
Brian May and Roger Taylor pre-Queen.
Smile 07-01-73, 20-01-73, 24-04-76
Smiler (3 appearances) 30-04-77, 29-09-77, 30-10-77
The Smirks (7 appearances) 10-06-78, 04-10-78, 11-10-78, 18-10-78, 30-10-78, 16-02-79, 21-03-79
Gordon Smith (5 appearances) 02-08-68, 11-09-68, 25-09-68, 07-10-68, 28-10-68
Hurricane Smith (1 appearance) 23-05-71
Smith, Perkins & Smith (2 appearances) 16-05-72, 29-06-72
Smokestack (2 appearances) 21-05-71, 22-06-71
Smooth Bitch (1 appearance) 09-05-71
Smurks (1 appearance) 18-02-78
Snafu (7 appearances) 27-11-73, 25-02-75, 27-03-75, 17-06-75, 05-08-75, 06-08-75, 14-10-75
Snake Eye (2 appearances) 09-05-72, 09-08-72
Snakebite (2 appearances) 07-05-77, 16-07-77
The Sneakers (6 appearances) 24-11-64, 01-12-64, 08-12-64, 15-12-64, 2-12-64, 29-12-64
Sneekers (1 appearance) 08-04-78
Sniff 'n' The Tears (4 appearances) 20-05-73, 31-05-73, 15-03-79, 04-07-79
Snips (1 appearance) 15-11-78
Snow Leopard (1 appearance) 06-06-74
Soft Boys (2 appearances) 25-05-78, 18-06-78
Cambridge band formed by Robyn Hitchcock and, at the trime of these dates, including on guitar Kimberley Rew. Hitchcock later formed The Egyptians, while Rew joined Katrina & The Waves.
Soft Machine (3 appearances) 08-07-69, 02-10-69, 17-02-70
Mick Softley (1 appearance) 03-08-70
Soho Jets (1 appearance) 22-07-76
Solid Gold Cadillac (1 appearance) 08-11-72
Solid Waste (1 appearance) 02-11-77
Soliluque (1 appearance) 01-06-74
Solution (2 appearances) 17-11-73, 09-04-76
Sorahan (2 appearances) 13-04-77, 27-07-77
Sore Throat (4 appearances) 03-06-78, 11-09-78, 12-02-79, 12-03-79
The Soul Agents (7 appearances) 06-06-66, 04-07-66, 18-07-66, 06-08-66, 13-08-66, 20-08-66, 27-08-66
Southern Comfort (1 appearance) 28-09-71
Southern Electric (1 appearance) 25-03-77
The Southern Ramblers (1 appearance) 07-12-66
The Span (1 appearance) 04-07-68
Spanker Onslow (1 appearance) 17-12-74
Spanner (1 appearance) 19-01-74
Spare Parts (1 appearance) 15-12-78
Sparks (4 appearances) 06-12-72, 14-12-72, 21-12-72, 28-12-72
Sparrow (5 appearances) 11-07-74,

25-07-74, 15-08-74, 13-09-74, 18-10-74

Roger Ruskin Spear (5 appearances) 28-06-70, 12-07-70, 02-08-70, 13-09-70, 27-09-70
Ex-Bonzo loony probably still playing intricate solos on his wah-wah rabbits.

Chris Spedding (1 appearance) 17-12-77

Speedometers (5 appearances) 31-01-78, 02-12-78, 03-05-79, 7-05-79, 9-04-78

Jeremy Spencer's Albatross (1 appearance) 06-03-75
Ex-Fleetwood Mac guitarist hinting heavily to remind punters of former glory.

Spice (15 appearances) 07-09-68, 19-10-68, 12-12-68, 04-01-69, 11-01-69, 18-01-69, 25-01-69, 01-02-69, 08-02-69, 15-02-69, 22-02-69, 01-03-69, 08-03-69, 15-03-69, 22-03-69

Spirogyra (3 appearances) 30-07-71, 25-06-73, 15-11-73

Spiteri (2 appearances) 19-06-73, 11-05-77

Spontaneous Combustion (3 appearances) 11-01-73, 21-02-73, 14-07-74

Spontaneous Music Ensemble (4 appearances) 08-10-69, 22-10-69, 29-10-69, 12-11-69

Spooky Tooth (11 appearances) 30-01-68, 12-03-68, 27-05-68, 24-06-68, 03-07-68, 07-08-68, 10-10-68, 24-10-68, 0/-11-68, 21-11-68, 09-01-69

Spoon (1 appearance) 23-04-72

The Sports (2 appearances) 09-04-79, 27-04-79

Spreadeagle (6 appearances) 13-08-71, 26-11-71, 24-05-72, 19-09-72, 16-10-72, 10-12-72

Spring (2 appearances) 26-07-70, 18-03-71

Spring Fever (1 appearance) 28-05-70
Spud (4 appearances) 30-07-75, 09-12-77, 17-03-78, 01-12-78

Squeeze (5 appearances) 25-06-77, 03-12-77, 13-01-78, 14-09-78, 22-12-78

Squire (3 appearances) 15-06-79, 22-07-79, 27-10-79

SS2 (1 appearance) 14-09-75
St Louis Union (1 appearance) 14-07-67

Stackridge (18 appearances) 09-07-70, 04-10-70, 30-11-70, 04-05-71, 12-08-71, 16-03-72, 17-05-72, 03-07-72, 21-08-72, 30-08-72, 23-10-72, 02-11-72, 31-12-72, 05-03-73, 05-06-73, 21-08-73, 19-02-74, 07-05-74

Tim Staffell (1 appearance) 25-10-73
Ex-Smile (May and Taylor's pre-Queen gig).

Chris Stainton (2 appearances) 19-08-74, 12-11-74

Stairway (1 appearance) 11-06-72
The Staks (2 appearances) 08-04-68, 11-04-68

Stalag 6 (1 appearance) 16-06-77
The Stalkers (7 appearances) 04-04-67, 22-04-67, 13-05-67, 10-06-67, 23-06-67, 01-07-67, 14-07-67

Stallion (2 appearances) 13-11-76, 26-02-77

Vivian Stanshall (2 appearances) 09-08-71, 10-08-71
Ex-Bonzo, mad person and leading GBE (Great British Eccentric).

The Star Jets (5 appearances) 04-09-78, 07-12-78, 21-07-79, 08-09-79, 25-06-78

Stardust (2 appearances) 22-10-73, 22-11-73

Stargang (1 appearance) 04-08-76
Cindy Starr & The Mopeds (2 appearances) 28-07-68, 09-02-69

Edwin Starr (1 appearance) 08-02-68
Starry Eyed & Laughing (1 appearance) 27-08-74

Stars (1 appearance) 05-04-76
Stateline (1 appearance) 09-07-77
The Statesides (1 appearance) 12-05-66

Status Quo (11 appearances) 25-04-70, 07-07-70, 25-07-70, 16-10-70, 09-04-71, 15-10-71, 01-12-71, 07-03-72, 26-06-72, 27-06-72, 28-11-72

Strapps (1 appearance) 05-05-77
Stealers Wheel (2 appearances) 05-07-71, 26-02-73

Steamhammer (21 appearances) 31-01-69, 04-03-69, 20-03-69, 04-04-69, 22-04-69, 02-05-69, 16-05-69, 06-06-69, 19-06-69, 30-06-69, 24-07-69, 04-09-69, 09-07-70, 02-09-70, 24-11-70, 02-07-71, 13-07-72, 08-07-72, 04-05-73, 15-06-73, 28-10-73

The Steampacket (17 appearances) 22-07-65, 18-08-65, 02-09-65, 30-09-65, 14-10-65, 23-11-65, 28-10-65, 23-12-65, 13-01-66, 27-01-66, 10-02-66, 24-02-66, 14-03-66, 25-04-66, 23-05-66, 27-06-66, 29-08-66
These gigs cover the life of this mighty outfit. It included Rod Stewart, Long John Baldry, Julie Driscoll and Brian Auger.

Steel Mill (12 appearances) 12-12-70, 09-01-71, 23-01-71, 03-02-71, 10-02-71, 17-02-71, 24-02-71, 03-03-71, 04-71, 17-04-71, 01-05-71, 22-12-71

Steppenwolf (1 appearance) 16-05-69
Cat Stevens (1 appearance) 21-02-67
John Stevens (2 appearances) 14-01-77, 03-03-77

Al Stewart (30 appearances) 01-09-65, 20-10-65, 03-11-65, 22-06-66, 09-03-66, 06-07-66, 03-08-66, 19-10-66, 09-11-66, 18-01-67, 01-02-67, 08-03-67, 07-06-67, 14-06-67, 21-06-67, 28-06-67, 05-07-67, 12-07-67, 19-07-67, 26-07-67, 02-08-67, 16-08-67, 23-08-67, 24-04-68, 07-06-72, 14-06-72, 21-06-72, 28-06-72, 05-07-72, 12-07-72

Rod Stewart (10 appearances) 10-12-64, 17-12-64, 24-12-64, 07-01-65, 14-01-65, 21-01-65, 28-01-65, 04-02-65, 11-02-65, 18-02-65

The Stickers (1 appearance) 31-12-79
Stickey George (1 appearance) 07-05-71

Sticky Wicket (1 appearance) 15-05-76

Still Life (2 appearances) 09-03-68, 25-03-68

Alan Stivell (1 appearance) 06-06-73
Stone Delight (1 appearance) 04-05-75
Stone Feather & Almanac (1 appearance) 15-06-70
Stone The Crows (4 appearances) 07-10-69, 11-11-70, 29-04-71, 13-08-71
Stone's Masonry (1 appearance) 30-01-67

Storm (1 appearance) 22-10-70
Stormsville Shakers (2 appearances) 03-11-66, 12-12-66

Straight Eight (9 appearances) 05-11-78, 26-11-78, 16-01-79, 01-02-79, 08-03-79, 06-04-79, 05-08-79, 02-09-79, 19-11-79

Straight Lace (1 appearance) 16-03-70
Straight Three (1 appearance) 15-05-78

Strange Days (7 appearances) 13-10-74, 25-10-74, 13-11-74, 27-11-74, 20-04-75, 11-07-75, 17-11-75

The Stranglers (2 appearances) 08-03-76, 07-11-76

Strapps (3 appearances) 21-03-77, 05-04-77, 18-04-77

Jack Straw (8 appearances) 07-09-74,

28-09-74, 12-10-74, 26-10-74, 15-11-74, 11-01-75, 22-02-75, 08-03-75

The Strawbs (3 appearances) 15-06-69, 22-06-69, 15-04-70

Stray (26 appearances) 15-01-71, 26-04-71, 16-06-71, 15-07-71, 23-09-71, 30-11-71, 15-02-72, 29-05-72, 22-08-72, 04-09-73, 20-11-73, 16-04-74, 04-06-74, 19-11-74, 28-12-74, 25-03-75, 27-05-75, 01-07-75, 03-10-75, 25-11-75, 27-04-76, 09-06-76, 24-11-76, 25-11-76, 27-12-76, 22-02-77

Stray Dog (6 appearances) 27-06-73, 04-07-73, 18-07-73, 01-08-73, 15-08-73, 29-08-73

Streetband (8 appearances) 26-01-77, 10-02-77, 11-02-77, 30-03-77, 22-06-77, 06-12-78, 25-01-79, 11-04-79
With vocalist Paul Young.

Strider (35 appearances) 10-12-72, 31-12-72, 10-01-73, 17-01-73, 24-01-73, 31-01-73, 12-04-73, 19-04-73, 25-04-73, 07-05-73, 18-05-73, 19-06-73, 20-07-73, 10-08-73, 14-09-73, 21-12-73, 29-01-74, 13-03-74, 26-03-74, 10-04-74, 07-05-74, 11-06-74, 28-06-74, 24-07-74, 07-08-74, 21-08-74, 03-09-74, 06-11-74, 24-12-74, 07-01-75, 06-01-76, 30-03-77, 10-06-77, 22-06-77, 19-07-77

At various times this outfit included vocalist Jenny Haan, later of Babe Ruth, and guitarist Gary Grainger, who went on to work with Rod Stewart.

Strife (15 appearances) 08-11-71, 14-11-72, 17-02-75, 15-09-75, 01-10-75, 19-01-76, 23-02-76, 08-04-76, 08-04-76, 05-05-76, 22-07-76, 13-08-76, 28-09-76, 02-02-77, 15-03-77

String Driven Thing (13 appearances) 21-09-72, 16-10-72, 14-01-74, 04-02-74, 27-05-74, 13-08-74, 28-10-74, 05-12-74, 20-01-75, 16-04-75, 20-08-75, 16-09-75, 09-12-75

StripJack (1 appearance) 17-12-76
Mike Stuart (2 appearances) 12-01-67, 25-07-68

Stud (12 appearances) 05-01-71, 02-03-71, 31-05-71, 23-07-71, 19-08-71, 02-11-71, 14-12-71, 04-01-72, 01-02-72, 19-06-72, 09-07-72, 23-07-72
Jim Cregan (gtr) went to Family, which was where bassist John Weider had come from.

Studio Six (11 appearances) 05-05-67, 29-06-67, 06-07-67, 03-08-67, 31-08-67, 07-09-67, 18-09-67, 05-10-67, 16-10-67, 05-02-68, 29-02-68

The Stukas (11 appearances) 13-03-77, 03-05-77, 11-06-77, 30-06-77, 08-07-77, 10-09-77, 08-10-77, 14-01-78, 06-02-78, 27-04-78, 07-05-78

Suburban Studs (2 appearances) 20-11-77, 27-11-77
Sugar Pie Desanto & The Shevelles (1 appearance) 10-08-65
Sugar Simone & Hummingbirds (1 appearance) 21-02-68
The Sugar Simone Show (2 appearances) 20-03-68, 27-03-68

Suicide (2 appearances) 05-11-76, 18-07-78
Red Sullivan (1 appearance) 25-01-67
Summer Set (12 appearances) 21-10-65, 05-11-65, 19-11-65, 03-03-66, 10-03-66, 18-03-66, 22-03-66, 09-06-66, 01-07-66, 15-07-66, 18-11-66, 25-11-66

Sun (3 appearances) 03-01-70, 01-01-72, 08-01-72
Suncharlot (1 appearance) 10-08-72
Sundance (3 appearances) 24-07-73, 03-07-74, 04-05-75
Sunday Gage (2 appearances) 22-02-74, 15-03-74

Sunflower Boogie Band (1 appearance) 22-06-73
Sunforest (7 appearances) 04-03-70, 18-03-70, 01-04-70, 08-04-70, 15-04-70, 13-05-70, 17-05-70

Sunrise (3 appearances) 19-07-72, 18-08-72, 01-11-72
Sunshine (1 appearance) 08-08-72
The Sunshine Garden (1 appearance) 16-03-68
Suntreader (1 appearance) 13-06-73

Supercharge (10 appearances) 05-06-76, 25-08-76, 01-09-76, 16-09-76, 19-12-77, 20-12-77, 23-03-78, 23-07-78, 05-10-78, 03-12-78

Supertramp (5 appearances) 14-07-70, 24-07-70, 16-02-71, 24-10-71, 11-07-72

John Surman (6 appearances) 25-05-69, 08-06-69, 29-06-69, 06-07-69, 13-07-69, 27-07-69

Sutherland Brothers (9 appearances) 03-12-71, 10-01-72, 24-01-72, 11-04-72, 29-06-72, 27-08-72, 29-12-72, 23-04-73, 02-07-73

Sutherland Brothers & Quiver (6 appearances) 10-12-73, 01-02-74, 26-07-74, 15-10-74, 23-12-74, 24-06-75

Pete Sutton (1 appearance) 08-05-74
SVT (1 appearance) 20-04-79
Swan Arcade (1 appearance) 26-04-75

Swank (1 appearance) 25-11-77
Swastika (1 appearance) 04-06-72
Sweet Marriage (2 appearances) 11-06-69, 23-06-69

Sweet Plum (1 appearance) 12-01-70
Sweet Slag (2 appearances) 03-04-70, 13-01-71

Sweet Water Canal (8 appearances) 09-01-70, 16-01-70, 23-01-70, 30-01-70, 06-02-70, 20-02-70, 27-02-70, 06-03-70

Sydd Arthur (1 appearance) 14-02-73
Syn (36 appearances) 26-08-66, 12-09-66, 23-09-66, 29-09-66, 10-10-66, 28-11-66, 06-12-66, 13-12-66, 20-12-66, 29-12-66, 03-01-67, 17-01-67, 24-01-67, 31-01-67, 07-02-67, 14-02-67, 21-02-67, 28-02-67, 01-04-67, 08-04-67, 15-04-67, 22-04-67, 29-04-67, 06-05-67, 13-05-67, 27-05-67, 10-06-67, 17-06-67, 24-06-67, 17-07-67, 06-08-67, 20-08-67, 07-09-67, 12-10-67, 02-11-67, 16-11-67
Chris Squire and Pete Banks went to Mabel Greer's Toyshop and thence to Yes.

Synthanesia (1 appearance) 28-07-69
Syrup (6 appearances) 27-01-71, 13-03-71, 27-03-71, 15-05-71, 10-07-71, 11-12-71

T

T2 (9 appearances) 06-05-70, 20-05-70, 07-08-70, 21-08-70, 28-08-70, 22-10-70, 29-08-71, 03-10-71, 19-12-71
Tages (1 appearance) 09-11-67
Tangerine Peel (1 appearance) 30-05-70

Tanz Der Youth (2 appearances) 25-07-78, 13-09-78
Tapestry (1 appearance) 01-07-71
Tarzan (2 appearances) 06-01-70, 20-01-70

Tasavallan Presidentti (4 appearances) 30-05-72, 19-03-73, 31-08-73, 16-11-73

Taste (38 appearances) 10-02-68, 26-03-68, 14-05-68, 17-05-68, 03-06-68, 17-06-68, 08-07-68, 22-07-68, 29-07-68, 12-08-68, 26-08-68, 09-

09-68, 23-09-68, 04-10-68, 25-10-68, 22-11-68, 13-12-68, 20-12-68, 31-12-68, 31-01-69, 07-02-69, 21-02-69, 07-03-69, 21-03-69, 04-04-69, 02-05-69, 23-05-69, 24-06-69, 04-07-69, 04-09-69, 19-09-69, 24-10-69, 21-11-69, 02-01-70, 03-03-70, 28-04-70, 21-07-70

James Taylor (1 appearance) 15-06-69

Jeremy Taylor (1 appearance) 08-04-70

The T-Bones (92 appearances) 26-06-64, 13-07-64, 23-07-64, 14-08-64, 21-08-64, 28-08-64, 18-09-64, 25-09-64, 02-10-64, 09-10-64, 16-10-64, 06-11-64, 13-11-64, 20-11-64, 27-11-64, 04-12-64, 11-12-64, 18-12-64, 01-01-65, 08-01-65, 15-01-65, 29-01-65, 05-02-65, 12-02-65, 19-02-65, 26-02-65, 05-03-65, 12-03-65, 19-03-65, 26-03-65, 02-04-65, 09-04-65, 16-04-65, 23-04-65, 30-04-65, 21-05-65, 28-05-65, 04-06-65, 11-06-65, 18-06-65, 25-06-65, 02-07-65, 09-07-65, 16-07-65, 06-08-65, 13-08-65, 20-08-65, 27-08-65, 03-09-65, 10-09-65, 17-09-65, 24-09-65, 01-10-65, 08-10-65, 15-10-65, 22-10-65, 29-10-65, 12-11-65, 26-11-65, 10-12-65, 31-12-65, 07-01-66, 14-01-66, 21-01-66, 04-02-66, 18-02-66, 25-02-66, 04-03-66, 18-03-66, 25-03-66, 01-04-66, 08-04-66, 15-04-66, 29-04-66, 06-05-66, 20-05-66, 03-06-66, 10-06-66, 17-06-66, 24-06-66, 22-07-66, 29-07-66, 09-08-66, 26-08-66, 02-09-66, 09-09-66, 16-09-66, 30-09-66, 07-10-66, 14-10-66, 21-10-66, 28-10-66
One of those 60s R&B bands that made just a handful of records but gigged like crazy, as this datesheet shows. Headed by vocalist Gary Farr, the group included at various times Lee Jackson and Keith Emerson, together later in The Nice.

TC's Big Boss Band (1 appearance) 25-11-65

Bram Tchaikovsky (1 appearance) 19-03-79

Bram Tchaikovsky's Battleaxe (1 appearance) 20-10-78

Rudi Tchaikovsky (3 appearances) 25-05-74, 31-08-74, 07-06-75

Tea (2 appearances) 05-05-75, 31-03-76

Tea & Symphony (6 appearances) 06-02-69, 14-01-72, 10-03-72, 14-04-72, 16-06-72, 07-07-72

The Tea Set (1 appearance) 03-09-66

Tear Gas (2 appearances) 08-02-72, 23-02-72

Teaser (4 appearances) 13-01-77, 05-03-77, 23-03-77, 14-04-77

Teazer (3 appearances) 16-10-76, 13-11-76, 02-02-79

Teenbeats (3 appearances) 14-09-79, 30-12-79, 25-08-79

Temple Creatures (2 appearances) 04-11-70, 02-12-70

Ten Years After (27 appearances) 20-06-67, 10-07-67, 22-07-67, 18-08-67, 28-08-67, 04-09-67, 22-09-67, 06-10-67, 20-10-67, 03-11-67, 10-11-67, 17-11-67, 08-12-67, 22-12-67, 05-01-68, 19-01-68, 06-02-68, 08-03-68, 22-03-68, 05-04-68, 04-07-68, 07-06-68, 16-08-68, 30-08-68, 26-12-68, 24-01-69, 25-02-69

Tennant & Morrison (2 appearances) 02-05-72, 11-08-72

Terra Nova (4 appearances) 09-07-79, 23-07-79, 06-08-79, 20-08-79

Terry Dactyl & The Dinosaurs (1 appearance) 28-07-72

Joe Tex (1 appearance) 02-08-66

Thackery (4 appearances) 25-05-68, 03-06-68, 20-06-68, 05-07-68

Thank You (1 appearance) 13-06-72

Thin Lizzy (8 appearances) 09-04-71, 28-06-73, 26-09-73, 13-11-73, 05-02-74, 09-07-74, 23-08-74, 08-10-74

Third Ear Band (1 appearance) 18-07-72

The Third Eye (8 appearances) 24-06-67, 07-07-67, 31-07-67, 05-08-67, 26-08-67, 30-09-67, 12-10-67, 28-10-67

Third World War (2 appearances) 14-05-71, 20-09-71

Thirsty Two (2 appearances) 11-06-72, 25-06-72

Gery Thompson (7 appearances) 01-07-65, 08-07-65, 15-07-65, 29-07-65, 05-08-65, 12-08-65, 19-08-65

Those Four (1 appearance) 08-10-78

The Thoughts (1 appearance) 09-03-67

Three Beard (1 appearance) 18-07-71

Throat (1 appearance) 23-01-75

Thunder (1 appearance) 11-10-74

Johnny Thunders & The Heartbreakers (1 appearance) 28-03-77

Tiger (1 appearance) 02-03-77

Steve Tilston (2 appearances) 25-10-71, 20-09-72

Tilted Cross (4 appearances) 22-11-69, 04-12-69, 11-12-69, 27-12-69

Timbre (1 appearance) 10-05-71

Time & Motion (1 appearance) 14-04-67

Timebox (42 appearances) 16-01-67, 03-03-67, 17-03-67, 07-04-67, 21-04-67, 25-05-67, 05-06-67, 12-06-67, 22-06-67, 01-08-67, 08-08-67, 22-08-67, 28-08-67, 05-09-67, 12-09-67, 19-09-67, 26-09-67, 03-10-67, 10-10-67, 19-10-67, 30-10-67, 17-12-67, 21-12-67, 23-01-68, 12-02-68, 19-03-68, 06-04-68, 13-04-68, 20-04-68, 04-05-68, 18-05-68, 25-05-68, 01-06-68, 08-06-68, 15-06-68, 03-10-68, 31-10-68, 28-11-69, 03-02-70, 17-02-70, 21-02-70, 24-02-70
Included Ollie Halsall (gtr) and Mike Patto (vox); subsequently changed name to Patto.

Timon (1 appearance) 29-04-71

Timothy (1 appearance) 19-08-71

Tintagel (3 appearances) 06-01-71, 10-04-72, 21-05-72

Tiny Clanger (2 appearances) 06-05-70, 06-06-71

Keith Tippett (8 appearances) 06-08-69, 13-08-69, 20-08-69, 27-08-69, 03-09-69, 10-09-69, 17-09-69, 24-09-69

Tir Na Nog (1 appearance) 02-08-72

Titanic (3 appearances) 08-02-71, 20-09-71, 02-06-74

Titus Groan (5 appearances) 17-01-70, 03-07-70, 10-07-70, 25-11-70, 21-03-71

Toast (4 appearances) 15-06-68, 24-10-68, 08-01-69, 05-02-70

Toe-Fat (1 appearance) 28-04-70
Ex-Rebel Rouser singer Cliff Bennett's mob.

Tomato (1 appearance) 06-06-74

Tonge (1 appearance) 11-05-75

Tonight (2 appearances) 15-02-78, 21-05-78

Tools (2 appearances) 15-07-77, 09-09-77

Tooting Fruities (2 appearances) 07-06-76, 08-06-76

Topaz (1 appearance) 06-11-76

Bernie Torme (7 appearances) 18-08-77, 14-09-77, 24-11-77, 04-01-78, 15-09-78, 02-10-78, 18-05-79

The Tourists (8 appearances) 24-05-78, 11-07-78, 31-07-78, 10-09-78, 24-09-78, 02-11-78, 13-12-78, 12-06-79
Annie and Dave then formed Eurythmics.

Tours (1 appearance) 27-11-79

Toyah (2 appearances) 12-08-79, 21-10-79

Trace (2 appearances) 28-03-75, 18-11-75

Lee Tracey (1 appearance) 29-04-70

Trader Horne (4 appearances) 04-02-71, 11-02-71, 18-02-71, 25-02-71

Traffic (4 appearances) 14-11-67, 30-01-68, 14-05-68, 03-09-68

The Train (1 appearance) 15-11-65

Tramline (13 appearances) 05-04-68, 10-05-68, 28-05-68, 28-06-68, 02-07-68, 16-07-68, 29-07-68, 16-08-68, 26-08-68, 02-09-68, 16-09-68, 27-09-68, 26-10-68
This lot featured future Whitesnake guitarist Micky Moody among their number.

Tranquility (1 appearance) 15-12-71

Trans Am (1 appearance) 25-11-78

Trapeze (19 appearances) 01-07-71, 25-09-72, 08-01-73, 15-01-73, 15-02-73, 23-03-73, 07-12-73, 02-01-74, 24-01-74, 22-02-74, 15-03-74, 07-04-74, 13-06-74, 15-07-74, 02-10-74, 18-06-75, 18-08-75, 27-07-77, 07-06-78
One-time Trapeze artist Glen Hughes was later to be found bassing in Deep Purple and sundry other heavy-metallurgists.

Trapper (1 appearance) 21 -06-75

Trash (3 appearances) 25-03-69, 25-04-69, 07-05-69

Pat Travers (4 appearances) 24-06-76, 31-08-76, 21-10-76, 31-12-76

Travis (2 appearances) 15-03-73, 23-08-73

Trees (3 appearances) 10-11-69, 04-05-70, 08-04-71

Tremeloes (2 appearances) 04-09-74, 16-10-74

The Triad (1 appearance) 02-06-66

The Tribe (11 appearances) 30-03-67, 04-05-67, 15-06-67, 01-07-67, 08-07-67, 15-07-67, 22-07-67, 29-07-67, 05-08-67, 12-08-67, 19-08-67

Trickster (1 appearance) 23-07-77

Trifle (7 appearances) 23-03-69, 13-04-69, 09-05-70, 06-06-70, 22-08-70, 26-09-70, 12-11-70

The Troggs (2 appearances) 26-07-66, 12-01-79

The Tropical Boot Company (1 appearances) 18-03-67

Trouble At Mill (1 appearance) 23-08-74

Robin Trower (3 appearances) 04-04-73, 24-04-73, 11-07-73

Tubeway Army (2 appearances) 19-02-78, 20-04-78

Tuesday (2 appearances) 31-08-74, 13-03-75

Tuesday's Children (3 appearances) 09-11-67, 28-12-67, 17-01-70

Dave Turner (1 appearance) 05-09-73

The Turnstyle (1 appearance) 03-05-69

Tush (1 appearance) 02-04-77

20th Century Steelband (1 appearance) 04-11-76

29th & Deerborn (2 appearances) 23-03-78, 05-10-78

Twink (1 appearance) 08-02-73

Twinkle Ripley (1 appearance) 15-03-73

Twist (1 appearance) 09-08-79

2001 (1 appearance) 05-05-69

The Tyla Gang (6 appearances) 03-11-75, 25-10-77, 10-11-77, 06-03-78, 15-05-78, 19-06-78

U

UFO (43 appearances) 22-02-71, 07-03-71, 14-03-71, 21-03-71, 28-03-71, 04-04-71, 18-04-71, 15-08-71, 21-11-71, 29-12-71, 17-01-72, 31-01-72, 27-03-

72, 31-05-72, 19-07-72, 06-08-72, 18-08-72, 28-08-72, 26-09-72, 03-11-72, 10-11-72, 17-11-72, 24-11-72, 01-12-72, 07-07-73, 29-07-73, 27-08-73, 23-12-73, 07-01-74, 16-05-74, 03-06-74, 10-07-74, 06-08-74, 08-09-74, 09-10-74, 27-12-74, 11-02-75, 15-06-75, 17-07-75, 25-08-75, 18-12-76, 19-12-76, 20-12-76
Long-lived rockers; their Marquee dates included guitarists Bernie Marsden and Michael Schenker at various times.

The Uglys (1 appearance) 11-10-65
Brum band with vocalist Steve Gibbons and later Fairport bassist Dave Pegg.

UK Subs (5 appearances) 22-01-79, 16-03-79, 16-10-79, 17-10-79, 18-10-79

The Ultimate (9 appearances) 21-07-66, 19-08-66, 021-09-66, 10-09-66, 08-10-66, 27-11-66, 16-12-66, 14-01-67, 23-01-67

Ultravox (19 appearances) 25-02-77, 25-03-77, 15-04-77, 12-05-77, 26-05-77, 16-06-77, 30-06-77, 14-07-77, 26-08-77, 31-12-77, 11-02-78, 12-02-78, 13-02-78, 19-08-78, 20-08-78, 21-08-78, 22-08-78, 23-08-78, 26-12-78

Undercarriage (3 appearances) 24-08-74, 07-12-74, 12-04-75

The Undertones (8 appearances) 12-11-78, 13-11-78, 19-02-79, 14-03-79, 01-08-79, 02-08-79, 03-08-79, 04-08-79

Unicorn (3 appearances) 26-10-76, 27-10-76, 28-10-76

Unit 4+2 (3 appearances) 11-03-72, 29-04-72, 27-05-72

Universe (6 appearances) 09-05-71, 11-06-71, 28-06-71, 03-08-71, 20-08-71, 12-09-71

The Untamed (1 appearance) 13-07-65

Unwanted (1 appearance) 20-06-77

Upp (13 appearances) 05-01-75, 16-02-75, 16-03-75, 02-05-75, 26-08-75, 28-08-75, 24-09-75, 13-11-75, 19-12-75, 19-03-76, 15-04-76, 09-11-76, 16-12-76

Uproar (1 appearance) 04-09-76

Urban Disturbance (1 appearance) 12-05-78

Uriah Heep (5 appearances) 19-05-70, 08-06-70, 10-08-70, 26-08-71, 09-11-71

V

Va-Va Voom (1 appearance) 27-08-77

The Vagabonds (1 appearance) 18-03-65

Valhalla (12 appearances) 14-12-75, 21-12-75, 28-12-75, 16-08-76, 23-08-76, 24-08-76, 06-09-76, 09-10-76, 30-10-76, 12-11-76, 04-07-77, 18-04-77

Valhalla UK (4 appearances) 14-02-70, 06-04-70, 13-04-70, 27-04-70

Van Der Graaf Generator (22 appearances) 27-11-68, 11-01-69, 30-01-69, 30-04-69, 19-04-70, 03-08-70, 26-07-70, 23-08-70, 06-09-70, 27-09-70, 18-10-70, 07-06-71, 07-07-71, 26-11-71, 27-07-76, 28-07-76, 29-07-76, 15-01-78, 16-01-78, 04-06-78, 05-06-78

Vanilla Fudge (1 appearance) 26-09-69

Vapour Trails (1 appearance) 16-07-77

The Vapours (5 appearances) 19-08-79, 01-09-79, 15-09-79, 06-10-79, 04-11-79

John Verity (2 appearances) 09-07-73, 07-12-73

Vermillion (1 appearance) 23-06-79
Mike Vernon (1 appearance) 07-04-72
The Versions (1 appearance) 18-05-67
VHF (1 appearance) 25-10-77
The Vibrations (1 appearance) 19-04-66
The Vibrators (8 appearances) 01-05-77, 30-07-77, 31-07-77, 01-08-77, 13-08-78, 14-08-78, 21-10-78, 22-10-78
Victim (2 appearances) 12-08-77, 17-10-77
Vikivaki (1 appearance) 06-05-76
Village (27 appearances) 14-08-68, 12-10-68, 29-10-68, 05-11-68, 21-11-68, 03-12-68, 20-12-68, 31-12-68, 10-01-69, 22-01-69, 01-02-69, 11-02-69, 27-03-69, 10-04-69, 17-04-69, 05-07-69, 12-07-69, 19-07-69, 26-07-69, 02-08-69, 09-08-69, 16-08-69, 23-08-69, 30-08-69, 06-09-69, 20-09-69, 27-09-69
Bassist Bruce Thomas went on to Quiver and Elvis Costello's Attractions.
Duke Vin's Sound-System (9 appearances) 02-06-64, 09-06-64, 16-06-64, 23-06-64, 30-06-64, 07-07-64, 14-07-64, 21-07-64, 28-07-64
Vin had come to England from Jamaica in 1954, one of the first to start a DJ sound-system here. He appeared in the 60s at the Flamingo as well as the Marquee, helping to spread the word on ska and reggae.
Gene Vincent (1 appearance) 22-09-71
Vinegar Joe (15 appearances) 29-09-71, 09-11-71, 07-12-71, 31-12-71, 06-01-72, 20-01-72, 10-02-72, 24-02-72, 30-03-72, 27-04-72, 30-05-72, 04-07-72, 01-08-72, 31-10-72, 23-12-72
Vineyard (2 appearances) 23-09-73, 09-11-74
Viola Wills (1 appearance) 01-06-75
The VIPs (9 appearances) 09-07-65, 26-07-65, 08-07-66, 12-08-66, 19-08-66, 01-09-66, 12-09-66, 17-10-66, 23-12-66
Vitas Dance (1 appearance) 21-10-79

W

Wages Of Sin (1 appearance) 02-06-67
T-Bone Walker (3 appearances) 28-01-65, 25-03-65, 15-10-65
The Wallace Collection (1 appearance) 31-07-69
Wally (5 appearances) 18-04-75, 12-05-75, 30-07-75, 29-09-75, 21-11-75
Walrus (2 appearances) 05-04-72, 19-04-72
Warhorse (4 appearances) 12-10-70, 29-03-71, 01-08-71, 28-11-71
Warlock (4 appearances) 23-03-74, 07-09-74, 31-05-75, 23-08-75
Warm Dust (2 appearances) 21-10-70, 04-12-70
Warm Jets (5 appearances) 24-05-79, 07-06-79, 05-07-79, 10-08-79, 06-09-79
Johnny Warman (1 appearance) 16-04-78
Harry Warren (2 appearances) 17-06-78, 14-10-78
Harry Warren & The Yum Yum Band (1 appearance) 10-03-75
Geno Washington (8 appearances) 28-03-67, 18-07-67, 17-10-67, 09-01-68, 04-04-70, 26-12-70, 07-05-75, 15-06-76
Wasps (2 appearances) 20-01-77, 22-04-77
Calmen Waters Blues Band (1 appearance) 22-08-69
Lloyd Watson (2 appearances) 02-08-

72, 16-08-72
Wayfarer (1 appearance) 12-02-71
Wayne County (1 appearance) 25-05-77
We Three Kings (1 appearance) 05-05-67
The Web (1 appearance) 19-05-67
Stan Webb (6 appearances) 11-09-74, 11-10-74, 17-12-74, 11-03-75, 22-04-75, 16-12-75
Stan Webb's Brokenglass (1 appearance) 20-05-75
Adrienne Webber (2 appearances) 20-07-73, 26-07-73
Aj Webber (4 appearances) 17-08-73, 23-10-73, 27-02-74, 16-07-75, 14-03-77
Max Webster (2 appearances) 08-06-79, 09-06-79
The Weightwatchers (1 appearance) 02-03-76
Wells Fargo (1 appearance) 21-01-73
West End (1 appearance) 11-10-79
West Farm Cottage (1 appearance) 20-12-71
Gavin Weston (2 appearances) 30-04-67, 06-01-71
Westpoint Supernaturals (2 appearances) 03-06-67, 26-06-67
Wheeler Django (1 appearance) 01-03-71
Wheels (1 appearance) 10-03-74
Whispering Smith (1 appearance) 09-06-72
White Lightning (1 appearance) 13-04-70
White Tam (2 appearances) 22-12-69, 12-01-70
White Trash (1 appearance) 21-10-69
Jaki Whitren (1 appearance) 30-06-74
The Who (29 appearances) 24-11-64, 01-12-64, 08-12-64, 15-12-64, 22-12-64, 29-12-64, 12-01-65, 26-01-65, 02-02-65, 09-02-65, 16-02-65, 23-02-65, 02-03-65, 09-03-65, 16-03-65, 23-03-65, 30-03-65, 06-04-65, 13-04-65, 20-04-65, 27-04-65, 25-05-65, 07-06-65, 13-07-65, 02-11-65, 05-12-65, 21-12-65, 23-04-68, 17-12-68
Wide Open (1 appearance) 28-12-70
Widowmaker (1 appearance) 31-07-76
Wild Angels (3 appearances) 27-06-70, 23-12-70, 02-07-76
Wild Horses (2 appearances) 07-03-79, 16-04-79, 17-04-79
Wild Turkey (25 appearances) 07-05-71, 29-07-71, 10-10-71, 16-08-72, 13-10-72, 02-01-73, 01-03-73, 22-03-73, 22-04-73, 30-05-73, 24-06-73, 01-07-73, 25-07-73, 16-08-73, 05-09-73, 24-10-73, 30-11-73, 01-12-73, 22-12-73, 30-01-74, 18-02-74, 25-03-74, 17-04-74, 09-05-74, 24-06-74
The Wild Wax Show (1 appearance) 02-07-76
The Wilde Flowers (1 appearance) 03-11-67
Wildmouth (1 appearance) 20-04-71
Derry Wilkie (1 appearance) 11-11-65
Sonny Boy Williamson (5 appearances) 24-12-63, 31-12-63, 10-02-64, 13-03-64, 30-12-64
Willis (3 appearances) 17-01-73, 24-01-73, 31-01-73
The Wimps (1 appearance) 29-08-79
Window (9 appearances) 19-02-77, 02-04-77, 07-05-77, 12-06-77, 20-01-78, 03-02-78, 17-02-78, 02-03-78, 16-03-78
Martin Windsor (1 appearance) 25-01-67
Wine (2 appearances) 21-03-69, 03-06-69

Pete Wingfield (1 appearance) 07-04-72
The Winkies (6 appearances) 02-04-74, 16-06-74, 17-07-74, 20-08-74, 02-09-74, 21-12-74
Winston's Fumbs (1 appearance) 11-07-67
The Wipers (1 appearance) 01-04-78
Wire (6 appearances) 04-08-77, 10-12-77, 02-02-78, 29-03-78, 22-11-78, 23-11-78
Wishbone Ash (10 appearances) 08-05-70, 04-06-70, 15-06-70, 16-09-70, 02-02-71, 04-05-71, 31-12-71, 17-03-73, 18-03-73, 29-10-77
Wishful Thinking (1 appearance) 01-07-66
Wisper (2 appearances) 16-03-72, 02-11-72
Jimmy Witherspoon (1 appearance) 28-11-68
Wolf (9 appearances) 22-11-71, 12-07-73, 08-08-73, 11-09-73, 06-11-73, 10-01-74, 01-04-74, 14-05-74, 06-06-74
Wolfrilla (1 appearance) 15-10-70
Woman (2 appearances) 04-01-75, 07-03-75, 25-09-75
Stevie Wonder (1 appearance) 07-02-66
Art Wood (1 appearance) 15-04-63
Woodfall (1 appearance) 04-12-71
Woody Woodmansey (11 appearances) 09-09-76, 03-10-76, 10-10-76, 17-10-76, 24-10-76, 31-10-76, 10-11-76, 09-12-76, 07-01-77, 14-02-77, 20-05-77
Bruce Woolley (1 appearance) 03-12-79
The Workshop (2 appearances) 28-07-67, 01-09-67
The World (3 appearances) 02-08-70, 13-09-70, 03-12-70
Wreckless Eric (2 appearances) 05-02-79, 20-12-79
Gary Wright (1 appearance) 12-01-72
Writing On The Wall (43 appearances) 04-10-69, 11-10-69, 18-10-69, 25-10-69, 03-11-69, 10-11-69, 17-11-69, 24-11-69, 01-12-69, 08-12-69, 15-12-69, 22-12-69, 29-12-69, 05-01-70, 13-01-70, 19-01-70, 26-01-70, 12-02-70, 26-02-70, 12-03-70, 26-03-70, 16-04-70, 30-04-70, 04-06-70, 06-08-70, 26-08-70, 31-10-71, 24-07-72, 06-05-73, 20-05-73, 03-06-73, 17-06-73, 08-07-73, 22-07-73, 16-09-73, 29-09-73, 04-11-73, 13-01-74, 27-01-74, 10-02-74, 24-02-74, 21-04-74, 26-05-74
WOTW manager Brian Waldman had run the Middle Earth club in Covent Garden.
Writz (1 appearance) 06-12-79
Derek Wyatt (1 appearance) 03-04-74
Wynder K Frog (18 appearances) 13-09-66, 20-09-66, 31-10-66, 10-11-66, 23-12-66, 06-01-67, 02-02-67, 07-03-67, 14-03-67, 11-04-67, 18-04-67, 25-04-67, 09-05-67, 30-05-67, 27-06-67, 24-07-67, 05-03-68, 17-10-68
Most of Wynder K Frog became The Grease Band, who went on to be Joe Cocker's fine backing group.

X, Y

X-Effects (1 appearance) 08-09-79
X-Ray Spex (7 appearances) 23-05-77, 06-08-77, 26-09-77, 06-10-77, 26-10-77, 18-11-77, 30-12-77
XTC (3 appearances) 23-11-77, 30-05-78, 31-05-78
This is pop.

The Yachts (4 appearances) 07-11-77, 05-03-78, 29-10-78, 19-06-79
The Yardbirds (43 appearances) 06-02-64, 13-02-64, 20-02-64, 27-02-64, 05-03-64, 13-03-64, 20-03-64, 27-03-64, 03-04-64, 10-04-64, 17-04-64, 01-05-64, 08-05-64, 15-05-64, 22-05-64, 29-05-64, 05-06-64, 12-06-64, 19-06-64, 03-07-64, 10-07-64, 17-07-64, 24-07-64, 29-07-64, 07-08-64, 04-09-64, 11-09-64, 23-10-64, 30-10-64, 22-01-65, 01-02-65, 15-02-65, 08-03-65, 29-03-65, 26-04-65, 03-05-65, 17-05-65, 08-06-65, 06-07-65, 12-10-65, 15-03-66, 03-05-66, 13-06-66
On the first date here you would have seen Eric Clapton in the line-up; by the March '65 gigs God was out and Beck was in; and that last date in 66 might well have had Jimmy Page on board. See Led Zeppelin for later Marquee moves...
Thomas Yates (1 appearance) 29-07-70
Yellow (1 appearance) 05-11-70
Yellow Bird (3 appearances) 17-08-74, 05-04-75, 07-02-76
Yellowstone & Voice (1 appearance) 18-10-72
Yes (38 appearances) 05-08-68, 17-08-68, 06-09-68, 19-09-68, 28-09-68, 02-11-68, 13-11-68, 27-11-68, 17-12-68, 01-01-69, 08-01-69, 15-01-69, 22-01-69, 29-01-69, 05-02-69, 12-02-69, 19-02-69, 26-02-69, 05-03-69, 12-03-69, 19-03-69, 02-04-69, 09-04-69, 14-05-69, 28-05-69, 11-06-69, 25-06-69, 02-07-69, 07-09-69, 09-07-69, 16-07-69, 23-07-69, 30-07-69, 07-08-69, 14-08-69, 30-10-69, 26-12-69, 10-04-70, 18-08-70
Covering the period from their formation to the arrival of Steve Howe (August '70 gig).
Pete York (1 appearance) 16-07-71
Young Blood (1 appearance) 24-06-68
An early outing for the percussive power of drummer Cozy Powell.
Young Bucks (7 appearances) 23-02-78, 19-11-78, 07-01-79, 14-01-79, 21-01-79, 28-01-79, 24-03-79
The Young Ones (8 appearances) 11-03-78, 10-08-78, 11-08-78, 09-09-79, 16-09-79, 23-09-79, 30-09-79, 07-10-79
Roy Young (2 appearances) 27-09-72, 30-10-73

Z

Zaine Griff (9 appearances) 02-09-78, 13-10-78, 31-10-78, 17-11-78, 04-12-78, 30-01-79, 01-03-79, 05-04-79, 24-08-79
Zaine Griff & Screemer (2 appearances) 22-05-77, 29-05-77
Zal (1 appearance) 22-03-78
Zebidee (1 appearance) 29-09-67
Zeus (4 appearances) 18-12-67, 28-09-72, 20-11-72, 03-02-73
Zhain (2 appearances) 15-06-74, 10-08-74
Zior (3 appearances) 23-05-70, 13-09-71, 22-12-71
Zoe (1 appearance) 23-11-73
Zoo (1 appearance) 16-05-71
Zzebra (12 appearances) 20-07-74, 01-09-74, 15-09-74, 29-09-74, 20-10-74, 11-11-74, 28-11-74, 09-12-74, 14-02-75, 19-03-75, 16-06-75, 02-10-75
This jazz-flavoured band have one major claim to fame: they are virtually guaranteed the last entry in any widely-drawn A-Z of British rock history. Luckily for them, ZZ Top never played the Marquee.

This listing details on a day-by-day basis all the pop bands that played at the Marquee from April 1962 to December 1979. It works in conjunction with the A-Z listing of the bands that can be found on pages 148-163. If more than one band is shown with the same date, the first band is the headliner.

April 1962
Fr 06 Alexis Korner (with Chris Barber)
W 11 Cyril Davies (with Chris Barber)
May 1962
Th 10 Blues Incorporated
Th 17 Blues Incorporated
Th 24 Blues Incorporated
Th 31 Blues Incorporated
June 1962
Th 07 Blues Incorporated
Th 14 Blues Incorporated
Th 21 Blues Incorporated
Th 28 Blues Incorporated
July 1962
Th 05 Blues Incorporated
Th 12 Blues Incorporated
Th 19 Blues Incorporated
Th 26 Blues Incorporated
August 1962
Th 02 Blues Incorporated
Th 09 Blues Incorporated
Th 16 Blues Incorporated
Th 23 Blues Incorporated
Th 30 Blues Incorporated
September 1962
Th 06 Blues Incorporated
Th 13 Blues Incorporated
Th 20 Blues Incorporated
Th 27 Blues Incorporated
October 1962
Th 04 Blues Incorporated
Th 11 Blues Incorporated
Th 11 Ronnie Jones
Th 18 Blues Incorporated
Th 18 Ronnie Jones
Th 25 Blues Incorporated
November 1962
Th 01 Blues Incorporated
Th 08 Blues Incorporated
Th 15 Blues Incorporated
Th 22 Blues Incorporated
Th 29 Blues Incorporated
December 1962
M 03 Blues Incorporated
M 03 Graham Bond
M 06 Blues Incorporated
Su 09 "Manne-Hug Quartet"
M 10 Blues Incorporated
M 10 Graham Bond
M 13 Blues Incorporated
M 17 Blues Incorporated
M 17 Graham Bond
M 20 Blues Incorporated
M 24 Blues Incorporated
Th 27 Blues Incorporated
M 31 Blues Incorporated
January 1963
Th 03 Cyril Davies R&B Group
M 07 Blues By Six
M 07 Big Pete Deuchar's Country Blues
Th 10 Cyril Davies All-Star R&B Group
Th 10 The Rollin' Stones
M 14 Blues By Six
M 14 Big Pete Deuchar's Country Blues
Th 17 Cyril Davies All-Star R&B Group
Th 17 The Rollin' Stones
M 21 Blues By Six
M 21 Big Pete Deuchar's Country Blues
Th 24 Cyril Davies All-Stars
Th 24 The Rollin' Stones
M 28 Big Pete Deuchar's Country Blues
M 28 Blues By Six
Th 31 Cyril Davies All-Stars
Th 31 The Rollin' Stones
February 1963
M 04 Big Pete Deuchar's Country Blues
M 04 Blues By Six
Th 07 Cyril Davies All-Stars

M 11 Big Pete Deuchar's Country Blues
M 11 Blues By Six
Th 14 Cyril Davies All-Stars
M 18 Big Pete Deuchar's Country Blues
M 18 Blues By Six
Th 21 Cyril Davies All-Stars
M 25 Big Pete Deuchar's Country Blues
M 25 Blues By Six
Th 28 Cyril Davies All-Stars
March 1963
M 04 Big Pete Deuchar's Country Blues
M 04 Blues By Six
Th 07 Cyril Davies All-Stars
M 11 Big Pete Deuchar's Country Blues
Th 14 Cyril Davies All-Stars
M 18 Big Pete Deuchar's Country Blues
M 18 Mann-Hugg Blues Brothers
Th 21 Cyril Davies All-Stars
M 25 Big Pete Deuchar's Country Blues
M 25 Mann-Hugg Blues Brothers
Th 28 Cyril Davies All-Stars
April 1963
M 01 Mann-Hugg Blues Brothers
M 01 Big Pete Deuchar's Country Blues
Th 04 Cyril Davies All-Stars
M 08 Big Pete Deuchar's Country Blues
M 08 Mann-Hugg Blues Brothers
Th 11 Cyril Davies All-Stars
Sa 13 Graham Bond
M 15 Mann-Hugg Blues Brothers
M 15 Art Wood R&B Combo
Th 18 Cyril Davies All-Stars
M 22 Big Pete Deuchar's Country Blues
M 22 Mann-Hugg Blues Brothers
Th 25 Cyril Davies All-Stars
M 29 Mann-Hugg Blues Borthers
M 29 Big Pete Deuchar's Country Blues
May 1963
Th 02 Cyril Davies All-Stars
M 06 Big Pete Deuchar's Country Blues
M 06 Mann-Hugg Blues Brothers
M 09 Cyril Davies All-Stars
M 13 Mann-Hugg Blues Brothers
M 13 Big Pete Deuchar's Country Blues
Th 16 Cyril Davies All-Stars
M 20 Big Pete Deuchar's Country Blues
M 20 Graham Bond Quintet
Th 23 Cyril Davies All-Stars
M 27 Mann-Hugg Blues Brothers
M 27 Big Pete Deuchar's Country Blues
Th 30 Cyril Davies All-Stars
June 1963
M 03 Big Pete Deuchar's Country Blues
M 03 Mann-Hugg Blues Brothers
Th 06 Cyril Davies All-Stars
M 10 Mann-Hugg Blues Borthers
Th 13 Cyril Davies All-Stars
M 17 Mann-Hugg Blues Brothers
M 24 Mann-Hugg Blues Brothers
Th 27 Cyril Davies All-Stars
Th 30 Cyril Davies All-Stars
July 1963
M 01 Mann-Hugg Blues Brothers
Th 04 Cyril Davies All-Stars
M 08 Mann-Hugg Blues Brothers
Th 11 Cyril Davies All-Stars
M 15 (Mann-Hugg) Blues Brothers
M 15 The Roosters

Th 18 Cyril Davies All-Stars
M 22 (Mann-Hugg) Blues Brothers
Th 25 Cyril Davies All-Stars
M 29 (Mann-Hugg) Blues Brothers
M 29 Chris Farlowe
August 1963
Th 01 Cyril Davies All-Stars
M 05 (Mann-Hugg) Blues Brothers
Th 08 Cyril Davies All-Stars
M 12 (Mann-Hugg) Blues Brothers
Tu 13 The Brian Auger Trinity
Th 15 Cyril Davies All-Stars
M 19 Manfred Mann
M 19 (Mann-Hugg) Blues Brothers
Th 22 Cyril Davies All-Stars
M 26 Manfred Mann
M 26 (Mann-Hugg) Blues Brothers
Th 29 Cyril Davies All-Stars
September 1963
M 02 Manfred Mann
Th 05 Cyril Davies All-Stars
M 09 Manfred Mann
Th 12 Cyril Davies All-Stars
Sa 14 The Brian Auger Trinity
M 16 Manfred Mann
M 19 Cyril Davies All-Stars
M 23 Manfred Mann
Th 26 Cyril Davies All-Stars
M 30 Manfred Mann
October 1963
Th 03 Cyril Davies All-Stars
M 07 Manfred Mann
Th 10 Cyril Davies All-Stars
M 14 Manfred Mann
M 14 Hogsnort Rupert R&B Band
Th 17 Cyril Davies All-Stars
M 21 Manfred Mann
Th 24 Cyril Davies All-Stars
M 28 Manfred Mann
Th 31 Cyril Davies All-Stars
November 1963
M 04 Manfred Mann
M 04 John Mayall's Bluesbreakers
Th 07 Cyril Davies All-Stars
Su 10 The Brian Auger Trinity
M 11 Manfred Mann
M 14 Cyril Davies All-Stars
M 18 Manfred Mann
M 18 John Mayall's Bluesbreakers
Th 21 Cyril Davies All-Stars
Sa 23 The Brian Auger Trinity
M 25 Manfred Mann
M 25 Zoot Money R&B Group
Th 28 Cyril Davies All-Stars
December 1963
M 02 Manfred Mann
M 02 John Mayall's Bluesbreakers
M 05 Cyril Davies All-Stars
M 09 Manfred Mann
Th 12 Cyril Davies All-Stars
M 16 Manfred Mann
M 16 John Mayall's Bluesbreakers
Th 19 Cyril Davies All-Stars
M 23- Manfred Mann
M 23 Zoot Money R&B Group
Tu 24 Sonny Boy Williamson
Tu 24 Cyril Davies All-Stars
Su 29 The Brian Auger Trinity
M 30 Manfred Mann
M 30 John Mayall's Bluesbreakers
Tu 31 Sonny Boy Williamson
January 1964
Th 02 Cyril Davies All-Stars
M 06 Manfred Mann
Th 09 (Cyril Davies) All-Stars
M 13 Manfred Mann
Th 16 (Cyril Davies) All-Stars
M 20 Manfred Mann
Th 23 (Cyril Davies) All-Stars
Su 26 The Brian Auger Trinity
M 27 Manfred Mann
Th 30 (Cyril Davies) All-Stars
February 1964
M 03 The Cheynes

M 03 John Mayall's Bluesbreakers
Tu 04 Red Price and the Blue Beats
Th 06 Long John Baldry and the
Hoochie Coochie Men
Th 06 Long John Baldry and the
Hoochie Coochie Men
M 10 Sonny Boy Williamson
M 10 Manfred Mann
M 10 The Cheynes
Tu 11 Red Price and the Blue Beats
Th 13 Long John Baldry and the
Hoochie Coochie Men
Th 13 The Yardbirds
M 17 The Cheynes
M 17 John Mayall's Bluesbreakers
Tu 18 Red Price and the Blue Beats
Th 20 Long John Baldry and the
Hoochie Coochie Men
Th 20 The Yardbirds
Su 23 The Brian Auger Trinity
M 24 The Cheynes
M 24 John Mayall's Bluesbreakers
Tu 25 Red Price and the Blue Beats
Th 27 Long John Baldry and the
Hoochie Coochie Men
Th 27 The Yardbirds

March 1964
M 02 The Cheynes
M 02 John Mayall's Bluesbreakers
Tu 03 Lester Dawson and the Blue
Beats
Th 05 Long John Baldry and the
Hoochie Coochie Men
Th 05 The Yardbirds

The removal from Oxford Street to
Wardour Street took place in this gap.
Frr 13 Sonny Boy Williamson
Fr 13 Long John Baldry and the
Hoochie Coochie Men
Fr 13 The Yardbirds
M 16 The Cheynes
M 16 Zoot Money's Big Roll Band
Tu 17 Lester Dawson & the Blue Beats
Th 19 Long John Baldry and the
Hoochie Coochie Men
Fr 20 The Yardbirds
M 23 The Cheynes
M 23 John Mayall's Bluesbreakers
Tu 24 Lester Dawson & the Blue Beats
Th 26 Long John Baldry and the
Hoochie Coochie Men
Fr 27 The Yardbirds
M 30 Manfred Mann
M 30 The Cheynes
Tu 31 Lester Dawson and the Blue
Beats

April 1964
Th 02 Long John Baldry and the
Hoochie Coochie Men
Th 02 Andy McKinley and the see see
riders
Fr 03 The Yardbirds
Fr 03 The Impulsions
M 06 Manfred Mann
M 06 John Mayall's Bluesbreakers
Tu 07 Lester Dawson and the Blue
Beats
Th 09 Long John Baldry and the
Hoochie Coochie Men
Th 09 Andy McKinley and the See
See Riders
Fr 10 The Yardbirds
Fr 10 The Impulsions
M 13 Manfred Mann
M 13 The Mark Leeman Five
Th 16 Long John Baldry and the
Hoochie Coochie Men
Th 16 Andy McKinley and the See
See Riders
Fr 17 The Yardbirds
Fr 17 The Impulsions
M 20 Manfred Mann
Tu 21 Lester Dawson and the Blue
Beats
Th 23 Long John Baldry and the

Hoochie Coochie Men
Fr 24 Andy McKinley and the see see
riders
M 27 The Migil Five
M 27 John Mayall's Bluesbreakers
Tu 28 Lester Dawson and the Blue
Beats
Th 30 Long John Baldry and the
Hoochie Coochie Men
Th 30 Andy McKinley and the see see
riders

May 1964
Fr 01 The Yardbirds
Fr 01 The Authentics
Su 03 Champion Jack Dupree
M 04 Manfred Mann
Tu 05 Cyko and the Red Devils
Tu 05 Fritz and the Blue Beats
Th 07 The Cheynes
Th 07 The Bluebirds
Fr 08 The Yardbirds
Fr 08 The Authentics
M 11 Manfred Mann
M 11 John Mayall's Bluesbreakers
Tu 12 Cyko and the Red Devils
Tu 12 Fritz and the Blue Beats
Th 14 The Cheynes
Th 14 The Bluebirds
Fr 15 The Yardbirds
Fr 15 The Authentics
M 18 Manfred Mann
M 18 John Mayall's Bluesbreakers
Tu 19 Cyko and the Red Devils
Tu 19 Fritz and the Blue Beats
Th 21 Memphis Slim
Th 21 Long John Baldry and the
Hoochie Coochie Men
Fr 22 The Yardbirds
Fr 22 The Authentics
M 25 The Migil Five
Tu 26 Cyko and the Red Devils
Tu 26 Fritz and the Blue Beats
Th 28 Long John Baldry and the
Hoochie Coochie Men
Fr 29 The Yardbirds
Fr 29 The Authentics

June 1964
M 01 The Mark Leeman Five
M 01 The Bluebirds
Tu 02 The Blue Beats
Tu 02 Duke Vin's Sound-System
Th 04 Long John Baldry and the
Hoochie Coochie Men
Th 04 The Grebbels
Fr 05 The Yardbirds
Fr 05 The Authentics
M 08 Manfred Mann
M 08 The Mark Leeman Five
Tu 09 The Blue Beats
Tu 09 Duke Vin's Sound-System
Th 11 Long John Baldry and the
Hoochie Coochie Men
Th 11 The Bluebirds
Fr 12 The Yardbirds
Fr 12 The Authentics
M 15 Manfred Mann
M 15 The Mark Leeman Five
Th 16 The Blue Beats
Tu 16 Duke Vin's Sound-System
Th 18 Long John Baldry and the
Hoochie Coochie Men
Th 18 The Bluebirds
Fr 19 The Yardbirds
Fr 19 The Authentics
M 22 Manfred Mann
M 22 The Mark Leeman Five
Tu 23 The Blue Beats
Tu 23 Duke Vin's Sound-System
Th 25 Long John Baldry and the
Hoochie Coochie Men
Th 25 The Bluebirds
Fr 26 The T-Bones
Fr 26 The Authentics
M 29 Manfred Mann

M 29 The Mark Leeman Five
Tu 30 The Blue Beats
Tu 30 Duke Vin's Sound-System

July 1964
Th 02 Long John Baldry and the
Hoochie Coochie Men
Th 02 The Grebbels
Fr 03 The Yardbirds
Fr 03 The Authentics
M 06 Manfred Mann
M 06 The Mark Leeman Five
Tu 07 Dick Charlesworth's Big Blues
Tu 07 Duke Vin's Sound-System
Th 09 Long John Baldry and the
Hoochie Coochie Men
Th 09 The Grebbels
Fr 10 The Yardbirds
Fr 10 The Authentics
M 13 The T-Bones
Tu 14 Dick Charlesworth's Big Blues
Tu 14 Duke Vin's Sound-System
Th 16 Long John Baldry and the
Hoochie Coochie Men
Th 16 The Grebbels
Fr 17 The Yardbirds
Fr 17 The Authentics
M 20 Manfred Mann
Tu 21 Dick Charlesworth's Big Blues
Tu 21 Duke Vin's Sound-System
Th 23 The T-Bones
Th 23 The Grebbels
Fr 24 The Yardbirds
Fr 24 The Authentics
M 27 Manfred Mann
Tu 28 Dick Charlesworth's Big Blues
Tu 28 Duke Vin's Sound-System
Fr 29 The Yardbirds
Fr 29 The Authentics

August 1964
M 03 The Mike Cotton Sound
M 03 The Night Shift
Tu 04 Dick Charlesworth's Big Blues
Th 06 Long John Baldry and the
Hoochie Coochie Men
Th 06 The Grebbels
Fr 07 The Yardbirds
Fr 07 The Brakemen
M 10 Manfred Mann
M 10 John Mayall's Bluesbreakers
Tu 11 Dick Charlesworth's Big Blues
Th 13 Long John Baldry and the
Hoochie Coochie Men
Th 13 The Grebbels
Fr 14 The T-Bones
Fr 14 The Authentics
M 17 Manfred Mann
Tu 18 Dick Charlesworth's Big Blues
Th 20 Long John Baldry and the
Hoochie Coochie Men
Th 20 The Grebbels
Fr 21 The T-Bones
Fr 21 David John and the Mood
M 24 Manfred Mann
Tu 25 Dick Charlesworth's Big Blues
Th 27 Memphis Slim
Fr 28 The T-Bones
Fr 28 The Authentics
M 31 Manfred Mann
M 31 The Mark Leeman Five

September 1964
Tu 01 Dick Charlesworth's Big Blues
W 02 The Exotics
Th 03 The Moody Blues
Th 03 The Night Shift
Fr 04 The Yardbirds
Fr 04 The Dissatisfieds
M 07 Manfred Mann
Tu 08 Dick Charlesworth's Big Blues
Th 10 Long John Baldry and the
Hoochie Coochie Men
Th 10 The Exotics
Fr 11 The Yardbirds
Fr 11 The Moody Blues
M 14 Manfred Mann

Tu 15 Dick Charlesworth's Big Blues
Th 17 Long John Baldry and the
Hoochie Coochie Men
Fr 18 The T-Bones
Fr 18 The Clique
M 21 Manfred Mann
Tu 22 Dick Charlesworth's Big Blues
W 23 The Exotics
Th 24 The Moody Blues
Th 24 The Night Shift
Fr 25 The T-Bones
Fr 25 The Barbarians
M 28 Manfred Mann
Tu 29 Dick Charlesworth's Big Blues

October 1964
Th 01 Little Walter
Th 01 Long John Baldry and the
Hoochie Coochie Men
Fr 02 The T-Bones
Fr 02 The Dissatisfieds
Su 04 The Moody Blues
M 05 Manfred Mann
Tu 06 Dick Charlesworth's Big Blues
Th 08 The Mike Cotton Sound
Th 08 The Night Shift
Fr 09 The T-Bones
Fr 09 The Dissatisfieds
M 12 Manfred Mann
Tu 13 Dick Charlesworth's Big Blues
Th 15 Long John Baldry and the
Hoochie Coochie Men
Fr 16 The T-Bones
Fr 16 The Night Shift
M 19 Manfred Mann
Tu 20 Dick Charlesworth's Big Blues
Th 22 Long John Baldry and the
Hoochie Coochie Men
Fr 23 The Yardbirds
M 26 Manfred Mann
Tu 27 Dick Charlesworth's Big Blues
Th 29 Long John Baldry and the
Hoochie Coochie Men
Fr 30 The Yardbirds
Fr 30 The Night Shift

November 1964
M 02 Manfred Mann
M 02 The Mark Leeman Five
Tu 03 Dick Charlesworth's Big Blues
Tu 03 Bobby Breen and The Outsiders
Th 05 Long John Baldry and the
Hoochie Coochie Men
Fr 06 The T-Bones
M 09 Manfred Mann
M 09 The Mark Leeman Five
Tu 10 Dick Charlesworth's Big Blues
Tu 10 Bobby Breen and The Outsiders
Th 12 Long John Baldry and the
Hoochie Coochie Men
Th 12 The Muleskinners
Fr 13 The T-Bones
M 16 Manfred Mann
M 16 The Mark Leeman Five
Tu 17 Dick Charlesworth's Big Blues
Tu 17 Bobby Breen and The Outsiders
Th 19 Long John Baldry and the
Hoochie Coochie Men
Th 19 The Night Shift
Fr 20 The T-Bones
M 23 The Moody Blues
M 23 The Muleskinners
Tu 24 The Who
Tu 24 The Sneakers
Th 26 Long John Baldry and the
Hoochie Coochie Men
Th 26 Howlin' Wolf
Fr 27 The T-Bones
M 30 Manfred Mann

December 1964
Tu 01 The Who
Tu 01 The Sneakers
W 02 The Brian Auger Trinity
Th 03 Long John Baldry and the
Hoochie Coochie Men
Fr 04 The T-Bones

Fr 04 The Muleskinners
M 07 The Moody Blues
M 07 The Mark Leeman Five
Tu 08 The Who
Tu 08 The Sneakers
W 09 The Brian Auger Trinity
Th 10 The Sheffields
Th 10 Rod Stewart
Fr 11 The T-Bones
Fr 11 David John and the Mood
M 14 The Moody Blues
M 14 The Mark Leeman Five
Tu 15 The Who
Tu 15 The Sneakers
W 16 The Brian Auger Trinity
Th 17 Jimmy Powell and the Five Dimensions
Th 17 Rod Stewart
Fr 18 The T-Bones
M 21 The Moody Blues
M 21 The Mark Leeman Five
Tu 22 The Who
Tu 22 The Sneakers
W 23 The Brian Auger Trinity
Th 24 Long John Baldry and the Hoochie Coochie Men
Th 24 Rod Stewart
M 28 Manfred Mann
M 28 The Mark Leeman Five
Tu 29 The Who
Tu 29 The Sneakers
W 30 Sonny Boy Williamson
W 30 The Brian Auger Trinity
W 30 Long John Baldry and the Hoochie Coochie Men

January 1965
Fr 01 The T-Bones
Fr 01 The Ingoes
M 04 The Moody Blues
M 04 The Mark Leeman Five
W 06 The Brian Auger Trinity
Th 07 Long John Baldry and the Hoochie Coochie Men
Th 07 Rod Stewart with The Soul Agents
Fr 08 The T-Bones
Fr 08 The Muleskinners
M 11 The Mark Leeman Five
Tu 12 The Who
W 13 The Brian Auger Trinity
Th 14 Rod Stewart with The Soul Agents
Th 14 Alex Harvey Soul Band
Fr 15 The T-Bones
M 18 Mark Leeman Five
Th 21 Rod Stewart with the Soul Agents
Th 21 Jimmy Powell and the Five Dimensions
Fr 22 The Yardbirds
M 25 The Mark Leeman Five
Tu 26 The Who
W 27 The Brian Auger Trinity
Th 28 T-Bone Walker
Th 28 Rod Stewart with The Soul Agents
Fr 29 The T-Bones

Februray 1965
M 01 The Yardbirds
M 01 The Mark Leeman Five
Tu 02 The Who
Th 04 Long John Baldry and the Hoochie Coochie Men
Th 04 Rod Stewart with The Soul Agents
Fr 05 The T-Bones
M 08 The Moody Blues
Tu 09 The Who
Th 11 Long John Baldry and the Hoochie Coochie Men
Th 11 Rod Stewart with The Soul Agents
Fr 12 The T-Bones
M 15 The Yardbirds

Tu 16 The Who
Th 18 Rod Stewart with The Soul Agents
Th 18 Jimmy Powell and the Five Dimensions
Fr 19 The T-Bones
Sa 20 The Brian Auger Trinity
M 22 The Moody Blues
M 22 The Mark Leeman Five
Tu 23 The Who
Th 25 Buddy Guy
Th 25 Long John Baldry and the Hoochie Coochie Men
Fr 26 The T-Bones

March 1965
M 01 Spencer Davis Group
M 01 The Mark Leeman Five
Tu 02 The Who
Th 04 Long John Baldry and the Hoochie Coochie Men
Th 04 Alex Harvey Soul Band
Fr 05 (Gary Farr and) The T-Bones
M 08 The Yardbirds
M 08 The Mark Leeman Five
Tu 09 The Who
Th 11 Long John Baldry and the Hoochie Coochie Men
Th 11 Alex Harvey Soul Band
Fr 12 (Gary Farr and) The T-Bones
M 15 Manfred Mann
M 15 The Mark Leeman Five
Tu 16 The Who
Th 18 The Mike Cotton Sound
Th 18 The Vagabonds
Fr 19 (Gary Farr and) The T-Bones
M 22 The Moody Blues
M 22 The Mark Leeman Five
Tu 23 The Who
Th 25 T-Bone Walker
Fr 26 (Gary Farr and) The T-Bones
M 29 The Yardbirds
M 29 The Mark Leeman Five
Tu 30 The Who

April 1965
Th 01 Long John Baldry and the Hoochie Coochie Men
Th 01 Alex Harvey Soul Band
Fr 02 (Gary Farr and) The T-Bones
M 05 Manfred Mann
Tu 06 The Who
Th 08 Long John Baldry and the Hoochie Coochie Men
Th 08 Alex Harvey Soul Band
Fr 09 (Gary Farr and) The T-Bones
M 12 Manfred Mann
Tu 13 The Who
Th 15 Long John Baldry and the Hoochie Coochie Men
Th 15 Alex Harvey Soul Band
Fr 16 (Gary Farr and) The T-Bones
M 19 The Moody Blues
M 19 The Mark Leeman Five
Tu 20 The Who
Th 22 Long John Baldry and the Hoochie Coochie Men
Th 22 Alex Harvey Soul Band
Fr 23 (Gary Farr and) The T-Bones
M 26 The Yardbirds
M 26 The Mark Leeman Five
Tu 27 The Who
Th 29 Long John Baldry and the Hoochie Coochie Men
Th 29 Alex Harvey Soul Band
Fr 30 (Gary Farr and) The T-Bones

May 1965
M 03 The Yardbirds
M 03 The Mark Leeman Five
Tu 04 Spencer Davis Group
Tu 04 Julian Covey and the Machine
Th 06 Long John Baldry and the Hoochie Coochie Men
Th 06 Alex Harvey Soul Band
Fr 07 Elkie Brooks
Fr 07 The Crow

Fr 07 The Mike Cotton Sound
M 10 The Moody Blues
Tu 11 Manfred Mann
Tu 11 The Mark Leeman Five
Th 13 Long John Baldry and the Hoochie Coochie Men
Th 13 Alex Harvey Soul Band
Fr 14 The Ivy League
M 17 The Yardbirds
Tu 18 Jimmy James and The Vagabonds
Tu 18 The Mark Leeman Five
Th 20 Long John Baldry and the Hoochie Coochie Men
Th 20 Alex Harvey Soul Band
Fr 21 (Gary Farr and) The T-Bones
M 24 Manfred Mann
Tu 25 The Who
Tu 25 The Mark Leeman Five
Th 27 Memphis Slim
Th 27 Alex Harvey Soul Band
Th 27 Long John Baldry and the Hoochie Coochie Men
Fr 28 (Gary Farr and) The T-Bones
M 31 Jimmy James and The Vagabonds

June 1965
Tu 01 The Moody Blues
Tu 01 The Muleskinners
Th 03 Long John Baldry and the Hoochie Coochie Men
Th 03 Alex Harvey Soul Band
Fr 04 (Gary Farr and) The T-Bones
M 07 The Who
M 07 Jimmy James and The Vagabonds
Tu 08 The Yardbirds
Tu 08 The Mark Leeman Five
Th 10 Long John Baldry and the Hoochie Coochie Men
Th 10 Alex Harvey Soul Band
Fr 11 (Gary Farr and) The T-Bones
M 14 Solomon Burke
M 14 Jimmy James and The Vagabonds
M 14 The Mike Cotton Sound
Tu 15 Spencer Davis Group
Tu 15 The Mark Leeman Five
Th 17 Long John Baldry and the Hoochie Coochie Men
Th 17 Alex Harvey Soul Band
Fr 18 (Gary Farr and) The T-Bones
Su 20 Tommy Quickly
Su 20 The Remo Four
M 21 Jimmy James and The Vagabonds
M 21 Ronnie Jones and the Blue Jays
Th 24 Long John Baldry and the Hoochie Coochie Men
Th 24 Alex Harvey Soul Band
Fr 25 (Gary Farr and) The T-Bones
Fr 25 The Crow
M 28 Jimmy James and The Vagabonds
Tu 29 Spencer Davis Group
Tu 29 The Mark Leeman Five

July 1965
Th 01 Alex Harvey Soul Band
Th 01 Gery L Thompson and the Sidewinders
Fr 02 (Gary Frar and) The T-Bones
Fr 02 The Poor Souls
M 05 The Animals
M 05 Jimmy James and The Vagabonds
Tu 06 The Yardbirds
Tu 06 The Mark Leeman Five
Th 08 The Graham Bond Organisation
Th 08 Gery L Thompson and the Sidewinders
Fr 09 (Gary Farr and) The T-Bones
Fr 09 The VIPs
M 12 Jimmy James and The

Vagabonds
Tu 13 The Who
Tu 13 The Mark Leeman Five
Tu 13 The Untamed
Th 15 Alex Harvey Soul Band
Th 15 Gery L Thompson and the Sidewinders
Fr 16 (Gary Farr and) The T-Bones
M 19 Manfred Mann
M 19 Jimmy James and The Vagabonds
Tu 20 Spencer Davis Group
Tu 20 The Mark Leeman Five
Th 22 The Steampacket
Fr 23 The Moody Blues
Fr 23 The Crow
M 26 Jimmy James and The Vagabonds
M 26 The VIPs
Th 29 The Graham Bond Organisation
Th 29 Gery L Thompson and the Sidewinders

August 1965
M 02 Jimmy James and The Vagabonds
Tu 03 Spencer Davis Group
Tu 03 The Mark Leeman Five
W 04 Long John Baldry
Th 05 The Mike Cotton Sound
Th 05 Gery L Thompson and the Sidewinders
Fr 06 (Gary Farr and) The T-Bones
Fr 09 Jimmy James and The Vagabonds
Tu 10 Sugar Pie Desanto and the Shevelles
Tu 10 The Mark Leeman Five
Th 12 The Graham Bond Organisation
Th 12 Gery L Thompson and the Sidewinders
Fr 13 (Gary Farr and) The T-Bones
Fr 13 (John Lee's) Groundhogs
M 16 Jimmy James and The Vagabonds
M 16 (Boz and) The Boz People
Tu 17 Manfred Mann
Tu 17 The Mark Leeman Five
W 18 Long John Baldry
Th 19 The Steampacket
Th 19 Gery L Thompson and the Sidewinders
Fr 20 (Gary Farr and) The T-Bones
M 23 Jimmy James and The Vagabonds
Tu 24 Lulu and the Luvvers
Tu 24 The Mark Leeman Five
Th 26 The Graham Bond Organisation
Th 26 (Boz and) The Boz People
Fr 27 (Gary Farr and) The T-Bones
M 30 Jimmy James and The Vagabonds
M 30 (John Lee's) Groundhogs
Tu 31 The Moody Blues
Tu 31 The Mark Leeman Five

September 1965
W 01 Al Stewart
Th 02 The Steampacket
Th 02 (Boz and) The Boz People
Fr 03 (Gary Farr and) The T-Bones
M 06 Jimmy James and The Vagabonds
M 06 The Crowd
Tu 07 The Mark Leeman Five
Th 09 The Graham Bond Organisation
Th 09 (Boz and) The Boz People
Fr 10 (Gary Farr and) The T-Bones
M 13 Jimmy James and The Vagabonds
Tu 14 Manfred Mann
Tu 14 The Mark Leeman Five

Th 16 Spencer Davis Group
Th 16 The Bo Street Runners
Fr 17 (Gary Farr and) The T-Bones
M 20 Jimmy James and The Vagabonds
M 20 The Sidewinders
Tu 21 Spencer Davis Group
Tu 21 The Mark Leeman Five
W 22 The Silkie
Th 23 The Graham Bond Organisation
Th 23 (Boz and) The Boz People
Fr 24 (Gary Farr and) The T-Bones
Fr 24 The Crowd
M 27 Jimmy James and The Vagabonds
M 27 The Mark Leeman Five
Tu 28 The Moody Blues
Th 30 The Steampacket

October 1965
Fr 01 (Gary Farr and) The T-Bones
Fr 01 The Blues Train
M 04 Jimmy James and The Vagabonds
M 04 Boz and the Boz People
Tu 05 The Alan Price Set
Tu 05 The Crowd
Th 07 The Graham Bond Organisation
Fr 08 (Gary Farr and) The T-Bones
Fr 08 David Bowie and the Lower Third
M 11 Jimmy James and The Vagabonds
M 11 The Uglys
Tu 12 The Yardbirds
Tu 12 The Mark Leeman Five
Th 14 The Steampacket
Th 14 Boz and the Boz People
Fr 15 T Bone Walker
Fr 15 (Gary Farr and) The T-Bones
M 18 Jimmy James and The Vagabonds
Tu 19 Spencer Davis Group
Tu 19 The Mark Leeman Five
W 20 Al Stewart
Th 21 The Graham Bond Organisation
Th 21 Summer Set
Fr 22 (Gary Farr and) The T-Bones
Fr 22 The Blues Roots
M 25 Jimmy James and The Vagabonds
M 25 (John Lee's) Groundhogs
Tu 26 Manfred Mann
Tu 26 The Mark Leeman Five
Th 28 The Steampacket
Fr 29 (Gary Farr and) The T-Bones

November 1965
M 01 Jimmy James and The Vagabonds
M 01 Roscoe Brown Combo
Tu 02 The Who
Tu 02 The Mark Leeman Five
W 03 Al Stewart
Th 04 The Graham Bond Organisation
Th 04 (John Lee's) Groundhogs
Fr 05 Summer Set
Fr 05 David Bowie and the Lower Third
M 08 Jimmy James and The Vagabonds
M 08 The Banshees
Tu 09 Spencer Davis Group
Tu 09 The Mark Leeman Five
Th 11 The Alan Price Set
Th 11 Derry Wilkie and the Pressmen
Fr 12 (Gary Farr and) The T-Bones
M 15 Jimmy James and The Vagabonds
M 15 The Train
Tu 16 Spencer Davis Group
Tu 16 The Mark Leeman Five

Th 18 The Graham Bond Organisation
Fr 19 David Bowie and the Lower Third
Fr 19 Summer Set
M 22 Jimmy James and The Vagabonds
Tu 23 The Steampacket
Th 25 The Alan Price Set
Th 25 TC's Big Boss Band
Fr 26 (Gary Farr and) The T-Bones
M 29 Jimmy James and The Vagabonds
Tu 30 The Animals

December 1965
Th 02 The Graham Bond Organisation
Th 02 Boz & The Sidewinders
Tu 05 The Who
Tu 05 The Boys
M 06 Ronnie Jones and the Blue Jays
Tu 07 Spencer Davis Group
Tu 07 Alex Harvey Group
W 08 Phil Ochs
Tu 09 The Alan Price Set
Th 09 The Mark Leeman Five
Fr 10 (Gary Farr and) The T-Bones
Fr 10 The In Crowd
M 13 Jimmy James and The Vagabonds
M 13 Roscoe Brown Combo
Tu 14 The Action
Tu 14 The Mark Leeman Five
Th 16 The Alan Price Set
Th 16 Bluesology
Fr 17 The Mike Cotton Sound
M 20 Jimmy James and The Vagabonds
Tu 21 The Who
Tu 21 The Mark Leeman Five
Th 23 The Steampacket
Th 23 Jimmy Cliff Big Sound
Fr 24 The Action
Fr 24 Roscoe Brown Combo
Tu 28 Manfred Mann
Tu 28 The Mark Leeman Five
Th 30 The Action
Fr 31 (Gary Farr and) The T-Bones
Fr 31 The Mark Leeman Five

January 1966
M 03 The Mark Leeman Five
Tu 04 The Action
Th 06 The Alan Price Set
Fr 07 (Gary Farr and) The T-Bones
M 10 Jimmy James and The Vagabonds
M 10 The Mark Leeman Five
Tu 11 Spencer Davis Group
Tu 11 Alex Harvey Group
Th 13 The Steampacket
Fr 14 (Gary Farr and) The T-Bones
M 17 Jimmy James and The Vagabonds
Tu 18 The Action
Th 20 The Alan Price Set
Fr 21 (Gary Farr and) The T-Bones
M 24 Jimmy James and The Vagabonds
M 24 The Mark Leeman Five
Tu 25 Manfred Mann
M 27 The Steampacket
Fr 28 The Action
M 31 Jimmy James and The Vagabonds

February 1966
W 02 Al Stewart
Th 02 Dave Anthony's Moods
Fr 04 (Gary Farr and) The T-Bones
M 07 Little Stevie Wonder
M 07 The Sidewinders
Th 08 The Action
Tu 08 Roscoe Brown Combo
Th 10 The Steampacket
Th 10 Jimmy Cliff Big Sound

Fr 11 David Bowie and the Lower Third
Su 13 Georgie Fame
M 14 Jimmy James and The Vagabonds
M 14 The Mark Leeman Five
Tu 15 The Action
Tu 15 The Bo Street Runners
Th 17 The Alan Price Set
Fr 18 (Gary Farr and) The T-Bones
M 21 Jimmy James and The Vagabonds
M 21 The Mark Leeman Five
Tu 22 Spencer Davis Group
Tu 22 Bluesology
Th 24 The Steampacket
Th 24 Jimmy Cliff Big Sound
Fr 25 (Gary Farr and) The T-Bones
M 28 The Mark Leeman Five

March 1966
Tu 01 Manfred Mann
Th 03 Jimmy James and The Vagabonds
Th 03 Summer Set
Fr 04 (Gary Farr and) The T-Bones
M 07 The Graham Bond Organisation
Tu 08 Spencer Davis Group
Tu 08 Jimmy Cliff and the New Generation
W 09 Al Stewart
Th 10 The Mark Leeman Five
Th 10 Summer Set
M 14 The Steampacket
Tu 15 The Yardbirds
Tu 15 The Clayton Squares
Th 17 The Mark Leeman Five
Th 17 The Objects
Fr 18 (Gary Farr and) The T-Bones
Fr 18 Summer Set
M 21 Jimmy James and The Vagabonds
M 21 Boz "and new group"
Tu 22 The Small Faces
Tu 22 Summer Set
Th 24 The Mark Leeman Five
Fr 25 (Gary Farr and) The T-Bones
M 28 The Mike Cotton Sound
Tu 29 The Action
Tu 29 Loose Ends
Th 30 The Mark Leeman Five
Th 30 The Bo Street Runners

April 1966
Fr 01 (Gary Farr and) The T-Bones
Fr 01 The Move
M 04 Jimmy James and The Vagabonds
Tu 05 The Action
Th 07 The Mark Leeman Five
Th 07 The Move
Fr 08 (Gary Farr and) The T-Bones
Fr 08 Sands
Su 10 David Bowie and the Buzz
M 11 John Mayall's Bluesbreakers
M 11 The James Royal Set
Tu 12 Manfred Mann
Tu 12 Bluesology
Th 14 The Mark Leeman Five
Th 14 The Objects
Fr 15 (Gary Farr and) The T-Bones
Fr 15 Roscoe Brown Combo
Su 17 David Bowie and the Buzz
M 18 The Lovin' Spoonful
Tu 19 Jimmy James and The Vagabonds
Tu 19 The Vibrations
Th 21 The Mark Leeman Five
Th 21 The Bo Street Runners
Fr 22 Sands
Fr 22 Bluesology
Su 24 David Bowie and the Buzz
Su 24 Georgie Fame
M 25 The Steampacket
M 25 The Herd

Tu 26 The Action
Tu 26 The Clayton Squares
Th 28 The Mark Leeman Five
Th 28 The Alan Bown Set
Fr 29 (Gary Farr and) The T-Bones
Fr 29 The Objects

May 1966
Su 01 David Bowie and the Buzz
M 02 The Graham Bond Organisation
M 02 Blues Syndicate
Tu 03 The Yardbirds
Tu 03 The Clayton Squares
Th 05 The Mark Leeman Five
Th 05 The Emeralds
Fr 06 (Gary Farr and) The T-Bones
Fr 06 Sands
Su 08 David Bowie and the Buzz
M 09 John Lee Hooker
Tu 10 Spencer Davis Group
Tu 10 Jimmy Cliff Sound
Th 12 Jimmy James and The Vagabonds
Th 12 The Statesides
Fr 13 The Move
Fr 13 Sands
Su 15 David Bowie and the Buzz
M 16 The Mark Leeman Five
M 16 The Bo Street Runners
Tu 17 Patti La Belle and her Belles
Tu 17 The Clayton Squares
Th 19 The Action
Th 19 The Herd
Fr 20 (Gary Farr and) The T-Bones
Su 22 David Bowie and the Buzz
M 23 The Steampacket
M 23 Sands
Tu 24 The Alan Price Set
Tu 24 The Clayton Squares
Th 26 The Bo Street Runners
Th 26 Loose Ends
Fr 27 The Move
Fr 27 Sands
Su 29 Champion Jack Dupree
Su 29 David Bowie and the Buzz
M 30 John Mayall's Bluesbreakers
Tu 31 Ben E King
Tu 31 The Clayton Squares

June 1966
Th 02 The Move
Th 02 The Triad
Fr 03 (Gary Farr and) The T-Bones
Fr 03 The Objects
Su 05 David Bowie and the Buzz
M 06 The Graham Bond Organisation
M 06 The Soul Agents
Tu 07 Manfred Mann
Tu 07 The Alan Bown Set
Th 09 Tony Rivers and the Castaways
Th 09 Summer Set
Fr 10 (Gary Farr and) The T-Bones
Su 12 David Bowie and the Buzz
M 13 Jimmy James and The Vagabonds
Tu 14 Spencer Davis Group
Tu 14 Jimmy Cliff Sound
Th 16 John Mayall's Bluesbreakers
Th 16 The Amboy Dukes
Fr 17 (Gary Farr and) The T-Bones
M 20 Shotgun Express
M 20 Sands
Tu 21 The Yardbirds
Tu 21 The Clayton Squares
Th 23 The Move
Th 23 The Rift
Fr 24 (Gary Farr and) The T-Bones
Fr 25 Bluesology
M 27 The Steampacket
M 27 The Herd
Tu 28 The Small Faces
Tu 28 Sands
Th 30 The Action
Tu 30 The Alan Bown Set

July 1966
Fr 01 Summer Set
Fr 01 Wishful Thinking
Su 03 David Bowie and the Buzz
M 04 The Graham Bond Organisation
M 04 The Soul Agents
Tu 05 The Alan Price Set
Th 05 The James Royal Set
W 06 Al Stewart
Th 07 The Move
Th 07 Sands
Fr 08 The VIPs
Fr 08 Bluesology
Su 10 Simon And Garfunkel
M 11 Jimmy James and The Vagabonds
M 11 Jimmy Brown Sound
Tu 12 The Action
Tu 12 The Creation
Th 14 The Move
Th 14 Bluesology
Fr 15 Summer Set
Fr 15 The Majority
Su 17 Julie Felix
M 18 Solomon Burke
M 18 The Soul Agents
Tu 19 Spencer Davis Group
Tu 19 The Habits
Th 21 The Move
Th 21 The Ultimate
Fr 22 (Gary Farr and) The T-Bones
Fr 22 Graham Bell Trend
M 25 John Mayall's Bluesbreakers
Tu 26 The Troggs
Tu 26 The Clayton Squares
Th 28 The Move
Th 28 The Herd
Fr 29 (Gary Farr and) The T-Bones
Fr 29 The Objects

August 1966
Tu 02 Joe Tex and his American Band
Tu 02 The Clayton Squares
W 03 Al Stewart
Th 04 The Move
Th 04 Sands
Sa 06 The Soul Agents
Sa 06 Bluesology
Su 07 Tony Rivers and the Castaways
Su 07 The Factotum
M 08 The Graham Bond Organisation
Tu 09 (Gary Farr and) The T-Bones
Tu 09 The Clayton Squares
Th 11 The Move
Th 11 Bluesology
Fr 12 The VIPs
Sa 13 The Soul Agents
Sa 13 The Game
Su 14 The Bo Street Runners
M 15 John Mayall's Bluesbreakers
M 15 James Royal Set
Tu 16 Cream
Tu 16 The Clayton Squares
Th 18 The Move
Th 18 Sands
Fr 19 The VIPs
Fr 19 The Ultimate
Sa 20 The Soul Agents
Sa 20 The James Royal Set
Su 21 David Bowie and the Buzz
M 22 The Artwoods
M 22 The Herd
Tu 23 The Action
Tu 23 The Clayton Squares
Th 25 The Move
Fr 26 (Gary Farr and) The T-Bones
Fr 26 Syn
Sa 27 The Soul Agents
Sa 27 Episode Six
Su 28 David Bowie and the Buzz
M 29 The Steampacket
M 29 The Alan Bown Set
Tu 30 Jimmy James and The

Vagabonds
Tu 30 The Clayton Squares

September 1966
Th 01 The VIPs
Th 01 The Herd
Fr 02 (Gary Farr and) The T-Bones
Fr 02 The Ultimate
Sa 03 Victor Brox Blues Train
Sa 03 The Tea Set
Su 04 John Mayall's Bluesbreakers
Su 04 The Race
M 05 The Alan Bown Set
Tu 06 The Action
Tu 06 Graham Bell Trend
Th 08 The Move
Th 08 Ml-Five
Fr 09 (Gary Farr and) The T-Bones
Fr 09 Loose Ends
Sa 10 The Herd
Sa 10 The Ultimate
Su 11 Blues Incorporated
M 12 The VIPs
M 12 Syn
Tu 13 Jimmy James and The Vagabonds
Tu 13 Wynder K Frog
Th 15 The Move
Th 15 The Bo Street Runners
Fr 16 (Gary Farr and) The T-Bones
Sa 17 Episode Six
Sa 17 The Good-Goods
M 19 The Alan Bown Set
M 19 The James Royal Set
Tu 20 Spencer Davis Group
Tu 20 Wynder K Frog
Th 22 The Move
Th 22 Julian Covey and the Machine
Fr 23 The Action
Fr 23 Syn
Sa 24 John McCoy's Crawdaddies
M 26 Jimmy James and The Vagabonds
M 26 Bluesology
Tu 27 Cream
Tu 27 The Herd
Th 29 The Move
Th 29 Syn
Fr 30 (Gary Farr and) The T-Bones
Th 30 The Blue Monks

October 1966
Sa 01 The Herd
Sa 01 Sands
Su 02 (Alexis Korner's) Free At Last
M 03 The Artwoods
M 03 Ml-Five
Tu 04 John Mayall's Bluesbreakers
Tu 04 The Race
Th 06 The Move
Th 06 Embers West
Fr 07 (Gary Farr and) The T-Bones
Fr 07 Bluesology
Sa 08 The Bunch
Sa 08 The Ultimate
M 10 The Alan Bown Set
M 10 Syn
Tu 11 Jimmy James and The Vagabonds
Tu 11 Episode Six
Th 13 The Move
Th 13 Sands
Fr 14 (Gary Farr and) The T-Bones
Fr 14 Graham Bell Trend
Sa 15 The Herd
Sa 15 The Barry Lee Show
M 17 The VIPs
M 17 Sonny Childe and the TNTs
Tu 18 The Action
Tu 18 Episode Six
W 19 Al Stewart
Th 20 The Move
Th 20 Bluesology
Fr 21 (Gary Farr and) The T-Bones
Fr 21 John Andrews and the Lonely Ones

Sa 22 The Herd
Sa 22 Mark Barry
M 24 Brian Auger Trinity
M 24 Victor Brox Blues Train
Tu 25 Cliff Bennett and the Rebel Rousers
Tu 25 Episode Six
Th 27 The Move
Th 27 The Good-Goods
Fr 28 (Gary Farr and) The T-Bones
Fr 28 Sands
Sa 29 The Herd
Sa 29 Bluesology
M 31 The Alan Bown Set
M 31 Wynder K Frog

November 1966
Tu 01 Spencer Davis Group
Tu 01 Episode Six
W 02 Long John Baldry
Th 03 (Alexis Korner's) Free At Last
Th 03 Stormsville Shakers
Fr 04 Sands
Fr 04 Duffy Power's Nucleus
Sa 05 The Herd
Sa 05 The Crazy World of Arthur Brown
M 07 The Artwoods
M 07 Embers West
Tu 08 Cream
Tu 08 The Race
W 09 Al Stewart
Th 10 Paul Butterfield
Th 10 Wynder K Frog
Fr 11 John Mayall's Bluesbreakers
Fr 11 Savoy Brown Blues Band
Sa 12 The Herd
Sa 12 Bluesology
Su 13 David Bowie and the Buzz
M 14 The Alan Bown Set
M 14 Ml-Five
Tu 15 Cliff Bennett and the Rebel Rousers
Tu 15 Episode Six
W 16 Gerry Lockran
Th 17 The Move
Th 17 Dave Anthony's Moods
Fr 18 Jimmy James and The Vagabonds
Fr 18 Summer Set
Sa 19 The Herd
Sa 19 Roscoe Brown Combo
Su 20 (Alexis Korner's) Free At Last
Su 20 The Race
M 21 Brian Auger and the Other Thing
M 21 The Iveys
Tu 22 The Action
Tu 22 Episode Six
Th 24 The Move
Th 24 Roscoe Brown Combo
Fr 25 Sands
Fr 25 Summer Set
Sa 26 The Herd
Sa 27 The Ultimate
M 28 The Alan Bown Set
M 28 Syn
Tu 29 Manfred Mann
Tu 29 The Longboatmen

December 1966
Th 01 The Graham Bond Organisation
Th 01 The Bunch
Fr 02 The Fenmen
Fr 02 The Majority
Sa 03 The Herd
Sa 03 John's Children
M 05 The Artwoods
M 05 Nite People
Tu 06 Jimmy James and The Vagabonds
Tu 06 Syn
W 07 Gerry Lockran
W 07 Gooch
W 07 The Southern Ramblers

Th 08 John Mayall's Bluesbreakers
Th 08 The Race
Fr 09 Sands
Fr 09 The Iveys
Sa 10 The Herd
Sa 10 Neat Change
M 12 Sonny Childe and the TNTs
M 12 Stormsville Shakers
Tu 13 (Eric Burdon and) The Animals
Tu 13 Syn
Th 15 (Alexis Korner's) Free At Last
Th 15 Ram Holder's Messenger
Fr 16 Sands
Fr 16 The Ultimate
Sa 17 The Herd
Sa 17 Mark Barry
Su 18 Theodore Bikel
M 19 The Alan Bown Set
Tu 20 Spencer Davis Group
Tu 20 Syn
Th 22 Pink Floyd
Th 22 The Iveys
Fr 23 The VIPs
Fr 23 Nite People
Fr 23 The Deep Feeling Band
Fr 23 Wynder K Frog
Sa 24 The Herd
Sa 24 Neat Change
M 26 The Brian Auger Trinity
M 26 Amen Corner
Tu 27 John Mayall's Bluesbreakers
Tu 27 The Race
Th 29 Pink Floyd
Th 29 Syn
Fr 30 Long John Baldry
Fr 30 Bluesology
Fr 30 The Good-Goods
Sa 31 Jimmy James and The Vagabonds
Sa 31 Neat Change
Sa 31 The Bunch

January 1967
M 02 The Herd
M 02 Nite People
Tu 03 Tony Rivers and the Castaways
Tu 03 Syn
Th 05 Pink Floyd
Th 05 The Eyes of Blue
Fr 06 Herbie Goins and the Night-Timers
Fr 06 Wynder K Frog
Sa 07 Neat Change
Sa 07 Robert Hirst and the Big Taste
M 09 The Herd
Sa 09 The Bunch
Tu 10 Cream
Tu 10 Catch 22
Th 12 The Artwoods
Th 12 Mike Stuart Span
Fr 13 Sands
Fr 13 Roscoe Brown Combo
Sa 14 Neat Change
Sa 14 The Ultimate
Su 15 Champion Jack Dupree
Su 15 Savoy Brown Blues Band
M 16 The Herd
M 16 Richard Henry
M 16 Timebox
Tu 17 Zoot Money's Big Roll Band
Tu 17 Syn
W 18 Al Stewart
Th 19 Pink Floyd
Th 19 Marmalade
Fr 20 Sonny Childe and the TNTs
Fr 20 Felder's Orioles
Sa 21 Neat Change
Sa 21 The Bunch
M 23 The Herd
M 23 The Ultimate
Tu 24 Jimi Hendrix
Tu 24 Syn
W 25 Martin Windsor
W 25 Red Sullivan
Th 26 Herbie Goins and the Night-

Timers
Th 26 Jimmy Cliff and the Shakedown
    Sound
Fr 27 Sands
Fr 27 Mark Barry
Sa 28 Neat Change
Sa 28 The Parking Lot
M 30 John Mayall's Bluesbreakers
M 30 Stone's Masonry
Tu 31 Jimmy James and The
    Vagabonds
Tu 31 Syn

February 1967
W 01 Al Stewart
Th 02 Wynder K Frog
Th 02 The Deep Feeling Band
Fr 03 The Action
Fr 03 Marmalade
Sa 04 Neat Change
Sa 04 The Mirage
M 06 The Herd
M 06 The Motivation
Tu 07 Spencer Davis Group
Tu 07 Syn
Th 09 Herbie Goins and the Night-
    Timers with the Satin Dolls
Th 09 The In Crowd
Fr 10 Sonny Childe and the TNTs
Fr 10 The Goodtime Band
Sa 11 Neat Change
Sa 11 Robert Hirst and the Big Taste
Su 12 The Rick'n'Beckers
M 13 The Herd
M 13 Philip Goodhand-Tait and the
    Stormsville Shakers
Tu 14 Tony Rivers and the Castaways
Tu 14 Syn
Th 16 John Mayall's Bluesbreakers
Th 16 Cock-A-Hoop
Fr 17 Sands
Fr 17 The Condors
Sa 18 Neat Change
Sa 18 The Love Affair
Su 19 The Bonzo Dog Doo-Dah Band
M 20 The Birds' Birds
M 20 The Majority
Tu 21 Cat Stevens
Tu 21 George Bean and the Runners
Tu 21 Syn
Th 23 Herbie Goins and the Night-
    Timers with the Satin Dolls
Th 23 The In Crowd
Fr 24 Maxine Brown
Fr 24 The Q Set
Sa 25 Robert Hirst and the Big Taste
Sa 25 Neat Change
Su 26 The Rick'n'Beckers
M 27 The Herd
M 27 Roscoe Brown Combo
Tu 28 The Alan Bown Set
Tu 28 Syn

March 1967
W 01 Champion Jack Dupree
Th 02 Neat Change
Th 02 The Bunch
Fr 03 Peter Jay and the Jaywalkers
Fr 03 Timebox
Sa 05 The Moving People
Sa 05 The Rumble Band
M 06 The Herd
M 06 The Motivation
Tu 07 Tony Rivers and the Castaways
Tu 07 Wynder K Frog
W 08 Long John Baldry
W 08 Al Stewart
Th 09 Pink Floyd
Th 09 The Thoughts
Fr 10 The Chicago Line
Fr 10 Savoy Brown Blues Band
Sa 11 1-2-3
Sa 11 Skip Bifferty
Su 12 John Mayall's Bluesbreakers
Sa 12 Cock-A-Hoop
M 13 The Herd

M 13 Philip Goodhand-Tait and the
    Stormsville Shakers
Tu 14 Jimmy James and The
    Vagabonds
Tu 14 Wynder K Frog
Th 16 Marmalade
Th 16 Nite People
Fr 17 The Long John Baldry Show
Fr 17 Timebox
Fr 17 Bluesology
Sa 18 1-2-3
Sa 18 The Tropical Boot Company
Su 19 The Bonzo Dog Doo-Dah Band
M 20 Savoy Brown Blues Band
M 20 Cock-A-Hoop
Tu 21 Cream
Tu 21 Family
Th 23 Marmalade
Th 23 The Fancy Bred
Fr 24 Peter Jay and the Jaywalkers
Fr 24 Richard Kent Style
Sa 25 1-2-3
Sa 25 C Jam Blues
Su 26 Dandy and the Wypp Dancers
Su 26 Laurel Aitken
Su 26 The Bees
Su 26 The Scenery
M 27 Robert Hirst and the Big Taste
Tu 28 Geno Washington and the Ram
    Jam Band
Tu 28 The Amboy Dukes
Th 30 Marmalade
Th 30 The Tribe
Fr 31 Neat Change
Fr 31 The Children

April 1967
Sa 01 Syn
Sa 01 The Footprints
M 03 The Herd
M 03 Tony Knight's Chessmen
Tu 04 The Action
Tu 04 The Stalkers
Th 06 Marmalade
Th 06 The Fancy Bred
Fr 07 1-2-3
Fr 07 Timebox
Sa 08 Syn
Sa 08 The Love Affair
M 10 The Herd
M 10 Fleur De Lys
Tu 11 The Jeff Beck Group
Tu 11 Wynder K Frog
Th 13 Marmalade
Th 13 Nite People
Fr 14 Tony Rivers and the Castaways
Fr 14 Time and Motion
Sa 15 Syn
Sa 15 C Jam Blues
M 17 The Herd
Tu 18 Chris Farlowe and the
    Thunderbirds
Tu 18 Wynder K Frog
Th 20 Savoy Brown Blues Band
Th 20 Cock-A-Hoop
Fr 21 The Long John Baldry Show
Fr 21 Timebox
Sa 22 Syn
Sa 22 The Stalkers
M 24 The Herd
M 24 Family
Tu 25 Jimmy James and The
    Vagabonds
Tu 25 Wynder K Frog
Th 27 John Mayall's Bluesbreakers
Th 27 Blues City Shakedown
Fr 28 1-2-3
Fr 28 The Goodtime Band
Sa 29 Syn
Sa 29 Skip Bifferty
Su 30 Jesse Fuller
Su 30 Jo Ann Kelly
Su 30 Paul Layton
Su 30 Peter Baughen
Su 30 Weston Gavin

May 1967
M 01 The Herd
M 01 Skip Bifferty
Tu 02 The Alan Bown Set
Tu 02 Darlings
Th 04 Marmalade
Th 04 The Tribe
Fr 05 The Creation
Fr 05 Studio 6
Sa 06 Syn
Sa 06 We Three Kings
Su 07 The Bonzo Dog Doo Dah Band
M 08 Neat Change
M 08 The Five Proud Walkers
Tu 09 Prince Buster
Tu 09 The Bees
Tu 09 Wynder K Frog
Th 11 Marmalade
Th 11 The Fancy Bred
Fr 12 1-2-3
Fr 12 Roscoe Brown Combo
Sa 13 Syn
Sa 13 The Stalkers
M 15 The Herd
M 15 Nite People
Tu 16 John Mayall's Bluesbreakers
Tu 16 Family
Th 18 Marmalade
Th 18 The Versions
Fr 19 The Mike Cotton Sound
Fr 19 The Web
Sa 20 Darlings
M 22 Neat Change
M 22 Nite People
Tu 23 Cream
Tu 23 Family
Th 25 1-2-3
Th 25 Timebox
Fr 26 Terry Reid
Fr 26 Peter Jay and the Jaywalkers
Fr 26 The Seychelles
Su 27 Syn
Sa 27 The Bluesyard
M 29 Savoy Brown Blues Band
M 29 Cock-A-Hoop
Tu 30 Spencer Davis Group
Tu 30 Wynder K Frog

June 1967
Th 01 Marmalade
Th 01 The Epics
Fr 02 Sands
Fr 02 The Wages Of Sin
Sa 03 The Love Affair
Sa 03 The Westpoint Supernaturals
M 05 The Herd
M 05 Timebox
Tu 06 The Jeff Beck Group
Tu 06 Nite People
W 07 The New Songs
W 07 Al Stewart
W 07 Picadilly Line
Th 08 Denny Laine and his Electric
    String Band
Th 08 The Pyramid
Fr 09 The Long John Baldry Show
Fr 09 C Jam Blues
Sa 10 Syn
Sa 10 The Stalkers
M 12 Procol Harum
M 12 Timebox
Tu 13 The Action
Tu 13 The Prime Apples
W 14 The New Songs
W 14 Al Stewart
W 14 Picadilly Line
Th 15 Marmalade
Th 15 The Tribe
Fr 16 Family
Fr 16 Le Gay
Sa 17 Syn
Sa 17 The Love Affair
M 19 The Herd
M 19 John Evan Smash
Tu 20 John Lee Hooker

Tu 20 Savoy Brown Blues Band
Tu 20 Ten Years After
W 21 The New Songs
W 21 Al Stewart
W 21 Picadilly Line
Th 22 Neat Change
Th 22 Timebox
Fr 23 The Creation
Fr 23 The Stalkers
Sa 24 Syn
Sa 24 The Third Eye
M 26 Robert Hirst and the Big Taste
M 26 The Westpoint Supernaturals
Tu 27 John Mayall's Bluesbreakers
Tu 27 Wynder K Frog
W 28 The New Songs
W 28 Al Stewart
W 28 Picadilly Line
Th 29 Marmalade
Th 29 Studio Six
Fr 30 Terry Reid
Fr 30 Peter Jay and the Jaywalkers
Fr 30 The Erection

July 1967
Sa 01 The Tribe
Sa 01 The Stalkers
Su 02 Playground
M 03 The Herd
M 03 Derek Savage Foundation
Tu 04 Alan Bown
Tu 04 Nite People
W 05 The New Songs
W 05 Al Stewart
W 05 Picadilly Line
Th 06 Marmalade
Th 06 Studio Six
Fr 07 The Creation
Fr 07 The Third Eye
Sa 08 The Tribe
Sa 08 The Love Affair
M 10 Family
M 10 Ten Years After
Tu 11 The Move
Tu 11 Winston's Fumbs
W 12 The New Songs
W 12 Al Stewart
W 12 Picadilly Line
Th 13 Marmalade
Th 13 Nite People
Fr 14 St Louis Union
Fr 14 The Stalkers
Sa 15 The Tribe
Sa 15 The Monopoly
Su 16 The Bonzo Dog Doo-Dah Band
M 17 Syn
M 17 Darlings
Tu 18 Geno Washington and the Ram
    Jam Band
Tu 18 The Amboy Dukes
W 19 The New Songs
W 19 Al Stewart
W 19 Picadilly Line
Th 20 Marmalade
Th 20 The Iveys
Fr 21 Terry Reid
Fr 21 Peter Jay and the Jaywalkers
Fr 21 The Illusions
Sa 22 The Tribe
Sa 22 Ten Years After
M 24 Wynder K Frog
M 24 Richard Kent Style
Tu 25 Dave Dee, Dozy, Beaky, Mick
    & Tich
Tu 25 Nite People
W 26 The New Songs
W 26 Al Stewart
W 26 Picadilly Line
Th 27 Marmalade
Th 27 The Love Affair
Fr 28 The Long John Baldry Show
Fr 28 The Workshop
Sa 29 The Tribe
Sa 29 Darlings
Su 30 Playground

M 31 The Herd
M 31 The Third Eye

August 1967

Tu 01 The Action
Tu 01 Timebox
W 02 The New Songs
W 02 Al Stewart
W 02 Picadilly Line
Th 03 Marmalade
Th 03 Studio Six
Fr 04 The Creation
Fr 04 John Evan Smash
Sa 05 The Tribe
Sa 05 The Third Eye
Su 06 Syn
M 07 Family
M 07 Cock-A-Hoop
Tu 08 (Eric Burdon and) The Animals
Tu 08 Timebox
W 09 Picadilly Line
Th 10 Marmalade
Th 10 Blossom
Fr 11 Robert Hirst and the Big Taste
Sa 12 The Tribe
Sa 12 Impact Blues
Su 13 Adam's Recital
M 14 The Long John Baldry Show
M 14 Jimmy Powell
Tu 15 (Peter Green's) Fleetwood Mac
Tu 15 Chicken Shack
W 16 Al Stewart
W 16 Picadilly Line
Th 17 Marmalade
Th 17 The Love Affair
Fr 18 Tony Rivers and the Castaways
Fr 18 Ten Years After
Sa 19 The Tribe
Sa 19 Nite People
Su 20 Syn
M 21 Arthur Brown
M 21 Studio Six
Tu 22 Alan Bown
Tu 22 Timebox
W 23 Picadilly Line
W 23 Al Stewart
Th 24 Marmalade
Th 24 The Iveys
Fr 25 Terry Reid
Fr 25 Peter Jay and the Jaywalkers
Fr 25 Mud
Sa 26 The Dream
Sa 26 The Third Eye
Su 27 Playground
M 28 John Mayall's Bluesbreakers
M 28 Ten Years After
Tu 29 Amen Corner
Tu 29 Timebox
W 30 Picadilly Line
W 30 Mox & John LaMont
Th 31 Marmalade
Th 31 The Love Affair

September 1967

Fr 01 Robert Hirst and the Big Taste
Fr 01 The Workshop
Sa 02 The Dream
Su 03 The Bonzo Dog Doo-Dah Band
M 04 Arthur Brown
M 04 Ten Years After
Tu 05 (Peter Green's) Fleetwood Mac
Tu 05 Timebox
W 06 Picadilly Line
Th 07 Syn
Th 07 Studio Six
Fr 08 Denny Laine and his Electric String Band
Fr 08 The Gods
Sa 09 The Dream
Sa 09 Herbal Mixture
M 11 Arthur Brown
M 11 Nite People
Tu 12 Georgie Fame
Tu 12 Timebox
W 13 Picadilly Line
Th 14 Marmalade

Th 14 The Love Affair
Fr 15 The Long John Baldry Show
Fr 15 The Remo Four
Sa 16 The Dream
Sa 16 The Iveys
M 18 Arthur Brown
M 18 Studio Six
Tu 19 The Move
Tu 19 Timebox
W 20 Picadilly Line
Th 21 Marmalade
Th 21 Ray King Soul Band
Fr 22 Ten Years After
Fr 22 Ian Lloyd Bluesmen
Sa 23 The Dream
Sa 23 Mud
Su 24 Orange Bicycle
Su 24 Pandemonium
M 25 Robert Hirst and the Big Taste
M 25 Chris Shakespear Movement
Tu 26 The Jeff Beck Group
Tu 26 Timebox
W 27 Picadilly Line
Th 28 Marmalade
Th 28 The Love Affair
Fr 29 (Peter Green's) Fleetwood Mac
Fr 29 Zebidee
Sa 30 The Dream

October 1967

M 02 The Nice
M 02 Nite People
Tu 03 The Action
Tu 03 Timebox
Th 05 Maxine Brown
Th 05 Studio Six
Th 05 The Q Set
Fr 06 Ten Years After
Fr 06 Black Cat Bones
Sa 07 The Gods
Sa 07 Herbal Mixture
M 09 Robert Hirst and the Big Taste
M 09 Jon
Tu 10 Alan Bown
Tu 10 Timebox
Th 12 Syn
Th 12 The Third Eye
Fr 13 Chicken Shack
Fr 13 Ian Lloyd Bluesmen
Sa 14 Neat Change
Sa 14 The Iveys
M 16 The Nice
M 16 Studio Six
Tu 17 Geno Washington and the Ram Jam Band
Tu 17 The Amboy Dukes
Th 19 The Long John Baldry Show
Th 19 Timebox
Fr 20 Ten Years After
Fr 20 Eliokafanati
Sa 21 Neat Change
Sa 21 The Open Mind
M 23 The Action
M 23 Nite People
Tu 24 Jimi Hendrix
Tu 24 The Nice
Th 26 Marmalade
Th 26 The Love Affair
Fr 27 (Peter Green's) Fleetwood Mac
Fr 27 Ian Lloyd Bluesmen
Sa 28 Neat Change
Th 28 The Third Eye
M 30 Ben E King
M 30 The Senate
M 30 Timebox
Tu 31 John Mayall's Bluesbreakers
Tu 31 Chicken Shack

November 1967

Th 02 Syn
Th 02 The Quik
Fr 03 Ten Years After
Fr 03 The Wilde Flowers
Sa 04 Neat Change
Sa 04 The Open Mind

M 06 The Nice
M 06 Herbal Mixture
Tu 07 The Herd
Tu 07 Nite People
Th 09 Tages
Th 09 Tuesday's Children
Fr 10 Ten Years After
Fr 10 Black Cat Bones
Sa 11 Neat Change
Sa 11 John Morgan Blues Band
M 13 The Nice
M 13 The Open Mind
Tu 14 Traffic
Tu 14 The Remo Four
Th 16 Syn
Th 16 The Love Affair
Fr 17 Ten Years After
Fr 17 Shakey Vic's
Sa 18 Neat Change
Sa 18 The Sensory Armada
M 20 Aynsley Dunbar Retaliation
M 20 Chicken Shack
Tu 21 Amen Corner
Tu 21 The Love Affair
Th 23 The Long John Baldry Show
Th 23 Nite People
Fr 24 (Peter Green's) Fleetwood Mac
Fr 24 Black Cat Bones
Sa 25 Neat Change
Sa 25 Herbal Mixture
M 27 The Nice
M 27 The Sensory Armada
Tu 28 Cream
Tu 28 The Remo Four
Th 30 Marmalade
Th 30 The Iveys

December 1967

Fr 01 Savoy Brown Blues Band
Fr 01 Shakey Vic's Big City Blues Band
Sa 02 Neat Change
M 04 Chicken Shack
M 04 The Boilerhouse
Tu 05 The Electric Prunes
Tu 05 The Open Mind
Th 07 The Amboy Dukes
Th 07 The Pride and Joy Buzz Band
Fr 08 Ten Years After
Fr 08 Cock-A-Hoop
Sa 09 Mabel Greer's Toyshop
M 11 Simon Dupree and the Big Sound
M 11 Jon
Tu 12 The Jeff Beck Group
Tu 12 Nite People
Th 14 The Remo Four
Th 14 Bag O' Blues
Fr 15 Aynsley Dunbar Retaliation
Fr 15 Shakey Vic's Big City Blues Band
Sa 16 Neat Change
Sa 16 Herbal Mixture
Su 17 Timebox
M 18 The Nice
M 18 Zeus
Tu 19 (Eric Burdon and) The Animals
Tu 19 Eire Apparent
Th 21 Timebox
Th 21 Clouds
Fr 22 Ten Years After
Fr 22 The New Nadir
Sa 23 Neat Change
Sa 23 The Open Mind
Tu 26 John Mayall's Bluesbreakers
Tu 26 The Boilerhouse
Th 28 The Amboy Dukes
Th 28 Tuesday's Children
Fr 29 (Peter Green's) Fleetwood Mac
Fr 29 The Boilerhouse
Sa 30 Neat Change
Sa 30 Mud
Su 31 Marmalade
Su 31 Black Cat Bones

Su 31 Nite People

January 1968

M 01 The Nice
M 01 Mabel Greer's Toyshop
Tu 02 Simon Dupree and the Big Sound
Tu 02 Nite People
Th 04 Skip Bifferty
Th 04 The Pride and Joy Buzz Band
Fr 05 Ten Years After
Fr 05 Skye Wine
Sa 06 The Ivys
Sa 06 The Open Mind
Su 07 Blue Rivers & his Maroons
M 08 The Nice
M 08 Human Instinct
Tu 09 Geno Washington and the Ram Jam Band
Tu 09 Ferris Wheel
Th 11 Marmalade
Th 11 The Breakthru
Fr 12 Aynsley Dunbar Retaliation
Fr 12 Black Cat Bones
Sa 13 The Gods
Sa 13 The Cat's Pajamas
Su 14 Blue Rivers & his Maroons
M 15 The Nice
M 15 The Open Mind
Tu 16 Eddie Boyd
Tu 16 Aynsley Dunbar Retaliation
Tu 16 Navy Blue
Th 18 Skip Bifferty
Th 18 The Pride and Joy Buzz Band
Fr 19 Ten Years After
Fr 19 The Spirit of John Morgan
Sa 20 The Gods
Sa 20 Mabel Greer's Toyshop
Su 21 Blue Rivers & his Maroons
M 22 The Nice
M 22 Granny's Intentions
Tu 23 Timebox
Th 25 Neat Change
Th 25 The Ivys
Fr 26 Aynsley Dunbar Retaliation
Fr 26 Skye Wine
Sa 27 The Gods
Sa 27 Circus
Su 28 Blue Rivers & his Maroons
M 29 Fairport Convention
M 29 Nite People
Tu 30 Traffic
Tu 30 Spooky Tooth

February 1968

Th 01 Marmalade
Th 01 Jon
Fr 02 Savoy Brown Blues Band
Fr 02 Jethro Tull
Sa 03 The Ivys
Sa 03 The Open Mind
M 05 Neat Change
M 05 Studio Six
Tu 06 Ten Years After
Tu 06 Dr K's Blues Band
W 07 The John Dummer Blues Band
Th 08 Edwin Starr
Th 08 Robert Plant and the Band of Joy
Th 08 The JJ Sound
Fr 09 Eddie Boyd
Fr 09 Black Cat Bones
Fr 09 Jethro Tull
Sa 10 The Gods
Sa 10 Taste
M 12 Timebox
M 12 Clouds
Tu 13 John Mayall's Bluesbreakers
Tu 13 The New Nadir
W 14 Human Instinct
Th 15 Skip Bifferty
Th 15 The Pride and Joy Buzz Band
Fr 16 Jethro Tull
Fr 16 The Spirit of John Morgan
Sa 17 The Gods
Sa 17 The Mylton Rhode

Su 18 Blue Rivers & his Maroons
M 19 Neat Change
M 19 The Open Mind
Tu 20 The Jeff Beck Group
Tu 20 Nite People
W 21 Sugar Simone and the
Hummingbirds
Th 22 Skip Bifferty
Th 22 The Plague
Fr 23 Tim Rose
Fr 23 Aynsley Dunbar Retaliation
Fr 23 Robert Plant and the Band of
Joy
Sa 24 The Gods
Sa 24 Le Gay
Su 25 Blue Rivers & his Maroons
M 26 The Nice
M 26 London
Tu 27 The Move
Tu 27 The Attack
W 28 Blossom
Th 29 Marmalade
Th 29 Studio Six

March 1968
Fr 01 Savoy Brown Blues Band
Fr 01 Chicken Shack
Sa 02 The Gods
Sa 02 The Glass Menagerie
Su 03 Blue Rivers & his Maroons
M 04 The Nice
M 04 The New Nadir
Tu 05 Jimmy James Show
Tu 05 Jimmy Cliff Show
Tu 05 Wynder K Frog
W 06 Carolyn Hester
Th 07 Nite People
Th 07 Granny's Intentions
Fr 08 Ten Years After
Fr 08 The Spirit of John Morgan
Sa 09 Still Life
Sa 09 The Open Mind
Su 10 Blue Rivers & his Maroons
M 11 The Nice
M 11 The Attack
Tu 12 Procol Harum
Tu 12 Spooky Tooth
W 13 Brave New World
W 13 Lee Hawkins Group
Th 14 Skip Bifferty
Th 14 The Klubs
Fr 15 Aynsley Dunbar Retaliation
Fr 15 Jethro Tull
Sa 16 The Gods
Sa 16 The Sunshine Garden
Su 17 Blue Rivers & his Maroons
M 18 The Nice
M 18 The Exception
Tu 19 Timebox
W 20 The Sugar Simone Show
Th 21 Marmalade
Th 21 The Open Mind
Fr 22 Ten Years After
Fr 22 The New Nadir
Sa 23 The Gods
Sa 23 The Iveys
Su 24 Blue Rivers & his Maroons
M 25 The Nice
M 25 Still Life
Tu 26 John Mayall's Bluesbreakers
Tu 26 Taste
W 27 The Sugar Simone Show
Th 28 Skip Bifferty
Th 28 Granny's Intentions
Fr 29 Fleetwood Mac
Fr 29 Jethro Tull
Sa 30 The Gods
Sa 30 Mud
Su 31 Blue Rivers & his Maroons

April 1968
M 01 The Nice
M 01 The Glass Menagerie
Tu 02 The Foundations
Tu 02 The Beatstalkers
W 03 Jade Hexagram

W 03 Hearts 'n' Souls
Th 04 Skip Bifferty
Th 04 Rainbow Reflection
Fr 05 Ten Years After
Fr 05 Tramline
Sa 06 Timebox
Sa 06 Black Cat Bones
Su 07 Blue Rivers & his Maroons
M 08 Nite People
M 08 The Staks
Tu 09 The Jeff Beck Group
Tu 09 The New Nadir
Th 11 The Nice
Th 11 The Staks
Fr 12 Aynsley Dunbar Retaliation
Fr 12 The Spirit of John Morgan
Sa 13 Arthur Brown
Sa 13 Timebox
Su 14 Blue Rivers & his Maroons
M 15 The Bonzo Dog Doo-Dah Band
M 15 Jethro Tull
Tu 16 John Mayall's Bluesbreakers
Tu 16 The Boilerhouse
Th 18 Marmalade
Th 18 Granny's Intentions
Fr 19 Savoy Brown Blues Band
Fr 19 The New Nadir
Sa 20 Timebox
Sa 20 The Cortinas
Su 21 Blue Rivers & his Maroons
M 22 Nite People
M 22 The Open Mind
Tu 23 The Who
W 24 Al Stewart
W 24 Fairport Convention
Th 25 Skip Bifferty
Th 25 The Exception
Fr 26 The Nice
Fr 26 Black Cat Bones
Sa 27 The Beatstalkers
Su 27 Pandemonium
Su 28 Blue Rivers & his Maroons
Su 28 The House of Lords
M 29 The Gods
M 29 The Glass Menagerie
Tu 30 Long John Baldry

May 1968
Th 02 The Nice
Th 02 Mabel Greer's Toyshop
Fr 03 Jethro Tull
Fr 03 The New Nadir
Sa 04 Timebox
Sa 04 The Spirit of John Morgan
Su 05 Blue Rivers & his Maroons
M 06 Nite People
M 06 The Breakthru
Tu 07 Manfred Mann
Tu 07 The Glass Menagerie
W 08 Hearts 'n' Souls
Th 09 The Gods
Th 09 Granny's Intentions
Fr 10 Aynsley Dunbar Retaliation
Fr 10 Tramline
Sa 11 Dick Morrisey Unit
Sa 11 Clouds
M 13 Neat Change
M 13 The Exception
Tu 14 Traffic
Tu 14 Taste
W 15 The Mushrooms
Th 16 Joe Cocker
Th 16 Granny's Intentions
Fr 17 Jethro Tull
Fr 17 Taste
Sa 18 Timebox
Sa 19 Circus
M 20 Nite People
M 20 Rivers Invitation
Tu 21 The Nice
Tu 21 Dick Morrisey Unit
W 22 Tom Rush
Th 23 Marmalade
Th 23 Granny's Intentions
Fr 24 Ten Years After

Fr 24 Duster Bennett
Sa 25 Timebox
Sa 25 Thackery
M 27 Spooky Tooth
M 27 Rivers Invitation
Tu 28 John Mayall's Bluesbreakers
Tu 28 Tramline
W 29 The Sharrons
Th 30 The Gods
Th 30 Juniors Eyes
Fr 31 Jethro Tull
Fr 31 The Spirit of John Morgan

June 1968
Sa 01 Timebox
Sa 01 The Exception
M 03 Taste
M 03 Thackery
Tu 04 The Counts
Tu 04 The Selofane
W 05 The Riot Squad
Th 06 The Nice
Th 06 The Red Light District
Fr 07 Ten Years After
Fr 07 Giant Marrowfat
Sa 08 Timebox
Sa 08 Neat Change
M 10 Nite People
M 10 The Cortinas
Tu 11 Family
Tu 11 Granny's Intentions
W 12 Mud
Th 13 Marmalade
Th 13 Gun
Fr 14 Jethro Tull
Fr 14 Duster Bennett
Sa 15 Timebox
Sa 15 Toast
Su 16 The Mushrooms
Su 16 The Sharrons
M 17 Taste
M 17 The Red Light District
Tu 18 John Mayall's Bluesbreakers
Tu 18 Black Cat Bones
W 19 The Sharrons
Th 20 The Nice
Th 20 Thackery
Fr 21 Taste
Fr 21 Free
Sa 22 The Glass Menagerie
Sa 22 The Exception
M 24 Spooky Tooth
M 24 The Red Light District
Tu 25 Joe Cocker
Tu 25 The Cheese
W 26 Don Lusher
W 26 Red Star
Th 27 Marmalade
Th 27 The Breakthru
Fr 28 Jethro Tull
Fr 28 Tramline
Sa 29 The Beatstalkers
Sa 29 The Cheese
Su 30 The House of Lords

July 1968
M 01 Nite People
M 01 Granny's Intentions
Tu 02 Simon Dupree and the Big
Sound
Tu 02 Tramline
W 03 Spooky Tooth
W 03 The Glass Menagerie
Th 04 The Nice
Th 04 The House of Lords
Th 04 The Span
Fr 05 Jethro Tull
Fr 05 Thackery
Sa 06 Neat Change
Sa 06 Gun
M 08 Taste
M 08 Black Cat Bones
Tu 09 Family
Tu 09 The Beatstalkers
W 10 Joe Cocker
W 10 The Red Light District

Th 11 The Beatstalkers
Th 11 Dream Police
Fr 12 Aynsley Dunbar Retaliation
Fr 12 Duster Bennett
Sa 13 Neat Change
Sa 13 The Iveys
Su 14 The House of Lords
M 15 Nite People
M 15 The Glass Menagerie
Tu 16 Tim Rose
Tu 16 Tramline
W 17 Joe Cocker
W 17 Gun
Th 18 The Nice
Th 18 The Red Light District
Fr 19 Jethro Tull
Fr 19 Dynaflow Blues Band
Sa 20 Neat Change
Sa 20 The Groop
Su 21 The House of Lords
Su 21 The Reaction
M 22 Taste
M 22 Duster Bennett
Tu 22 Tony Rivers and the Castaways
Tu 23 The Cortinas
W 24 Joe Cocker
W 24 Granny's Intentions
Th 25 The Beatstalkers
Th 25 Mike Stuart Span
Fr 26 Jethro Tull
Fr 26 Black Cat Bones
Sa 27 Neat Change
Sa 27 The Open Mind
Su 28 Cindy Starr & The Mopeds
M 29 Taste
M 29 Tramline
Tu 30 The Herd
Tu 30 Granny's Intentions
W 31 Joe Cocker
W 31 The Glass Menagerie

August 1968
Th 01 The Beatstalkers
Th 01 The Group
Fr 02 Savoy Brown Blues Band
Fr 02 Gordon Smith
Sa 03 Neat Change
M 05 Nite People
M 05 Yes
Tu 06 Arthur Brown
Tu 06 East of Eden
W 07 Spooky Tooth
W 07 Clouds
Th 08 The Nice
Th 08 The Glass Menagerie
Fr 09 Jethro Tull
Fr 09 Black Cat Bones
Sa 10 Neat Change
Sa 10 The Boots
M 12 Taste
M 12 Keef Hartley
Tu 13 John Mayall's Bluesbreakers
Tu 13 Duster Bennett
W 14 Joe Cocker
W 14 Village
Th 15 The Beatstalkers
Th 15 The Open Mind
Fr 16 Ten Years After
Fr 16 Tramline
Sa 17 Neat Change
Sa 17 Yes
Su 18 The House of Lords
M 19 Nite People
M 19 The Cortinas
Tu 22 Tony Rivers and the Castaways
Tu 20 The Glass Menagerie
W 21 Joe Cocker
W 21 The Open Mind
Th 22 The Nice
Th 22 East of Eden
Fr 23 Jethro Tull
Fr 23 Duster Bennett
Sa 24 July
Sa 24 Young Blood
Su 25 The House of Lords

M 26 Taste
M 26 Tramline
Tu 27 Marmalade
W 27 Gun
W 28 Joe Cocker
W 28 Clouds
Th 29 The Beatstalkers
Th 29 Dream Police
Fr 30 Ten Years After
Fr 30 Keef Hartley
Sa 31 The Boots
Sa 31 The Open Mind

September 1968
Su 01 The House of Lords
Su 02 Tramline
M 02 Black Cat Bones
Tu 03 Traffic
Tu 03 East of Eden
W 04 Eclection
W 04 Keef Hartley
Th 05 The Nice
Th 05 The Red Light District
Fr 06 Joe Cocker
Fr 06 Yes
Sa 07 The Cortinas
Sa 07 Spice
Su 08 The House of Lords
M 09 Taste
M 09 Chicago Blues Band
Tu 10 Spencer Davis Group
Tu 10 Terry Reid
W 11 Eclection
W 11 Gordon Smith
Th 12 Joe Cocker
Th 12 July
Fr 13 Aynsley Dunbar Retaliation
Fr 13 Lots
Sa 14 Dream Police
Sa 14 The Open Mind
Su 15 The House of Lords
M 16 Black Cat Bones
M 16 Tramline
Tu 17 Family
Tu 17 East of Eden
W 18 Fairport Convention
W 18 Duster Bennett
Th 19 The Nice
Th 19 Yes
Fr 20 Jethro Tull
Fr 20 Love Sculpture
Sa 21 Dream Police
Sa 21 Kippington Lodge
Su 22 The House of Lords
M 23 Taste
M 23 Keef Hartley
Tu 24 The Jeff Beck Group
Tu 24 The Red Light District
W 25 Fairport Convention
W 25 Gordon Smith
Th 26 Joe Cocker
Th 26 Granny's Intentions
Fr 27 Tramline
Fr 27 Chicago Blues Band
Sa 28 Dream Police
Sa 28 Yes
Su 29 The House of Lords
M 30 Canned Heat
M 30 Keef Hartley

October 1968
Tu 01 Savoy Brown Blues Band
Tu 01 Love Sculpture
W 02 Fairport Convention
W 02 Duster Bennett
Th 03 Timebox
Fr 04 Taste
Fr 04 Pegasus
Sa 05 Dream Police
Sa 05 Kippington Lodge
Su 06 The House of Lords
M 07 Free
M 07 Gordon Smith
Tu 08 The Moody Blues
Tu 08 Keef Hartley
W 09 Fairport Convention

Th 10 Spooky Tooth
Th 10 Ashton, Gardner & Dyke
Fr 11 Jethro Tull
Fr 11 The Spirit of John Morgan
Sa 12 Dream Police
Sa 12 Village
Su 13 The House of Lords
M 14 Free
M 14 The Red Light District
Tu 15 Jimmy James and the Vagabonds
W 16 Love Sculpture
W 16 Dr K's Blues Band
Th 17 Wynder K Frog
Th 17 Kippington Lodge
Fr 18 Led Zeppelin (as The "new" Yardbirds)
Fr 18 Sleepy
Sa 19 Dream Police
Sa 19 Spice
Su 20 The House of Lords
M 21 Free
M 21 Duster Bennett
Tu 22 Family
Tu 22 Love Sculpture
W 23 Eclection
W 23 Pegasus
Th 24 Spooky Tooth
Th 24 Toast
Fr 25 Taste
Fr 25 The Spirit of John Morgan
Sa 26 Tramline
Sa 26 Kippington Lodge
Su 27 The House of Lords
M 28 Free
M 28 Gordon Smith
Tu 29 Julie Driscoll
Tu 29 The Brian Auger Trinity
Tu 29 Village
W 30 Fairport Convention
W 30 Dr K's Blues Band
Th 31 Timebox
Th 31 East of Eden

November 1968
Fr 01 (Jon Hiseman's) Colosseum
Fr 01 Pegasus
Sa 02 Dream Police
Sa 02 Yes
Su 03 The House of Lords
M 04 Free
M 04 The John Dummer Blues Band
Tu 05 The Nice
Tu 05 Village
W 06 Eclection
W 06 East of Eden
Th 07 Spooky Tooth
Th 07 Andromeda
Fr 08 The Spirit of John Morgan
Fr 08 Pegasus
Sa 09 Dream Police
Sa 09 The Cortinas
Su 10 The House of Lords
M 11 Black Cat Bones
M 11 Ashton, Gardner & Dyke
Tu 12 Muddy Waters
Tu 12 Free
W 13 Love Sculpture
W 13 Yes
Th 14 Joe Cocker
Th 14 Clouds
Fr 15 Keef Hartley
Fr 15 Pegasus
Sa 16 Dream Police
Sa 16 Clouds
Su 17 The House of Lords
M 18 Free
M 18 The Spirit of John Morgan
Tu 19 Muddy Waters
Tu 19 Bobby Parker
W 20 Love Sculpture
W 20 East of Eden
Th 21 Spooky Tooth
Th 21 Village
Fr 22 Taste

Fr 22 The John Dummer Blues Band
Sa 23 Dream Police
Sa 23 Sarsparilla
Su 24 The House of Lords
M 25 Free
M 25 Pegasus
Tu 26 Jethro Tull
Tu 26 Bakerloo Blues Line
W 27 Yes
W 27 Van Der Graaf Generator
Th 28 Jimmy Witherspoon
Th 28 The Spirit of John Morgan
Fr 29 Aynsley Dunbar Retaliation
Fr 29 Bobby Parker
Sa 30 Dream Police
Sa 30 Octopus

December 1968
Su 01 The House of Lords
M 02 Free
M 02 Woody Kearn
Tu 03 Family
Tu 03 Village
Th 05 Joe Cocker
Th 05 Slam Creepers
Fr 06 Love Sculpture
Fr 06 Food
Sa 07 Dream Police
Sa 07 Sleepy
Su 08 Blue Rivers & his Maroons
M 09 Free
M 09 Steve Miller's Delivery
Tu 10 Led Zeppelin
Tu 10 Bakerloo Blues Line
Th 12 East of Eden
Fr 13 Taste
Fr 13 The Spirit of John Morgan
Sa 14 Dream Police
Sa 14 Andromeda
Su 15 Blue Rivers & his Maroons
M 16 Free
Tu 17 The Who
Tu 17 Yes
Th 19 Joe Cocker
Th 19 Clouds
Fr 20 Taste
Fr 20 Village
Sa 21 Dream Police
Sa 21 Steve Miller's Delivery
Su 22 The House of Lords
M 23 Free
M 23 Pegasus
Tu 24 Aynsley Dunbar Retaliation
Tu 24 The John Dummer Blues Band
Th 26 Ten Years After
Th 26 East of Eden
Fr 27 Chicken Shack
Fr 27 The Spirit of John Morgan
Sa 28 Dream Police
Sa 28 Just William
Tu 31 Taste
Tu 31 Village

January 1969
W 01 Yes
W 01 Octopus
Th 02 John Mayall's Bluesbreakers
Th 02 The John Dummer Blues Band
Fr 03 (Jon Hiseman's) Colosseum
Fr 03 Earth
Sa 04 Spice
Sa 04 Clouds
Su 05 The Explosives
Tu 07 Aynsley Dunbar Retaliation
W 08 Yes
W 08 Toast
Th 09 Spooky Tooth
Th 09 Woody Kearn
Fr 10 Bakerloo Blues Line
Fr 10 Village
Sa 11 Spice
Sa 11 Van Der Graaf Generator
Su 12 The House of Lords
Tu 14 The Jeff Beck Group
Tu 14 Andromeda

W 15 Yes
W 15 Procession
Th 16 Free
Th 16 Shakey Vic's Big City Blues Band
Fr 17 Savoy Brown Blues Band
Fr 17 Pegasus
Sa 18 Spice
Sa 18 Octopus
Su 19 The Explosives
Tu 21 Marmalade
Tu 21 Clouds
W 22 Yes
W 22 Village
Th 23 Joe Cocker
Th 23 Andromeda
Fr 24 Ten Years After
Fr 24 Woody Kearn
Sa 25 Spice
Sa 25 The Beatstalkers
Su 26 The Exception
Tu 28 The Nice
Tu 28 Killing Floor
W 29 Yes
W 29 Clouds
Th 30 Mortimer
Th 30 Van Der Graaf Generator
Fr 31 Taste
Fr 31 Steamhammer

February 1969
Sa 01 Spice
Sa 01 Village
Su 02 The House of Lords
Tu 04 Love Sculpture
Tu 04 The Eyes of Blue
W 05 Yes
W 05 Caravan
Th 06 Locomotive
Th 06 Bakerloo
Th 06 Earth
Th 06 Roy Everett
Th 06 Tea and Symphony
Fr 07 Taste
Fr 07 Groundhogs
Sa 08 Spice
Sa 08 Procession
Su 09 Cindy Starr & The Mopeds
Tu 11 Mick Abrahams
Tu 11 Village
W 12 Yes
W 12 Octopus
Th 13 Free
Th 13 Pegasus
Fr 14 (Jon Hiseman's) Colosseum
Fr 14 The Spirit of John Morgan
Sa 15 Spice
Sa 15 Octopus
Su 16 Black Velvet
Tu 18 Gun
Tu 18 Caravan
W 19 Yes
W 19 The Spirit of John Morgan
Th 20 Aynsley Dunbar Retaliation
Th 20 The Eyes of Blue
Fr 21 Taste
Fr 21 Pegasus
Sa 22 Spice
Sa 22 Andromeda
Su 23 The House of Lords
Tu 25 Ten Years After
Tu 25 The Spirit of John Morgan
W 26 Yes
W 26 Clouds
Th 27 Juniors Eyes
Th 27 Rainbows
Fr 28 Bakerloo
Fr 28 Earth

March 1969
Sa 01 Spice
Sa 01 The Elastic Band
Su 02 The House of Lords
M 04 Freddy King
Tu 04 Steamhammer
Tu 04 The John Dummer Blues Band

W 05 Yes
W 05 Circus
Th 06 Terry Reid
Th 06 Clouds
Fr 07 Taste
Fr 07 The Outsiders
Sa 08 Spice
Sa 08 The Shoo String Band
Su 09 The House of Lords
Tu 11 Bakerloo
Tu 11 Locomotive
Tu 11 Earth
Tu 11 Roy Everett
W 12 Yes
W 12 Killing Floor
Th 13 Terry Reid
Th 13 Black Sabbath
Fr 14 Chicken Shack
Fr 14 The John Dummer Blues Band
Sa 15 Spice
Sa 15 Circus
Su 16 The House of Lords
Tu 18 (Jon Hiseman's) Colosseum
Tu 18 The Spirit of John Morgan
W 19 Yes
W 19 Clouds
Th 20 Terry Reid
Th 20 Steamhammer
Fr 21 Taste
Fr 21 Wine
Sa 22 Spice
Sa 22 Procession
Su 23 Trifle
Tu 25 Trash
Tu 25 Clouds
W 26 Rainbows
W 26 Procession
Th 27 Terry Reid
Th 27 Village
Fr 28 Led Zeppelin
Fr 28 The Eyes of Blue
Sa 29 Country Joe and the Fish
Su 30 The House of Lords

April 1969
Tu 01 Love Sculpture
Tu 01 Pegasus
W 02 Yes
W 02 Harsh Reality
Th 03 Terry Reid
Th 03 Hard Meat
Fr 04 Taste
Fr 04 Steamhammer
Sa 05 Procession
Sa 05 The Shoo String Band
Su 06 The House of Lords
M 07 The Spirit of John Morgan
M 07 The John Dummer Blues Band
Tu 08 Harmony Grass
Tu 08 The Cymbaline
W 09 Yes
W 09 The Elastic Band
Th 10 Elmer Gantry
Th 10 Village
Fr 11 Chicken Shack
Fr 11 The Eyes of Blue
Sa 12 Procession
Sa 12 Octopus
Su 13 Trifle
Tu 15 Terry Reid
Tu 15 The John Dummer Blues Band
W 16 Rainbows
W 16 Entire Sioux Nation
Th 17 The Spirit of John Morgan
Th 17 Village
Fr 18 Mick Abrahams
Fr 18 Blodwyn Pig
Fr 18 Circus
Sa 19 The Eyes of Blue
Sa 19 Pegasus
Su 20 Mouse & the Traps
Tu 22 (Jon Hiseman's) Colosseum
Tu 22 Steamhammer
W 23 Rainbows
W 23 Clouds

Th 24 Elmer Gantry
Th 24 Hard Meat
Fr 25 Trash
Fr 25 Pegasus
Sa 26 My Dear Watson
Sa 26 Sarolta with The Turnstile
Su 27 Jason Crest
Tu 29 Mick Abrahams
Tu 29 Blodwyn Pig
Tu 29 The Elastic Band
W 30 Van Der Graaf Generator
W 30 The Eyes of Blue

May 1969
Th 01 The Spirit of John Morgan
Th 01 Clouds
Fr 02 Taste
Fr 02 Steamhammer
Sa 03 The Klubs
Sa 03 The Turnstile
Su 04 Groundhogs
Tu 06 Alan Bown
Tu 06 The Maddening Crowd
W 07 Trash
W 07 Junco Partners
Th 08 Terry Reid
Th 08 Grail
Fr 09 Bakerloo
Fr 09 2001
Sa 10 Procession
Sa 10 Mandrake Paddlesteamer
Su 11 Lowell Fulson
Su 11 Sam Apple Pie
Su 11 Steve Miller's Delivery
Tu 13 Emanon
Tu 13 Circus
W 14 Yes
W 14 Peter Cooper
Th 15 Terry Reid
Th 15 Leviathan
Fr 16 Steppenwolf
Fr 16 Terry Reid
Fr 16 Hard Meat
Fr 16 King Crimson
Fr 16 Steamhammer
Sa 17 Procession
Sa 17 Pegasus
Su 18 Ron Geesin
Tu 20 Blodwyn Pig
Tu 20 Grail
W 21 The Spirit of John Morgan
W 21 Sam Apple Pie
Th 22 Terry Reid
Th 22 Hardmeat
Fr 23 Savoy Brown Blues Band
Fr 23 Junco Partners
Sa 24 Procession
Sa 24 The Maddening Crowd
Su 25 New Paths
Su 25 King Crimson
Su 25 John Surman Octet
M 26 (Jon Hiseman's) Colosseum
M 26 Circus
Tu 27 Taste
Tu 27 Rich and Grimes with Babylon
W 28 Yes
W 28 The Maddening Crowd
Th 29 Howlin' Wolf
Th 29 McKenna Mendelson Mainline
Th 29 The John Dummer Blues Band
Fr 30 Blodwyn Pig
Fr 30 Sam Apple Pie
Sa 31 Procession
Sa 31 The Eyes of Blue

June 1969
Su 01 New Paths
Su 01 King Crimson
Su 01 Circus
Tu 03 Aynsley Dunbar Retaliation
Tu 03 Wine
W 04 The Spirit of John Morgan
W 04 Pegasus
Th 05 Terry Reid
Th 05 Man
Fr 06 The Jeff Beck Group

Fr 06 Steamhammer
Sa 07 Procession
Sa 07 Kippington Lodge
Su 08 New Paths
Su 08 King Crimson
Su 08 John Surman Octet
Tu 10 The Nice
Tu 10 Circus
W 11 Yes
W 11 Sweet Marriage
Th 12 Terry Reid
Th 12 Joint
Fr 13 Chicken Shack
Fr 13 Groundhogs
Sa 14 Procession
Sa 14 Audience
Su 15 The Strawbs
Su 15 David Bowie
Su 15 James Taylor
M 16 Procession
M 16 Audience
Tu 17 Family
Tu 17 Grail
W 18 The Spirit of John Morgan
W 18 Leviathan
Th 19 Freddy King
Th 19 Killing Floor
Th 19 Steamhammer
Fr 20 Il Jackson
Fr 20 Circus
Sa 21 Procession
Sa 21 Joint
Su 22 The Strawbs
Su 22 Paper Bubble
Su 22 Tony Crerar
M 23 Juniors Eyes
M 23 Sweet Marriage
Tu 24 Taste
Tu 24 Pegasus
W 25 Yes
W 25 Mandrake Paddlesteamer
Th 26 The Spirit of John Morgan
Th 26 Brainbox
Fr 27 Blodwyn Pig
Fr 27 Mick Abrahams
Fr 27 Groundhogs
Sa 28 Procession
Sa 28 Octopus
Su 29 King Crimson
Su 29 John Surman Octet
M 30 John Mayall
M 30 Steamhammer

July 1969
Tu 01 (Jon Hiseman's) Colosseum
Tu 01 Grail
W 02 Yes
W 02 Andromeda
Th 03 The Spirit of John Morgan
Th 03 Babylon
Fr 04 Taste
Fr 04 Groundhogs
Sa 05 Village
Sa 05 Kippington Lodge
Su 06 New Paths
Su 06 King Crimson
Su 06 John Surman Octet
M 07 Eclection
M 07 Grail
Tu 08 Soft Machine
Tu 08 Circus
W 09 Yes
W 09 Hard Meat
Th 10 The Spirit of John Morgan
Th 10 Samson
Fr 11 Blodwyn Pig
Fr 11 Andromeda
Sa 12 Village
Sa 12 Leviathan
Su 13 New Paths
Su 13 King Crimson
Su 13 John Surman Octet
M 14 The Liverpool Scene
M 14 Grail
Tu 15 Marmalade

Tu 15 Dream Police
W 16 Yes
W 16 Kippington Lodge
Th 17 The Spirit of John Morgan
Th 17 The Mooche
Fr 18 Keef Hartley
Fr 18 Circus
Sa 19 Village
Sa 19 Samson
Su 20 New Paths
Su 20 King Crimson
M 21 Eclection
M 21 Grail
Tu 22 Chicken Shack
Tu 22 Groundhogs
W 23 Yes
W 23 Leviathan
Th 24 Steamhammer
Th 24 The Glass Menagerie
Fr 25 Blodwyn Pig
Fr 25 Circus
Sa 26 Village
Sa 26 Imagination
Su 27 New Paths
Su 27 King Crimson
Su 27 John Surman Octet
M 28 The Liverpool Scene
M 28 Synthanesia
Tu 29 The Brian Auger Trinity
Tu 29 Circus
W 30 Yes
W 30 Hard Meat
Th 31 The Spirit of John Morgan
Th 31 The Wallace Collection

August 1969
Fr 01 (Jon Hiseman's) Colosseum
Fr 01 Circus
Sa 02 Village
Sa 02 Pegasus
Su 03 King Crimson
M 04 Eclection
M 04 Cressida
Tu 05 Family
Tu 05 Samson
W 06 New Paths
W 06 Circus
W 06 Keith Tippett
Th 07 Yes
Th 07 Leviathan
Fr 08 The Spirit of John Morgan
Fr 08 The Breakthru
Sa 09 Village
Sa 09 Cuby's Blues Band
Su 10 King Crimson
M 11 (Keith Relf's) Renaissance
M 11 Man
Tu 12 Harmony Grass
Tu 12 Playground
W 13 New Paths
W 13 Circus
W 13 Keith Tippett
Th 14 Yes
Th 14 Samson
Fr 15 Blodwyn Pig
Fr 15 Grail
Sa 16 Village
Sa 16 Babylon
Su 17 King Crimson
M 18 (Keith Relf's) Renaissance
M 18 The Breakthru
Tu 19 Love Sculpture
Tu 19 Groundhogs
W 20 New Paths
W 20 Circus
W 20 Keith Tippett
Th 21 Clouds
Th 21 The Mooche
Fr 22 The Spirit of John Morgan
Fr 22 Calmen Waters Blues Band
Sa 23 Village
Sa 23 Affinity
Su 24 King Crimson
M 25 Eclection
Tu 26 (Noel Redding's) Fat Mattress

Tu 26 The Glass Menagerie
W 27 Circus
W 27 Keith Tippett
Th 28 Clouds
Th 28 Babylon
Fr 29 Blodwyn Pig
Fr 29 Samson
Sa 30 Village
Sa 30 Jasper
Su 31 Hardin & York
Su 31 Griffin

September 1969
M 01 (Keith Relf's) Renaissance
M 01 The Open Mind
Tu 02 Aynsley Dunbar Retaliation
Tu 02 Groundhogs
W 03 New Paths
W 03 Circus
W 03 Keith Tippett
Th 04 Steamhammer
Th 04 Grail
Fr 05 Taste
Fr 05 Man
Sa 06 Village
Sa 06 The Mooche
Su 07 Jo Ann Kelly
Su 07 Brett Marvin and the
   Thunderbolts
M 08 Clouds
M 08 Babylon
Tu 09 Deep Purple
Tu 09 Samson
W 10 New Paths
W 10 Circus
W 10 Keith Tippett
Th 11 The Spirit of John Morgan
Th 11 The Elastic Band
Fr 12 Atomic Rooster
Fr 12 Gypsy
Sa 13 The Glass Menagerie
Sa 13 Imagination
Su 14 Principal Edwards Magic
   Theatre
Su 14 Pete Brown with Piblokto!
M 15 (Keith Relf's) Renaissance
M 15 Grail
Tu 16 Grapefruit
Tu 16 Groundhogs
W 17 New Paths
W 17 Circus
W 17 Keith Tippett
Th 18 Hardin & York
Th 18 Entire Sioux Nation
Fr 19 Taste
Fr 19 Andwella's Dream
Sa 20 Village
Sa 20 Gypsy
Su 21 Jo Ann Kelly
Su 21 Brett Marvin and the
   Thunderbolts
M 22 Clouds
M 22 Samson
Tu 23 Blossom Toes
Tu 23 Mike Hart and the Business
W 24 New Paths
W 24 Circus
W 24 Keith Tippett
Th 25 The Glass Menagerie
Th 25 The Open Mind
Fr 26 Vanilla Fudge
Fr 26 Grail
Sa 27 Village
Sa 27 Gracious
Su 28 Radha Krishna Temple
M 29 Eclection
M 29 Gypsy
Tu 30 Blodwyn Pig
Tu 30 Ground

October 1969
W 01 Mixed Media
W 01 Big Finger
W 01 Circus
W 01 Incandescant Mantle
W 01 The Occasional Word

Th 02 Soft Machine
Th 02 Samson
Fr 03 Keef Hartley
Fr 03 Shades
Sa 04 Writing on the Wall
Sa 04 Julian's Treatment
M 06 (Keith Relf's) Renaissance
M 06 Grail
Tu 07 Family
Tu 07 Emily Muff
Tu 07 Stone the Crows
W 08 Mixed Media
W 08 Circus
W 08 Incandescant Mantle
W 08 Spontaneous Music Ensemble
Th 09 The Glass Menagerie
Th 09 The Mooche
Fr 10 Savoy Brown Blues Band
Sa 11 Writing on the Wall
Su 12 Magna Carta
M 13 Blossom Toes
M 13 Big Finger
Tu 14 The Brian Auger Trinity
Tu 14 Samson
W 15 Mixed Media
W 15 Circus
Th 16 Atomic Rooster
Th 16 Audience
Fr 17 Hardin & York
Fr 17 Grail
Sa 18 Writing on the Wall
Sa 18 Arcadium
M 20 (Keith Relf's) Renaissance
M 20 The Elastic Band
Tu 21 White Trash
Tu 21 Gypsy
W 22 Mixed Media
W 22 Circus
W 22 Spontaneous Music Ensemble
Th 23 The Glass Menagerie
Th 23 Rare Bird
Fr 24 Taste
Fr 24 Groundhogs
Sa 25 Writing on the Wall
Sa 25 The Eyes of Blue
M 27 Clouds
M 27 Audience
Tu 28 (Jon Hiseman's) Colosseum
Tu 28 Audience
W 29 Mixed Media
W 29 Circus
W 29 Spontaneous Music Ensemble
Th 30 Yes
Th 30 Samson
Fr 31 Graham Bond
Fr 31 Class

November 1969
Sa 01 Igginbottom
Sa 01 Shades
M 03 Writing on the Wall
M 03 Arcadium
Tu 04 Atomic Rooster
Tu 04 Samson
W 05 Mixed Media
W 05 Circus
Th 06 Howlin' Wolf
Th 06 Groundhogs
Th 06 Junco Partners
Fr 07 (Keith Relf's) Renaissance
Fr 07 Grail
Sa 08 Affinity
Sa 08 Cressida
M 10 Writing on the Wall
M 10 Trees
Tu 11 Aynsley Dunbar Retaliation
Tu 11 Igginbottom
W 12 Mixed Media
W 12 Circus
W 12 Spontaneous Music Ensemble
Th 13 Freddy King
Th 13 Shades
Fr 14 Hardin & York
Fr 14 Black Sabbath
Sa 15 Affinity

Sa 15 The Mooche
M 17 Writing on the Wall
M 17 Skin Alley
Tu 18 Juicy Lucy
Tu 18 Made In Sweden
W 19 Mixed Media
W 19 Circus
Th 20 Clouds
Fr 21 Taste
Fr 21 Mike Hart and the Business
Sa 22 The Glass Menagerie
Sa 22 Tilted Cross
M 24 Writing on the Wall
M 24 Hawkwind
Tu 25 Blossom Toes
Tu 25 Grail
W 26 Mixed Media
W 26 Circus
Th 27 Jo Ann Kelly
Th 27 Bob Hall
Fr 28 Hardin & York
Fr 28 Timebox
Sa 29 Shades
Sa 29 Medicine Hat

December 1969
M 01 Writing on the Wall
M 01 Arcadium
Tu 02 The Spirit of John Morgan
Tu 02 Cuby's Blues Band
W 03 Mixed Media
Th 04 The Ring of Truth
Th 04 Tilted Cross
Fr 05 Hardin & York
Fr 05 Cressida
Sa 06 Quatermass
Sa 06 Ashcan
M 08 Writing on the Wall
M 08 The Big Fir
Tu 09 Blossom Toes
Th 09 Rare Bird
W 10 Mixed Media
Th 11 Clouds
Th 11 Tilted Cross
Fr 12 Hardin & York
Fr 12 Fat Daughter
Sa 13 Kippington Lodge
Sa 13 Smile
M 15 Writing on the Wall
M 15 Grope
Tu 16 Savoy Brown Blues Band
Tu 16 Dry Ice
W 17 Mixed Media
Th 18 (Tony McPhee and the)
   Groundhogs
Th 18 Jellybread
Fr 19 Alan Bown
Fr 19 Audience
Sa 20 Kippington Lodge
Sa 20 Cressida
M 22 Writing on the Wall
M 22 Tam White
Tu 23 Colosseum
W 24 Keef Hartley
W 24 Mike Hart and the Business
Fr 26 Yes
Fr 26 Man
Sa 27 The John Dummer Blues Band
Sa 27 Tilted Cross
Su 28 Magna Carta
Su 28 Cosmos
Su 28 Jon Betmead
Su 28 The Paupers
M 29 Writing on the Wall
M 29 Arcadium
Tu 30 Harmony Grass
Tu 30 Mandrake
W 31 Family
W 31 Audience
W 31 Emily Muff

January 1970
Fr 02 Taste
Fr 02 Skin Alley
Sa 03 Sam Gopal
Sa 03 Sun

Su 04 Magna Carta
M 05 Writing on the Wall
M 05 Scratch
Tu 06 The Graham Bond Initiation
Tu 06 Tarzan
W 07 Mixed Media
Th 08 Rare Bird
Th 08 Little Free Rock
Fr 09 Sweet Water Canal
Fr 09 Lace
Sa 10 The John Dummer Blues Band
Sa 10 Jo Anne Kelly
Su 11 Magna Carta
M 12 Sweet Plum
M 12 Tam White
Tu 13 Writing on the Wall
Tu 13 Hard Meat
W 14 Mixed Media
Th 15 The Spirit of John Morgan
Th 15 Armada
Fr 16 Sweet Water Canal
Fr 16 Affinity
Sa 17 Tuesday's Children
Sa 17 Titus Groan
M 19 Writing on the Wall
Tu 20 Aynsley Dunbar Retaliation
Tu 20 Tarzan
W 21 Mixed Media
Th 22 Rare Bird
Th 22 Forum
Fr 23 Sweet Water Canal
Fr 23 Nucleus
Sa 24 Andwella's Dream
Sa 24 Gorman Ghost
M 26 Writing on the Wall
M 26 Arcadium
Tu 27 Chicken Shack
Tu 27 Jellybread
W 28 Mixed Media
Th 29 (Tony McPhee and the)
   Groundhogs
Th 29 Daddy Longlegs
Fr 30 Sweet Water Canal
Fr 30 Nucleus
Sa 31 May Blitz
Sa 31 Egg

February 1970
Tu 03 David Bowie
Tu 03 Juniors Eyes
Tu 03 Timebox
W 04 Keef Hartley and his band
W 04 Genesis
Th 05 Rare Bird
Th 05 Toast
Fr 06 Sweet Water Canal
Fr 06 Hard Meat
Tu 10 Blodwyn Pig
Tu 10 Grail
Tu 10 Trevor Billmuss
W 11 Anything Acoustic
W 11 Colin Scott
W 11 Hunter Muskett
Th 12 Writing on the Wall
Th 12 Skin Alley
Fr 13 Aynsley Dunbar's Blue Whale
Fr 13 Gracious
Sa 14 The Business
Sa 14 Valhalla UK
M 16 Julian's Treatment
M 16 My Cake
Tu 17 Soft Machine
Tu 17 Timebox
W 18 Hunter Muskett
W 18 Anything Acoustic
W 18 Magna Carta
Th 19 Rare Bird
Th 19 Genesis
Fr 20 Hard Meat
Fr 20 Sweet Water Canal
Sa 21 Timebox
M 23 Julian's Treatment
Tu 24 The Graham Bond Initiation
Tu 24 Timebox
W 25 Anything Acoustic

W 25 Spencer Davis
W 25 Hunter Muskett
Th 26 Writing on the Wall
Th 26 Red Star
Fr 27 Hard Meat
Fr 27 Sweet Water Canal
Sa 28 The Foundations
Sa 28 Cardboard Orchestra

March 1970
M 02 Julian's Treatment
Tu 03 Taste
Tu 03 Anno Domini
W 04 Anything Acoustic
W 04 Sunforest
Th 05 Caravan
Th 05 Griffin
Fr 06 Sweet Water Canal
Fr 06 Nucleus
Sa 07 Consortium
Sa 07 Silas
M 09 Julian's Treatment
Tu 10 The Liverpool Scene
Tu 10 PC Kent
W 11 Anything Acoustic
W 11 Derek Brimstone
Th 12 Writing on the Wall
Th 12 Morning
Fr 13 (Tony McPhee and the)
        Groundhogs
Fr 13 Silas
Sa 14 Nucleus
Sa 14 Armada
M 16 Black Sabbath
M 16 Grisby Dyke
M 16 Straight Lace
Tu 17 (Jon Hiseman's) Colosseum
W 18 Anything Acoustic
W 18 Alan Hull
W 18 Continuum
W 18 Sunforest
Th 19 Rare Bird
Th 19 Patto
Fr 20 Christine Perfect
Fr 20 Requiem
Sa 21 Nucleus
M 23 Julian's Treatment
Tu 24 Hard Meat
Tu 24 Hardin & York
W 25 Anything Acoustic
W 25 The Famous Jug Band
Th 26 Writing on the Wall
Th 26 Grail
Fr 27 Arthur Brown
Fr 27 Slade
Sa 28 Matthews Southern Comfort
Sa 28 Silas
Su 29 Alex Harvey Hair Band
M 30 The Spirit of John Morgan
M 30 Armada
Tu 31 Atomic Rooster
Tu 31 Big Toe

April 1970
W 01 Orange Blossom
W 01 Sunforest
Th 02 Caravan
Fr 03 Nucleus
Fr 03 Sweet Slag
Sa 04 Geno Washington and the Ram
        Jam Band
M 06 Valhalla UK
Tu 07 Juicy Lucy
Tu 07 Patto
W 08 Jeremy Taylor
W 08 Sunforest
Th 09 Rare Bird
Th 09 Salt 'n' Pepper
Fr 10 Yes
Fr 10 Slade
Fr 10 Trevor Billmuss
Sa 11 Harmony Grass
Su 12 Audience
Su 12 Jan Dukes De Grey
M 13 Valhalla UK
M 13 White Lightning

Tu 14 The Liverpool Scene
Tu 14 Hookfoot
W 15 Magna Carta
W 15 The Strawbs
W 15 Colin Scott
W 15 Sunforest
Th 16 Writing on the Wall
Th 16 Business
Fr 17 Humble Pie
Fr 17 Morning
Sa 18 Jimmy James
Su 19 Van Der Graaf Generator
Su 19 Jan Dukes De Grey
M 20 Julian's Treatment
M 20 Black August
Tu 21 Fat Mattress
Tu 21 Gypsy
Th 23 Rare Bird
Th 23 Birth
Fr 24 Nucleus
Fr 24 Armada
Sa 25 Status Quo
Su 26 Audience
Su 26 Farm
M 27 Valhalla UK
M 27 Mungo Jerry
Tu 28 Taste
Tu 28 Toe-Fat
W 29 Ian Tracey and the Tributes
Th 30 Writing on the Wall
Th 30 Gracious

May 1970
Fr 01 Nucleus
Fr 01 Patto
Sa 02 Napolcon
Su 03 Van Der Graaf Generator
M 04 Skin Alley
M 04 Trees
Tu 05 East of Eden
Th 06 Rare Bird
W 06 T?
Th 06 Actress
W 06 Tiny Clanger
Fr 08 Slade
Fr 08 Wishbone Ash
Sa 09 Trifle
Su 10 Kevin Ayers & the Whole
        World
Su 10 Quiver
M 11 Cressida
M 11 Fairfield Parlour
Tu 12 Keef Hartley
W 13 Long John Baldry
W 13 Sunforest
Th 14 Black Sabbath
Th 14 Bakerloo
Fr 15 The Spirit of John Morgan
Fr 15 Granny's Intentions
Sa 16 Harmony Grass
Su 17 Audience
Su 17 Sunforest
M 18 Gracious
M 18 Ginger Johnson
M 18 Little Free Rock
Tu 19 Hardin & York
Tu 19 Uriah Heep
W 20 T2
W 20 Castle Farm
Th 21 Groundhogs
Th 21 Quatermass
Fr 22 Affinity
Fr 22 Granny's New Intentions
Sa 23 Zior
Su 24 If
Su 24 Kelly James
M 25 Justine
Tu 26 Chicken Shack
Tu 26 Adolphus Rebirth
W 27 Satisfaction
W 27 My Cake
Th 28 Caravan
Th 28 Spring Fever
Fr 29 Arthur Brown
Fr 29 Pacific Drift

Sa 30 Tangerine Peel
Su 31 Daddy Longlegs

June 1970
M 01 Argent
M 01 Amory Kane
Tu 02 Humble Pie
Tu 02 Da Da
W 03 Blodwyn Pig
Th 04 Writing on the Wall
Th 04 Wishbone Ash
Fr 05 Elton John
Fr 05 Business
Sa 06 Trifle
Su 07 Raven
Su 07 Brethren
M 08 Gracious
M 08 Uriah Heep
Tu 09 Brinsley Schwarz
Tu 09 Patto
W 10 Luv Machine
Th 11 Heavy Jelly
Th 11 Jackie Lomax
Th 11 Quiver
Fr 12 Slade
Fr 12 Clark Hutchinson
Sa 13 Harmony Grass
Su 14 Genesis
Su 14 Junco Partners
M 15 Wishbone Ash
M 15 Clang Feather and Almanac
Tu 16 Keef Hartley
Tu 16 High Broom
W 17 Keith Christmas
W 17 Gary Farr
Th 18 Caravan
Th 18 Patto
Fr 19 Pete Brown with Piblokto!
Fr 19 Mayfields Mule
Sa 20 Jimmy James
M 22 Climax Chicago Blues Band
M 22 Mirrors
Tu 23 Judus Jump
Tu 23 Samson
W 24 Peter Green
W 24 Ginger Johnson's African
        Drummers
W 24 Little Free Rock
Th 25 Groundhogs
Th 25 Granny's New Intentions
Fr 26 Atomic Rooster
Fr 26 Deep Joy
Sa 27 The Wild Angels
Su 28 Audience
Su 28 Amazing Blondel
Su 28 Roger Ruskin Spear's Giant
        Kinetic Wardrobe
M 29 Gracious
Tu 30 Hardin & York

July 1970
W 01 Nova Carmina
W 01 Childe Rolande
W 01 Stephen Delft
Th 02 Caravan
Th 02 Mandragon
Fr 03 The Pink Fairies
Fr 03 Titus Groan
Sa 04 Custer's Track
Su 05 Rumpelstiltskin
Su 05 Gin House
M 06 Medicine Head
M 06 Jellybread
Tu 07 Status Quo
W 08 Black Sabbath
W 08 Harry The Horse
Th 09 Steamhammer
Th 09 Stackridge
Fr 10 The Pink Fairies
Fr 10 Titus Groan
Sa 11 Napoleon
Su 12 Genesis
Su 12 Osibisa
Su 12 Roger Ruskin Spear's Giant
        Kinetic Wardrobe
M 13 May Blitz

M 13 Bob Downes Open Music
Tu 14 Keef Hartley
Tu 14 Supertramp
W 15 Slade
W 15 Gentle Giant
Th 16 Black Widow
Th 16 Eric Leese
Fr 17 The Love Affair
Fr 17 Key Largo
Sa 18 Dream Police
Su 19 Audience
Su 19 Da Da
M 20 Kripple Vision
M 20 Heads Hands & Feet
Tu 21 Taste
Tu 21 Deep Joy
W 22 Granny's New Intentions
W 22 Rat
Th 23 Edgar Broughton
Th 23 Noir
Fr 24 Groundhogs
Fr 24 Supertramp
Fr 25 Status Quo
Su 26 Van Der Graaf Generator
Su 26 Spring
M 27 Justine
Tu 28 Hardin & York
W 29 Thomas Yates & Ron Henderson
Th 30 Caravan
Fr 31 MC5
Fr 31 Grail

August 1970
Sa 01 Custer's Track
Su 02 The World
Su 02 Neil Innes & Dennis Cowan
Su 02 Roger Ruskin Spear's Giant
        Kinetic Wardrobe
M 03 Rock Workshop
M 03 Nick Softley
Tu 04 Humble Pie
Tu 04 Cochise
W 05 Made In Sweden
Th 06 Armada
Th 06 Granny's New Intentions
Fr 07 T2
Sa 08 Custer's Track
Su 09 Brethren
M 10 Uriah Heep
M 10 Czar
Tu 11 Derek and the Dominos
W 12 Slade
Th 13 Granny's New Intentions
Fr 14 Fat Mattress
Fr 14 Deep Joy
Sa 15 Harmony Grass
Su 16 Audience
Su 16 Black August
M 17 Duster Bennett
M 17 Blitzkrieg
Tu 18 Yes
W 19 Childe Rolande
W 19 Mister Fox
W 19 Stephen Delft
Th 20 Granny's New Intentions
Th 20 Armada
Fr 21 T2
Fr 21 Patto
Sa 22 Trifle
Su 23 Van Der Graaf Generator
Su 23 Trevor Billmuss
M 24 Climax Chicago Blues Band
M 24 Mirrors
Tu 25 Jackson Heights
W 26 Writing on the Wall
W 27 Granny's New Intentions
Th 27 Trevor Billmuss
Fr 28 T2
Fr 28 Anno Domini
Sa 29 Dream Police
Su 30 Genesis
Su 30 Amazing Blondel
M 31 Gracious
M 31 Justine

September 1970

Tu 01 Rare Bird	Tu 20 Judas Jump	Tu 15 Blodwyn Pig	M 22 UFO
Tu 01 Salamander	Tu 20 Idle Race	Tu 15 Main Horse Airlines	M 22 Distant Jim
W 02 Steamhammer	W 21 Warm Dust	W 16 Little Free Rock	Tu 23 Hardin & York
W 02 Mandragon	W 21 Kripple Vision	W 16 Shades	Tu 23 Demick & Armstrong
Th 03 Granny's New Intentions	Th 22 T2	Th 17 Karakorum	W 24 Steel Mill
Th 03 Interns	Th 22 Storm	Fr 18 Atomic Rooster	Th 25 Comus
Fr 04 Hardin & York	Fr 23 Fat Mattress	Fr 18 Ricotti & Alberqueque	Th 25 Paul Brett Sage
Fr 04 Blend	Fr 23 Deep Joy	Sa 19 Asrail	Th 25 Trader Horne
Sa 05 The Nashville Teens	Sa 24 Custer's Track	M 21 Medicine Head	Fr 26 Anno Domini
Su 06 Van Der Graaf Generator	Su 25 Audience	Tu 22 Groundhogs	Fr 26 Shide and Acorn
M 07 LA	Su 25 Skinny Cat	W 23 The Wild Angels	Sa 27 Lockjaw
M 07 Skid Row	M 26 Requiem	Th 24 Anno Domini	**March 1971**
W 09 Stephen Delft	M 26 Boris & Teargas	Sa 26 Geno Washington and the Ram	M 01 Paul Korda
Th 10 Granny's New Intentions	Tu 27 Airforce	Jam Band	M 01 Django Wheeler
Th 10 Armada	Tu 27 Deep Joy	M 28 Julian's Treatment	M 01 Patriarch of Glastonbury's Band
Sa 12 Custer's Track	W 28 Affinity	M 28- Wide Open	Tu 02 Stud
Su 13 The World	W 28 Flare	Tu 29 Hardin & York	Tu 02 Arc
Su 13 Roger Ruskin Spear's Giant	Th 29 Barclay James Harvest	W 30 Little Free Rock	W 03 Steel Mill
Kinetic Wardrobe	Th 29 Duster Bennett	W 30- Ginger Johnson's African	Th 04 Comus
M 14 Gentle Giant	Fr 30 Everyone	Drummers	Th 04 Paul Brett Sage
Tu 15 Black Sabbath	Fr 30 Howl	Th 31 Custer's Track	Fr 05 Terry Reid
Tu 15 The Dog That Bit People	Sa 31 Mucky Duck	**January 1971**	Fr 05 Nimbo
W 16 Wishbone Ash	**November 1970**	Sa 02 Salt of the Earth	Sa 06 The Crew
W 16 Arcadium	M 02 Alan Bown	Tu 05 Stud	Su 07 Sandhams Village
Th 17 Granny's New Intentions	M 02 Hate	Tu 05 Anno Domini	Su 07 Brewers Droop
Th 17 Armada	Tu 03 Van Der Graaf Generator	W 06 Weston Gavin	Su 07 Legend
Fr 18 Blodwyn Pig	Tu 03 Lindisfarne	W 06 Stephen Delft	Su 07 Little Free Rock
Fr 18 Hammer	W 04 Childe Rolande	W 06 Tintagel	Su 07 UFO
Sa 19 Custer's Track	W 04 Stephen Delft	Th 07 Patto	M 08 The Pink Fairies
Su 20 Lindisfarne	W 04 Temple Creatures	Fr 08 Audience	Tu 09 If
M 21 Heads Hands & Feet	Th 05 East of Eden	Fr 08 America	Tu 09 Karakorum
M 21 Gracious	Th 05 Yellow	Sa 09 Steel Mill	Th 11 Humble Pie
Tu 22 Keef Hartley	Fr 06 Bacon Fat	Su 12 Daddy Longlegs	Th 11 Paul Brett Sage
Tu 22 Aardvark	Fr 06 Ricotti & Albuqerque	W 13 Sweet Slag	Fr 12 Anno Domini
W 23 Andy Roberts and Everyone	Sa 07 Mucky Duck	W 13 Eliot	Fr 12 Demick & Armstrong
W 23 Shelagh McDonald	M 09 Legend	Th 14 Karakorum	Sa 13 Syrup
Th 24 Granny's New Intentions	M 09 Dear Mr Tyme	Fr 15 Stray	Su 14 Sandhams Village
Fr 25 The Faces	Tu 10 Jackson Heights	Fr 15 Junkyard Angel	Su 14 Balloon & Banana
Fr 25 Fail Safe	Tu 10 Genesis	Sa 16 Jessop & Co	Su 14 Danta
Sa 26 Trifle	W 11 Stone the Crows	Tu 19 Mott The Hoople	Su 14 Gilberto Gil
Su 27 Van Der Graaf Generator	W 11 Kiss	Tu 19 Blondel	Su 14 UFO
Su 27 Roger Ruskin Spear's Giant	Th 12 Trifle	W 20 Little Free Rock	Su 14 Dusky Ruth
Kinetic Wardrobe	Th 12 Ginger	W 20 Distant Jim	M 15 Cochise
M 28 Bram Stoker	Fr 13 Mick Abrahams Band	Th 21 David O'List Band	M 15 Skin Alley
M 28 Hate	Fr 13 Autumn	Fr 22 Terry Reid	Tu 16 Ashton, Gardner & Dyke
Tu 29 Groundhogs	Sa 14 Custer's Track	Fr 22 Kiss	Th 18 Keef Hartley
Tu 29 Jellybread	M 16 Sin	Sa 23 Steel Mill	Th 18 Spring
W 30 Mott The Hoople	M 16 Maggot	Tu 26 The Pink Fairies	Fr 19 Gilberto Gil
W 30 Bronco	Tu 17 Keef Hartley	Tu 26 Hawkwind	Fr 19 Demick & Armstrong
October 1970	W 18 Satisfaction	W 27 Mandrake	Sa 20 The Crew
Th 01 Dream Police	Th 19 East of Eden	W 27 Syrup	Su 21 Sandhams Village
Th 01 Iron Prophet	Th 19 Fagin	Th 28 Man	Su 21 Little Free Rock
Fr 02 East of Eden	Fr 20 The Faces	Fr 29 Brian Auger's Oblivion Express	Su 21 Mandrake
Fr 02 Fagin	Sa 21 Anno Domini	Fr 29 David O'List Band	Su 21 Titus Groan
Sa 03 Mucky Duck	M 23 Ben	Sa 30 The Crew	Su 21 UFO
Su 04 Genesis	M 23 Room	**February 1971**	M 22 The Pink Fairies
Su 04 Stackridge	Tu 24 Steamhammer	M 01 The Faces	Tu 23 Led Zeppelin
M 05 Gary Farr	Tu 24 Bubastis	M 01 (Doris Henderson's) Eclection	Th 25 Egypt
M 05 Skin Alley	W 25 Comus	Tu 02 Wishbone Ash	Th 25 Poor Son
Tu 06 Lifetime	W 25 Demon Fuzz	Tu 02 Gordon Giltrap	Sa 27 Syrup
Tu 06 Deep Joy	W 25 Heron	W 03 Steel Mill	Su 28 Sandhams Village
W 07 Stephen Delft	W 25 Titus Groan	Th 04 Comus	Su 28 Little Free Rock
W 07 Casey	Th 26 Dream Police	Th 04 Trader Horne	Su 28 Puckless Blend
Th 08 Slade	Fr 27 Fat Mattress	Fr 05 Barclay James Harvest	Su 28 Pure Wing
Th 08 Grizelda	Fr 27 Mr Proud	Sa 06 Custer's Track	Su 28 UFO
Fr 09 Atomic Rooster	Sa 27 Custer's Track	M 08 Titanic	M 29 Graham Bond's Magick
Fr 09 Blitzkrieg	M 30 Stackridge	M 08 Puckless Blend	M 29 Warhorse
Su 11 May Blitz	**December 1970**	Tu 09 Humble Pie	Th 30 Heads Hands & Feet
Su 11 Comus	Tu 01 Heads Hands & Feet	W 10 Steel Mill	**April 1971**
M 12 Jimmy Campbell	W 02 Temple Creatures	Th 11 Comus	Th 01 Argent
M 12 Clear Blue Sky	W 02 Elyse	Th 11 Trader Horne	Th 01 Satisfaction
M 12 Warhorse	W 02 Saffron & Friends	Fr 12 Argent	Fr 02 Lancaster
Tu 13 Every Which Way	Th 03 The World	Fr 12 Wayfarer	Fr 02 Gnome Sweet Gnome
Tu 13 Lindisfarne	Fr 04 Warm Dust	Sa 13 Axiom	Sa 03 Steel Mill
W 14 Climax Chicago Blues Band	Fr 04 Duffy	M 15 Patriarch of Glastonbury's Band	Su 04 Sandhams Village
W 14 Mirrors	Sa 05 Flame	M 15 Childe Rolande	Su 04 Balloon & Banana
Th 15 Dream Police	Tu 08 Rare Bird	Tu 16 Chicken Shack	Su 04 Little Free Rock
Th 15 Wolfrilla	Tu 08 Bloodson	Tu 16 Supertramp	Su 04 UFO
Fr 16 Status Quo	Th 10 Dream Police	W 17 Steel Mill	M 05 Patriarch of Glastonbury's Band
Sa 17 Deep Joy	Fr 11 Andwella's Dream	Th 18 Comus	Tu 06 Mungo Jerry
Su 18 Van Der Graaf Generator	Fr 11 Dog Feet	Th 18 Trader Horne	Tu 06 Paul Brett Sage
Su 18 Hackensack	Sa 12 Steel Mill	Fr 19 Renaissance	Th 08 Trees
M 19 Gracious	M 14 Gracious	Fr 19 Medicine Head	Th 08 Pluto
M 19 Rocking Chair	M 14 Budgie	Sa 20 Custer's Track	Fr 09 Status Quo

Fr 09 Thin Lizzy
Sa 10 Custer's Track
Su 11 Sandhams Village
Su 11 Balloon & Banana
Su 11 Gilberto Gil
Su 11 Hackensack
Su 11 Little Free Rock
M 12 Hardin & York
M 12 Highly Inflammable
Tu 13 Atomic Rooster
Tu 13 (Doris Henderson's) Eclection
Fr 16 Audience
Fr 16 Journey
Sa 17 Steel Mill
Su 18 Sandhams Village
Su 18 Balloon & Banana
Su 18 Gilberto Gil
Su 18 Hackensack
Su 18 Little Free Rock
Su 18 UFO
M 19 Fairfield Parlour
M 19 National Anthem
Tu 20 Mick Abrahams
Tu 20 Wildmouth
Th 22 Skin Alley
Th 22 Egg
Fr 23 Renaissance
Sa 24 Custers Track
Su 25 Sandhams Village
Su 25 Gilberto Gil
Su 25 Ginger Johnson's African
          Drummers
Su 25 Gnome Sweet Gnome
Su 25 Hackensack
M 26 Stray
M 26 Blitzkrieg
Tu 27 Ashton, Gardner & Dyke
Tu 27 Accrington Stanley
Th 29 Stone the Crows
Th 29 Timon
Fr 30 Nucleus

May 1971
Sa 01 Steel Mill
Su 02 Sandhams Village
Su 02 Gilberto Gil
Su 02 Nigger
Su 02 Pure Wing
M 03 Patriarch of Glastonbury's Band
M 03 Jonathon Coudrille
Tu 04 Wishbone Ash
Tu 04 Stackridge
Th 06 Genesis
Th 06 Mythica
Fr 07 Wild Turkey
Fr 07 Stickey George
Sa 08 Custers Track
Su 09 Sandhams Village
Su 09 Bubastis
Su 09 Smooth Bitch
Su 09 Universe
M 10 Leaf Hound
M 10 Timbre
Tu 11 Terry Reid
Tu 11 Gnidrolog
Th 13 Patto
Th 13 Good Habit
Fr 14 Third World War
Fr 14 Hokus Poke
Sa 15 Syrup
Su 16 Sandhams Village
Su 16 Byzantium
Su 16 Gilberto Gil
Su 16 Nigger
Su 16 Zoo
Tu 18 Rory Gallagher
Tu 18 Da Da
Th 20 Lancaster
Th 20 Ray Russell & Rock Workshop
Fr 21 Medicine Head
Fr 21 Smokestack
Sa 22 Mumma Bear
Su 23 Sandhams Village
Su 23 Bubastis
Su 23 Hurricane Smith

Su 23 Killing Floor
M 24 Argent
M 24 Egypt
Tu 25 Ashton, Gardner & Dyke
Tu 25 Accrington Stanley
Th 27 Arthur Brown
Th 27 Bubastis
Fr 28 Anno Domini
Fr 28 Feather
Sa 29 Halfbreed
Su 30 Sandhams Village
Su 30 Gollum
Su 30 Max Merritt & The Meteors
Su 30 Nigger
M 31 Stud
M 31 Feather

June 1971
Tu 01 Stray
Tu 01 Raw Material
W 02 The Magazine
Th 03 Diable Coxhill
Th 03 Miller Brothers
Fr 04 Renaissance
Fr 04 On
Sa 05 The Crew
Su 06 Sandhams Village
Su 06 Demon Fuzz
Su 06 Scapa Flow
Su 06 Tiny Clanger
M 07 Patriarch of Glastonbury's Band
Tu 08 Keef Hartley
W 09 Ram Jam Holder & His Black
          London Blues
Th 10 Quadrille
Th 10 Crazy Mabel
Fr 11 Patto
Fr 11 Universe
Sa 12 Les Flambeaux
Su 13 Keef Hartley Big Band
Su 14 Keef Hartley Big Band
Tu 15 Hardin & York
Tu 15 Eggs Over Easy
W 16 Terri Quaye
Th 17 Satisfaction
Th 17 Crocodile
Fr 18 Skid Row
Fr 18 Nick Pickett
Su 20 Sandhams Village
Su 20 9.30 Fly
Su 20 Jerico Jones
M 21 Amazing Blondel
M 21 Carol Grimes with Uncle Dog
Tu 22 Medicine Head
Tu 22 Smokestack
Th 24 Climax Chicago
Th 24 David Rees
Fr 25 If
M 28 The Pink Fairies
M 28 Universe
Tu 29 Mungo Jerry
Tu 29 Jerico Jones

July 1971
Th 01 Trapeze
Th 01 Tapestry
Fr 02 Steamhammer
Fr 02 Kahn
Sa 03 Custer's Track
Su 04 Sandhams Village
Su 04 Bram Stoker
Su 04 Origin
M 05 Lindisfarne
M 05 Stealers Wheel
Tu 06 Van Der Graaf Generator
W 07 Bell And Arc
W 07 Birth Control
Th 08 Audience
Th 08 Jackson Heights
Fr 09 Genesis
Fr 09 Cosmosis
Sa 10 Syrup
Su 11 Sandhams Village
M 12 Heads Hands & Feet
M 12 Cosmosis
Tu 13 Chicken Shack

Tu 13 Gnome Sweet Gnome
W 14 Ginger Johnson's African
          Highlife Band
Th 15 Stray
Th 15 Origin
Fr 16 Pete York Percussion Band
Sa 17 Callum Bryce
Su 18 Sandhams Village
Su 18 Shades
Su 18 Three Beard
M 19 FELA
M 19 Ginger Baker
Tu 20 Rory Gallagher
Tu 20 Cochise
W 21 Ram John Holder & His Bootleg
          Blues
Th 22 Slade
Fr 23 Stud
Fr 23 Fruup
Su 25 Chango
Su 25 Diabolus
M 26 Assagai
Tu 27 Terry Reid
Tu 27 Gnidrolog
W 28 Happy Days
Th 29 Wild Turkey
Th 29 Cigarette & Burning Boots
Fr 30 Patto
Fr 30 Spirogyra
Sa 31 Custer's Track

August 1971
Su 01 Warhorse
M 02 Patriarch of Glastonbury's Band
M 02 Charon
M 02 Saffron
Tu 03 Hardin & York
Tu 03 Universe
Th 05 Ashton, Gardner & Dyke
Th 05 Curtis Muldoon
Fr 06 Gnome Sweet Gnome
Fr 06 Sattva
Su 08 Blonde on Blonde
M 09 King Crimson
M 09 Vivian Stanshall
Tu 10 King Crimson
Tu 10 Vivian Stanshall
Th 12 Stackridge
Fr 13 Stone the Crows
Fr 13 Spreadeagle
Sa 14 Gonzales
Su 15 UFO
M 16 Audience
Tu 17 Medicine Head
Tu 17 Gringo
W 18 Nelson
Th 19 Stud
Th 19 Timothy
Fr 20 Patto
Fr 20 Universe
Sa 21 Custer's Track
Su 22 Pete Brown with Piblokto!
Su 22 Bubastis
M 23 The Pink Fairies
Tu 24 Renaissance
Tu 24 Glencoe
Th 26 Uriah Heep
Fr 27 Man
Fr 27 BB Blunder
Sa 28 Callum Bryce
Su 29 T2
M 30 Fleetwood Mac
M 30 Nick Pickett
Tu 31 Fleetwood Mac
Tu 31 Nick Pickett

September 1971
Th 02 Gnome Sweet Gnome
Th 02 Albert Monk
Fr 03 Morgan
Fr 03 Jonathan Kelly
Sa 04 Penance Rock Mission
Su 05 Caravan
Su 05 Fusion Orchestra
Su 05 Patto
M 06 Patriarch of Glastonbury's Band

Tu 07 Van Der Graaf Generator
Th 09 The Grease Band
Fr 10 Lindisfarne
Fr 10 Greasy Bear
Sa 11 Nicky James Band
Su 12 Universe
Su 12 Shango
M 13 Zior
M 13 Bill Fay and the Reverend Dawn
Tu 14 Skidrow
Tu 14 Nick Picket
Th 16 Cliff Bennett's Rebellion
Fr 17 Ashton, Gardner & Dyke
Fr 17 Curtis Muldoon
Sa 18 Slade
Su 19 Beggars Opera
Su 19 Gravy Train
M 20 Titanic
M 20 Third World War
Tu 21 Keef Hartley
Tu 21 Nazareth
W 22 Gene Vincent
Th 23 Stray
Th 23 Flying Hat Band
Fr 24 Hardin & York
Fr 24 Opal Butterfly
Sa 25 Custer's Track
Su 26 Origin
Su 26 On
M 27 Hurricane
M 27 Freddie 'Fingers' Lee
Tu 28 Southern Comfort
Tu 28 Khan
Tu 29 Renaissance
Th 29 Vinegar Joe

October 1971
Fr 01 Amazing Blondel
Fr 01 Claire Hamill
Su 03 T2
Su 03 Fireweed
M 04 Rory Gallagher
M 04 Million
Tu 05 Rory Gallagher
Tu 05 Million
Th 07 Armada
Th 07 Burnt Oak
Fr 08 Gnome Sweet Gnome
Fr 08 Sattva
Su 10 Wild Turkey
Su 10 Fresh Maggots
M 11 Morgan
M 11 Sattva
Tu 12 Manfred Mann
Th 14 Armada
Th 14 Burnt Oak
Fr 15 Status Quo
Fr 15 Open Road
Sa 16 Country Jug
Su 17 9.30 Fly
Su 17 Nothineverappens
Tu 19 Audience
W 20 America
W 20 Linda Lewis
W 20 National Head Band
Th 21 Armada
Th 21 Burnt Oak
Fr 22 Max Merritt & The Meteors
Fr 22 Kahva Jute
Su 24 Supertramp
M 25 Morgan
M 25 Steve Tilston
Tu 26 Terry Reid
Tu 26 Crocodile
W 27 Gypsy
W 27 Jackal
Th 28 Armada
Th 28 Burnt Oak
Fr 29 King Biscuit Boy
Fr 29 Brewers Droop
Su 31 Writing on the Wall
Su 31 Mr Moses Schoolband

November 1971
M 01 Skid Row
M 01 Nick Pickett

Tu 02	Stud
Tu 02	Anno Domini
W 03	Gnidrolog
W 03	Raw Material
Th 04	Morgan
Th 04	City Waites
Fr 05	Redwing
Fr 05	Jackal
Sa 06	Nimbus
Su 07	Pete Brown with Piblokto!
M 08	Strife
M 08	Beggars Death
M 08	Fernhill
Tu 09	Uriah Heep
Tu 09	Vinegar Joe
W 10	Hookfoot
W 10	Marianne Segal
W 10	Philip Goodhand-Tait
Th 11	Morgan
Th 11	Old Nick
Fr 12	Nazareth
Fr 12	Burnt Oak
Sa 13	Crew
Su 14	Blonde on Blonde
M 15	Skid Row
Tu 16	Bell And Arc
Tu 16	Grass
W 17	Natural Acoustic Band
W 17	Shape of the Rain
Th 18	Morgan
Th 18	Infant
Fr 19	Patto
Fr 19	Robert Lee Band
Sa 20	Odd Fox
Su 21	UFO
M 22	Skid Row
M 22	Wolf
Tu 23	Mick Abrahams
Tu 23	David Elliot
W 24	Freedom
W 24	Gentle Giant
Th 25	Morgan
Th 25	Shacklock
Fr 26	Van Der Graaf Generator
Fr 26	Spreadeagle
Sa 27	Custer's Track
Su 28	Warhorse
M 29	Skid Row
Tu 30	Stray

December 1971

W 01	Status Quo
W 01	Heron
Th 02	Max Merritt & The Meteors
Fr 03	Brinsley Schwarz
Fr 03	Sutherland Brothers
Sa 04	Woodfall
Su 05	Jellybread
Su 05	Pugmaho
M 06	Skid Row
M 06	Barabbas
Tu 07	Manfred Mann's Earthband
Tu 07	Vinegar Joe
W 08	Running Man
W 08	Raw Material
Th 09	Beggars Opera
Th 09	Merlin
Fr 10	Black Widow
Fr 10	Meridian
Sa 11	Syrup
M 13	Skid Row
M 13	Nick Pickett
Tu 14	Stud
W 15	Long John Baldry
W 15	Leslie Duncan
W 15	Tranquility
Th 16	Morgan
Th 16	Jonathan Kelly
Fr 17	Caravan
Fr 17	Khan
Su 19	T2
Su 19	Anna Purna
M 20	JSD Band
M 20	West Farm Cottage
Tu 21	Keef Hartley

W 22	Killing Floor
W 22	Steel Mill
W 22	Zior
Th 23	The Pink Fairies
Fr 24	Slade
M 27	Hardin & York
M 27	March Hare
Tu 28	If
Tu 28	Rising Sun
W 29	UFO
Th 30	Morgan
Th 30	Ben
Fr 31	Wishbone Ash
Fr 31	Joe Brown's Home Brew
Fr 31	Vinegar Joe

January 1972

Sa 01	Sun
M 03	Tony Hazzard
Tu 04	Stud
Tu 04	Shackrock
W 05	Armada
Th 06	Vinegar Joe
Th 06	Good Habit
Fr 07	Climax Chicago
Fr 07	Errol Dickson
Sa 08	Sun
M 10	Brinsley Schwarz
M 10	Sutherland Brothers
Tu 11	Renaissance
W 12	Gary Wright's Wonderwheel
W 12	Jerico Jones
Th 13	Morgan
Th 13	Carol Grimes with Uncle Dog
Fr 14	Eddie "Guitar" Burns
Fr 14	Tea and Symphony
Sa 15	Custer's Track
M 17	UFO
M 17	John Danbrough Band
Tu 18	Nazareth
Tu 18	Byzantium
W 19	Armada
W 19	Hok Cottage
Th 20	Vinegar Joe
Th 20	Gringo
Fr 21	Brewers Droop
Fr 21	Nighthawks
Sa 22	Pendulum
M 24	Brinsley Schwarz
M 24	Sutherland Brothers
Tu 25	Paul Jones and his Band
Tu 25	Gonzales
Tu 25	Mason Alley
W 26	Armada
W 26	Burnt Oak
Th 27	Morgan
Th 27	Jackal
Fr 28	Duster Bennett
Fr 28	Zoot Money
M 31	UFO

February 1972

Tu 01	Stud
Tu 01	Shacklock
W 02	Morgan
Th 02	Carol Grimes with Uncle Dog
Th 03	Beggars Opera
Th 03	Gully Foyle
Fr 04	JB Hutto
Fr 04	Killing Floor
Sa 05	Crew
M 07	Skid Row
M 07	Nick Pickett
Tu 08	The Long John Baldry Road Show
Tu 08	Ashman Reynolds
Tu 08	Million
Tu 08	Tear Gas
W 09	Danta
W 09	Evensong
Th 10	Vinegar Joe
Th 10	Jopal
Fr 11	Brett Marvin and the Thunderbolts
Sa 12	Air Fiesta
M 14	Skid Row

M 14	Nick Pickett
Tu 15	Stray
Tu 15	Red Dirt
W 16	Curtis Muldoon
W 16	Bullitt
Th 17	Beggars Opera
Th 17	Jade Warrior
Fr 18	JB Hutto
Sa 19	Custer's Track
M 21	Morgan
Tu 22	Flash
W 23	Alex Harvey
W 23	Tear Gas
Th 24	Vinegar Joe
Th 24	November
Fr 25	Lightnin' Slim
Fr 25	Jellybread
M 28	Gary Moore
M 28	Nick Pickett
Tu 29	Hardin & York
Tu 29	March Hare

March 1972

W 01	Alex Harvey
W 01	Sleaz Band
Th 02	Morgan
Fr 03	Brunning Hall Blues Band
Fr 03	Praeger & Rye
Sa 04	Crew
M 06	Armada
Tu 07	Status Quo
Tu 07	Flying Hat Band
W 08	Focus
W 08	Iguana
W 08	John Bryant
Th 09	Skin Alley
Th 09	Akido
Fr 10	Irwin Helfer
Fr 10	Tea and Symphony
Sa 11	Unit 4+2
M 13	JSD Band
Th 16	Stackridge
Th 16	Wisper
Fr 17	Bond & Brown
Fr 17	Killing Floor
M 20	Morgan
Tu 21	Paul Jones and his Band
Tu 21	Good Habit
Tu 21	Mason Alley
W 22	Tony Capstick
W 22	Andy Anderson
W 22	Hedgehog High
W 22	Pete Scott
W 22	The Callies
Th 23	JSD Band
Fr 24	Brewers Droop
Fr 24	Nighthawks
Sa 25	Custer's Track
M 27	UFO
M 27	Crow
Tu 28	Caravan
Tu 28	Life Blud
W 29	Running Man
W 29	Dando Shaft
Th 30	Vinegar Joe
Th 30	Cast Iron
Fr 31	Brett Marvin and the Thunderbolts

April 1972

Sa 01	The Pieces Fit
Su 02	Skid Row
Su 02	Main Horse Airline
M 03	East of Eden
M 03	Shacklock
Tu 04	Assagai
Tu 04	Rowan Oak
W 05	Alex Harvey
W 05	Walrus
Th 06	Morgan
Th 06	Gracious
Fr 07	Jellybread
Fr 07	Michigan Rag
Fr 07	Mike Vernon
Fr 07	Pete Wingfield
Sa 08	Object

Su 09	Rory Gallagher
M 10	Gwenyway
M 10	Tintagel
M 10	Wendy Hoile
Tu 11	Sutherland Brothers
W 12	Natural Acoustic Band
W 12	Gnidrolog
Th 13	Assagai
Th 13	Continuum
Fr 14	King Earle Boogie Band
Fr 14	Tea and Symphony
Sa 15	Crew
Su 16	Skid Row
Su 16	Jonesy
M 17	Gwenyway
M 17	Griffin
M 17	Wendy Hoile
Tu 18	Heads Hands & Feet
Tu 18	Junkyard Angel
W 19	Walrus
W 19	Burnt Oak
Th 20	Armada
Th 20	Bitch
Fr 21	Errol Dickson
Sa 22	Brave New World
Su 23	Gwenyway
Su 23	Listen
Su 23	Spoon
M 24	Skid Row
M 24	Jonesy
Tu 25	Mahatma Kane Jeeves
Tu 25	Blitzkrieg
W 26	Cottonwood
W 26	Grace
Th 27	Vinegar Joe
Th 27	Camel
Fr 28	Victor Brox Blues Band
Fr 28	Duffy Power
Sa 29	Unit 4+2
Su 30	Gwenyway
Su 30	Dell
Su 30	Plaincover

May 1972

M 01	Patto
Tu 02	Marmalade
Tu 02	Tennant & Morrison
W 03	Nazareth
Th 04	JSD Band
Th 04	Nichelson
Fr 05	Brewers Droop
Sa 06	Freight
Su 07	Gwenyway
Su 07	Slump
Su 07	Wendy Hoile
M 08	Gary More
Tu 09	Flash
Tu 09	Snake Eye
W 10	Skid Row
W 10	Fruup
Th 11	Peter Sarstedt
Fr 12	King Earle Boogie Band
Fr 12	Brunning Hall
Sa 13	Crew
Su 14	Gwenyway
Su 14	Dell
M 15	Morgan
Tu 16	Heads Hands & Feet
Tu 16	Smith, Perkins & Smith
W 17	Stackridge
W 17	Fumble
Th 18	Armada
Th 18	Bono
Fr 19	Duster Bennett
Fr 19	Brunning Hall
Sa 20	Muscles
Su 21	Gwenyway
Su 21	Tintagel
M 22	Gary Moore
M 22	Nick Pickett
Tu 23	Audience
Tu 23	Glencoe
W 24	Capability Brown
W 24	Spreadeagle
Th 25	Cottonwood

Th 25	Burnt Oak	
Fr 26	Boogie Woogie Red and Baby Boy Warren	
Fr 26	Brunning Hall	
Sa 27	Unit 4+2	
Su 28	David Essex & His Band	
Su 28	Burnt Oak	
M 29	Stray	
M 29	Cat Iron	
Tu 30	Vinegar Joe	
Tu 30	Tasavallan Presidentti	
W 31	UFO	
W 31	Roxy Music	

June 1972

Th 01 Mahatma Kane Jeeves
Fr 02 Doctor Ross
Fr 02 Brunning Hall
Sa 03 The Pieces Fit
Su 04 Skid Row
Su 04 Swastika
M 05 Nazareth
M 05 Alex Harvey
M 05 Sleaz Band
Tu 06 Flash
Tu 06 Cat Iron
W 07 Al Stewart and his Band
Th 08 Patto
Th 08 Music
Fr 09 Lightnin' Slim
Fr 09 Brunning Hall
Fr 09 Whispering Smith
Su 11 Listen
Su 11 Stairway
Su 11 Thirsty Two
M 12 Morgan
Tu 13 Raymond Froggatt
Tu 13 Thank You
W 14 Al Stewart and his Band
Th 15 If
Th 15 Glencoe
Fr 16 Tea and Symphony
Fr 16 Brunning Hall
Su 18 Skid Row
Su 18 Fruup
M 19 Stud
M 19 Jonesy
Tu 20 Amon Duul II
W 21 Al Stewart and his Band
Th 22 Mahatma Kane Jeeves
Fr 23 Jellybread
Fr 23 Michigan Rag
Sa 24 Crew
Su 25 Carrots Rock Workshop
Su 25 Dockyard
Su 25 Listen
Su 25 Thirsty Two
M 26 Status Quo
M 26 Burnt Oak
Tu 27 Status Quo
Tu 27 Pugmaho
W 28 Al Stewart and his Band
Th 29 Sutherland Brothers
Th 29 Smith, Perkins & Smith
Fr 30 Brett Marvin and the Thunderbolts
Fr 30 Brunning Hall Blues Band

July 1972

Su 02 Skid Row
Su 02 Fruup
M 03 Stackridge
Tu 04 Vinegar Joe
W 05 Al Stewart and his Band
Th 06 Mahatma Kane Jeeves
Th 06 Collusion
Fr 07 Major Wiley
Fr 07 Tea and Symphony
Sa 08 The Pieces Fit
Su 09 Stud
Su 09 Bruno AD
M 10 Rare Bird
M 10 Al Matthews
Tu 11 Mick Abrahams Band
Tu 11 Supertramp
W 12 Al Stewart and his Band

Th 13 Steamhammer
Th 13 Jonesy
Fr 14 Climax Chicago
Fr 14 Brunning Hall
Sa 15 Flesh
Su 16 Skid Row
Su 16 Bono
M 17 Gary Moore
M 17 Nick Pickett
Tu 18 Third Ear Band
Tu 18 Camel
W 19 UFO
W 19 Sunrise
Th 20 Mahatma Kane Jeeves
Th 20 Copperfield
Fr 21 The John Dummer Blues Band
Fr 21 Brunning Hall
Sa 22 One Night Stand
Su 23 Stud
Su 23 Quicksand
M 24 Man
M 24 Writing on the Wall
Tu 25 East of Eden
Tu 25 Babe Ruth
W 26 Renaissance
W 26 Cat Iron
Th 27 Mahatma Kane Jeeves
Th 27 Renia
Fr 28 Terry Dactyl & The Dinosaurs
Fr 28 Brett Marvin and the Thunderbolts
Fr 28 Brunning Hall
Sa 29 Equity
Su 30 Skid Row
Su 30 Fruup
M 31 Gary Moore
M 31 Nick Pickett

August 1972

Tu 01 Vinegar Joe
Tu 01 Glencoe
W 02 Tir Na Nog
W 02 Lloyd Watson
Th 03 Mahatma Kane Jeeves
Th 03 Philharmonic Rock Duo
Fr 04 Brewers Droop
Fr 04 Brunning Hall
Sa 05 Indigo
Su 06 UFO
Su 06 Beckett
M 07 Jackson Heights
M 07 Affinity
Tu 08 Steamhammer
Tu 08 Sunshine
W 09 Audience
W 09 Snake Eye
Th 10 Mahatma Kane Jeeves
Th 10 Sunchariot
Fr 11 Focus
Fr 11 Tennant & Morrison
Sa 12 Flesh
M 14 Nazareth
M 14 Jade Warrior
Tu 15 Renaissance
W 15 Cat Iron
W 16 Wild Turkey
W 16 Lloyd Watson
Th 17 Fusion Orchestra
Th 17 Mahatma Kane Jeeves
Fr 18 UFO
Fr 18 Sunrise
Sa 19 Flesh
Su 20 Patto
Su 20 Cottonwood
M 21 Stackridge
M 21 Cat Iron
Tu 22 Stray
W 23 If
W 23 Bitch
Th 24 The Pretty Things
Th 24 Orphan
Fr 25 Bond & Brown
Fr 25 Brunning Hall
Sa 26 The Pieces Fit
Su 27 Sutherland Brothers

M 28 UFO
M 28 Al Matthews
Tu 29 Slade
W 30 Stackridge
W 30 FF&Z
Th 31 Mahatma Kane Jeeves
Th 31 Quadrille

September 1972

Fr 01 Medicine Head
Fr 01 Brunning Hall
Sa 02 Palomino
Su 03 Mick Abrahams Band
Su 03 Damp Savannah
M 04 Juicy Lucy
Tu 05 East of Eden
W 06 Brush
Th 07 Mahatma Kane Jeeves
Th 07 Land

Melody Maker was not published this week because of an industrial dispute. This meant the regular Marquee ad did not appear, and thus this gap in the listing.

Th 14 Mahatma Kane Jeeves
Th 14 Land
Fr 15 Hardin, York & Fenwick
Fr 15 Brunning Hall
M 18 Long John Baldry
M 18 Byzantium
Tu 19 Genesis
Tu 19 Spreadeagle
W 20 Rab Noakes
W 20 Peter Hammill
W 20 Steve Tilston
Th 21 Capability Brown
Th 21 String Driven Thing
Fr 22 Mick Abrahams Band
Fr 22 Brunning Hall
Sa 23 Inside Out
Sa 23 Rat
M 25 Trapeze
M 25 Poem
Tu 26 UFO
Tu 26 Cottonwood
W 27 Roy Young Band
Th 28 Mahatma Kane Jeeves
Th 28 Zeus
Fr 29 Dick Heckstall-Smith Band
Fr 29 Mike Maran

October 1972

M 02 Brush
M 02 Kerry Scott
Tu 03 Medicine Head
W 04 Savoy Brown
W 04 Saturnalia
Th 05 Mahatma Kane Jeeves
Th 05 Judas Priest
Fr 06 Bond & Brown
Fr 06 Brunning Hall
M 09 Climax Chicago
M 09 Redwing
Tu 10 Chicken Shack
W 11 Alex Harvey Band
W 11 Sammy
Th 12 Fusion Orchestra
Th 12 Rat
Fr 13 Wild Turkey
Fr 13 Asgard
Sa 14 March Hare
Sa 14 Kinane
M 16 Capability Brown
M 16 Spreadeagle
M 16 String Driven Thing
Tu 17 Caravan
Tu 17 Sandgate
W 18 Geordie
W 18 Schunge
W 18 Yellowstone & Voice
Th 19 Mahatma Kane Jeeves
Th 19 Biggles
Fr 20 Brewers Droop
Fr 20 Brunning Hall

Sa 21 Inside Out
M 23 Stackridge
Tu 24 Flash
Tu 24 Racoon
W 25 The Average White Band
Th 26 Jonesy
Th 26 Kerry Scott
Fr 27 Champion Jack Dupree
Fr 27 Brunning Hall
Sa 28 Slider
M 30 Colin Blunstone
Tu 31 Vinegar Joe
Tu 31 Fumble

November 1972

W 01 D'Abo Band
W 01 Sunrise
Th 02 Stackridge
Th 02 Wisper
Fr 03 UFO
Sa 04 Flesh
M 06 Brush
M 06 Kerry Scott
Tu 07 Screaming Lord Sutch
Tu 07 Dr Marigold
Tu 07 Rock Rebellion
W 08 Gnidrolog
W 08 Solid Gold Cadillac
Th 09 Morgan
Fr 10 UFO
Fr 10 Ankh
Su 11 Mahatma Kane Jeeves
M 13 Patto
M 13 Schy
Tu 14 Chicken Shack
Tu 14 Strife
W 15 Beggars Opera
Th 16 Morgan
Fr 17 UFO
Sa 18 Mahatma Kane Jeeves
M 20 Fusion Orchestra
M 20 Zeus
Tu 21 Nazareth
W 22 Brewers Droop
W 22 Natural Acoustic Band
Th 23 Morgan
Fr 24 UFO
Fr 24 Elder Kindred
Sa 25 Mahatma Kane Jeeves
M 27 Jackson Heights
M 27 Rimmington
Tu 28 Status Quo
Tu 28 Greenslade
W 29 Byzantium
W 29 Jade Warrior
Th 30 Morgan
Th 30 Henry Schifter

December 1972

Fr 01 UFO
Sa 02 March Hare
M 04 Alex Harvey Band
Tu 05 Brush
W 05 Sammy
Th 06 Sparks
Fr 07 Morgan
Sa 09 Mahatma Kane Jeeves
Su 10 Strider
M 11 Climax Chicago
Tu 12 Chicken Shack
Th 14 Sparks
Fr 15 Babe Ruth
Sa 16 Mahatma Kane Jeeves
Su 17 Jonesy
M 18 Capability Brown
M 18 Spreadeagle
Tu 19 Nazareth
Th 21 Sparks
Fr 22 Patto
Sa 23 Vinegar Joe
Sa 23 Al Matthews
Sa 23 Mahatma Kane Jeeves
W 27 Babe Ruth
Th 28 Sparks
Fr 29 Sutherland Brothers
Sa 30 Mahatma Kane Jeeves

Su 31 Stackridge
Su 31 Strider

January 1973
Tu 02 Wild Turkey
Tu 02 Ro Ro
W 03 Jonesy
Th 04 Mick Abrahams
Th 04 Cottonwood
Th 04 Hemlock
Fr 05 Climax Chicago
Sa 06 Mahatma Kane Jeeves
Su 07 Smile
M 08 Trapeze
Tu 09 Caravan
Tu 09 Sandgate
W 10 Strider
Th 11 Babe Ruth
Th 11 Spontaneous Combustion
Fr 12 Jonesy
Sa 13 Mahatma Kane Jeeves
M 15 Trapeze
M 15 Beckett
Tu 16 Badger
Tu 16 Ro Ro
W 17 Strider
W 17 Willis
Th 18 Alex Harvey Band
Fr 19 Daddy Longlegs
Fr 19 Allan Lee Shaw
Sa 20 Mahatma Kane Jeeves
Sa 20 Smile
Su 21 Wells Fargo
M 23 Patto
Tu 22 Chicken Shack
W 24 Strider
W 24 Willis
Th 25 Nazareth
Fr 26 Q
Sa 27 Mahatma Kane Jeeves
Sa 27 Charlie
M 29 Babe Ruth
Tu 30 Savoy Brown
W 31 Strider
W 31 Willis

February 1973
Th 03 Fusion Orchestra
Th 03 Zeus
Fr 04 Patto
Sa 03 Rushwood
Sa 03 Orphan
M 05 Jackson Heights
Tu 06 Stackridge
W 07 Beggars Opera
W 07 Sammy
Th 08 Twink
Fr 09 Jonesy
Sa 10 King Crimson
Su 11 King Crimson
M 12 Mick Abrahams
Tu 13 Planxty
Tu 13 Iguana
W 14 Patto
W 14 Sydd Arthur
Th 15 Trapeze
Th 15 Fruup
Fr 16 Jonesy
Sa 17 Mahatma Kane Jeeves
Sa 17 A Million People
M 19 Glencoe
Tu 20 Rare Bird
Tu 20 Al Matthews
W 21 Babe Ruth
W 21 Spontaneous Combustion
Th 22 The Average White Band
Fr 23 Dick Heckstall-Smith Band
Fr 23 Nick Pickett
Sa 24 Mahatma
M 26 Stealers Wheel
W 28 Climax Chicago
W 28 Jade

March 1973
Tu 01 Wild Turkey
Fr 02 Brush
Sa 03 Mahatma

Su 04 Black Velvet
M 05 Babe Ruth
Tu 06 Chicken Shack
W 07 Alex Harvey
W 07 Rushwood
Th 08 If
Fr 09 Greenslade
Sa 10 Mahatma
M 12 Capability Brown
Tu 13 Saturnalia
W 14 Nazareth
W 14 Rushwood
Th 15 Travis
Th 15 Levinsky
Th 15 Twinkle Ripley
Fr 16 Climax Chicago
Fr 16 Cockney Rebel
Sa 17 Wishbone Ash
Su 18 Wishbone Ash
M 19 Tasavallan Presidentti
Tu 20 McGuinness Flint
W 21 Jo'Burg Hawk
Th 22 Wild Turkey
Fr 23 Trapeze
Sa 24 Flesh
Su 25 Kala
Su 25 Hunter Muskett
Su 25 Paul Brett
M 26 Fusion Orchestra
Tu 27 Edgar Broughton
W 28 Atlantis
Th 29 The Average White Band
Th 29 Cat Iron
Fr 30 Jonesy
Sa 31 Rushwood

April 1973
Su 01 Isis
M 02 Babe Ruth
Tu 03 Spencer Davis Band
W 04 Robin Trower
Th 05 The Quiverland Brothers
Fr 06 Greenslade
Sa 07 Mahatma
M 09 Queen
Tu 10 Nazareth
W 11 Chicken Shack
Th 12 Strider
Fr 13 Medicine Head
Fr 13 Nick Pickett
Sa 14 Rushwood
M 16 Ange
Tu 17 Alex Harvey Band
W 18 Jo'Burg Hawk
Th 19 Strider
Fr 20 Savoy Brown
Fr 20 Bronx Cheer
Sa 21 McGuinness Flint
Sa 21 Nick Pickett
Su 22 Wild Turkey
M 23 Caravan
M 23 Sutherland Brothers
Tu 23 Quiver
W 24 Robin Trower Band
Th 25 Strider
Th 25 Burnt Oak
Fr 27 Brett Marvin and the
       Thunderbolts
Sa 28 Rushwood
Sa 28 Sidewinder
Su 29 Dark Star
M 30 Jonesy

May 1973
Tu 01 Babe Ruth
Tu 01 Alquin
W 02 Spencer Davis Band
Th 03 Greenslade
Fr 04 Steamhammer
Sa 05 March Hare
Su 06 Writing on the Wall
M 07 Strider
Tu 08 Roy Buchanan
W 09 Beggars Opera
Th 10 The Average White Band
Fr 11 Dick & The Firemen

Sa 12 Mahatma
M 14 The John Dummer Band
Tu 15 Alex Harvey Band
W 16 Beggars Opera
Th 17 Skin Alley
Fr 18 Strider
Sa 19 Flesh
Su 20 Writing on the Wall
Su 20 Sniff 'n' the Tears
M 21 Budgie
M 21 Ruby
Tu 22 Greenslade
W 23 Capability Brown
Th 24 Good Habit
Fr 25 Jonesy
Sa 26 Mahatma
Su 27 Beckett
Su 27 Burnt Oak
M 28 Chicken Shack
M 28 Bronx Cheer
Tu 29 East of Eden
Tu 29 Ace
W 30 Wild Turkey
Th 31 The Average White Band
Th 3 Sniff 'n' the Tears

June 1973
Fr 01 Medicine Head
Fr 01 Duffy
Sa 02 Mahatma
Su 03 Writing on the Wall
Su 03 Regeneration
M 04 Good Habit
Tu 05 Stackridge
Tu 05 James Hogg Band
W 06 Alan Stivell
Th 07 Brown's Home Brew
Fr 08 JSD Band
Sa 09 Shangoe
Su 10 Terry Reid
M 11 Terry Reid
Tu 12 Gong
W 13 Suntreader
Th 14 Ellis
Fr 15 Steamhammer
Sa 16 Mahatma
Sa 16 Dark Star
Su 17 Writing on the Wall
M 18 JSD Band
M 18 Bill Barclay & Lucas &
       McCulloch
Tu 19 Strider
Tu 19 Spiteri
W 20 Alex Harvey Band
Th 21 Fumble
Fr 22 Brewers Droop
Fr 22 Sunflower Boogie Band
Sa 23 Flesh
Sa 23 Burnt Oak
Su 24 Wild Turkey
M 25 Caravan
M 25 Spirogyra
Tu 26 Chicken Shack
Tu 26 Bronx Cheer
W 27 Stray Dog
Th 28 Thin Lizzy
Th 28 Oxo Whitney
Fr 29 Greenslade
Sa 30 Ruby

July 1973
Su 01 Wild Turkey
M 02 Sutherland Brothers
M 02 Quiver
M 02 Ace
Tu 03 Babe Ruth
W 04 Stray Dog
Th 05 Beckett
Fr 06 Axis
Sa 07 UFO
Su 08 Writing on the Wall
Su 08 Slack Alice
M 09 Mahatma
M 09 John Verity Band
Tu 10 Jack The Lad
W 11 Robin Trower Band

W 11 Leo Sayer
Th 12 (Darryl Way's) Wolf
Fr 13 McGuinness Flint
Sa 14 Fumble
Su 15 Fusion Orchestra
M 16 Mahatma
M 16 Riff Raff
Tu 17 Andy Brown
W 18 Stray Dog
Th 19 Gary Moore Band
Th 19 Elrick
Fr 20 Strider
Fr 20 Adrienne Webber
Sa 21 Climax Chicago
Sa 21 Cold River Lady
Su 22 Writing on the Wall
Su 22 Burnt Oak
M 23 Mahatma
M 23 Queen
Tu 24 Caravan
Tu 24 Sundance
W 25 Wild Turkey
W 25 Dizzy
Th 26 Spencer Davis Band
Th 26 Adrienne Webber
Fr 27 Axis
Fr 27 Buckley
Sa 28 Flesh
Su 29 UFO
Su 29 Hous Hin
M 30 Glencoe
M 30 Simon's Fancy
Tu 31 Bedlam

August 1973
W 01 Stray Dog
Th 02 Eric Burdon
Fr 03 Eric Burdon
Sa 04 Eric Burdon
Su 05 Beckett
M 06 Marmalade
M 06 Simon's Fancy
Tu 07 East of Eden
Tu 07 Public Foot The Roman
W 08 (Darryl Way's) Wolf
Th 09 Ellis
Th 09 Dark Star
Fr 10 Strider
Sa 11 Flesh
Su 12 Mahatma
Su 12 Simon's Fancy
M 13 Alquin
Tu 14 Sharks
Tu 14 747
W 15 Stray Dog
Th 16 Wild Turkey
Fr 17 Greenslade
Fr 17 Aj Webber
Sa 18 The Heavy Metal Kids
Su 19 Silverhead
Su 19 Rossocks
M 20 Axis
M 20 Simon's Fancy
Tu 21 Stackridge
Tu 21 Sassafras
W 22 Capability Brown
W 22 Gryphon
Th 23 Sandgate
Th 23 Travis
Fr 24 Ange
Sa 25 Flesh
Sa 25 Dark Star
M 27 UFO
M 27 Ruby
Tu 28 Jack The Lad
W 29 Stray Dog
Th 30 The Average White Band
Fr 31 Tasavallan Presidentti
Fr 31 Dave Ellis

September 1973
Sa 01 Flesh
Su 02 Mahatma
M 03 Camel
Su 04 Stray
W 05 Wild Turkey

W 05 Dave Turner
Th 06 Capability Brown
Fr 07 Chicken Shack
Sa 08 Climax Chicago
Su 09 Mahatma
M 10 Bedlam
M 10 Ruby
Tu 11 (Darryl Way's) Wolf
Tu 11 Little Big Band
W 12 Geordie
Th 13 Glencoe
Fr 14 Strider
Sa 15 Flesh
Sa 15 The Mo Bacon Band
Su 16 Writing on the Wall
M 17 Beckett
Tu 18 Alex Harvey Band
Tu 18 Mark Maran
W 19 McGuinness Flint
Th 20 The Alan Price Set
Th 20 Highway
Fr 21 Brett Marvin and the
    Thunderbolts
Sa 22 Flesh
Su 23 Gary Moore Band
Su 23 Vineyard
M 24 Golden Earring
M 24 Mike Silver
Tu 25 Edgar Broughton
Tu 25 Al Matthews
W 26 Thin Lizzy
Th 27 Beggars Opera
Fr 28 Climax Blues Band
Sa 29 Writing on the Wall
Su 30 Flesh

October 1973
M 01 Ace
M 01 Refuge
Tu 02 Jon Hiseman's Tempest
W 03 Bitch
Th 04 Fumble
Fr 05 Brian Auger's Oblivion Express
Fr 05 Highway
Sa 06 Dark Star
Su 07 Hackensack
Su 07 Riff Raff
M 08 Ace
M 08 Canton Trig
Tu 09 Sharks
W 10 Prelude
W 10 Fruup
Th 11 Birth Control
Th 11 Coast Road Drive
Fr 12 Chicken Shack
Fr 12 Bronx Cheer
Su 14 Gary Moore Band
Su 14 Elrick
M 15 Ace
M 15 Canton Trig
Tu 16 East of Eden
W 17 Heavy Heart
M 22 Ace
M 22 Stardust
Tu 23 Greenslade
Tu 23 Aj Webber
W 24 Wild Turkey
W 24 Boys
Th 25 Fusion Orchestra
Th 25 Tim Staffell
Fr 26 Ange
Sa 27 Flesh
Su 28 Steamhammer
M 29 Marmalade
Tu 30 Roy Young
W 31 Heavy Heart

November 1973
Sa 01 Mahatma
Th 01 Skin Alley
Fr 02 Beggars Opera
Sa 03 Dark Star
Su 04 Writing on the Wall
M 05 Capability Brown
M 05 Crow
Tu 06 (Darryl Way's) Wolf

Tu 06 Rusty Butler
W 07 Brewers Droop
Th 08 Beckett
Fr 09 Longdancer
Sa 10 Flesh
Su 11 Orme
M 12 Gryphon
Tu 13 Thin Lizzy
W 14 Heavy Heart
Th 15 Camel
Th 15 Spirogyra
Fr 16 Tasavallan Presidentti
Sa 17 Solution
Su 18 Mahatma
Su 18 Quadrille
M 19 Jack The Lad
Tu 20 Stray
Tu 20 Rusty Butler
W 21 Bedlam
W 21 Barry Dransfield
Th 22 Ace
Th 22 Stardust
Fr 23 Reign
Fr 23 Zoe
Sa 24 Flesh
Su 25 Hackensack
M 26 Principal Edwards
Tu 27 Snafu
W 28 Heavy Heart
Th 29 If
Th 29 Dave Ellis
Fr 30 Wild Turkey

December 1973
Sa 01 Wild Turkey
Su 02 Amity
Su 02 Rococo
M 03 Ellis
M 03 Slowhand
Tu 04 Sharks
W 05 Magma
Th 06 Ace
Fr 07 Trapeze
Fr 07 John Verity
Sa 08 Flesh
Sa 08 Quadrille
Su 09 Bedlam
M 10 Sutherland Brothers & Quiver
Tu 11 Jon Hiseman's Tempest
W 12 Heavy Heart
Th 13 Hummingbird
Fr 14 Babe Ruth
Sa 15 Dark Star
Su 16 Nucleus
Su 16 Hookfoot
M 17 Tim Hardin
Tu 18 Manfred Mann's Earthband
W 19 JSD Band
Th 20 Silverhead
Fr 21 Strider
Sa 22 Wild Turkey
Su 23 UFO
M 24 Flesh
M 24 Quadrille
Th 27 The Pink Fairies
Th 27 Bronx Cheer
Fr 28 Camel
Sa 29 The Heavy Metal Kids
Su 30 Gary Moore Band
M 31 Fumble
M 31 Edison Lighthouse

January 1974
W 02 Trapeze
W 02 Fable
Th 03 Quadrille
Fr 04 Capability Brown
Sa 05 Dark Star
Su 06 Mahatma
M 07 Hookfoot
Tu 08 The Average White Band
W 09 Jack The Lad
Th 10 (Darryl Way's) Wolf
Th 10 Davies & Murrell
Fr 11 Greep
Sa 12 Quadrille

Su 12 Writing on the Wall
Sa 12 Dixie
M 14 String Driven Thing
Tu 15 Sharks
Tu 15 Charlie and the Wide Boys
W 16 Babe Ruth
Th 17 Camel
Fr 18 Brett Marvin and the
    Thunderbolts
Sa 19 Mahatma
Sa 19 Spanner
Su 20 Bedlam
M 21 Beckett
Tu 22 (The New) Savoy Brown
W 23 Jack The Lad
W 23 Chilli Willi & The Red Hot
    Peppers
Th 24 Trapeze
Th 24 Fable
Fr 25 Quadrille
Fr 25 Randy
Sa 26 Hustler
Su 27 Writing on the Wall
M 28 Spencer Davis Band
Tu 29 Strider
W 30 Wild Turkey
Th 31 Jonathan Kelly's Outside

February 1974
Fr 01 Sutherland Brothers & Quiver
Sa 02 Hellraiser
Su 03 Karass
M 04 String Driven Thing
M 04 Contraband
Tu 05 Thin Lizzy
W 06 Jack The Lad
W 06 Chilli Willi & The Red Hot
    Peppers
Th 07 The Pink Fairies
Th 07 Keith Christmas
Fr 08 Camel
Fr 08 Keith Christmas
Sa 09 Dark Star
Su 10 Writing on the Wall
M 11 Budgie
M 11 Judas Priest
Tu 12 Fumble
Tu 12 Shepstone & Dibbens
W 13 Fusion Orchestra
Th 14 Quadrille
Th 14 Bearded Lady
Fr 15 Mahatma
Sa 16 Procession
Su 17 The Heavy Metal Kids
M 18 Wild Turkey
M 18 Charlie and the Wide Boys
Tu 19 Stackridge
W 20 Jack The Lad
W 20 Chilli Willi & The Red Hot
    Peppers
Th 21 Hustler
Fr 22 Trapeze
Fr 22 Sunday Gage
Sa 23 Fable
Su 24 Writing on the Wall
M 25 Beckett
M 25 Mike Maran
Tu 26 Hardin & York
W 27 Mahatma
W 27 Aj Webber
Th 28 Quadrille
Th 28 Bearded Lady

March 1974
Fr 01 Philip Goodhand-Tait
Fr 01 Martin Carter
Sa 02 Osborne's Greep
Su 03 Jo'Burg Hawk
M 04 Ace
Tu 05 Hustler
W 06 Badger
Th 07 UFO
Fr 08 Capability Brown
Fr 08 Darien Spirit
Sa 09 Peaches
Su 10 Hookfoot

Su 10 Wheels
M 11 Refugee
Tu 12 Sharks
W 13 Strider
Th 14 Camel
Fr 15 Trapeze
Fr 15 Sunday Gage
Sa 16 Procession
Sa 16 Mr Big
Su 17 Magma
M 18 Ace
Tu 19 Alquin
W 20 Babe Ruth
Th 21 Hustler
Fr 22 Blodwyn Pig
Sa 23 Grand Slam
Sa 23 Warlock
Su 24 Mahatma
Su 24 Ironside
M 25 Wild Turkey
Tu 26 Strider
W 27 Climax Blues Band
Th 28 Hackensack
Fr 29 Capability Brown
Fr 29 Darien Spirit
Sa 30 Be-Bop Deluxe
Sa 30 Mothers Pride
Su 31 Charlie and the Wide Boys

April 1974
M 01 (Darryl Way's) Wolf
M 01 Elysium
Tu 02 The Winkies
W 03 Sandgate
W 03 Derek Wyatt
Th 04 Brett Marvin and the
    Thunderbolts
Th 04 Gnasher
Fr 05 The Heavy Metal Kids
Sa 06 Bronx Cheer
Sa 06 Rod Felton
Su 07 Trapeze
M 08 Chilli Willi & The Red Hot
    Peppers
Tu 09 Greenslade
W 10 Strider
Th 11 Refugee
Fr 12 Fumble
Sa 13 Hustler
Su 14 Medicine Head
M 15 Medicine Head
Tu 16 Stray
W 17 Wild Turkey
Th 18 Jack The Lad
Fr 19 Spencer Davis Group
Fr 19 Mahatma
Sa 20 Dark Star
Su 21 Writing on the Wall
M 22 Fusion Orchestra
Tu 23 Blodwyn Pig
W 24 Capability Brown
Th 25 Dizzy
Th 25 Flux
Fr 26 Quadrille
Fr 26 Mankind
Sa 27 Procession
Su 28 Randy
M 29 The Heavy Metal Kids
Tu 30 Jon Hiseman's Tempest

May 1974
W 01 Esperanto
Th 02 Kiki Dee
Fr 03 Rory Gallagher & His Band
Sa 04 Rory Gallagher & His Band
Su 05 Rory Gallagher & His Band
M 06 Coast Road Drive
Tu 07 Stackridge
W 07 Strider
Th 08 Dizzy
Th 08 Pete Sutton
Fr 09 Wild Turkey
Sa 10 Osborne's Greep
Sa 10 Mother Sun
Su 11 Groundhogs
M 12 Good Habit

Tu 14 Wolf
W 15 Jack The Lad
Th 16 UFO
Th 16 Curly
Fr 17 Brett Marvin and the
      Thunderbolts
Sa 18 Mothers Pride
Su 19 Quicksand
M 20 Bees Make Honey
Tu 21 Michael Chapman
W 22 McGuinness Flint
Th 23 Global Village Trucking
      Company
Fr 24 Hustler
Sa 25 Peaches
Sa 25 Rudi Tchaikovsky
Su 26 Writing on the Wall
M 27 String Driven Thing
Tu 28 Fumble
W 29 The Heavy Metal Kids
Th 30 Camel

June 1974
Sa 01 Steve Brown Band
Sa 01 Soliloque
Su 02 Titanic
M 03 UFO
Tu 04 Stray
W 05 Esperanto
Th 06 Wolf
Th 06 Snow Leopard
Fr 07 Longdancer
Fr 07 Kerry Scott
Sa 08 Locomotive GT
Sa 08 Tomato
Su 09 Budgie
Su 09 Judas Priest
M 10 Hustler
Tu 11 Strider
W 12 Jack The Lad
Th 13 Trapeze
Fr 14 Capability Brown
Sa 15 Randy Pie
Sa 15 Zhain
Su 16 The Winkies
M 17 Esperanto
Tu 18 Refugee
W 19 Seventh Wave
Th 20 Camel
Fr 21 Fusion Orchestra
Sa 22 Procession
Su 23 Rock Rebellion
M 24 Wild Turkey
Tu 25 Bobbie McGee and Me
W 26 Jack The Lad
Th 27 Hustler
Fr 28 Strider
Fr 28 Procession
Sa 29 Bronx Cheer
Sa 29 Piggy
Su 30 Jo Ann Kelly
Su 30 Doris Anderson
Su 30 Jaki Whitren
Su 30 Joan Armatrading

July 1974
M 01 Savoy Brown
M 01 Rod Felton
Tu 02 Savoy Brown
Tu 02 Rod Felton
W 03 Babe Ruth
W 03 Sundance
Th 04 Jonathan Kelly's Outside
Fr 05 The Heavy Metal Kids
Sa 06 Jailbait
Sa 06 Cosmetix
Su 07 Casablanca
Su 07 Highway
M 08 Esperanto
Tu 09 Thin Lizzy
W 10 UFO
Th 11 Sparrow
Fr 12 Ange
Sa 13 Halcyon
Sa 13 Hush
Su 14 Spontaneous Combustion

M 15 Trapeze
Tu 16 Blodwyn Pig
Tu 16 Budlipp Springer
W 17 The Winkies
Th 18 Beckett
Th 18 Steve Brown Band
Fr 19 Esperanto
Sa 20 Zzebra
Sa 20 Blaze
Su 21 Brett Marvin and the
      Thunderbolts
M 22 Kevin Coyne
Tu 23 Geordie
W 24 Strider
Th 25 Sparrow
Fr 26 Sutherland Brothers & Quiver
Fr 26 Michael Chapman
Sa 27 Grand Slam
Sa 27 Martin Plum
Su 28 Hustler
M 29 Gypsy
Tu 30 Sharks
W 31 Fumble

August 1974
Th 01 Chilli Willi & The Red Hot
      Peppers
Fr 02 JSD Band
Sa 03 Greep
Su 04 Rowdies
M 05 GT Moore & The Reggae
      Guitars
Tu 06 UFO
W 07 Strider
Th 08 Esperanto
Fr 09 Amazing Blondel
Sa 10 Half Human Band
Sa 10 Zhain
Su 11 Bill Barclay
M 12 String Driven Thing
Tu 13 Blodwyn Pig
W 14 Hustler
Th 15 Sparrow
Fr 16 The Heavy Metal Kids
Sa 17 Mother Sun
Sa 17 Yellow Bird
Su 18 Camel
M 19 Chris Stainton's Tundra
M 19 Tony Kelly
Tu 20 The Winkies
W 21 Strider
Th 22 Beckett
Fr 23 Thin Lizzy
Fr 23 Trouble at Mill
Sa 24 Procession
Sa 24 Undercarriage
M 26 Fusion Orchestra
Tu 27 Starry Eyed & Laughing
Tu 27 Mike Cooper
W 28 Greenslade
Th 29 Kevin Coyne
Fr 30 Chilli Willi & The Red Hot
      Peppers
Sa 31 Rudi Tchaikovsky
Sa 31 Tuesday

September 1974
Su 01 Zzebra
M 02 The Winkies
Tu 03 Strider
W 04 The Tremeloes
Th 05 Sam Apple Pie
Th 05 Rock Rebellion
Fr 06 The Heavy Metal Kids
Sa 07 Jack Straw
Sa 07 Warlock
Su 08 UFO
M 09 Esperanto
Tu 10 Seventh Wave
W 11 The Stan Webb Band
Th 12 Jonathan Kelly's Outside
Fr 13 Sparrow
Sa 14 Gravy Train
Sa 14 Blaze
Su 15 Zzebra
M 16 Charlie and the Wide Boys

Tu 17 Fumble
W 18 Hustler
Th 19 Judas Priest
Th 19 Daddy Longlegs
Fr 20 Amazing Blondel
Sa 21 Grand Slam
Su 22 Brett Marvin and the
      Thunderbolts
M 23 Quadrille
Tu 24 Sharks
W 25 Fusion Orchestra
Th 26 Jonathan Kelly's Outside
Fr 27 Seventh Wave
Sa 28 Jack Straw
Sa 28 Orange
Su 29 Zzebra
M 30 The Jess Roden Band

October 1974
Tu 01 Be-Bop Deluxe
W 02 Trapeze
Th 03 Beckett
Fr 04 John Baldry
Sa 05 Mother Sun
Sa 05 Magic
Su 06 Jonathan Kelly's Outside
M 07 Dr Feelgood
Tu 08 Thin Lizzy
Tu 08 Jackie Lynton
W 09 UFO
Th 10 Alberto Y Lost Trios Paranoias
Fr 11 The Stan Webb Band
Fr 11 Thunder
Sa 12 Jack Straw
Sa 12 Gygato
Su 13 Strange Days
M 14 GT Moore & The Reggae
      Guitars
Tu 15 Sutherland Brothers & Quiver
W 16 The Tremeloes
W 16 Paul Carmen
Th 17 Nutz
Fr 18 Sparrow
Sa 19 Grand Slam
Su 20 Zzebra
M 21 Decameron
Tu 22 Seventh Wave
W 23 Hustler
Th 24 Alberto Y Lost Trios Paranoias
Fr 25 Strange Days
Sa 26 Jack Straw
Su 27 Raymond Froggatt Band
Su 27 Dolphins
M 28 String Driven Thing
Tu 29 Camel
Tu 29 Nick Pickett
W 30 Esperanto
Th 31 Brett Marvin and the
      Thunderbolts

November 1974
Fr 01 Judas Priest
Sa 02 Cosmetix
Su 03 Jonathan Kelly's Outside
M 04 Ariel
Tu 05 The Heavy Metal Kids
W 06 Strider
Th 07 Fumble
Fr 08 Blackfoot Sue
Sa 09 Vineyard
Sa 09 Kiss
Su 10 Country Joe McDonald
M 11 Zzebra
Tu 12 Chris Stainton's Tundra
Tu 12 Mike Hugg
W 13 Strange Days
Th 14 Slack Alice
Th 14 Daylight Robbery
Fr 15 Jack Straw
Fr 15 Keef Hartley's Dog Soldier
Sa 16 Mothers Pride
Su 17 Zoot Money's Big Roll Band
M 18 Fusion Orchestra
Tu 19 Stray
Tu 20 Babe Ruth
Th 21 Hustler

Fr 22 Rare Bird
Sa 23 Steve Brown Band
Su 24 Kevin Coyne
M 25 Headstone
Tu 26 Groundhogs
W 27 Strange Days
Th 28 Zzebra
Fr 29 Ariel
Sa 30 Sheerwater
Sa 30 Orange

December 1974
Su 01 Sassafras
Su 01 Long Vehicle
M 02 Dr Feelgood
Tu 03 Ronnie Lane & Slim Chance
Tu 03 Bees Make Honey
W 04 Ronnie Lane & Slim Chance
W 04 Bees Make Honey
Th 05 String Driven Thing
Fr 06 Keith Christmas Band
Sa 07 Blaze
Sa 07 Undercarriage
Su 08 Sam Apple Pie
M 09 Zzebra
Tu 10 The Jess Roden Band
W 11 Jonathan Kelly's Outside
Th 12 Moonrider
Fr 13 Ross Stag
Su 15 McGuinness Flint
M 16 JSD Band
Tu 17 The Stan Webb Band
Tu 17 Spanker Onslow
W 18 Rare Bird
Th 19 Beckett
Fr 20 Medicine Head
Sa 21 The Winkies
Su 22 Fusion Orchestra
M 23 Sutherland Brothers & Quiver
Tu 24 Strider
Tu 24 Overtown
Fr 27 UFO
Sa 28 Stray
Su 29 Amazing Blondel
M 30 Edgar Broughton
Tu 31 The Heavy Metal Kids

January 1975
Th 02 Dr Feelgood
Fr 03 Seventh Wave
Sa 04 Woman
Su 05 Upp
M 06 Hustler
Tu 07 Strider
W 08 Sassafras
Th 09 Cozy Powell's Hammer
Fr 10 Kilburn & the High Roads
Sa 11 Jack Straw
Sa 11 Punchin' Judy
Su 12 The Average White Band
M 13 Headstone
Tu 14 Dog Soldier
W 15 Overtown
Th 16 Fumble
Fr 17 Ducks Deluxe
Sa 18 Grand Slam
Su 19 Alberto Y Lost Trios Paranoias
M 20 String Driven Thing
Tu 21 Babe Ruth
W 22 Nutz
Th 23 Grand Slam
Th 23 Throat
Fr 24 Keith Christmas Band
Sa 25 Orange
Sa 25 Palm Beach Express
Su 26 Nicol & Marsh Easy Street
Su 26 Sailor
M 27 Shanghai
Tu 28 Medicine Head
W 29 Overtown
Th 30 East of Eden
Fr 31 Jackie Lynton's Grande

February 1975
Sa 01 Grand Slam
Sa 01 Harp
Su 02 The Equals

M 03 Slack Alice
Tu 04 Rare Bird
W 05 Curly
Th 06 (Jill Saward's) Fusion Orchestra
Fr 07 Alberto Y Lost Trios Paranoias
Sa 08 Greep
Sa 08 Jugglers
Su 09 Kleptomania
M 10 Gordon Giltrap Band
Tu 11 UFO
W 12 Overtown
Th 13 Kiki Dee Band
Fr 14 Zzebra
Sa 15 The Heavy Metal Kids
Sa 15 Grand Slam
Su 16 Upp
M 17 Strife
Tu 18 Kilburn & the High Roads
W 19 Ange
Th 20 Tim Rose
Th 20 The Movies
Fr 21 Nutz
Sa 22 Jack Straw
Sa 22 Second Front
Su 23 Global Village Trucking Company
M 24 Blackfoot Sue
Tu 25 Snafu
W 26 Overtown
Th 27 (Jill Saward's) Fusion Orchestra
Th 27 Baby
Fr 28 Ducks Deluxe

March 1975
Sa 01 Grand Slam
Sa 01 Janus
Su 02 Isaac Guillory's Pure Chance
M 03 Back Door
Tu 04 Savoy Brown
W 05 Pulsar
W 05 Conny Condell
Th 06 Jackie Lynton's Grande
Th 06 Jeremy Spencer's Albatross
Fr 07 Woman
Sa 08 Jack Straw
Su 09 Casablanca
M 10 The Kursaal Flyers
M 10 Warren Harry & the Yum Yum Band
Tu 11 The Stan Webb Band
W 12 Groundhogs
Th 13 Sassafras
Th 13 Tuesday
Fr 14 Magna Carta
Sa 15 Jailbait
Sa 15 Jugglers
Su 16 Upp
M 17 Perigeo
Tu 18 Brinsley Schwarz
W 19 Zzebra
Th 20 (Jill Saward's) Fusion Orchestra
Fr 21 Ducks Deluxe
Sa 22 Palm Beach Express
Sa 22 Hot Rock
Su 23 A Band Called O
M 24 Kilburn & the High Roads
Tu 25 Stray
W 26 Ange
Th 27 Snafu
Fr 28 Trace
Sa 29 The One
Sa 29 Daga Band
Su 30 Budgie
M 31 Budgie

April 1975
Tu 01 Medicine Head
W 02 Judas Priest
W 02 National Flag
Fr 04 Sandgate
Sa 05 Yellow Bird
Sa 05 Child
Su 06 GT Moore & The Reggae Guitars
M 07 Blackfoot Sue
Tu 08 Fumble

W 09 Steve Gibbons Band
Th 10 Magna Carta
Fr 11 The One
Sa 12 Steve Brown Band
Sa 12 Undercarriage
Su 13 Overtown
M 14 Alberto Y Lost Trios Paranoias
Tu 15 Savoy Brown
W 16 String Driven Thing
Th 17 Ariel
Fr 18 Wally
Sa 19 Orange
Sa 19 Clemen Pull
Su 20 Strange Days
M 21 Slack Alice
Tu 22 The Stan Webb Band
W 23 Dick & The Firemen
W 23 Chance of a Lifetime
Th 24 Nutz
Th 24 National Flag
Fr 25 The One
Fr 25 National Flag
Sa 26 Jailbait
Sa 26 Swan Arcade
Su 27 Overtown
M 28 Curly
Tu 29 Edgar Broughton
W 30 Judas Priest
W 30 Asylum

May 1975
Th 01 (Jill Saward's) Fusion Orchestra
Fr 02 Upp
Sa 03 Chris Hinze Combination
Sa 03 Poodles
Su 04 Sundance
Su 04 Stone Delight
M 05 Tea
Tu 06 Ken Bloxham & Emas
W 07 Geno Washington Band
Th 08 Hustler
Fr 09 Ariel
Fr 09 Harlot
Sa 10 Dogs
Sa 10 Courtesan
Su 11 Nicol & Marsh
Su 11 Tonge
M 12 Wally
Tu 13 East of Eden
W 14 Skid Row
Th 15 Cozy Powell's Hammer
Fr 16 Judas Priest
Sa 17 Palm Beach Express
Sa 17 Poodles
Su 18 Sandgate
M 19 Ducks Deluxe
Tu 20 Stan Webb's Brokenglass
W 21 Gonzales
Th 22 The Neutrons
Fr 23 Good Habit
Sa 24 National Flag
Sa 24 Scylla
Su 25 Ariel
M 26 Fruup
Tu 27 Stray
W 28 Blackfoot Sue
W 28 Consortium
Th 29 GT Moore & The Reggae Guitars
Th 29 Amity
Fr 30 Magna Carta
Sa 31 Dogs
Sa 31 Warlock

June 1975
Su 01 Viola Wills
M 02 Sassafras
Tu 03 Savoy Brown
W 04 A Band Called O
Th 05 Equinox
Fr 06 Frive Hand Reel
Fr 06 Cold River Lady
Sa 07 Rudi Tchaikovsky
Sa 07 Mynd
Su 08 Paradise
M 09 The Kursaal Flyers

Tu 10 Medicine Head
W 11 Alberto Y Lost Trios Paranoias
Th 12 Ariel
Fr 13 Judas Priest
Sa 14 Sheerwater
Sa 14 Skyfield
Su 15 UFO
M 16 Zzebra
Tu 17 Snafu
W 18 Trapeze
Th 19 Shanghai
Fr 20 Ducks Deluxe
Sa 21 Trapper
Sa 21 Mantis
Su 22 Harlot
Su 22 National Flag
M 23 Curly
Tu 24 Sutherland Brothers & Quiver
W 25 Hustler
Th 26 Upp
Fr 27 Back Door
Sa 28 Orange
Sa 28 Daga Band
Su 29 National Flag
Su 29 Harlot
M 30 Global Village Trucking Company

July 1975
Tu 01 Stray
W 02 Five Hand Reel
Th 03 Amazing Blondel
Fr 04 Tim Hardin
Sa 05 Palm Beach Express
Sa 05 Mynd
Su 06 Harlot
Su 06 National Flag
M 07 Slack Alice
Tu 08 Babe Ruth
W 09 Jack The Lad
Th 10 Savoy Brown
Fr 11 Strange Days
Fr 11 Dragon Fly
Sa 12 Clemen Pull
Sa 12 Benefit
Su 13 National Flag
Su 13 Harlot
M 14 Mike Heron's Reputation
Tu 15 Fumble
W 16 Philip Goodhand-Tait
W 16 Aj Webber
W 16 Tony Reeves
Th 17 UFO
Fr 18 Good Habit
Sa 19 Agnes Strange
Su 20 Harlot
Su 20 National Flag
M 21 The Kursaal Flyers
Tu 22 Medicine Head
W 23 Sassafras
Th 24 Nutz
Fr 25 Mike Chapman
Sa 26 Poodles
Sa 26 IPOH
Su 27 Harlot
Su 27 Guinever
M 28 Chris Farlowe & Friends
Tu 29 A Band Called O
Tu 29 Reds Whites & Blues
W 30 Wally
W 30 Spud
Th 31 East of Eden

August 1975
Fr 01 Jet
Sa 02 Rasputin
Su 03 FBI
M 04 Cheeks
Tu 05 Snafu
W 06 Snafu
Th 07 Amazing Blondel
Fr 08 Moonrider
Fr 08 Max Merritt
Sa 09 Consortium
Sa 09 Biffo
Su 10 FBI

M 11 Chapman-Whitney Streetwalkers
Tu 12 Chapman-Whitney Streetwalkers
W 13 Chapman-Whitney Streetwalkers
Th 14 Hardin & York
Fr 15 Good Habit
Sa 16 Gasworks
Su 17 FBI
M 18 Trapeze
Tu 19 Babe Ruth
W 20 String Driven Thing
Th 21 Motorhead
Fr 22 National Flag
Sa 23 Warlock
M 25 UFO
Tu 26 Tim Hardin
W 27 Mike Heron's Reputation
Th 28 Upp
Fr 29 Nutz
Sa 30 Palm Beach Express
Su 31 FBI

September 1975
Tu 02 Judas Priest
W 03 Alberto Y Lost Trios Paranoias
Th 04 East Of Eden
Fr 05 Clancy
Sa 06 Consortium
Su 07 Clemen Pull
M 08 Gong
Tu 09 Gong
W 10 Gong
Th 11 Medicine Head
F 12 Slack Alice
Sa 13 Palm Beach Express
Su 14 Clemen Pull
Su 14 SS2
M 15 Strife
Tu 16 String Driven Thing
W 17 Gonzales
Th 18 National Flag
Fr 19 FBI
Sa 20 Daga Band
Su 21 Clemen Pull
Su 21 SF2
M 22 The Kursaal Flyers
Tu 23 Fumble
W 24 Upp
Th 25 Woman
Fr 26 Shanghai
Sa 27 Jailbait
Su 28 Clemen Pull
Su 28 SF2
M 29 Wally
Tu 30 Nutz

October 1975
W 01 Strife
Th 02 Zzebra
Fr 03 Stray
Sa 04 Dogs
Sa 04 Benefit
Su 05 Hobo
Su 05 Sky
M 06 Good Habit
Tu 07 Seventh Wave
W 08 FBI
Th 09 Clancy
Fr 10 National Flag
Sa 11 Consortium
Su 12 Hobo
M 13 Alkatraz
Tu 14 Snafu
Tu 14 Duke, Duke & the Dukes
W 15 The Kursaal Flyers
Th 16 Moonrider
Fr 17 Graham Bell's Stotts
Fr 17 Rubber Rhino
Sa 18 Poodles
Sa 18 Bouncer
Su 19 Hobo
M 20 Neil Innes' Fatso
Tu 21 Medicine Head
W 22 Alberto Y Lost Trios Paranoias

W 22 Reds Whites & Blues
Th 23 Mick Abrahams Band
Fr 24 Boxer
Sa 25 Gasworks
Su 26 Hobo
M 27 A Band Called O
Tu 28 Nutz
W 29 Kraan
Th 30 The Pink Fairies
Fr 31 Clive Jones

November 1975
Sa 01 Consortium
Su 02 Poodles
M 03 The Tyla Gang
Tu 04 Andy Fraser Band
W 05 Judas Priest
Th 06 Mike Heron's Reputation
Fr 07 (Ian Carr's) Nucleus
Sa 08 Giggles
Sa 08 Razorbacks
Su 09 Poodles
M 10 Jack The Lad
Tu 11 Scorpions
Tu 11 Mother Superior
W 12 Motorhead
Th 13 Upp
Fr 14 Paul Joses' Band
Sa 15 Burglar Bill
Su 16 Poodles
M 17 Strange Days
Tu 18 Trace
W 19 Gonzales
Th 20 Sassafras
Fr 21 Wally
Sa 22 Gasworks
Sa 22 Hungry Horse
Su 23 Poodles
Su 23 Burlesque
M 24 John Baldry
Tu 25 Stray
W 26 Slack Alice
Th 27 National Flag
Fr 28 Dirty Tricks
Sa 29 Bearded Lady
Su 30 Poodles

December 1975
M 01 Bunny
Tu 02 Keef Hartley
Tu 02 Mike Harrison
W 03 Tony Sheridan and Band
W 03 Gimme Hope
Th 04 Fumble
Fr 05 Dirty Tricks
Sa 06 City Boy
Su 07 Clemen Pull
M 08 Banco
Tu 09 String Driven Thing
W 10 Alkatraz
Th 11 National Flag
Su 14 Clemen Pull
Su 14 Valhalla
M 15 Frogmorton
Tu 16 The Stan Webb Band
Tu 16 Kircus
W 17 Medicine Head
W 17 Kircus
Th 18 Babe Ruth
Th 18 Brewster
Fr 19 Upp
Fr 19 Fastbuck
Su 21 Clemen Pull
Su 21 Valhalla
M 22 Brand X
Tu 23 Seventh Wave
W 24 FBI
Sa 27 Giggles
Su 28 Clemen Pull
Su 28 Valhalla
M 29 The Pink Fairies
Tu 30 A Band Called O
W 31 The Heavy Metal Kids

January 1976
Fr 02 Seventh Wave
Sa 03 Fogg

Su 04 Nova
M 05 Poodles
Tu 06 Strider
W 07 The Diversions
Th 08 Mick Abrahams
Fr 09 Graham Bell's Stotts
Sa 10 Giggles
Su 11 Nova
M 12 Carol Grimes' London Boogie
Band
Tu 13 The Kursaal Flyers
W 14 Dirty Tricks
Th 15 Halfbreed
Fr 16 National Flag
Sa 17 Giggles
Su 18 Nova
M 19 Strife
Tu 20 Gryphon
W 21 Locus
Th 22 Magna Carta
Fr 23 Gonzales
Sa 24 Giggles
Su 25 Nova
M 26 Agnes Strange
Tu 27 Nutz
W 28 Oscar
Th 29 Halfbreed
Fr 30 FBI
Sa 31 Giggles

February 1976
Su 01 Palm Beach Express
M 02 Clancy
Tu 03 Fumble
W 04 (Ian Carr's) Nucleus
Th 05 Mick Abrahams
Fr 06 Tim Hardin
Sa 07 Yellow Bird
Sa 07 Razorbacks
Su 08 Palm Beach Express
M 09 Hobo
Tu 10 Mr Big
W 11 Ange
Th 12 Eddie & the Hotrods
Th 12 Sex Pistols
Fr 13 Dana Gillespie
Sa 14 Asylum
Su 15 Palm Beach Express
M 16 Savoy Brown
Tu 17 Nutz
W 18 Kilburn & the High Roads
Th 19 National Flag
Th 19 Cock Sparrow
Fr 20 Back Door
Sa 21 Bearded Lady
Sa 21 Hooker
Su 22 Palm Beach Express
M 23 Strife
Tu 24 The Enid
W 25 Gonzales
Th 26 Mike Heron's Reputation
Fr 27 Druid
Sa 28 Giggles
Su 29 Palm Beach Express

March 1976
M 01 Poodles
Tu 02 The Weightwatchers
W 03 Halfbreed
Th 04 Gryphon
Fr 05 National Flag
Sa 06 D Dancer
Su 07 Asylum
M 08 The Pink Fairies
M 08 The Stranglers
Tu 09 The Pink Fairies
Tu 09 The Count Bishops
W 10 Moon
Th 11 Sam Apple Pie
Fr 12 Clancy
Sa 13 Giggles
Sa 13 Mantis
Su 14 Asylum
M 15 Graham Bell
M 15 Cirkus
Tu 16 FBI

W 17 Magna Carta
Th 18 Sassafras
Fr 19 Upp
Sa 20 Jailbait
Sa 20 Razorbacks
Su 21 Asylum
M 22 A Band Called O
W 24 Mike Heron's Reputation
Th 25 The Enid
Fr 26 National Flag
Sa 27 Rococo
Su 28 Asylum
M 29 Scorpions
Tu 30 Doctors of Madness
W 31 Tea

April 1976
Th 01 Gordon Giltrap
Th 01 Krazy Kat
Fr 02 Little Bob Story
Fr 02 Count Bishops & The Rockets
Sa 03 Gasworks
Sa 03 Razorbacks
Su 04 Arbre
Su 04 Felix
M 05 Gonzales
M 05 Stars
Tu 06 Fruup
W 07 Five hand Reel
W 07 Hedgehog Pie
Th 08 Strife
Th 08 Heartbreaker
Fr 09 Solution
Fr 09 Lalla Harrison
Sa 10 Bearded Lady
Sa 10 Matt Black Sunday
Su 11 Druid
M 12 Back Door
Tu 13 John Grimaldi Band
Th 15 Upp
Th 15 Hungry Horse
Fr 16 The Enid
Sa 17 Babe Ruth
Su 18 Fumble
M 19 Manfred Mann's Earthband
Tu 20 Manfred Mann's Earthband
W 21 Manfred Mann's Earthband
Th 22 Colosseum II
Fr 23 Colosseum II
Sa 24 Gryphon
Sa 24 Smile
Su 25 Eddie & the Hot Rods
M 26 Racing Cars
Tu 27 Stray
Tu 27 Fastbuck
W 28 The Nashville Teens
Th 29 Kilburn & the High Roads
Th 29 Hungry Horse
Fr 30 National Flag
Fr 30 Curly

May 1976
Sa 01 Mahjun
Su 02 Giggles
M 03 Druid
Tu 04 Medicine Head
Tu 04 Cock Sparrow
W 05 Strife
W 05 Krakatoa
Th 06 Roogalator
Th 06 Vikivaki
Fr 07 Russ Ballard
Sa 08 Clemen Pull
Sa 08 Mantis
Su 09 Giggles
M 10 Druid
Tu 11 Back Street Crawler
Tu 11 AC/DC
W 12 Back Street Crawler
W 12 AC/DC
Th 13 Mick Abrahams Band
Th 13 Harpoon
Fr 14 Tim Hardin
Fr 14 Copra
Sa 15 Cirkus
Sa 15 Sticky Wicket

Su 16 Giggles
M 17 Druid
Tu 18 The Jess Roden Band
W 19 The Jess Roden Band
Th 20 The Jess Roden Band
Fr 21 Roogalator
Fr 21 Cruiser
Sa 22 Bearded Lady
Sa 22 No Dice
Su 23 Giggles
Su 23 Captain Clapham
M 24 Druid
Tu 25 Back Door
Tu 25 Scrapyard
W 26 Jack The Lad
Fr 28 National Flag
Fr 28 Montana Red
Sa 29 Salt
Sa 29 Razorbacks
Su 30 Giggles
M 31 Druid

June 1976
Tu 01 The Noel Redding Band
W 02 The Noel Redding Band
Th 03 Caledonia
Fr 04 AC/DC
Sa 05 Supercharge
M 07 Graham Parker & The Rumour
M 07 Bank Of England Brass
M 07 Tooting Fruities
Tu 08 Graham Parker & The Rumour
Tu 08 Bank Of England Brass
Tu 08 Tooting Fruities
W 09 Stray
Th 10 Little Bob Story
Fr 11 Mr Big
Fr 11 Ronji Southern Band
Sa 12 Bearded Lady
Sa 12 Bouncer
Su 13 Steve Gibbons Band
Su 13 Blaze
M 14 Fruup
Tu 15 Geno Washington and the Ram
Jam Band
W 16 Colosseum II
Th 17 Clancy
Th 17 Seventh Heaven
Fr 18 Gryphon
Fr 18 Razorbacks
Sa 19 Scarecrow
Sa 19 Mountain Ash
Su 20 Fumble
Su 20 Montana Red
M 21 Poodles
Tu 22 Automatic Man
W 23 Automatic Man
Th 24 Pat Travers Band
Fr 25 The Enid
Sa 26 The Count Bishops
Sa 26 Bouncer
Su 27 Giggles
M 28 John Dowie & The Big Girl's
Blouse
Tu 29 Moon
W 30 Steve Gibbons Band

July 1976
Th 01 Carol Grimes' London Boogie
Band
Th 01 Obie Clayton Band
Fr 02 The Wild Angels
Fr 02 The Wild Wax Show
Sa 03 The Smiggs Band
Su 04 Sam Apple Pie
Su 04 Razorbacks
M 05 Nutz
M 05 Heartbreaker
Tu 06 The Bobby Harrison Band
W 07 Palm Beach Express
W 07 Nick Pickett
Th 08 The Enid
Fr 09 Eddie & the Hot Rods
Fr 09 Riviera Feedback
Sa 10 Bearded Lady
Sa 10 Mantis

Su 11 Giggles
Su 11 Captain Cook's Dog
M 12 Hedgehog Pie
Tu 13 Doctors of Madness
W 14 A Band Called O
Th 15 Automatic Man
Fr 16 Automatic Man
Sa 17 Salt
Sa 17 Razorbacks
Su 18 Poodles
Su 18 Rippa
M 19 Five Hand Reel
Tu 20 Moon
W 21 Back Door
W 21 Sammy Mitchell's Three-Piece Suite
Th 22 Strife
Th 22 Soho Jets
Fr 23 FBI
Sa 24 HeartBreaker
Sa 24 Amberband
Su 25 Roogalator
M 26 AC/DC
Tu 27 Van Der Graaf Generator
W 28 Van Der Graaf Generator
Th 29 Van Der Graaf Generator
Fr 30 Brand X
Sa 31 Widowmaker

August 1976
M 02 AC/DC
Tu 03 The Pink Fairies
W 04 Back Door
W 04 Stargang
Th 05 Dirty Tricks
Th 05 Razorbacks
Fr 06 FBI
Sa 07 Bearded Lady
Sa 07 Ritzy
Su 08 Giggles
Su 08 Jerry The Ferret
M 09 AC/DC
Tu 10 Eddie & the Hot Rods
W 11 Sassafras
Th 12 Fumble
Fr 13 Strife
Fr 13 Razorbacks
Sa 14 Salt
Sa 14 Major Bull
Su 15 The Fabulous Poodles
Su 15 Polecat
M 16 AC/DC
M 16 Valhalla
Tu 17 Gryphon
W 18 Roogalator
Fr 20 The Enid
Sa 21 Clemen Pull
Su 22 Sam Apple Pie
Su 22 Heartbreaker
M 23 AC/DC
M 23 Valhalla
Tu 24 AC/DC
Tu 24 Valhalla
W 25 Supercharge
Th 26 Brand X
Fr 27 Moon
Sa 28 Scarecrow
Sa 28 Razorbacks
M 30 A Band Called O
M 30 The Dodgers
Tu 31 Pat Travers Band

September 1976
W 01 Supercharge
Th 02 Loving Awareness
Th 02 Handbag
Fr 03 Eddie & the Hot Rods
Fr 03 Razorbacks
Sa 04 The Count Bishops
Sa 04 Uproar
Su 05 The Foster Brothers
Su 05 Amberband
M 06 The Rhythm Traps
M 06 Valhalla
Tu 07 AC/DC
W 08 AC/DC

Th 09 Woody Woodmansey's U-Boat
Th 09 Oppo
Fr 10 Roogalator
Sa 11 Heartbreaker
Sa 11 Mantis
Su 12 The Foster Brothers
Su 12 Panama Scandal
M 13 Moon
Tu 14 Medicine Head
W 15 Back Door
W 15 Bethnal
Th 16 Supercharge
Fr 17 Eddie & the Hot Rods
Sa 18 Scarecrow
Sa 18 Jerry The Ferret
Su 19 The Foster Brothers
Su 19 Panama Scandal
M 20 Giggles
M 20 Captain Cook's Dog
Tu 21 Eddie & the Hot Rods
Tu 21 Heartbreaker
W 22 Loving Awareness
W 22 Michael Fury Band
Th 23 Carol Grimes' London Boogie Band
Th 23 Razorbacks
Fr 24 The Enid
Sa 25 Bearded Lady
Sa 25 Mantis
Su 26 The Foster Brothers
Su 26 Amberband
M 27 Roogalator
Tu 28 Strife
W 29 Back Door
Th 30 Remus Down Boulevard
Th 30 Jackie Lynton's Banned

October 1976
Fr 01 Loving Awareness
Sa 02 Heartbreaker
Sa 02 Bouncer
Su 03 Woody Woodmansey's U-Boat
Su 03 Oppo
M 04 Colosseum II
Tu 05 Colosseum II
W 06 John Coughlan's Diesel Band
Th 07 Phoenix
Th 07 Little Acre
Fr 08 Little River Band
Fr 08 Asaph
Sa 09 Dogwatch
Sa 09 Valhalla
Su 10 Woody Woodmansey's U-Boat
Su 10 Oppo
M 11 The Fabulous Poodles
Tu 12 The Enid
W 13 Back Door
W 13 Blue Angel
Th 14 Steve Gibbons Band
Th 14 Cock Sparrow
Fr 15 Roogalator
Sa 16 Razorbacks
Sa 16 Teazer
Su 17 Woody Woodmansey's U-Boat
M 18 Georgie Fame & the Blue Flames
M 18 Alfalpha
Tu 19 Georgie Fame & the Blue Flames
Tu 19 Alfalpha
W 20 Dead Fingers Talk
Th 21 Pat Travers Band
Fr 22 Nutz
Sa 23 Bearded Lady
Sa 23 Silent Sister
Su 24 Woody Woodmansey's U-Boat
Su 24 Pumphouse Gang
M 25 Babe Ruth
M 25 Heartbreaker
Tu 26 Groundhogs
Tu 26 Unicorn
W 27 Groundhogs
W 27 Unicorn
Th 28 Groundhogs
Th 28 Unicorn

Fr 29 Loving Awareness
Fr 29 The Jab
Sa 30 Heartbreaker
Sa 30 Valhalla
Su 31 Woody Woodmansey's U-Boat

November 1976
M 01 The Fabulous Poodles
Tu 02 The Enid
W 03 Racing Cars
Th 04 20th Century Steelband
Fr 05 Dirty Tricks
Fr 05 Suicide
Sa 06 Dogwatch
Sa 06 Topaz
Su 07 The Stranglers
M 08 Remus Down Boulevard
Tu 09 Upp
Tu 09 Panama Scandal
W 10 Woody Woodmansey's U-Boat
Th 11 Loving Awareness
Th 11 Lee Kosmin Band
Fr 12 Giggles
Fr 12 Valhalla
Sa 13 Stallion
Sa 13 Teazer
Su 14 The Foster Brothers
Su 14 Bouncer
M 15 AFT
W 17 Flying Aces
W 17 Red
Th 18 Motorhead
Th 18 Hungry Horse
Fr 19 Babe Ruth
Sa 20 Clemen Pull
Sa 20 Gloria Mundi
Su 21 Scorpions
Su 21 Razorbacks
M 22 Hinkley's Heroes
M 22 Isaac Guillory
M 22 Clemen Pull
M 22 Gloria Mundi
Tu 23 Hinkley's Heroes
Tu 23 Isaac Guillory
W 24 Stray
W 24 Jerry The Ferret
Th 25 Stray
Th 25 Oppo
Fr 26 Little Bob Story
Sa 27 Bearded Lady
Sa 27 Panama Scandal
Su 28 Meal Ticket
M 29 AFT
Tu 30 Charlie

December 1976
W 01 Racing Cars
Th 02 Nutz
Th 02 Consortium
Fr 03 Druid
Sa 04 Bearded Lady
Sa 04 Pumphouse gang
Su 05 Roogalator
M 06 Giggles
Tu 07 Bert Jansch
W 08 Loving Awareness
Th 09 Woody Woodmansey's U-Boat
Fr 10 Steve Gibbons Band
Fr 10 Jerry The Ferret
Sa 11 Oppo
M 13 AFT
M 13 Panama Scandal
Tu 14 Bert Jansch
W 15 A Band Called O
Th 16 Upp
Fr 17 StripJack
Sa 18 UFO
Su 19 UFO
M 20 UFO
Tu 21 Moon
W 22 Alberto Y Lost Trios Paranoias
Th 23 Alberto Y Lost Trios Paranoias
Fr 24 Loving Awareness
Fr 24 Oppo
M 27 Stray
Tu 28 Bert Jansch

W 29 Meal Ticket
Th 30 Sassafras
Fr 31 The Pat Travers Band

January 1977
M 03 AFT
Tu 04 Medicine Head
W 05 George Hatcher Band
Th 06 Racing Cars
Fr 07 Woody Woodmansey's U-Boat
Fr 07 Scarlet Strange
Sa 08 Screemer
Sa 08 Meridian
Su 09 Salt
M 10 Muscles
Tu 11 Bert Jansch
W 12 Roogalator
Th 13 Flying Aces
Th 13 Teaser
Fr 14 John Stevens Away
Fr 14 Red
Sa 15 Hungry Horse
Sa 15 Panama Scandal
Su 16 Salt
M 17 Muscles
Tu 18 Steve Gibbons Band
W 19 George Hatcher Band
W 19 A1
Th 20 Babe Ruth
Th 20 Wasps
Fr 21 Plummet Airlines
Fr 21 Gloria Mundi
Sa 22 Bearded Lady
Sa 22 The Jam
Su 23 Salt
M 24 Muscles
Tu 25 Remus Down Boulevard
W 26 Mr Big
W 26 Streetband
Th 27 Nasty Pop
Fr 28 Motorhead
Fr 28 Bandana
Su 30 Salt
M 31 Muscles
M 31 Lee Kosmin Band

February 1977
Tu 01 Moon
W 02 Strife
Th 03 Medicine Head
Th 03 Jenny Haan's Lion
Th 03 Skeater
Fr 04 The Fabulous Poodles
Fr 04 Silent Sister
Sa 05 Hungry Horse
Sa 05 Metro
Su 06 Bearded Lady
Su 06 Panama Scandal
M 07 Racing Cars
M 07 Simon Drake
Tu 08 Charlie
W 09 George Hatcher Band
Th 10 The Pink Fairies
Th 10 Streetband
Fr 11 The Pink Fairies
Fr 11 Streetband
Sa 12 Consortium
Sa 12 Duffy
Su 13 Bearded Lady
Su 13 Panama Scandal
M 14 Woody Woodmansey's U-Boat
M 14 Caribou
Tu 15 Bert Jansch
W 16 Krazy Kat
Th 17 Georgie Fame & the Blue Flames
Fr 18 Georgie Fame & the Blue Flames
Sa 19 Window
Sa 19 Gentlemen
Su 20 Bearded Lady
Su 20 Panama Scandal
M 21 Roogalator
Tu 22 Stray
Tu 22 Gloria Mundi
W 23 The Sensational Alex Harvey

Band
Th 24 The Sensational Alex Harvey
         Band
Fr 25 Ultravox
Sa 26 Stallion
Sa 26 Gloria Mundi
Su 27 Bearded Lady
Su 27 Panama Scandal
M 28 After The Fire

March 1977
Tu 01 Little Bob Story
W 02 Tiger
Th 03 John Stevens Away
Fr 04 Screemer
Sa 05 Hungry Horse
Sa 05 Teaser
Su 06 Lee Kosmin Band
M 07 George Hatcher Band
M 07 The Motors
Tu 08 Doctors of Madness
W 09 Gryphon
W 09 Reinhardt Boogie Band
Th 10 Nasty Pop
Fr 11 Nova
Sa 12 Heartbreaker
Sa 12 Second Avenue
Su 13 Lee Kosmin Band
Su 13 The Stukas
M 14 Back To Front
M 14 AJ Webber
Tu 15 Strife
Tu 15 Bandana
W 16 Meal Ticket
Th 17 Caledonia
Fr 18 Bandit
Sa 19 Jerry The Ferret
Sa 19 Bazooka Joe
Su 20 Plummet Airlines
M 21 Strapps
Tu 22 Charlie
W 23 Gryphon
W 23 Teaser
Th 24 Michael Chapman
Fr 25 Ultravox
Fr 25 Southern Electric
Sa 26 Scarecrow
Sa 26 Masterswitch
Su 27 Plummet Airlines
M 28 Johnny Thunders & the
         Heartbreakers
Tu 29 Heron
W 30 Strider
W 30 Streetband
Th 31 Generation X
Th 31 Gloria Mundi

April 1977
Fr 01 Motorhead
Fr 01 Valhalla
Sa 02 Window
Sa 02 Tush
Su 03 Plummet Airlines
M 04 Screemer
Tu 05 Bert Jansch
Th 05 Strapps
W 06 Nigel Benjamin's Assassins
W 06 Kites
Th 07 Meal Ticket
Fr 08 Michael Chapman
Sa 09 Michael Chapman
Su 10 Plummet Airlines
M 11 Edgar Broughton Childermass
M 11 Panama Scandal
Tu 12 Nutz
Tu 12 Dragons
W 13 Babe Ruth
W 13 Sorahan
Th 14 Fumble
Th 14 Teaser
Fr 15 Ultravox
Fr 15 Gloria Mundi
Sa 16 Killer
Sa 16 Mount
Su 17 Plummet Airlines
M 18 Strapps

M 18 Valhalla
Tu 19 Remus Down Boulevard
Tu 19 Jackie Lynton
W 20 Nasty Pop
Th 21 No Dice
Th 21 Alfalpha
Fr 22 Salt
Fr 22 Wasps
Sa 23 Brand X
Su 24 Plummet Airlines
M 25 The Motors
Su 26 Heron
W 27 Gryphon
W 27 The Good Stuff
Th 28 Rough Diamond
Fr 29 The Fabulous Poodles
Sa 30 Gloria Mundi
Sa 30 Smiler

May 1977
Su 01 The Vibrators
M 02 John Cale
Tu 03 The Kursaals
W 04 The Kursaals
Th 05 Strapps
Fr 06 Krazy Kat
Sa 07 Window
Sa 07 Snakebite
Su 08 Lee Kosmin Band
Su 08 The Stukas
M 09 The Motors
M 09 Hooker
Tu 10 Illusion
Tu 10 Nick Pickett
W 11 Jenny Haan's Lion
W 11 Spiteri
Th 12 Ultravox
Fr 13 Roogalator
Sa 14 Gloria Mundi
Sa 14 Bazooka
Su 15 Screemer
M 16 The Pirates
Tu 17 Medicine Head
W 18 The Count Bishops
Th 19 Lake
Fr 20 Woody Woodmansey's U-Boat
Sa 21 Panama Scandal
Su 22 Zaine Griff & Screemer
M 23 The Boys
M 23 X-Ray Spex
Tu 24 Moon
W 25 Wayne County
W 25 Electric Chair
W 25 The Police
Th 26 Ultravox
Fr 27 Heron
Sa 28 Killer
Sa 28 Montana Red
Su 29 Zaine Griff & Screemer
M 30 Fury
Tu 31 Bert Jansch

June 1977
W 01 Cado Belle
Th 02 Doctors of Madness
Fr 03 The Boomtown Rats
Fr 03 Sidewinder
Sa 04 Chelsea
Sa 04 Screwdriver
Su 05 Mungo Jerry
M 06 Meal Ticket
Tu 07 Nutz
Tu 07 Jackie Lynton
W 08 John Otway & Wild Willy
         Barret
Th 10 Strider
Th 10 Imperial Show Band
Fr 11 The Saints
Fr 11 The Stukas
Sa 12 Window
Sa 12 Fresh
M 13 Five Hand Reel
Tu 14 Sassafras
W 15 Fury
Th 16 Ultravox
Th 16 Stalag 6

Fr 17 Plummet Airlines
Fr 17 Amazorblades
Sa 18 The Cortinas
Su 19 Salt
M 20 Alternative TV
M 20 Unwanted
Tu 21 Remus Down Boulevard
W 22 Strider
W 22 Streetband
Th 23 After The Fire
Fr 24 The Police
Fr 24 The Lurkers
Sa 25 Squeeze
Su 26 Salt
M 27 George Hatcher Band
Tu 28 City Boy
Tu 28 Dinner at the Ritz
W 29 Heron
Th 30 Ultravox
Th 30 The Stukas

July 1977
Fr 01 No Dice
Sa 02 Gloria Mundi
Sa 02 Neo
Su 03 The Dammed
Su 03 Rings
M 04 The Dammed
M 04 Johnny Moped
Tu 05 The Dammed
W 06 The Dammed
W 06 The Adverts
Th 07 Mr Big
Th 07 Brainchild
Fr 08 Giggles
Fr 08 Easy
Sa 09 Stateline
Sa 09 Masterswitch
Su 10 Salt
M 11 Little Bob Story
M 11 Advertising
Tu 12 Nutz
W 13 The Saints
Th 14 Ultravox
Th 14 Neo
Fr 15 The Boomtown Rats
Fr 15 Tools
Sa 16 Vapour Trails
Sa 16 Snakebite
Su 17 Salt
M 18 Quantum Jump
Tu 19 Strider
Tu 19 Brainchild
W 20 Generation X
W 20 The Lurkers
Th 21 Deaf School
Fr 22 The Enid
Fr 22 Howard Bragen
Sa 23 Trickster
Sa 23 Boy Bastin
Su 24 Jenny Haan's Lion
Su 24 Imperial Storm Band
M 25 George Hatcher Band
Tu 26 Doctors of Madness
W 27 Trapeze
W 27 Sorahan
Th 28 Heron
Fr 29 Cado Belle
Fr 29 Andy Desmond
Sa 30 The Vibrators
Sa 30 Penetration
Su 31 The Vibrators
Su 31 Penetration

August 1977
M 01 The Vibrators
M 01 Penetration
W 03 The Boomtown Rats
Tu 02 The Darts
Th 04 The Buzzcocks
Th 04 Wire
Fr 05 Radio Stars
Sa 06 X-Ray Spex
M 08 The Boys
Tu 09 Rico
Tu 09 Major Wiley

W 10 Chelsea
Th 11 Edgar Broughton Childermass
Th 11 A1
Fr 12 Generation X
Fr 12 Victim
Sa 13 Michael Chapman
Su 14 Michael Chapman
M 15 Jenny Haan's Lion
M 15 Cruiser
Tu 16 Doctors of Madness
Tu 16 The New Hearts
W 17 The Cortinas
W 17 The Pop Group
Th 18 The Boomtown Rats
Th 18 Bernie Torme
Fr 19 Kingfish
Su 21 Eddie & the Hot Rods
M 22 Eddie & the Hot Rods
Tu 23 Eddie & the Hot Rods
W 24 Eddie & the Hot Rods
Th 25 Eddie & the Hot Rods
Fr 26 Ultravox
Sa 27 Scarecrow
Sa 27 Va-Va Voom
M 29 The Enid
Tu 30 George Hatcher Band
W 31 Illusion

September 1977
Th 01 Gloria Mundi
Fr 02 The Adverts
Fr 02 Buster James
Sa 03 The Stukas
Sa 03 Mean Street
Su 04 Roogalator
M 05 Radio Stars
Tu 06 Generation X
Tu 06 Jolt
W 07 John Martyn
Th 08 John Martyn
Fr 09 999
Fr 09 Tools
Sa 10 The Stukas
Sa 10 The Criminals
Su 11 The Tom Robinson Band
M 12 Bert Jansch
Tu 13 Generation X
W 14 The Boomtown Rats
W 14 Bernie Torme
Th 15 No Dice
Th 15 A1
Fr 16 The Fabulous Poodles
Sa 17 Grand Hotel
Sa 17 Japan
M 19 George Hatcher Band
Tu 20 Generation X
Tu 20 Johnny Curious & the Strangers
W 21 The Motors
Th 22 The Heavy Metal Kids
Fr 23 The Heavy Metal Kids
Sa 24 A1
Su 25 Gloria Mundi
M 26 X-Ray Spex
Tu 27 Generation X
W 28 The Motors
Th 29 Giggles
Th 29 Smiler
Fr 30 Radio Stars

October 1977
Sa 01 The Only Ones
Sa 01 Bazoomis
Su 02 Grand Hotel
Su 02 Cock Sparrow
M 03 Cherry Vanilla
M 03 Rage
Tu 04 The Buzzcocks
W 05 The Motors
Th 06 X-Ray Spex
Th 06 Dole Queue
Fr 07 Heron
Fr 07 A1
Sa 08 The Stukas
Sa 08 Bazooka Joe
Su 09 Grand Hotel
Su 09 Cock Sparrow

M 10 The Tom Robinson Band
Tu 11 The Foster Brothers
W 12 The Motors
Th 13 Illusion
Fr 14 Gloria Mundi
Sa 15 Radiators From Space
Su 16 Grand Hotel
Su 16 Prairie Dog
M 17 The New Hearts
M 17 Victim
Tu 18 Salt
W 19 Michael Chapman & Band
Th 20 Michael Chapman & Band
Fr 21 Sham 69
Fr 21 The Killjoys
Sa 22 Advertising
Sa 22 The Members
Su 23 Grand Hotel
M 24 The Tom Robinson Band
Tu 25 The Tyla Gang
Tu 25 VHF
W 26 X-Ray Spex
W 26 Jolt
Th 27 Quantum Jump
Fr 28 Gloria Mundi
Sa 29 Wishbone Ash
Su 30 Grand Hotel
Su 30 Smiler
M 31 The Saints

November 1977
Tu 01 The Saints
W 02 The Boys
W 02 Neo
W 02 Solid Waste
Th 03 The Boys
Th 03 Bazoomis
Th 03 The Lurkers
Fr 04 Rikki and the Last Days of Earth
Sa 05 The Depressions
Sa 05 Mean Street
Su 06 Illusion
Su 06 Krysia Kogcan
M 07 The Yachts
Tu 08 Roogalator
W 09 Five Hand Reel
W 09 Krysia Kogcan
Th 10 The Tyla Gang
Fr 11 Gloria Mundi
Fr 11 Skunks
Sa 12 Adam & The Ants
Su 13 Illusion
Su 13 Krysia Kogcan
M 14 The New Hearts
M 14 The Drones
Tu 15 Phil Rambow Band
W 16 English Assassins
Th 17 George Hatcher Band
Th 17 Fury
Fr 18 X-Ray Spex
Sa 19 Plummet Airlines
Sa 19 Bazoomis
Su 20 Suburban Studs
M 21 The Buzzcocks
M 21 The Flies
Tu 22 The Buzzcocks
Tu 22 The Flies
W 23 XTC
Th 24 Bernie Torme
Fr 25 Gloria Mundi
Fr 25 Swank
Sa 26 Adam & The Ants
Su 27 Suburban Studs
Su 27 The Members
M 28 Mungo Jerry
Tu 29 Roogalator
Tu 29 The Reaction
W 30 The Crabs
W 30 Monotone

December 1977
Th 01 Five Hand Reel
Fr 02 The Foster Brothers
Fr 02 Doll By Doll
Sa 03 Squeeze
Su 04 Grand Hotel

M 05 Racing Cars
Tu 06 Racing Cars
W 07 Greg Kihn
Th 08 London
Fr 09 Spud
Sa 10 Wire
Su 11 Adam & The Ants
M 12 No Dice
Tu 13 Salt
W 14 The Cortinas
Th 15 The Pirates
Fr 16 Bethnal
Sa 17 Chris Spedding
Su 18 Deaf School
M 19 Supercharge
Tu 20 Supercharge
W 21 Chelsea
W 21 Menace
Th 22 The Motors
Fr 23 The Motors
Sa 24 The Enid
Tu 27 Alberto Y Lost Trios Paranoias
W 28 Alberto Y Lost Trios Paranoias
Th 29 The Fabulous Poodles
Fr 30 X-Ray Spex
Sa 31 Ultravox

January 1978
M 02 The Boys
Tu 03 Bethnal
W 04 Dania Tarma
Th 05 Adam & The Ants
Fr 06 No Dice
Fr 06 Checkmate
Sa 07 Clayson and the Argonauts
Sa 07 Blitzkids
Su 08 Dynamite Day
Su 08 Zoot Money
Su 08 Friends
M 09 Slaughter & the Dogs
Tu 10 Bethnal
W 11 The Pirates
Th 12 Adam & The Ants
Fr 13 Squeeze
Sa 14 The Stukas
Sa 14 The Late Show
Su 15 Van Der Graaf Generator
M 16 Van Der Graaf Generator
Tu 17 Bethnal
W 18 Chelsea
Th 19 Adam & The Ants
Fr 20 Window
Sa 21 Fury
Su 22 The Police
M 23 The New Hearts
Tu 24 Bethnal
W 25 Salt
Th 26 Adam & The Ants
Fr 27 The Saints
Fr 27 Jolt
Sa 28 The Depressions
Sa 28 The Piranhas
Su 29 Roogalator
M 30 The Killjoys
Tu 31 Bethnal
Tu 31 The Speedometers

February 1978
W 01 Salt
Th 02 Wire
Fr 03 Window
Su 05 The Lurkers
M 06 The Stukas
M 06 The Look
Tu 07 Bethnal
W 08 The Crabs
W 08 Plastix
Th 09 No Dice
Fr 10 The New Hearts
Sa 11 Ultravox
Sa 11 The Doll
Su 12 Ultravox
Su 12 The Doll
M 13 Ultravox
M 13 The Doll
Tu 14 Bethnal

Tu 14 Cheap Stars
W 15 Tonight
Th 16 Rhode Island Red
Fr 17 Window
Sa 18 The Boyfriends
Sa 18 Smurks
Su 19 The Lurkers
Su 19 (Johnny Gee &) Tubeway Army
M 20 After The Fire
M 20 PTO
Tu 21 Bethnal
Tu 21 The Members
W 22 Gloria Mundi
W 22 NW10
Th 23 Salt
Th 23 Young Bucks
Fr 24 The Jam
Sa 25 The Jam
Su 26 The Rezillos
M 27 The Boys
M 27 Berlin & The Jerks
Tu 28 Bethnal
Tu 28 The Doll

March 1978
W 01 Krazy Kat
W 01 Gygafo
Th 02 Window
Fr 03 Gloria Mundi
Sa 04 The Automatics
Su 05 The Yachts
M 06 The Tyla Gang
Tu 07 Radiators From Space
W 08 The Boyfriends
Th 09 Meal Ticket
Fr 10 Meal Ticket
Sa 11 The Young Ones
Su 12 Pacific Eardrum
Su 12 Regulation Control
M 13 The Only Ones
Tu 14 Dire Straits
W 15 Gloria Mundi
Th 16 Window
Fr 17 Spud
Sa 18 The Automatics
Su 19 Hi-Fi
Su 19 Salt
M 20 The Heavy Metal Kids
Tu 21 Dire Straits
W 22 Zal
Th 23 Supercharge
Th 23 29th & Deerborn
Fr 24 The Pirates
Sa 25 The Pirates
Su 26 The Saints
M 27 Adam & The Ants
Tu 28 Dire Straits
W 29 Wire
Th 30 Slaughter & the Dogs
Fr 31 Gloria Mundi
Fr 31 The Dandies

April 1978
Sa 01 Rambling Strip
Sa 01 The Wipers
Su 02 Doctors of Madness
M 03 Head Waiter
Tu 04 Dynamite Days
W 05 Marseilles
W 05 Charlie Ainley Band
Th 06 Johnny Cougar
Fr 07 The Automatics
Sa 08 The Look
Sa 08 The Sneekers
Su 09 Dana Gillespie
Su 09 Better Looking
M 10 Doctors of Madness
M 10 Ritzi
Tu 11 Dire Straits
W 12 The Boyfriends
Th 13 The New Hearts
Fr 14 Adam & The Ants
Sa 15 Ozo
Sa 15 Dave Lewis Band
Su 16 Doctors of Madness
Su 16 Johnny Warman

M 17 After The Fire
M 17 Gypp
Tu 18 The Look
W 19 The Boyfriends
Th 20 The Lurkers
Th 20 Tubeway Army
Fr 21 The Automatics
Sa 22 The Late Show
Su 23 The Brakes
M 24 Radio Birdman
M 24 Neo
Tu 25 Electric Chairs
Tu 25 Levi & the Rockats
W 26 The Boyfriends
W 26 The News
Th 27 The Stukas
Fr 28 The New Hearts
Sa 29 The Speedometers
Sa 29 The News
Su 30 The Banned

May 1978
M 01 Rikki and the Last Days of Earth
Tu 01 Johnny Cougar
Tu 02 The Orphans
W 03 The Boyfriends
W 03 The Backbeats
Th 04 The Automatics
Fr 05 The Look
Fr 05 Mono
Sa 06 Johnny Moped
Su 06 Drug Addix
Su 07 The Stukas
M 08 Pere Ubu
M 08 Nico
M 08 Patrick Fitzgerald
Tu 09 Pere Ubu
Tu 09 Nico
Tu 09 Patrick Fitzgerald
W 10 Wilko Johnson
Th 11 Wilko Johnson
Fr 12 The Look
Fr 12 Urban Disturbance
Sa 13 Buster James Band
Su 14 Dead Fingers Talk
M 15 The Tyla Gang
M 15 Straight Three
Tu 16 Cherry Vanilla
Tu 16 The Members
W 17 After The Fire
Th 18 The Automatics
Fr 18 The Look
Sa 20 Clayson and the Argonauts
Su 21 Tonight
M 22 The Brakes
Tu 23 Chelsea
W 24 The Tourists
Th 25 Soft Boys
Fr 26 The Look
Sa 27 Hi-Fi
Sa 27 Enter
Su 28 The Lurkers
M 29 The Lurkers
Tu 30 XTC
W 31 XTC

June 1978
Th 01 The Automatics
Fr 02 Gruppo Sportivo
Fr 02 Next
Sa 03 Sore Throat
Su 04 Van Der Graaf Generator
M 05 Van Der Graaf Generator
Tu 06 Racing Cars
W 07 Trapeze
Th 08 The Automatics
Fr 09 The Rezillos
Sa 10 The Smirks
M 12 Ian Gillan Band
M 12 Killer
Tu 13 Ian Gillan Band
Tu 13 Killer
W 14 Ian Gillan Band
W 14 Killer
Th 15 The Automatics
Th 15 The News

Fr	16	Chelsea
Sa	17	Warren Harry
Su	18	Soft Boys
M	19	The Tyla Gang
Tu	20	After The Fire
W	21	Penetration
Th	22	The Automatics
Th	22	The News
Fr	23	The Killjoys
Sa	24	Adam & The Ants
Su	25	The Banned
Su	25	The Star Jets
M	26	Ramrod
Tu	27	The New Hearts
W	28	Champion
Th	29	The Automatics
Fr	30	The Rubinoos

July 1978

Sa	01	The Rubinoos
Su	02	The Rubinoos
M	03	The Rubinoos
Tu	04	The Movies
W	05	Dire Straits
W	05	Sandy McLelland and the Backline
Th	06	Dire Straits
Th	06	Sandy McLelland and the Backline
Fr	07	The Brakes
Sa	08	Apostrophe
Su	09	Meal Ticket
M	10	Ramrod
M	10	Harlow
Tu	11	The Tourists
W	12	Sonja Kristina
Th	13	Adam & The Ants
Th	13	Blitz
Fr	14	The New Hearts
Sa	15	The News
Su	16	Eric Bell
M	17	Johnny Moped
Tu	18	Suicide
W	19	Dead Fingers Talk
Th	20	Radio Stars
Fr	21	Radio Stars
Sa	22	Blast Furnace & The Heatwaves
Sa	22	The Business
Su	23	Supercharge
M	24	The Shirts
Tu	25	Tanz Der Youth
W	26	The Adverts
Th	27	The Adverts
Fr	28	Chelsea
Sa	29	Rumble Strip
Su	30	The Banned
M	31	The Tourists

August 1978

Tu	01	Michael Chapman
W	02	Michael Chapman
Th	03	The Enid
Fr	04	The Enid
Sa	05	The Enid
Su	06	Racing Cars
M	07	Steve Hillage
Tu	08	Steve Hillage
W	09	The New Hearts
Th	10	Wilko Johnson's Solid Senders
Th	10	The Young Ones
Fr	11	Wilko Johnson's Solid Senders
Fr	11	The Young Ones
Sa	12	The Business
Sa	12	The Reaction
Su	13	The Vibrators
M	14	The Vibrators
Tu	15	The Movies
W	16	Pacific Eardrum
Th	17	The Boyfriends
Fr	18	Ramrod
Sa	19	Ultravox
Su	20	Ultravox
M	21	Ultravox
Tu	22	Ultravox
W	23	Ultravox
Th	24	Bethnal
Fr	25	The Motors
Sa	26	Scarecrow
M	28	The Pirates
M	28	Blazer Blazer
Tu	29	The Pirates
Tu	29	Blazer Blazer
W	30	The Pirates
W	30	Blazer Blazer
Th	31	Blue Max

September 1978

Fr	01	Jackie Lynton H.D. Band
Sa	02	Zaine Griff
Sa	02	Lionheart
Su	03	Jolt
M	04	Star Jets
Tu	05	Adam & The Ants
W	06	Adam & The Ants
Th	07	The Dodgers
Fr	08	The Fall
Sa	09	The Police
Su	10	The Tourists
M	11	Sore Throat
Tu	12	Dead Fingers Talk
Tu	12	Out Of Nowhere
W	13	Tanz Der Youth
Th	14	Squeeze
Fr	15	Bernie Torme
Sa	16	The Business
Sa	16	Media
Su	17	Sandy McLelland and the Backline
M	18	Crawler
Tu	19	Roger The Cat
Tu	19	Blank Cheque
W	20	After The Fire
Th	21	Champion
Fr	22	Roy Hill Band
Sa	23	Showbiz Kids
Su	24	The Tourists
M	25	Hi-Fi
W	27	Racing Cars
Th	28	The Ian Gillan Band
Fr	29	The Ian Gillan Band
Sa	30	The News

October 1978

Su	01	The Cortinas
M	02	Bernie Torme
Tu	03	Punishment Of Luxury
Tu	03	Fame
W	04	The Smirks
Th	05	Supercharge
Th	05	29th & Deerborn
Fr	06	Sassafras
Sa	07	The Autographs
Sa	07	The Crooks
Su	08	Those Four
M	09	The Edge
Tu	10	The Drones
W	11	The Smirks
Th	12	Gruppo Sportivo
Fr	13	Zaine Griff
Sa	14	Warren Harry
Su	15	Eric Bell
M	16	Hi-Fi
M	16	Blue Screaming
Tu	17	Chelsea
W	18	The Smirks
Th	19	The Automatics
Fr	20	Bram Tchaikovsky's Battleaxe
Fr	20	Asfalto
Sa	21	The Vibrators
Su	22	The Vibrators
M	23	Hi-Fi
M	23	Nick Pickett
Tu	24	The Business
W	25	Cado Belle
Th	26	The Intellectuals
Fr	27	The Movies
Sa	28	Blazer Blazer
Su	29	The Yachts
M	30	The Smirks
Tu	31	Zaine Griff

November 1978

W	01	The Skids
Th	02	The Tourists
Fr	03	Dave Lewis Band
Sa	04	Salford Jets
Su	05	Straight Eight
M	06	Hi-Fi
Tu	07	The Business
W	08	The Edge
Th	09	The Intellectuals
Fr	10	Blast Furnace
Sa	11	The Reaction
Su	12	The Rezillos
Su	12	The Undertones
M	13	The Rezillos
M	13	The Undertones
Tu	14	Chelsea
W	15	Snips
Th	16	Gloria Mundi
Fr	17	Zaine Griff
Sa	18	Little Bo Bitch
Sa	18	The Idols
Su	19	Young Bucks
M	20	Grand Hotel
Tu	21	The Business
W	22	Wire
Th	23	Wire
Fr	24	The Fabulous Poodles
Sa	25	Trans Am
Sa	25	Fame
Su	26	Straight Eight
M	27	C Gas 5
Tu	28	Adam & The Ants
W	29	Adam & The Ants
Th	30	No Dice

December 1978

Fr	01	Spud
Sa	02	The Speedometers
Su	03	Supercharge
Su	03	Panties
M	04	Zaine Griff
Tu	05	Fischer Z
Tu	05	Redwood
W	06	Streetband
Th	07	Star Jets
Fr	08	Blazer Blazer
Sa	09	The Autographs
Su	10	Chas & Dave
M	11	The Boys
M	11	NW10
Tu	12	Ivor Biggun
W	13	The Tourists
W	13	The Cleavers
Th	14	Bert Jansch
Fr	15	After The Fire
Fr	15	Spare Parts
Sa	16	David Kubinec
Su	17	The Fall
M	18	Racing Cars
Tu	19	Blast Furnace
Tu	19	John Potter's Clay
W	20	Steve Gibbons Band
Th	21	Steve Gibbons Band
Fr	22	Squeeze
Sa	23	The Enid
Tu	26	Ultravox
W	27	Ian Gillan Band
Th	28	Ian Gillan Band
Fr	29	Ian Gillan Band
Sa	30	No Dice
Su	31	Radio Stars

January 1979

Tu	02	The Food Band
W	03	Eater
Th	04	The Edge
Fr	05	Gloria Mundi
Sa	06	Showbiz Kids
Su	07	Young Bucks
M	08	Little Bo Bitch
Tu	09	C Gas 5
W	10	Advertising
Th	11	The Drones
Fr	12	The Troggs
Sa	13	Neon Hearts
Sa	13	Raped
Su	14	Young Bucks
M	15	Rory Gallagher
Tu	16	Straight Eight
W	17	The Eric Bell Band
Th	18	Jab Jab
Fr	19	Dave Lewis Band
Sa	20	Magnets
Su	21	Young Bucks
M	22	UK Subs
Tu	23	The Business
Tu	23	The Accelerators
W	24	Fame
W	24	Eyes
Th	25	Streetband
Fr	26	David Kubinec's Excess
Sa	27	The Cure
Su	28	Young Bucks
M	29	Percy's Package
M	29	Angelic Upstarts
M	29	The Invaders
Tu	30	Zaine Griff
W	31	The Records

February 1979

Th	01	Straight Eight
Fr	02	Dave Lewis Band
Fr	02	Teazer
Sa	03	Showbiz Kids
Su	04	Little Bo Bitch
M	05	Wreckless Eric
Tu	06	The Extras
W	07	Doll By Doll
Th	08	The Skids
Fr	09	Joe Jackson Band
Sa	10	Screens
Su	11	Little Bo Bitch
M	12	Sore Throat
Tu	13	Punishment of Luxury
W	14	The Eric Bell Band
Th	15	After The Fire
Fr	16	The Smirks
Sa	17	The Flys
Su	18	Little Bo Bitch
M	19	The Undertones
Tu	20	The Extras
Fr	23	Dave Lewis Band
Fr	23	Paris
Su	25	Little Bo Bitch
M	26	Reggae Regular
Tu	27	The Edge
W	28	The Eric Bell Band

March 1979

Th	01	Zaine Griff
Fr	02	The Members
Sa	03	The Members
Su	04	The Cure
Su	04	Joy Division
M	05	Brush Sheils & Skid Row
Tu	06	No Dice
W	07	Wild Horses
Th	08	Straight Eight
Fr	09	The Extras
Sa	10	Rule the Roost
Su	11	The Cure
Su	11	Fashion
M	12	Sore Throat
Tu	13	Radio Stars
W	14	The Undertones
Th	15	Sniff 'n' the Tears
Fr	16	UK Subs
Sa	17	The Jags
Su	18	The Cure
Su	18	Local Operator
M	19	Bram Tchaikovsky
Tu	20	The Extras
W	21	The Smirks
Th	22	Inner Circle
Fr	23	Inner Circle
Sa	24	Young Bucks
Su	25	The Cure
Su	25	Scars
M	26	The Movies
Tu	27	The Leyton Buzzards
Tu	27	Daylight Robbery
W	28	The Skids
Th	29	The Skids

Fr 30 After The Fire
Sa 31 Lee Farden's Legionnaires

April 1979
Su 01 Fame
M 02 The Pretenders
Tu 03 The Pretenders
W 04 John Cooper Clark
Th 05 Zaine Griff
Fr 06 Straight Eight
Sa 07 Angletrax
Su 08 Lew Lewis Reformer
M 09 The Sports
Tu 10 Doll By Doll
W 11 Streetband
Th 12 Wilko Johnson's Solid Senders
Fr 13 Wilko Johnson's Solid Senders
Sa 14 Wilko Johnson's Solid Senders
Su 15 Wilko Johnson's Solid Senders
M 16 Wild Horses
Tu 17 Wild Horses
W 18 Doll By Doll
Th 19 Ramrod
Fr 20 SVT
Sa 21 Showbiz Kids
Su 22 The Magnums
M 23 The Extras
Tu 24 Giants
W 25 Black Slate
Th 26 Gary Holton's Gems
Fr 27 The Sports
Sa 28 Bobby Henry
Su 29 Fame
M 30 Lew Lewis Reformer

May 1979
Tu 01 Screens
W 02 China Street & Cygnets
Th 03 The Speedometers
Fr 04 Kenny
Sa 05 The Press
Su 06 The Jags
M 07 Punishment of Luxury
Tu 08 The Flys
W 09 The Doll
Th 10 Fashion
Fr 11 Angletrax
Su 12 Secret Affair
Su 13 The Jags
M 14 The Sinceros
Tu 15 Headboys
W 16 Fischer Z
Th 17 The Speedometers
Fr 18 Bernie Torme
Sa 19 Showbiz Kids
Su 20 The Jags
M 21 Greg Kihn
Tu 22 Cyanide
Tu 22 Cameras
W 23 After The Fire
Th 24 Warm Jets
Fr 25 The Knack
Sa 26 Secret Affair
Su 27 The Jags
M 28 Brian James's Brain
Tu 29 Headboys
W 30 CMB
Th 31 999
Th 31 Pinpoint

June 1979
Fr 01 999
Fr 01 Pinpoint
Sa 02 999
Sa 02 Pinpoint
M 04 The Sinceros
Tu 05 The Cramps
W 06 Blood Donor
Th 07 Warm Jets
Fr 08 Max Webster
Sa 09 Max Webster
Su 10 Linton Kwesi Johnson
Su 10 Rico
M 11 Linton Kwesi Johnson
M 11 Rico
Tu 12 The Tourists
W 13 Headboys

Th 14 The Knack
Fr 15 The Chords
Fr 15 Squire
Fr 15 The Mods
Sa 16 The Purple Hearts
Sa 16 Les E'Lite
Sa 16 Little Rooster
Su 17 The Chords
Su 17 Back To Zero
M 18 The Sinceros
Tu 19 The Yachts
Tu 19 The Opposition
W 20 Generation X
Th 21 Human League
Fr 22 Human League
Sa 23 Vermillion
Sa 23 The Acres
Sa 23 The Lightning Raiders
Su 24 Fame
M 25 The Pirates
Tu 26 The Pirates
W 27 The Pirates
Th 28 The Records
Fr 29 The Records
Sa 30 The Crooks

July 1979
Su 01 The Fabulous Poodles
M 02 The Sinceros
Tu 03 Simple Minds
W 04 Sniff 'n' the Tears
Th 05 Warm Jets
Fr 06 Little Bo Bitch
Sa 07 Screens
Su 08 Secret Affair
M 09 Terra Nova
Tu 10 Ian Gillan Band
W 11 Ian Gillan Band
Th 12 Ian Gillan Band
Fr 13 The Purple Hearts
Sa 14 Showbiz Kids
Su 15 Secret Affair
Su 15 Back To Zero
M 16 The Chords
M 16 57 Men
Tu 17 Fame
Tu 17 Roxette
W 18 Chelsea
Th 19 The Ruts
Fr 20 The Extras
Sa 21 Star Jets
Su 22 Secret Affair
Su 22 Squire
M 23 Terra Nova
Tu 24 The Purple Hearts
W 25 The Enid
Th 26 The Enid
Fr 27 The Enid
Sa 28 Reg Law Band
Su 29 The Fall
M 30 The Chords
Tu 31 The Merton Parkas
Tu 31 Small Hour

August 1979
W 01 The Undertones
W 01 The Donkeys
Th 02 The Undertones
Th 02 The Donkeys
Fr 03 The Undertones
Fr 03 The Donkeys
Sa 04 The Undertones
Sa 04 The Donkeys
Su 05 Straight Eight
M 06 Terra Nova
Tu 07 Simple Minds
W 08 Black Slate
Th 09 The Invaders
Th 09 Twist
Fr 10 Warm Jets
Sa 11 The Piranhas
Su 12 Toyah
Su 12 The Outpatients
M 13 The Ruts
Tu 14 The Ruts
W 15 Wilko Johnson's Solid Senders

Th 16 Wilko Johnson's Solid Senders
Fr 17 Wilko Johnson's Solid Senders
Sa 18 The Jags
Su 19 The Chords
Su 19 The Vapours
M 20 Terra Nova
Tu 21 The Buzzards
W 22 The Drones
Th 23 Punishment of Luxury
Fr 24 Zaine Griff
Sa 25 The Teenbeats
Sa 25 Scooter
M 27 The Prxxx Pirates
Tu 28 Interview
Tu 28 Live Wire
W 29 Chelsea
W 29 The Wimps
Th 30 Lew Lewis Reformer
Fr 31 Lew Lewis Reformer

September 1979
Sa 01 The Vapours
Su 02 Straight Eight
M 03 Slaughter & the Dogs
Tu 04 Shake
W 05 Small Hour
W 05 The Merton Parkas
Th 06 Warm Jets
Fr 07 Gloria Mundi
Sa 08 Star Jets
Sa 08 X-Effects
Su 09 The Young Ones
M 10 The Chords
Tu 11 Shake
W 12 The Merton Parkas
W 12 Small Hour
Th 13 Cowboy International
Fr 14 Chris Farlowe's Blues Power
Fr 14 The Teenbeats
Sa 15 The Vapours
Su 16 The Young Ones
M 17 The Brakes
Tu 18 Axis Point
W 19 The Merton Parkas
Th 20 The Members
Fr 21 The Members
Sa 22 The Lambrettas
Su 23 The Young Ones
M 24 The Brakes
Tu 25 The Chords
W 26 Phil Rambow Band
Th 27 The Merton Parkas
Fr 28 John Coughlan's Diesel Band
Sa 29 John Coughlan's Diesel Band
Su 30 The Young Ones

October 1979
M 01 999
Tu 02 999
W 03 999
Th 04 999
Fr 05 999
Sa 06 The Vapours
Sa 06 The News
Su 07 The Young Ones
M 08 The Brakes
Tu 09 The Mekons
W 10 Kevin Borich Express
W 10 The Business
Th 11 No Dice
Th 11 West End
Fr 12 The Motels
Sa 13 Fingerprintz
Su 14 Random Hold
M 15 The Brakes
Tu 16 UK Subs
W 17 UK Subs
Th 18 UK Subs
Fr 19 Iron Maiden
Fr 19 Praying Mantis
Su 20 Back To Zero
Su 21 Toyah
Su 21 Vitas Dance
M 22 The Pretenders
Tu 23 The Adverts
Tu 23 The Decoys

W 24 The Adverts
W 24 The Decoys
Th 25 Climax Blues Band
Fr 26 Climax Blues Band
Sa 27 Squire
Su 28 Random Hold
M 29 The Pretenders
Tu 30 The Piranhas
W 31 Punishment of Luxury

November 1979
Th 01 Original Mirrors
Fr 02 John's Boys
Fr 02 The Nips
Sa 03 The Books
Sa 03 Bauhaus
Su 04 The Vapours
M 05 The Pretenders
Tu 06 Little Bo Bitch
W 07 The Lurkers
Th 08 The Photos
Fr 09 The Jags
Sa 10 The Chords
Su 11 The Chords
M 12 The Pretenders
Tu 13 Random Hold
W 14 The Lurkers
W 14 Carpettes
Th 15 Original Mirrors
Fr 16 Cowboy International
Sa 17 Pinpoint
Su 18 The Fall
M 19 Straight Eight
Tu 20 Scream
W 21 The Lurkers
Th 22 Mobile
Fr 23 Moon Martin
Fr 23 The Ravens
Sa 24 Moon Martin
Sa 24 The Ravens
Su 25 Bethnal
Su 25 Bruce Henry
M 26 Bethnal
M 26 Bruce Henry
Tu 27 Tours
W 28 The Lurkers
W 28 Carpettes
Th 29 The Photos
Fr 30 London Zoo

December 1979
Sa 01 Extremist
Sa 01 KY and the Kays
Su 02 Metro
Su 02 Geno and the Sharks
M 03 Bruce Woolley
M 03 Echo Bravo
Tu 04 The Dickies
W 05 Girl
Th 06 Writz
Fr 07 The Merton Parkas
Sa 08 The Merton Parkas
Su 09 Iron Maiden
Su 09 Praying Mantis
M 10 Wilko Johnson's Solid Senders
W 12 Girl
Th 13 Simple Minds
Fr 14 Simple Minds
Sa 15 Magnum
Su 16 Samson
M 17 The Ruts
Tu 18 The Ruts
W 19 The Boys
Th 20 Wreckless Eric
Th 20 Billy Karloff and the Supremes
Fr 21 Doll By Doll
Sa 22 The Pretenders
Su 23 The Pretenders
M 24 The Enid
Th 27 Chris Farlowe
Fr 28 Girl
Sa 29 Live Wire
Su 30 The Teenbeats
M 31 Lew Lewis Reformer
M 31 Little Rooster
M 31 The Stickers

Page numbers in **bold** refer to illustrations

The author and publisher would like to thank: Charles Alexander; Andrew Bodnar; Julie Bowie; Laurence Canty; Annette Carson; Andy Davis (Record Collector); Ealing Central Library; Pete Frame; Dave Gelly; Giorgio Gomelsky; Michael Heatley; Bob Henrit; Frances Hounsell (Greenford Library); Steve Howe; Ken Jones (National Jazz Foundation Archive); Martin Kinch; Steve Maycock (Sotheby's); Chas McDevitt; David Nathan (National Jazz Foundation Archive); Jon Newey; Geoff Nicholls; Mark Paytress; Harold Pendleton; Ian Purser; Mike Rejsa; Phil Richardson; Jim Roberts; Pete Sarfas (Audio Archives); Andrew Simons; Miki Slingsby; Phil Smee (Strange Things); Carolyn Starren (Local Studies, Royal Borough of Kensington & Chelsea Libraries); Sally Stockwell; Paul Trynka; Chris Verness; Charlie Whitney; Jon Wilton (Redfern's).

Special thanks to Johnny Black.

Photographs were supplied by the following (number indicates page). Pictorial Press Ltd: Who 4-5; main 15; Jazz Cellar 18-19; 2-ls main 26-7; 2-ls & Harris 30-1; inset 35; Harris 36-7, Stones 50-1, Fame 55; Small Faces 72-3, dancing & inset 74-5; Floyd 82-3, Hendrix 87, Hendrix & Floyd 88; UFO 90-1, both 94-5; main 96, dancing 99, Tiles 100, both 103; main & inset bottom 106-7. Redfern's (BB=Bob Baker; CA=C Andrews; GB=Glenn A Baker; DB=Dick Barnatt; JB=James Barron; ID=Ian Dickson; EE=Erica Echenberg; MG=Mick Gold; CG=Caroline Greville-Morris; CM=Chris Mills; MO=Michael Ochs; DR=David Redfern; RR=Rick Richards; SR=Steve Richards; BS=Brian Shuel; GW=Graham Wiltshire): Barber 21 (DR); both 28 (RR); Taylor 34-5 (RR); Jansch 39 (DR); MacColl 40 (BS); Troubadour both 42-3 (BS); Davies & Korner 47 (DR); dancing 53 (DR); Blue Flames 54 (CA); main 56-7 (DR); main 62-3 (DB); Who 65 (BB); Washington 67 (JB); main & inset 70-1 (DR); Yardbirds 76-7 (MO); Cream 78-9 (BS); Zeppelin 110-11 (GW); Dury 112 (MG); main 114-5 (CM); Ducks 117 (GB); main 118-9 (EE); main 120-1 (ID); Clash 126-7 (EE); Jones 129 (DB); Damned 130-1 (EE); Jam 134 (EE); both 136-7 (EE); Jordan 138 (SR); Ant 139 (CG); Siouxsie 140 (EE); Costello 142 (ID); Marquee 146-7 (GEMS).

Other illustrated items including advertisements, magazines, newspapers, record sleeves etc, came from the collections of Tony Bacon, Balafon, Chas McDevitt, The National Jazz Foundation Archive (Loughton, England), and The National Sound Archive (London, England).

Maps are based on Nick Gibbard's Postermaps.

BIBLIOGRAPHY Richard Barnes "Mods!" Eel Pie 1979. **Ashley Brown** (ed) "History Of Rock" Orbis (part-work) 1983. **Peter Cadle** "Nights In The Cellar: Bunjies Coffee House" Bunjies undated c1995. **Stanley Cohen** "Folk Devils And Moral Panics: The Creation Of Mods And Rockers" MacGibbon & Kee 1972. **Ray Davies** "X-Ray, The Unauthorized Autobiography" Viking 1994. **Mike Dewe** "Skiffle Craze" Planet 1998. **Daniel Farson** "Soho In The Fifties" Michael Joseph 1987. **John Fordham** "Let's Join Hands And Contact The Living: Ronnie Scott And His Club" Elm Tree 1986. **Pete Frame** "The Beatles And Some Other Guys: Rock Family Trees Of The Early Sixties" Omnibus 1997; "Complete Rock Family Trees" Omnibus 1993; "Harp Beat Rock Gazetteer Of Great Britain" Banyan 1989. **George Gimarc** "Punk Diary 1970-1979, An Eyewitness Account Of The Punk Decade" Vintage 1994. **Jim Godbolt** "Jazz In Britain 1919-50" Quartet 1984. **Marcus Gray** "London's Rock Landmarks" Omnibus 1985. **Jonathon Green** "Days In The Life, Voices From The London Underground 1961-71" Pimlico 1998. **Dick Heckstall-Smith** "The Safest Place In The World: A Personal History Of British R&B" Quartet 1989. **James Henke** & Parke Puterbaugh (eds) "I Want To Take You Higher: The Psychedelic Era 1965-1969" Chronicle 1997. **David Heslam** "NME Rock'n'Roll Decades: The Seventies" Octopus 1992. **Terry Hounsome** "Rock Record 7, Directory Of Albums & Musicians" Record Researcher 1997. **Vernon Joynson** "Tapestry Of Delights: Comprehensive Guide To British Music Of The Beat, R&B, Psychedelic And Progressive Eras 1963-76" Borderline 1995. **Colin Larkin** (ed) "Guinness Encyclopedia of Popular Music" Guinness 1992. **Norman Lebrecht** "Music In London, A History and Handbook" Aurum 1992. **Crail Low** & Lucy Minto

"Handbook Guide To Rock & Pop in London" Handbook 1997. **John Lydon** "Rotten: No Irish, No Blacks, No Dogs" Hodder & Stoughton 1993. **Ewan MacColl** "Journeyman" Sidgwick & Jackson 1990. **Dave Marsh** "Before I Get Old: The Story of The Who" Plexus 1983. **George Martin** with Jeremy Hornsby "All You Need Is Ears" Macmillan 1979. **Chas McDevitt** "Skiffle: The Definitive Inside Story" Robson 1997. **Joe McMichael** & Irish Jack Lyons "Who Concert File" Omnibus 1997. **George Melly** "Owning Up" Weidenfeld & Nicholson 1965; "Revolt Into Style" Allen Lane 1970. **Barry Miles** "Paul McCartney: Many Years From Now" Secker & Warburg 1997. Barry Miles & Andy Mabbett "Pink Floyd, The Visual Documentary" Omnibus 1994. **Simon Napier-Bell** "You Don't Have To Say You Love Me" New English Library 1983. **John Platt** "London's Rock Routes" Fourth Estate 1985. John Platt, Chris Dreja, Jim McCarty "Yardbirds" Sidgwick & Jackson 1983. **Terry Rawlings** & Keith Badman "Good Times Bad Times, The Definitive Diary Of The Rolling Stones 1960-69" Complete Music 1997. **Marc Roberty** "Eric Clapton Scrapbook" Citadel 1994. **Johnny Rogan** "Starmakers And Svengalis" Futura 1988. **Dave Russell** "Popular Music in England 1840-1914, A Social History" Manchester University Press 1987. **Jon Savage** "England's Dreaming: Sex Pistols And Punk Rock" Faber 1991. **Ann Scanlon** "Those Tourists Are Money: The Rock'n'Roll Guide To Camden" Tristia 1997. **Nicholas Schaffner** "Saucerful Of Secrets: The Pink Floyd Odyssey" Sidgwick & Jackson 1991. **Percy A Scholes** "Oxford Companion To Music" OUP 1947. **Harry Shapiro** "Alexis Korner" Bloomsbury 1996; "Graham Bond: The Mighty Shadow" Guinness 1992. Harry Shapiro & Caesar Glebbeek "Jimi Hendrix: Electric Gypsy" Heinemann 1990. **Piet Shreuders**, Mark Lewisohn, Adam Smith "Beatles London" Hamlyn 1994. **Ray Stevenson** (ed) "Sex Pistols File" Omnibus 1984. **Chris Twomey** "XTC: Chalkhills And Children" Omnibus 1992. **Mike Watkinson**/Pete Anderson "Crazy Diamond: Syd Barrett And The Dawn Of Pink Floyd" Omnibus 1991. **Ben Weinreb** & Christopher Hibbert "London Encyclopedia" Macmillan 1995. **Bruce Welch** "Rock'n'roll I Gave You The Best Years Of My Life: A Life In The Shadows" Viking 1989.

SECTION 1 PLEASURE GARDENS AND JAZZ CLUBS (pages 8-21)
1 Compiled from three separate interviews on BBC Radio 2 programmes: Coffee Bar Kids produced by Robin Quinn, broadcast 1996; Rock Island Line: The Story Of Skiffle written/produced by Barbara Wallace, broadcast c1995; and A Viper's Tale broadcast c1995.
2 Roger North Memoires Of Music 1728.
3 Weinreb & Hibbert The London Encyclopedia.
4 Russell Popular Music In England.
5 Jazz Illustrated May 1950.
6 Melody Maker August 1932.
7 Melody Maker June 21st 1941.
8 J B Priestley Angel Pavement 1930.
9 Melody Maker July 17th 1937.
10 Melody Maker June 21st 1941.
11 Independent Magazine September 20th 1996.
12 Melody Maker October 3rd 1942.
13 Melly Owning-Up.
14 Melody Maker July 29th 1950.
15 Jazz News August 1963.
16 Record Collector April 1998.
17 Interview with author October 1998.
18 Interview with author October 1998.
19 Interview with author October 1998.
20 Jazz News March 29th 1961.

SECTION 2 VIPERS, SKIFFLE, STEELE AND ROCK (pages 22-37)
21 BBC Radio 2 A Viper's Tale broadcast c1995.
22 Shapiro Alexis Korner.
23 BBC Radio 2 A Viper's Tale broadcast c1995.
24 BBC Radio 2 A Viper's Tale broadcast c1995.
25 Cadle Nights In The Cellar.
26 BBC Radio 2 A Viper's Tale broadcast c1995.
27 BBC Radio 2 Rock Island Line: The Story Of Skiffle written/produced by Barbara Wallace, broadcast c1995.
28 BBC Radio 2 Rock Island Line: The Story Of Skiffle written/produced by Barbara Wallace, broadcast c1995.
29 BBC Radio 2 Rock Island Line: The Story Of Skiffle written/produced by Barbara Wallace, broadcast c1995.
30 Welch Rock'n'Roll.
31 Martin All You Need Is Ears.
32 Melody Maker May 31st 1958.
33 Melody Maker May 31st 1958.
34 Rogan Starmakers And Svengalis.
35 Farson Soho In The Fifties.

36 Melody Maker September 15th 1956.

SECTION 3 FOLK: FINGERS-IN-EARS TO ELECTRIC GUITARS (pages 38-45)
37 MacColl Journeyman.
38 John Hasted Alternative Memoirs c1992.
39 BBC Radio 2 Rock Island Line: The Story Of Skiffle written/produced by Barbara Wallace, broadcast c1995.
40 Melody Maker June 10th 1961.
41 Shapiro Alexis Korner.
42 Melody Maker August 28th 1965.
43 Melody Maker September 30th 1967.
44 Melody Maker February 11th 1967.
45 Melody Maker July 29th 1967.

SECTION 4 BRITISH R&B: BORN IN THE LONDON CLUBS (pages 46-77)
46 Melody Maker July 29th 1950.
47 Shapiro Alexis Korner.
48 Jazz News January 10th 1962.
49 Beat Instrumental February 1965.
50 Frame The Beatles And Some Other Guys.
51 Barnes Mods!.
52 Jazz News January 16th 1963.
53 Interview with author October 1998.
54 Jazz News October 31st 1962.
55 Davies X-Ray.
56 Jazz News November 21st 1962.
57 Interview with author February 1999.
58 Roger St. Pierre, Blues & Soul, c1980.
59 BBC Radio 2 Georgie Fame produced by Oliver Jones, broadcast January 1999.
60 Interview with author February 1999.
61 Platt Yardbirds.
62 Sleevenote, Five Live Yardbirds, 1964.
63 Platt Yardbirds.
64 Melody Maker March 30th 1963.
65 Peter Leslie Fab: The Anatomy Of A Phenomenon 1964.
66 Melody Maker March 30th 1963.
67 Melody Maker October 26th 1963.
68 Melody Maker October 26th 1963.
69 Barnes Mods!.
70 Rolling Stone December 21st 1972.
71 Cohen Folk Devils & Moral Panics.
72 Barnes Mods!.
73 Marquee Club Newsletter, Jazzbeat Jan 1964.
74 Jazzbeat February 1964.
75 Jazzbeat September 1964.
76 Interview with author October 1998.

77 Interview with author October 1998.
78 Interview with author October 1998.
79 Marquee Club Newsletter, Jazzbeat April 1964.
80 Melody Maker May 5th 1973.
81 John Fisher Murray Tour Of The Thames 1845.
82 Zigzag #5, circa September 1969.
83 Comstock Lode #7, c1979.
84 Sleevenote to The Legendary Cyril Davies with Alexis Korner's Breakdown Group... 1970.
85 Comstock Lode #7, c1979.
86 Melody Maker April 10th 1976.
87 Heckstall-Smith The Safest Place In The World.
88 Davies X-Ray.
89 Weekend Telegraph April 16th 1965.
90 Melly Revolt Into Style.
91 Miles Paul McCartney.
92 Melody Maker April 10th 1976.

SECTION 5 LIGHTSHOWS, PSYCHEDELIA AND JAMMING AT THE SPEAK (pages 78-111)
93 Watkinson & Anderson Crazy Diamond.
94 Encounter October 1967.
95 Encounter October 1967.
96 Green Days In The Life.
97 Etchingam Through Gypsy Eyes.
98 Napier-Bell You Don't Have To Say.
99 Melly Revolt Into Style.
100 Melly Revolt Into Style.
101 Record Mirror December 10th 1966.
102 BBC Radio 1 Tribute to Jimi Hendrix broadcast September 1980.
103 Melody Maker April 10th 1976.
104 Shapiro & Glebbeek Jimi Hendrix.
105 Miles Paul McCartney.
106 Melody Maker September 30th 1967.
107 Melody Maker April 10th 1976.
108 Green Days In The Life.
109 Schaffner Saucerful Of Secrets.
110 Interview with author February 1999.
111 Watkinson & Anderson Crazy Diamond.
112 Interview with author February 1999.
113 Encounter October 1967.
114 Watkinson & Anderson Crazy Diamond.
115 Melody Maker August 12th 1967.
116 Melody Maker May 6th 1967.
117 Watkinson & Anderson Crazy Diamond.
118 Green Days In The Life.
119 Melody Maker August 5th 1967.
120 Green Days In The Life.
121 Richard Neville Playpower 1971.

122 Melody Maker August 19th 1967.
123 Jo Cruikshank, Green Days In The Life.
124 Interview with author December 1998.
125 NME May 20th 1967.
126 Disc & Music Echo December 2nd 1967.
127 Interview with author December 1998.
128 Melody Maker April 10th 1976.
129 Green Days In The Life.
130 Beat Instrumental November 1966.
131 Melody Maker September 12th 1970.
132 Interview with author December 1998.
133 Melody Maker May 15th 1971.

SECTION 6 GOOD-TIME MUSIC IN THE PUBLIC BAR TONIGHT (pages 112-117)
134 Melody Maker October 2nd 1971.
135 Beat Instrumental March 1974.

SECTION 7 PUNK, PISTOLS AND THE SEVENTIES (pages 118-143)
136 Caroline Coon, Melody Maker Oct 2nd 1976.
137 Let It Rock June 1975.
138 Melody Maker July 28th 1975.
139 Melody Maker July 28th 1975.
140 Melody Maker April 13th 1974.
141 Melody Maker August 3rd 1974.
142 Melody Maker July 6th 1974.
143 Zigzag May 1976.
144 NME February 19th 1976.
145 Lydon Rotten.
146 Sounds April 24th 1976.
147 Savage England's Dreaming.
148 Savage England's Dreaming.
149 Melody Maker October 2nd 1976.
150 Melody Maker October 2nd 1976.
151 Melody Maker October 2nd 1976.
152 Sideburns December 1976.
153 NME July 2nd 1977.
154 Twomey XTC.
155 Melody Maker January 22nd 1977.
156 Clerk The Book Of The Damned.
157 Clerk The Book Of The Damned.
158 Heslam NME Rock'n'Roll Decades.
159 The History Of Punk #103.
160 Melly Revolt Into Style.

"No one goes on stage unless they want to show off. Look at me: I'm up here, you're down there, and I'm cleverer than you because you paid to see me do this."
Rat Scabies, 1979.